Criminal Procedure

PAUL MARCUS
Haynes Professor of Law
College of William and Mary

MELANIE D. WILSON
Dean and Roy L. Steinheimer, Jr., Professor of Law
Washington and Lee University, Lexington, Virginia

JOËLLE ANNE MORENO
Professor of Law
Florida International University College of Law, Miami, Florida

Twenty-First Edition

WEST ACADEMIC

860 Blue Gentian Road, Suite 350
Eagan, MN 55121
1-877-888-1330

Published in the United States of America

ISBN: 979-8-89209-209-8

We dedicate this Edition to:

Sarah F. Katis, Melanie Wilson's mother, who passed away in January of 2026, after a joy-filled life of tenacity.

And to the future lawyers who will stand in courtrooms not yet built, arguing cases not yet imagined:

May you find strength in the law's promise of justice, even when that promise feels distant.

May our efforts remind you that justice lives only through those brave enough to defend it.

And may you be supported in your life and work, as Joëlle Moreno has been, by the love of those you hold dear—to Ken, Adam & Nathan.

Summary of Contents

Capsule Summary

I. CONSTITUTIONAL PRINCIPLES

A. THE BILL OF RIGHTS

The first 10 amendments to the Constitution (the Bill of Rights) include a number of provisions limiting the government's power over criminal procedure (*e.g.*, the ***Fourth Amendment*** prohibits unreasonable searches and seizures; the ***Fifth Amendment*** prohibits double jeopardy, compelled self-incrimination, and deprivations of life, liberty, or property without due process; the ***Sixth Amendment*** requires a speedy and public trial and grants a right to the assistance of counsel).

1. Selective Incorporation

Many of the individual rights guaranteed by the Bill of Rights are applicable to the states only via the Fourteenth Amendment's Due Process Clause, which requires "fundamental fairness" in state criminal proceedings.

Such rights include:

a. ***The prohibition against unreasonable searches and seizures and the exclusionary rule*** (Fourth Amendment);

b. ***The bar against double jeopardy*** and the privilege against forced ***self-incrimination*** (Fifth Amendment);

c. ***The rights to a speedy and public trial,*** to a ***jury trial*** (including the right to ***a unanimous verdict of guilt***), to ***confront witnesses*** and ***compulsory process*** to obtain witnesses, to ***counsel*** in felony and some misdemeanor cases (Sixth Amendment); and

d. ***The prohibition against cruel and unusual punishment*** (Eighth Amendment).

2. Rights Not Incorporated

Not all provisions of the Bill of Rights apply to the states:

a. ***The Fifth Amendment right to indictment*** for capital and infamous crimes does not apply; and

b. ***The Eighth Amendment prohibition against excessive bail*** may or may not apply to the states.

B. EXCLUSION OF EVIDENCE

1. General Principles of the Exclusionary Rule

To deter government agents from violating constitutional protections, the Supreme Court adopted the exclusionary rule. Under the rule, ***evidence obtained by an unconstitutional search or seizure*** generally is ***not admissible*** at a criminal trial ***as proof of guilt***. Be careful, though, because evidence obtained unlawfully may be used for impeachment, and the Court has narrowed the definition of an illegal search or seizure in various cases and contexts. *Note*: The exclusionary rule applies in both state ***and*** federal actions.

2. General Scope

Under the exclusionary rule, all evidence unconstitutionally obtained must be excluded—including evidence acquired directly or indirectly from the unconstitutional search or arrest (*i.e.,* "fruit of the poisonous tree").

a. Dissipation of the Taint

Evidence otherwise inadmissible under the exclusionary rule may be admitted if the prosecution proves by a preponderance of the evidence, in one of the following ways, that the taint from the government's unconstitutional acts has dissipated:

(1) ***Inevitable Discovery***—police would have discovered the evidence regardless of the illegal action through other, lawful means;

(2) ***Independent Source***—police obtained the evidence from an independent, untainted source; or

(3) ***Confessions***—confessions obtained in violation of a person's Fifth Amendment right against compelled self-incrimination generally will be excluded from evidence, but confessions obtained in violation of a defendant's Fourth Amendment rights (*e.g.*, confessions arising during or as a result of an unconstitutional search) may be admissible if there is a weak link between the evidence and the unconstitutional police conduct (*e.g.,* the prosecutor can show that defendant's confession was an act of free will).

b. Identification Exception

If the police seize the defendant illegally and use the seizure to assist in identifying the victim, the court need not exclude the resulting evidence.

c. Witness's Statement Exception

In cases where the ultimate evidence obtained is a statement of a third-party witness, courts are likely to find that the taint of illegality has been eliminated because of the free will individuals exercise in deciding whether to talk with police or to testify.

3. Enforcement of the Exclusionary Rule

The issue of whether to exclude evidence is normally raised at a ***pretrial suppression hearing.*** The judge decides, by a ***preponderance of the evidence,*** whether the evidence was constitutionally obtained. At the hearing, the defendant may testify, and her testimony may ***not*** be used later at trial to prove her guilt.

4. Exceptions to the Exclusionary Rule

a. Impeachment Exception

Unconstitutionally obtained evidence may be used at trial to impeach the credibility of a witness, but not to prove her guilt. However, a truly involuntary confession (*e.g.*, one coerced by threat of force or promises that coerce a confession) is inadmissible for any purpose. Similarly, immunized testimony may not be used for impeachment purposes.

b. Post-Conviction Federal Habeas Corpus Proceeding

If the state provided the defendant with a full and fair hearing of an unreasonable search and seizure claim, the defendant cannot raise the exclusionary question again later in a federal habeas corpus proceeding.

c. Private Party Search Exception

The Fourth and Fifth Amendments apply only to government action. Therefore, courts will ***not*** exclude evidence obtained by a private party acting independently of state or federal law enforcement.

d. Civil Proceedings Exception

The exclusionary rule does not apply in civil proceedings.

e. Police Good Faith Exception

In certain circumstances, the exclusionary rule does not apply when police officers act in the objectively reasonable belief that their conduct is not violating the defendant's rights. Thus, the rule does not apply when there has been good faith reliance by the police on a facially valid law or, under most circumstances, on a defective, but facially valid, search warrant. The exclusionary rule also does not apply even if police conduct a search or make an arrest relying on negligently maintained police records. However, police may not successfully rely on the good faith exception in all instances (*e.g.*, when the affiant lied in the supporting affidavit or the warrant is facially defective).

f. Grand Jury Exception

Grand jury witnesses may not refuse to answer questions based on illegally seized evidence.

g. State Law/Agency Rule Exception

If the search does not violate the Constitution and only violates state law or agency rule, the defendant is not entitled to exclusion of the evidence.

h. Parole Revocation Proceeding Exception

The exclusionary rule does not apply in parole revocation proceedings.

i. Knock and Announce Rule Violation

Exclusion is not an available remedy for violations of the Fourth Amendment knock and announce rule pertaining to the execution of a search warrant. (See *infra,* p. 24.)

5. Effect of Exclusionary Rule Violation

If the defendant has made a timely motion to suppress, it is error for the court to admit unconstitutionally obtained evidence. Admission of such evidence will result in a reversal on appeal if the defendant is convicted ***unless:*** (i) the defendant ***waived*** the error by failing to object to the use of the unconstitutionally obtained evidence; ***or*** (ii) the error is found, beyond a reasonable doubt, to be ***"harmless"***—*i.e.,* the illegally-obtained evidence did not contribute to the conviction.

6. Retroactivity

If a Supreme Court decision interprets or delineates constitutional rights, the decision will be applied retroactively to all ***convictions affected by the decision*** that are ***not yet final*** or that are ***pending on direct review***.

II. THE FOURTH AMENDMENT

A. ARREST AND OTHER DETENTIONS

1. Introduction

The Fourth Amendment prohibits ***the government*** from conducting ***unreasonable*** searches (intrusions on a person or their papers, houses, or effects) to gather information or an invasion of a person's reasonable expectations of privacy. It also prohibits unreasonable seizures (a meaningful interference by the government with a person's papers, houses, or "effects," or (in the case of a person) a show of police authority to which a person submits).

2. Arrests

An arrest is a Fourth Amendment seizure that occurs when a ***person is taken into custody against her will***. It requires a physical application of force by a police officer with the intent to restrain ***or*** submission to an officer's show of force.

a. Probable Cause Requirement

No arrest is valid unless there is probable cause—*i.e.*, a reasonable belief that this suspect has committed or is about to commit a crime. Probable cause turns on the assessment of probabilities given the totality of the circumstances. Probable cause is incapable of exact quantification.

b. Effect of Invalid Arrest

An unconstitutional arrest, by itself, has no impact on a subsequent criminal prosecution, although evidence found during a search incident to an unlawful arrest should be suppressed.

Note: An arrest is not unconstitutional merely because the grounds stated at the time of the arrest were erroneous or even if state law did not provide for arrest under the circumstances, provided the police had probable cause to make the arrest.

c. Arrest Warrant Not Required Except for Home Arrests

The Fourth Amendment reasonableness standard does not require that a warrant be obtained prior to an arrest in a public place, provided there is probable cause to make the arrest.

(1) Arrests in Public Places

A police officer may make a warrantless arrest in a public place when she has ***reasonable grounds (probable cause) to believe a felony has been committed*** by a particular person or when a ***misdemeanor has been committed in her presence***.

(2) Arrests in the Home

The Supreme Court imposes a presumption that warrantless, in-home arrests are unreasonable and, therefore, invalid under the Fourth Amendment, unless exigent circumstances are present or the arrestee consents.

(a) Exception—Hot Pursuit

If probable cause exists, the police may, without a warrant, pursue a suspect into his home if necessary to prevent danger to others, the suspect's escape, or the destruction of evidence. However, the pursuit of a fleeing misdemeanor suspect does not categorically qualify as an exigent circumstance justifying an officer's warrantless entry into a home.

(b) Exception—Emergency Assistance

Police may enter a home without a warrant to render emergency aid to an injured occupant or to protect an occupant from imminent injury.

(c) Announcement Requirement

Generally, a police officer must announce her authority and purpose before using force to enter a home to make an arrest. Police should wait a reasonable time after announcing before forcibly entering. Most jurisdictions allow officers to make a "no-knock" entry only if the officers have a reasonable belief that an announcement would endanger the officers, prompt a suspect's escape, or allow the destruction of evidence. Some jurisdictions issue no-knock warrants authorizing police entry without warning. In any case, failure to knock and announce will not result in the exclusion of evidence.

(d) **Scope of Search**

A warrant to arrest in a home does not authorize a full search of the home. Police must stop searching once the suspect is found. But when police enter with an arrest warrant, they may conduct a cursory sweep of the home for safety reasons, if they have a reasonable belief (reasonable suspicion) that others are hiding to ambush them. The cursory sweep may not be for evidence—only for people who may pose a danger to police.

(e) **Third-Party Premises**

A search warrant is required for the arrest of a suspect in another person's home.

(3) **Obtaining a Warrant**

To obtain an arrest warrant, a police officer's affidavit, containing facts showing the commission of an offense and the accused's responsibility for it, must be presented to a neutral judicial officer who determines its sufficiency.

3. **Force**

There is a Fourth Amendment "seizure" when a police officer uses deadly force to apprehend a suspect. An officer may not use deadly force unless it is reasonable to do so under the circumstances (*e.g.*, where a suspect might pose a danger to himself or others). A person is also "seized" when police shoot her intending to restrain her, even if she does not submit to police control and escapes. The seizure lasts only as long as she is restrained and does not continue during an escape.

4. **Stops and Other Detentions**

Not all seizures need to be supported by full probable cause. Limited seizures—stops and detentions may be justified on a lesser showing. **Terry v. Ohio**, 392 U.S. 1 (1968).

a. **Limited Detention—Stop and Frisk**

(1) **Stop (Seizure)**

Police officers may ***briefly*** detain (seize) a person for questioning without probable cause if they ***observe unusual conduct*** leading to a ***"reasonable suspicion"*** that criminal activity may be afoot, and the officer is ***able to point to specific and articulable facts to justify*** that suspicion. Even if the officer's reasonable belief is incorrect, that belief will support a brief detention (seizure). The officer must consider the ***totality of the circumstances*** and must have a ***particularized, objective basis*** for suspecting the particular person stopped of criminal activity. The investigatory stop must be ***temporary*** and ***no longer than necessary to effectuate its purpose*** (*i.e.*, to confirm or dispel the officer's suspicion). A traffic stop that is prolonged for seven or eight minutes to conduct a dog sniff without cause violates the Fourth Amendment. On the other hand, if the police have a reasonable suspicion that luggage contains narcotics, this will support a ***temporary*** detention of the unopened luggage for investigative purposes.

(2) **Frisk**

During a stop, an officer may conduct a limited pat-down search ("frisk") of a person's ***outer clothing*** for a ***weapon*** only if the officer ***reasonably suspects*** that the suspect is armed and dangerous. An officer may also "frisk" a passenger compartment of a car with reasonable suspicion to believe that it contains a weapon that the suspect can reach.

Note: The permissible frisk of a person or car is limited in scope and cannot rise to the level of a full search.

(3) **Stop and Identify Statutes**

Requiring loiterers to give police "credible and reliable identification" is unconstitutionally vague if it is unclear what is sufficient for identification. The Due Process Clause prohibits regulations that fail to give persons reasonable notice of what is prohibited. However, merely requiring a person who has been lawfully stopped to state his name is constitutional as long as the police have reasonable suspicion to make the stop.

Note: The requirement to provide a name does not originate with the Fourth Amendment, which imposes obligations only on the government, but with a separate state or federal law.

b. **Automobile Stops**

Police officers may not stop (seize) a single vehicle for the sole purpose of checking the driver's license or the vehicle's registration unless they have reasonable suspicion or probable cause to believe that the driver is unlicensed or the car is unregistered.

(1) **Pretextual Stops**

If an officer has probable cause to stop a vehicle, the officer may do so even if the officer's motive is to investigate whether some other law—for which the officer lacks any suspicion—has been violated.

(2) **Seizure of Occupants**

An automobile stop constitutes a seizure of the automobile's driver as wall as any passengers.

(3) **Roadblocks**

The Supreme Court has upheld roadblock searches—made without individualized suspicion that the driver has violated some law—when the roadblock stops cars on the basis of some neutral, articulable standard (*e.g.*, every car, every third car, etc.) ***and*** the roadblock is designed to serve law enforcement purposes related to automobiles and/or their mobility (*e.g.*, drunk driving).

(4) **Ordering Persons out of a Vehicle**

If a police officer has lawfully stopped a vehicle, the officer may, without further justification, order the occupants (driver and passengers) to get out.

Note: Such roadside detentions must be brief (*i.e.*, no longer than it takes the officer to issue a citation or otherwise address the basis for the stop)

c. **Detention During Search Permissible**

When executing a search warrant, police may detain persons present on the searched premises while the search is conducted. However, officers may not detain persons beyond the immediate vicinity of the premises or conduct a weapons pat down unless they have a reasonable and articulable suspicion that criminal activity is afoot and the detainee is armed.

d. Police Station Investigations

Generally, police officers must have probable cause to bring a suspect to the police station for questioning or fingerprinting. When police make an arrest for a serious crime and the arrest is supported by probable cause, police may also take a cheek swab of the arrestee for DNA as part of a routine booking procedure. The DNA sample can lawfully be analyzed and used to seek a match for any unsolved crimes.

5. Grand Jury Subpoena Exception

The Fourth Amendment requirement that searches and seizures be reasonable does not protect a person from being compelled by subpoena to appear before a grand jury. Thus, a grand jury subpoena to appear need not be based on probable cause or objective suspicion.

B. EVIDENTIARY SEARCH AND SEIZURE

1. Introduction

The Fourth Amendment prohibits ***the government*** from conducting ***unreasonable*** evidentiary searches and seizures. To be reasonable, most searches must be conducted pursuant to a warrant, which rests on probable cause. When conducting a search, police may usually look for: ***instrumentalities*** of crime, ***fruits*** of crime, ***contraband,*** or ***evidence*** of crime.

2. Governmental Conduct Requirement

The Fourth Amendment applies only to actions by ***government officials,*** unless a private person is acting on behalf of the government.

3. Reasonable Expectation of Privacy Requirement

A defendant can raise a Fourth Amendment claim only if he has ***standing,*** meaning a ***reasonable or legitimate expectation of privacy and has had their own rights violated***. Courts must look at the ***totality of circumstances*** to make that determination.

a. Standing

To have standing to challenge a search, a person must have a ***legitimate expectation of privacy,*** which is assessed under the totality of the circumstances. The Supreme Court has found standing when the place searched was the defendant's home, or a place he was staying overnight with the owner's permission, or a place the defendant had a right to possess with a right to exclude others. Anyone in an automobile stopped unconstitutionally may challenge the stop, and evidence obtained from the stop, but if an automobile is constitutionally stopped, a mere passenger does not have standing to challenge a search of the automobile just because the passenger was legitimately within the automobile. On the other hand, the driver of a rental car who has physical control of the car and can exclude others may have standing (*i.e.*, a reasonable expectation of privacy in the rental car) even when he is not listed in the rental agreement as an authorized driver of the car.

(1) Legitimately on Premises Alone—Insufficient

Someone merely present in a home with a homeowner's consent does not necessarily have standing to object to a search of the home.

(2) **Conspirators—No Automatic Standing**

A co-conspirator does not automatically have standing to object to the admission of evidence obtained illegally from another co-conspirator. He must show that his ***own expectation of privacy*** was violated.

b. **Items Exposed to the Public**

There is no reasonable expectation of privacy in items held out to the public (*e.g.*, handwriting, voice, bank records, location of car on public streets, the smell of one's luggage or automobile, etc.). However, despite the public nature of travel, police implicate the Fourth Amendment when they attach a GPS device to a suspect's car (an effect) and monitor the car's movements for an extended period or when they access historical cellphone data maintained by private wireless providers that creates a comprehensive record of the cell phone's movements over time.

(1) **Open Fields Doctrine**

Areas outside the curtilage of a home are considered open fields with no reasonable expectation of privacy. Searches of such areas do not violate the Fourth Amendment (*e.g.*, fields protected by fences and no trespassing signs; outbuildings) because they are deemed part of the "open field." In contrast, a front porch to a single-family home is considered part of the curtilage. Therefore, police may not walk a drug-detection dog onto the porch to sniff for odors of drugs emanating from within the home. Police also violate the Fourth Amendment when they trespass onto the curtilage to inspect a car or motorcycle parked on a private driveway.

(2) **Flyovers**

Items that can be viewed from airspace legally accessible under federal aviation regulations are subject to warrantless searches even within the curtilage.

(a) **Vision Enhancement**

The Court has allowed the warrantless use of powerful cameras—that are generally available to the public—to take photographs from legal airspace of ***industrial fields.*** However, the Court has prohibited the warrantless use of sense-enhancing technology (specifically, thermal imaging cameras) to gain information about the interior of a home that could not otherwise have been obtained without physical intrusion, at least where the technology in question is not in general public use. The difference between the two situations lies in the differing expectations of privacy.

(3) **Contraband**

There can be no legitimate expectation of privacy in contraband. Therefore, there is no unconstitutional search when contraband in luggage located in a public place or in a constitutionally stopped automobile is sniffed out by a narcotics detection dog.

4. **Searches Conducted Pursuant to a Warrant**

a. **Warrant Requirement**

Normally, a warrant is needed for a search or seizure (unless the action is within one of the established exceptions, *infra*). To be valid, a warrant must be based on probable cause, be supported by oath or affirmation, particularly describe what is to be searched or seized, and be issued by a neutral magistrate.

b. Probable Cause Requirement

No warrant may lawfully issue until an independent magistrate has determined that there is probable cause to issue the warrant.

Note: A warrant may be anticipatory—it is sufficient that there is probable cause to believe seizable evidence will be found at a future date, when the search is conducted. A warrant may also be contingent on a particular future condition (*e.g.*, delivery of a package to the suspect's address), although a contingent warrant is not valid until the condition has occurred. However, the duration of a warrant cannot be indefinite, and a search conducted long after the issuance of a warrant may be unlawful if the warrant is found to have been stale by the time of such search.

(1) Affidavits Based on Hearsay—Totality of the Circumstances

Credible hearsay ***may*** be used to establish probable cause. The validity of a warrant based on an informant's tip is determined by a ***totality of the circumstances*** test. All of the allegations in the affidavit, taken together, must permit the magistrate to make a commonsense evaluation that there is a fair probability that contraband or evidence of a crime will be found in a particular place.

(2) Challenging the Warrant

A warrant valid on its face may be challenged by the defendant, but the challenge must meet two requirements. First, the defense must establish that the affiant made false statements knowingly or recklessly. Second, the defense must show that, without the false statements, the affidavit fails to provide probable cause.

c. Precision Requirement

A warrant must describe with reasonable certainty the ***place*** to be searched and the ***items*** to be seized. It is not sufficient that such detail is in the affidavit underlying the warrant. However, a reasonable error in the description will not necessarily invalidate the search, and certain items (*e.g.*, narcotics, firearms) need not be identified with additional specificity.

d. Magistrate Requirements

A warrant must be issued by a ***neutral and detached*** magistrate, although in some jurisdictions the magistrate need not be trained as a lawyer. The magistrate is not neutral if she receives compensation for issuing warrants but no compensation for denying them. The magistrate is also required to review the supporting documentation and cannot merely "rubber stamp" a warrant application.

e. Third-Party Premises May Be Searched

Searches of property belonging to persons not suspected of a crime are permissible provided the search is conducted pursuant to a warrant based on probable cause to believe that evidence of someone's guilt (or other items subject to seizure) will be found.

f. Execution of Warrant

Generally, only police officers may execute a warrant (*e.g.*, the media or other third parties may not accompany the police), unless a third party's assistance is needed. Police officers must knock and announce their authority and purpose unless they have reasonable suspicion ***based on facts specific to the particular case***, that knocking and announcing would be ***dangerous or futile***, or that it would ***inhibit the***

investigation (*e.g.*, it would lead to the destruction of evidence), or during the execution of a lawfully issued no-knock warrant. However, failure to knock and announce will not result in exclusion of evidence.

During execution of the warrant, persons on the premises may ***not*** automatically be fully searched, but may be detained and even restrained in handcuffs. Police may search individuals present during execution of a search warrant only if they have independent grounds for the search (like reasonable, articulable suspicion that a person is armed and dangerous). The search of the premises cannot exceed the scope of the warrant, but an objectively reasonable error in execution does not invalidate a search. Generally, a separate search warrant is required to execute an arrest warrant on third-party premises.

5. Exceptions to Warrant Requirement

The Supreme Court has recognized exceptions to the warrant requirement when faced with special law enforcement needs, diminished expectations of privacy, minimal intrusions, or the like.

a. Search Incident to a Constitutional Arrest

The police may search a person without a warrant after a constitutional arrest. Such a search may be conducted pursuant to ***any custodial arrest***, even for minor violations of law.

(1) Arrest Must Be Constitutional

Most Supreme Court cases dealing with searches incident to arrest have indicated that the search must be "lawful," which the Supreme Court has recently held to mean "constitutional." To be constitutional, an arrest must be based on ***probable cause*** to arrest. The constitutionality of an arrest does not depend on whether, under the circumstances, state law authorized the arrest.

(2) Scope of Search

The search can be of the person arrested ***and*** the areas within the person's immediate reach. But the search may not extend to the contents of the arrestee's cellular phone.

(a) Protective Sweep

If police officers reasonably believe that dangerous accomplices may be present, they may conduct a "protective sweep" of the immediate area to ensure their safety.

(b) Automobile Occupants

After arresting an automobile occupant (or recent occupant), police officers may search the passenger compartment if they have reason to believe: (i) an unsecured arrestee may access the vehicle to obtain immediate control of a weapon, or (ii) if evidence of the offense of arrest reasonably might be found in the vehicle.

(3) Search Timing and Location

The search must be contemporaneous with the arrest. A search conducted at a different location and a significant time after the arrest generally cannot be justified by the arrest exception.

(a) **Exception—Station House Inventory Search**

When an arrestee is taken to the police station, police may make a full inventory search of the arrestee's person and all property in his possession (to protect the police and the property) if such a search is done pursuant to established procedures and not for investigatory purposes. Similarly, a full inventory search (including closed containers) can be made of impounded vehicles. Such inventory searches must be conducted pursuant to neutral established police procedures and cannot be used as "fishing expeditions" to gather evidence of other crimes. Also, provided the search is conducted as a routine part of booking for a serious charge, police may swab the inside of an arrestee's cheeks to obtain DNA.

b. **Automobile Exception**

A search of a vehicle (either on the road or at the police station) is valid if there is probable cause to believe that evidence of a crime will be found. The search may encompass the whole vehicle, as well as containers in the vehicle, if police have probable cause to believe evidence may be found somewhere in the car. However, if officers' probable cause is limited to a container within a vehicle, they may search only that container.

Note: The search need not be contemporaneous to the time the vehicle is stopped. The scope of the search is no narrower or broader than a magistrate could authorize in a warrant based on probable cause.

c. **Plain View Exception**

If officers are ***legitimately on the premises***, they may lawfully seize items that they discover on the premises ***in plain view*** that they have probable cause to believe are ***contraband or evidence*** of crime. The items need not be described in the warrant, but the illegal nature of the item must be immediately apparent without police manipulation.

d. ***Terry*** **Stop and Frisk Exception**

An officer may detain a suspect if the officer has an ***articulable, reasonable suspicion*** that the suspect is engaging in criminal activity. Reasonable suspicion need not be based on personal knowledge. The officer may question the suspect. If the officer reasonably believes the suspect may be armed, he is permitted to pat down the suspect's outer garments and to reach into garments **only if** the officer feels something that, based on its plain feel, he reasonably believes to be a weapon or has probable cause to believe is contraband.

(1) **Totality of Circumstances Considered**

In deciding whether to stop and frisk a person, the police may consider the totality of the circumstances.

Note: The Supreme Court has ruled that a person's ***unprovoked flight*** after seeing police in a high crime area gives officers reasonable suspicion for a stop. It is the combination of flight and high-crime area that gives rise to reasonable suspicion. Unprovoked flight by itself is insufficient.

(2) **Traffic Stops**

If police officers have lawfully stopped a vehicle for a traffic violation, they may search the passenger compartment for weapons **if** they reasonably believe the car contains weapons and the occupant can reach the weapon. Police officers may also order occupants out of the vehicle with no additional suspicion and frisk any occupant they reasonably suspect to be armed and dangerous.

(3) Stop

A *Terry* stop, which is a seizure, occurs when the police conduct is such that a reasonable person would believe that she is not free to leave and submits to police authority. To be valid, an investigatory stop must be for no longer than necessary to effectuate its purpose. If a stop is unreasonably long, it becomes an arrest and is unlawful unless there was probable cause for the arrest.

(4) Evidence Admissibility Standards

Evidence obtained during a *Terry* frisk will be admissible if, based on its plain feel during a frisk of the exterior of the suspect's clothing, the officer could reasonably have believed an item to be a ***weapon*** or the officer has probable cause to believe the item is ***contraband***.

(5) Stop and Identify Statutes

As long as police officers have reasonable suspicion to make a *Terry* stop, they may require the detainee to identify himself, if a state or local law requires, and the detainee may be arrested for failing to comply. *Note*: It is the state or local law that mandates identification, not the Fourth Amendment.

e. Consent Exception

Police may conduct a search without a warrant if the owner (or other person who reasonably appears to have authority over the property) ***voluntarily*** consents to the search (courts will consider all of the facts to determine whether consent was given voluntarily). The search may extend to any object or container that a reasonable officer would understand to be within the scope of the consent granted. The person giving consent controls the scope of the consent, including time constraints.

Note: Third party consent is invalid if the suspect against whom the search is directed is present and objects to the search, even if others give consent.

f. Emergency Exception

No warrant is needed if officers, in good faith, cannot obtain a warrant and need to conduct a search for the protection of themselves or others (*i.e.,* the emergency aid doctrine or the community caretaker exception) or evidence (*e.g.*, a threat of immediate physical danger exists, police are in hot pursuit of a dangerous suspect, rushing to scene of homicide, etc.).

g. Evanescent Evidence Exception

The warrantless seizure by police of breath evidence from someone suspected of driving drunk is reasonable. In contrast, police typically need a warrant for a blood draw because it is more intrusive. The taking of blood without a warrant must be determined case-by-case. Nevertheless, taking blood without a warrant from an unconscious suspect to test for intoxicants is usually deemed lawful.

6. Electronic Surveillance

Any form of electronic surveillance, including wiretapping, that violates a ***reasonable expectation of privacy*** constitutes a search.

a. Warrant Requirement

To be constitutionally valid, a warrant must describe with particularity the conversations to be heard, show probable cause to believe a crime has been or will be committed, limit the duration of the wiretap, and name the suspects whose conversations are to be overheard.

b. **Title III Compliance Requirement**

All electronic surveillances must comply with Title III of the 1968 Omnibus Crime Control and Safe Streets Act, which requires more than the constitutional minimum.

c. **Pen Registers**

The Fourth Amendment does not require police to obtain a warrant to place a pen register (a device that records numbers dialed from a particular phone), although a federal statute requires court approval of the pen register.

d. **Patriot Act**

The Patriot Act, adopted after the September 11, 2001, attacks on the World Trade Center and Pentagon extends pen register provisions to the Internet, provides for roving wiretaps under the Foreign Intelligence Surveillance Act ("FISA"), and subjects U.S. citizens to surveillance pursuant to FISA under specified conditions.

e. **"Uninvited" Ear**

A warrant is not required if the defendant made no attempt to keep his communication private.

f. **Unreliable Ear**

A person assumes the risk that the person with whom he is speaking is "unreliable"—*i.e.,* a government informer or undercover officer.

7. **Searches in Foreign Countries or at the Border**

The Fourth Amendment does not apply to searches and seizures by United States officials in foreign countries when a foreign citizen is involved. Border searches are permissible ***without a warrant or probable cause*** to enforce national boundaries. Searches near the border may also be proper on a showing of less than probable cause.

8. **Administrative Searches**

Generally, a warrant is required for a noncriminal-justice search (*i.e.,* for health and safety reasons—*e.g.,* an OSHA inspection), but the probable cause standard is relaxed and is satisfied by the showing of a ***general and neutral enforcement plan*** justifying the warrant.

a. **Airport Exception**

No warrant is required to search airline passengers before boarding an airplane.

b. **Welfare Inspections**

A warrant is not required for a welfare caseworker to enter a residence.

c. **Contaminated Food**

No warrant is required before seizing contaminated foods.

d. **Highly Regulated Industries**

No warrant is required to search highly regulated industries (*e.g.*, liquor, guns, strip mining, auto junkyards).

e. **Public Schools**

School officials need only ***reasonable suspicion*** to conduct limited, routine searches in the school. Reasonable grounds for a search will exist if the school official reasonably believes that the search will turn up evidence that the student has violated a school rule or the law. Nevertheless, a "strip search" of a student must be justified by the nature of the suspected infraction and consider the student's age and sex. Random warrantless drug testing of students participating in extracurricular activities has also been upheld.

f. Probationer's Home

No warrant is required for a probation officer or a police officer to search a probationer's home, where the probationer has agreed that as a condition of probation, he would submit to a search at any time. A similar rule has also been applied to a search of a parolee who agreed as a condition of parole to be searched at any time.

g. Government Employee's Desk and Pager

No warrant is required to search a government employee's desk, or even the text messages on his pager, if the search is reasonably related to the employee's work conduct and not excessive in scope.

h. Drug Testing

Where "special need" is present (*i.e.,* a reason beyond mere drug interdiction), the Court has not required a warrant when the government performs or requires drug testing of employees (*e.g.*, for railroad workers involved in accidents or drug interdiction agents who have access to drugs), or when a public school requires drug testing of students who participate in extracurricular activities.

9. General Evidence Gathering Limitation

Evidence obtained by means that "shock the conscience" of the court is inadmissible.

III. FIFTH AMENDMENT PRIVILEGE AGAINST COMPELLED SELF-INCRIMINATION

A. PRIVILEGE AGAINST COMPELLED SELF-INCRIMINATION

1. Constitutional Basis

The Fifth Amendment guarantees that "no person shall be compelled in any criminal case to be a witness against himself." This prohibition applies to both federal and state courts.

2. Purposes of the Privilege

The privilege is designed to ensure reliability in the criminal justice process, to avoid undue coercion, and to require the government to prove the defendant's guilt.

3. Who May Assert the Privilege

Only ***natural persons*** may assert the privilege (*i.e.,* not corporations), and it may be asserted only by those who may ***incriminate themselves*** (*i.e.*, one person cannot plead the Fifth to protect another).

4. When Privilege May Be Asserted

The privilege may be asserted in ***any proceeding*** (*e.g.,* criminal, civil, administrative) at which the government might compel testimony from the person asserting the privilege for use in a later prosecution. The privilege may be asserted at any stage of a proceeding. A criminal defendant may refuse to take the witness stand. All others can invoke the privilege only in response to individual questions.

5. **Scope of Privilege**

The privilege applies ***only to testimonial evidence*** and not to nontestimonial evidence (*e.g.,* lineup appearances), not to spoken words used solely for identification purposes, and not to "real" evidence (*e.g.,* blood samples, photographs, books, papers, documents, etc.).

6. **Compulsion Requirement**

The Fifth Amendment only bars the use of ***government compelled*** self-incriminating testimony.

a. **Reporting**

There is no Fifth Amendment privilege to refuse to keep records relevant to lawful administrative purposes (*e.g.*, one may not refuse to file a tax return, but may leave blank lines concerning source of income if the information would tend to incriminate).

b. **Registration**

The Fifth Amendment is violated by registration requirements: (i) aimed at a specific group; (ii) that is inherently suspect of criminal activity; and (iii) where the inquiry is into an area permeated with criminal statutes (*e.g.,* requiring gamblers to register as such).

c. **No Protection for False Statements**

The Fifth Amendment allows defendants to refuse to answer; it does not permit lying to avoid making an incriminating statement.

d. **Mental Illness**

Testimony is not compelled simply because it was prompted by mental illness; only ***official compulsion*** is proscribed.

7. **Burdening Assertion of Privilege**

A person cannot be penalized for asserting the privilege.

a. **No Penalties for Failure to Testify**

b. **Comments on Defendant's Post-*Miranda* Silence**

At trial, a prosecutor may not comment on the defendant's silence after receiving *Miranda* warnings (but a single comment on such silence may constitute harmless error). Nevertheless, a prosecutor may argue that a negative inference should be drawn from the silence of the defendant before arrest and before *Miranda* warnings may be used at trial.

c. **Comments on Defendant's Failure to Testify**

A prosecutor may not comment on the defendant's failure to testify at trial except in response to a defendant's claim that he was not given an opportunity to tell his side. The court must give a "no adverse inference" instruction if the defendant requests one and may do so even if the defendant objects. The Supreme Court has not decided whether a defendant is entitled to such an instruction during the penalty phase.

8. **Eliminating the Privilege**

The privilege does not apply if there is no possibility of incrimination because the witness has been granted ***immunity***, the ***statute of limitations*** has run, or the privilege has been knowingly, voluntarily, and intelligently ***waived***.

B. CONFESSIONS

1. Due Process "Voluntariness" Approach

Statements of a defendant may not be offered into evidence for any purpose at any time if they violate the voluntariness requirement of the Due Process Clause of the Fifth and Fourteenth Amendments.

a. Application

A judge must determine, by a preponderance of the evidence, that the statement was voluntarily made. The court will consider: (i) the defendant's personal characteristics (*e.g.*, age, education, intelligence); (ii) the nature of the detention (*e.g.*, conditions of confinement); (iii) the manner of interrogation (*e.g.*, length and number of sessions); and (iv) the use of offers, threats, promises, or deceptions. If a coerced confession is erroneously admitted, a resulting conviction will be overturned ***unless the error was harmless***.

2. Sixth Amendment Right to Counsel Approach

Even if the statement is "voluntary," it may be inadmissible if it violates the Sixth Amendment right to counsel. Generally, the right to counsel is violated if, after adversarial judicial proceedings have begun (*e.g.*, after indictment or arraignment), the police question the defendant outside the presence of counsel or without a valid waiver of the right to counsel. The right can also be violated when:

(i) ***The defendant is not explicitly questioned by a police officer***, but the statement was ***indirectly secured by the police*** outside the presence of counsel; or

(ii) ***The defendant's attorney is not present*** at the interrogation.

a. Offense Specific

The Sixth Amendment right to counsel is offense specific. Only statements relating to the crime charged are protected by invocation of the Sixth Amendment right. The Sixth Amendment right does not apply to an uncharged offense merely because it is factually intertwined with a charged offense for which the defendant has sought counsel. Offenses are considered different if one requires proof of an element that the other crime does not require.

3. Fifth Amendment Privilege Against Self-Incrimination Approach

In **Miranda v. Arizona**, the Court established the Fifth Amendment privilege against self-incrimination as a basis for determining the admissibility of a confession. Under *Miranda,* to offset the coercive atmosphere inherent in ***custodial police interrogation***, the Court requires the police to: (i) inform the suspect of his rights (to remain silent and to counsel, including appointed counsel for the indigent), (ii) warn him of the consequences of waiving those rights (anything said can be used against him at trial), and (iii) obtain a knowing and intelligent waiver; otherwise, generally any confession made by the suspect is ***inadmissible at trial to prove guilt.***

a. Failure to Give Warnings

(1) Public Safety Exception

A defendant's responses to brief and focused questions asked because of a reasonable concern for public safety may be admissible in court even though the defendant was in police custody at the time of questioning (interrogation) and was not given *Miranda* warnings.

(2) Subsequent Confession

If *Miranda* warnings are not given and a confession is obtained and then, during a subsequent interrogation, the suspect waives her *Miranda* rights and confesses again, the second confession is inadmissible if the "question first, warn later" strategy was intentional (*i.e.,* intended to get around *Miranda* requirements). Otherwise, the statement may be admissible.

b. Known Government Involvement

Miranda warnings need not be given prior to interrogation by someone whom the defendant does not know to be a government agent (*e.g.*, an undercover police officer).

c. Custody

Miranda applies only if the defendant is in custody. The standard may be difficult to apply, because courts must consider whether a reasonable person would have felt that they were not free to terminate the interrogation and leave **and** whether they were in an environment presenting the same inherently coercive pressures as the type of station house questioning in *Miranda*. The test is mostly objective. However, courts must consider the circumstances (such as the suspect's age, if it is known or apparent to the police officer) if such characteristics would affect how a reasonable person in the suspect's position would perceive things.

(1) *Terry* Stops

In their original limited form, *Terry* stops were not considered to be custodial, so no *Miranda* warnings were required. However, *Terry* stops have become more expansive and longer, so they might require *Miranda* warnings, depending on the circumstances.

(2) Traffic Stops

An ordinary traffic stop does not constitute custody, so no *Miranda* warnings are necessary.

d. Interrogation

A defendant's statements are subject to *Miranda* only if given in response to interrogation. This includes more than straight "questioning." The test for interrogation is whether the police officers knew, or should have known, that their words or actions were reasonably likely to elicit an incriminating response. Psychiatric exams to determine competency to stand trial constitute custodial interrogation, but grand jury questioning does not.

e. Resumption of Questioning

(1) If Defendant Wishes to Remain Silent

If after receiving warnings, the defendant tells the police that she wishes to remain silent, this request must be ***scrupulously honored*,** meaning at the least, that the interrogation must stop immediately and questioning may be resumed only after the passage of a significant period of time. Police should also advise the suspect of her rights again. Courts are divided on whether later questioning can be about the same crime. Invocation of the right to remain silent must be unambiguous and explicit (*i.e.,* a suspect's failure to sign a waiver form combined with his failure to speak and answer an officer's questions—even for hours—does not constitute an invocation of the right to silence).

(2) **If Defendant Requests Attorney**

If the defendant requests an attorney, ***all*** questioning must cease, even questioning regarding unrelated offenses, until a lawyer is made available to the suspect, unless the defendant initiates further discussion with the police. The defendant's initiation of discussion does not include questions about matters attendant to custody (*e.g.*, access to food or bathroom facilities). The invocation of the right to counsel remains in place for at least 14 days.

(3) **Ambiguities in Request**

Invocation of the right to counsel must be unambiguous and explicit. If the defendant's request is ambiguous, police may continue questioning the defendant.

f. **Waiver**

Miranda rights may be waived. The government must show by a preponderance of the evidence that the defendant ***knowingly and intelligently waived*** the privilege against self-incrimination. The court must examine all of the circumstances when determining whether a waiver was valid. However, once the warnings are given, the courts usually find waivers to be knowing and intelligent. If, under the circumstances, the waiver is ambiguous, the defendant must clarify her decision. The Court in *Miranda* originally described the government's burden to prove waiver as "heavy." Still, a suspect will be deemed to have waived when: 1) the police advise the suspect of her *Miranda* rights; 2) the suspect understands the rights; and 3) she makes an uncoerced statement.

g. **Impeachment**

Voluntary statements obtained in violation of *Miranda* ***may*** be used at trial to ***impeach*** a defendant who takes the stand, but silence may ***not*** be used to impeach a defendant who later takes the stand, unless the silence occurred prior to arrest or (if post-arrest) prior to *Miranda* warnings.

h. **Nontestimonial Fruits of an Unwarned Confession**

Physical evidence obtained as the fruit of an unwarned confession is admissible.

IV. PRETRIAL PROCEEDINGS

A. IDENTIFICATION PROCEDURES

1. Privilege Against Self-Incrimination

Acts such as being compelled to provide blood for intoxication testing, to stand in a lineup, or to utter specific words are not testimonial and thus do not violate the defendant's privilege against self-incrimination.

2. Right to Counsel

Generally, a defendant has a Sixth Amendment right to have an attorney present during pretrial identification proceedings only if they occur ***after an adversarial criminal proceeding*** (indictment, preliminary hearing, etc.) and involve the defendant's physical presence. Some states consider the issuance of an arrest warrant the beginning of the adversarial process.

a. **In-Court Identifications**

If a defendant is identified by a witness at a pretrial identification and the defendant's right to counsel was violated at the pretrial identification, the results of the identification are inadmissible at trial. However, a subsequent in-court identification is admissible if the prosecution can show that it has a source independent of the unlawful pretrial identification.

b. Harmless Error Test May Apply

If the right to counsel is denied during trial, the denial is almost always reversible error per se. However, a pretrial denial of the right does not require reversal if the error is found, beyond a reasonable doubt, to be harmless.

3. Due Process Clause

A pretrial identification procedure will violate due process if, in light of the totality of the circumstances, there is a substantial likelihood that the resulting identification is unreliable.

a. Factors Affecting Reliability

The courts consider ***all of the circumstances*** in determining reliability, including: (i) the witness's opportunity to view the suspect; (ii) the witness's degree of attention; (iii) the accuracy of the description; and (iv) the length of time between the crime and the identification.

4. Refusal to Cooperate

A trial judge may jail a defendant who refuses to participate in a court-ordered identification procedure.

B. PRELIMINARY HEARING

1. Introduction

A preliminary hearing is a judicial proceeding that occurs between arrest and trial, and may serve the following purposes.

2. Determine Probable Cause to Detain

The primary purpose of a preliminary hearing is to determine whether probable cause exists to believe that the defendant committed the crimes charged.

Note: In many jurisdictions, a preliminary hearing may be bypassed by a grand jury indictment, which establishes probable cause.

3. Initial Appearance to Set Bail

Before trial, the defendant will generally be entitled to a hearing within a few days after arrest: (i) to determine whether she should be freed on bail pending trial, (ii) to inform her of her rights, and (iii) to appoint counsel for her if she is indigent.

4. Bindover Hearing

A bindover hearing (or probable cause to prosecute hearing) reviews the prosecutor's decision to charge the defendant for sufficiency of evidence.

5. Limitations

Generally, no preliminary hearing is required: (i) if a grand jury returned the indictment, (ii) for misdemeanors, or (iii) if the defendant waives the right.

C. BAIL

1. Constitutional Basis

The Eighth Amendment provides that "excessive bail shall not be required." This does not guarantee a right to bail, only that if bail is granted, it shall not be excessive.

2. Function of Bail

Bail is designed to assure the presence of the defendant at trial. Thus, bail is excessive when it is set at an amount higher than reasonably calculated to assure the defendant's presence at trial.

3. Denial of Bail—Capital Cases

No right to bail exists in capital cases.

4. Denial of Bail—Preventive Detention

Many states (and Congress) allow courts to deny bail to defendants who are allegedly dangerous to society. Generally, if such preventive detention is applied, the affected defendant must receive an expedited trial date.

5. Appellate Review

Appealability of an order regarding bail varies from jurisdiction to jurisdiction, but if not immediately appealable, denial of bail can be raised in a habeas corpus petition.

6. Bail During Appeal

Under federal law, a defendant appealing a conviction can be released on bail only by showing that he is not likely to flee, does not pose a danger to the community, and that the appeal raises a substantial issue likely to result in a reversal, new trial, a sentence that does not include a term of imprisonment, or a reduced sentence to a term of imprisonment less than the total time already served plus the expected duration of the appeal.

7. Types of Bail

The predominant pretrial release system is the money bail system, where a bond is posted to assure the defendant's presence at trial. Some jurisdictions release defendants on their own recognizance or under specified conditions (*e.g.*, maintenance of employment).

D. INDICTMENT

1. Definition

An indictment is a written accusation, issued by a ***grand jury***, charging a person with a crime.

2. Use of Indictments

A defendant has a Fifth Amendment right to a grand jury indictment in all ***federal felony*** prosecutions. Although this right does not apply to state criminal prosecutions, many state constitutions have a similar provision.

3. Proceedings

Grand jury proceedings are secret, and the defendant has no right to appear personally or through counsel. Illegally obtained evidence and hearsay evidence ***may*** be used in a grand jury process. Once an indictment is returned, the prosecutor retains discretion whether to prosecute. But an indictment returned by a properly constituted grand jury conclusively determines probable cause for the charged crime(s).

4. Waiver

An accused can waive the right to a grand jury hearing in federal court in all but capital cases. Some states do not allow such waiver.

5. Special or Investigative Grand Jury

In extraordinary cases (usually involving organized crime or political corruption), an indictment may originate from a special grand jury's own investigation of criminal activity.

E. INFORMATION

1. Definition

An information is a written accusation prepared by a ***prosecutor***, used to charge persons with criminal offenses where a grand jury indictment is not required or has been waived. In many jurisdictions, the information is used more frequently than the indictment.

2. Limitations on Filing Information

Although not constitutionally required, most state and federal courts require the defendant to have a preliminary judicial examination before an information can be filed, and the information must reasonably inform the defendant of the charges so that an adequate defense may be prepared.

3. Joinder of Offenses and Defendants

Under federal law and the law of many states, an information (or indictment) can charge two or more offenses that are connected in their commission or are of the same character. Two or more defendants may be charged together if they participated in the same transaction or series of transactions.

F. RIGHT TO A SPEEDY TRIAL

1. Constitutional Basis

The Sixth Amendment provides that a defendant has a right to a speedy trial to avoid placing undue burdens on the defendant and to quickly dispose of criminal justice matters. Violation of the right requires dismissal of the charge, although the remedy is rarely applied.

2. When Right Attaches

For Sixth Amendment purposes, the only delays that are material are those that occur ***after*** the person has become an "***accused***" (*i.e.,* after arrest or formal charges). Any delays after the alleged commission of the crime, but before formal charging or arrest, do ***not*** raise speedy trial claims. However, the right attaches after formal charging even if the defendant does not know of the charges. Delays before arrest or formal charges may raise due process concerns.

3. Determining Unreasonableness of Delay

While many statutes specifically address the speedy trial question, for constitutional purposes there is ***no fixed time period*** that is determinative. Instead, a judge must consider factors such as: (i) the length of the delay; (ii) the reason for the delay (*e.g.*, by prosecutor, by accused); (iii) the defendant's assertion or nonassertion of the right; and (iv) any prejudice resulting from the delay.

4. Statutory Provisions

Many states have statutes dealing with speedy trial with fixed time periods for prosecution. The Federal Speedy Trial Act regulates federal prosecutions.

G. THE GOVERNMENT'S OBLIGATION TO DISCLOSE INFORMATION AND NOTICE OF DEFENSES

1. Constitutional Provisions

Under the Constitution (as opposed to numerous statutes and rules of criminal procedure), the prosecution has a duty to avoid using false evidence but only a limited obligation to disclose information to a defendant in a criminal trial.

2. Duty to Disclose Favorable Evidence

The prosecution has a duty to disclose material, exculpatory evidence to the defendant, even if the defendant does not request such evidence during discovery. This is known as the "*Brady* rule," named for the Supreme Court case **Brady v. Maryland**. If the prosecution fails to disclose material, exculpatory information under **Brady**, a conviction must be overturned if there is a ***reasonable probability*** that had the evidence been disclosed to the defendant, the result of the proceeding would have been different. Three elements must be shown to prove a **Brady** violation:

a. The evidence at issue is favorable to the accused because it is ***exculpatory or impeaches*** a prosecution witness;

b. The evidence was ***suppressed*** by the government willfully or inadvertently; and

c. The defendant's case was ***prejudiced*** as a result.

3. Defense Obligation to Disclose Information

Some states allow the prosecution to receive certain information (*e.g.*, advance notice of alibi defenses) from the defense prior to trial. In such cases, the defense must receive reciprocal discovery rights.

H. COMPETENCY TO STAND TRIAL AND AT TIME OF EXECUTION

1. Competency and Insanity Distinguished

Incompetency merely bars trial at this time and depends on the defendant's mental condition ***at the time of trial***. Insanity is a defense to the crime charged and is based on the defendant's mental condition ***at the time of the offense***.

2. Basis of Claim

The incompetency claim is based on the belief that, under the Due Process Clause, only persons competent to ***understand the charges*** against them and to ***assist counsel*** in the preparation of a defense may be tried, convicted, or sentenced.

Note: The standard of competency to waive counsel is different. A person may be found competent to stand trial but incompetent to waive counsel, although such a result is highly unusual.

3. Determining Competency

A defendant may not be declared incompetent without ***notice*** and a ***hearing***. A state may require a defendant to prove incompetency by a preponderance of the evidence. An indigent person has a right to a psychiatric exam at the government's expense if he can make a colorable showing that he might benefit from the insanity defense or if the government plans to use psychiatric evidence to prove potential future dangerousness at sentencing.

4. Effect of Finding Accused Incompetent

If the accused is found incompetent to stand trial, the criminal proceedings are suspended until the defendant is adjudged competent.

5. Incompetency at Time of Execution

A defendant may not be executed if he is incapable of understanding the nature and purpose of the punishment, although his inability to remember the events of his crime because of physical or mental deficits does not preclude his execution.

V. THE TRIAL

A. FAIR AND IMPARTIAL TRIAL

1. Constitutional Bases

A defendant has the right under the Sixth and Fourteenth Amendments to a fair trial by an impartial judge or jury.

2. Judge

Due process is violated if the judge is significantly ***prejudiced*** against the defendant or has a ***financial interest*** in the trial resulting in a finding of guilt.

3. Jury

A defendant has a right to a jury that is free from unfair influences or prejudice. A juror cannot: (i) have an interest in the trial results, (ii) have preconceived ideas about the verdict, (iii) be unduly influenced by pretrial publicity, or (iv) demonstrate racial or similar bias preventing the juror from remaining impartial.

a. Trying Defendant in Prison Clothing

Trying a defendant in prison clothing or in shackles can result in unfair jury prejudice and cannot constitutionally be compelled in most instances.

b. Trial Disruption

Televising a trial is unconstitutional ***if*** it disrupts the trial.

c. Pretrial Publicity

Excessive pretrial publicity prejudicial to the defendant may require a change of venue or a retrial.

4. Venue

The Sixth Amendment guarantees a trial in the State and district in which the crime "shall have been committed." The remedy for conducting a criminal trial in the wrong venue is to retry the accused in the proper venue.

B. JOINT TRIALS

1. Joinder of Defendants

Generally, multiple defendants may be tried jointly if they are charged with participating in the same act or transaction that constitutes the offense.

2. Severance of Defendants

A defendant is entitled to a separate trial if either co-defendant is unduly ***prejudiced*** by the joinder (*e.g.*, if the jury will not be able to keep the defendants separate and evidence is significantly more powerful against one defendant, or if the government seeks to use a confession by one defendant that implicates the other). The harmless error test applies.

3. Joinder of Offenses

Offenses (felonies, misdemeanors, or both) may be joined if they are of the same character, are based on the same act or transaction, or are part of a common scheme or plan.

4. Severance of Offenses

If a defendant is prejudiced by a joinder, a court has the ***discretion*** to grant a severance. Decisions on severance involve a balancing of the efficiency and economy of a joint trial against any prejudicial impact on the defendant. The harmless error test applies.

5. Confessions by Non-Testifying Codefendants

One of the most common forms of prejudice created by joint trials arises when a non-testifying codefendant has confessed and implicated a codefendant. The use of such a confession at trial requires adequate redaction to protect the non-testifying defendant, or the trial must be severed.

C. RIGHT TO A JURY TRIAL

1. Constitutional Bases

The right to trial by jury is guaranteed by the Sixth Amendment and is applied to the states via the Fourteenth Amendment.

2. When Right Attaches

The right to a jury trial applies in cases in which the authorized punishment for the charged offense is ***more than six months' imprisonment***. A jury trial is rarely required for punishments of less than six months' imprisonment, although the Court has found a right to jury trial for a $52 million criminal contempt fine. There is no right to a jury trial in juvenile proceedings.

3. Jury Size and Unanimity Requirements

a. Federal Court

In federal criminal trials, unless the parties and court agree otherwise, generally a ***12-person*** jury is required, and the verdict must be unanimous.

b. State Court

The Supreme Court has imposed on state courts a ***minimum of six jury members***. Unanimity is required, no matter the number of jurors.

4. Fair Cross-Section Requirement

While no particular composition is required for any jury, the basic rule is that a defendant is entitled to have the jury selected from a fair cross-section of the community.

a. Use of Peremptory Challenges

Peremptory challenges may not be used to exclude potential jurors because of race or gender. Challenging the use of peremptory challenges based on prejudice (an equal protection violation) involves three steps:

(i) The defendant must show facts or circumstances that ***raise an inference that the exclusion was based on race or gender***;

(ii) The challenged party must then come forward with a ***race/gender-neutral explanation*** for the strike; and

(iii) The judge must then determine whether the challenged party's explanation was the ***genuine reason for striking the juror or a pretext for unlawful discrimination***.

Note: A defendant's right to due process and peremptory challenges is not violated merely because a defendant is forced to exercise a peremptory challenge to remove a potential juror after the court erroneously refuses to remove the juror for cause.

5. Right to Impartial Jury

a. Objections to Capital Punishment

States may not automatically exclude potential jurors who say that they are opposed to the death penalty. However, jurors may be excluded for cause who state that they could ***never*** impose the death penalty or that their views would ***substantially impair*** their performance as a juror. If a juror is improperly excluded, a resulting death sentence must be set aside.

b. Favoring Capital Punishment

A potential juror who says that she would impose the death penalty upon any guilty verdict in a capital case must be excluded because that person has indicated an inability to follow instructions regarding mitigating circumstances.

c. Failure to Exclude the Racially Prejudiced

If race is ***inextricably bound up*** in the controversy, the defendant is entitled to questioning on voir dire regarding racial prejudice. The mere fact that the defendant and victim are of different races does not give the defendant the right to such questioning except in capital cases.

6. Waiver of Jury Trial

The defendant may waive the right to a jury trial provided the waiver is ***expressly and intelligently*** made.

D. RIGHT TO A PUBLIC TRIAL

1. Constitutional Provisions

The Sixth Amendment guarantees that a criminal trial shall be open to the public.

2. Closed Trial

The public and the media can demand that a trial be kept open unless there is some compelling reason to hold a closed trial. Any closure must be narrowly tailored to remedy the specific problem behind the closure. There also is a rebuttable presumption that pretrial hearings should be open.

E. RIGHT TO COUNSEL

1. Constitutional Basis

All persons have a Sixth Amendment right to an attorney in criminal prosecutions, regardless of ability to pay.

2. Rights of Indigent Persons to Appointment of Counsel

If a defendant is indigent, counsel may be appointed at state expense in many criminal cases (although some states require, as a condition of probation, that the defendant repay the state if she can afford to do so). In determining indigency, most courts will consider factors such as: (i) the defendant's income, indebtedness, assets, and dependents; (ii) the nature of the charge; and (iii) bond expenses.

3. Cases in Which Right to Counsel Exists

a. Right to Counsel at Trial

The right to counsel exists in ***criminal prosecutions*** when ***actual imprisonment is imposed*** upon conviction or when a defendant receives a suspended prison sentence that is to be imposed if probation is revoked.

(1) Assistance Other than Counsel

In all courts, the defendant may obtain investigative, transcription, expert, or other services necessary for an adequate defense.

(2) Joint Representation

A defendant may have to share a lawyer with a co-defendant if no conflict of interest exists.

b. Right to Counsel in Non-Trial Proceedings

In non-trial proceedings, a lawyer is required at ***any critical stage***, such as arraignments, preliminary hearings, identification proceedings after the adversary process has started. Counsel is also required at the ***first*** automatic appeal of a conviction. A defendant is ***not*** entitled to counsel at grand jury proceedings or probation or parole hearings.

4. Impact of Violation of Right to Counsel

The failure to provide counsel at trial when required is per se a ***reversible error*** (**a structural error**). Similarly, erroneous disqualification of privately retained counsel results in automatic reversal. However, failure to provide counsel at non-trial stages is subject to the harmless error rule.

5. Waiver

A defendant may waive the right to counsel and represent herself. This right is also guaranteed by the Sixth Amendment. The judge must decide whether the defendant is competent to make an ***intelligent and voluntary*** waiver of the right to legal counsel, and whether the defendant is competent to represent herself. The standard for competency to waive counsel is higher than the standard for competency to stand trial, but the Court has not specified the exact standard. The trial judge must determine competency regarding self-representation based on an assessment of the defendant's emotional and psychological state. Rarely will defendants be found not competent to represent themselves. *Note*: There is no constitutional right to self-representation for oral arguments on appeal.

6. Ineffective Assistance of Counsel

The Sixth Amendment entitles a defendant to be represented by a lawyer who will render effective aid, but there is no right to have the lawyer of the defendant's choice. A defendant may claim ineffective assistance in cases where the lawyer did not render ***reasonably competent service*** and, as a result, the defendant was wrongly convicted or received more jail time than he should have (even as a result of a plea of guilty).

a. Standard of Reasonableness

Convictions are not often set aside on the ground of ineffective assistance of counsel. Generally, the defendant must show deficient performance by counsel, and that, but for that deficiency, the trial results would probably have been different.

b. No Right to Particular Lawyer

An indigent defendant is not entitled to the particular lawyer of his own choosing in order for assistance to be effective. *Note*: Generally, the accused is entitled to her lawyer of choice, if she has retained her own counsel.

c. **Right Limited While Testifying**

The Sixth Amendment right to counsel includes the right to consult with counsel during trial, but there is no right to consult with counsel while testifying or during short breaks (*e.g.*, 15 minutes) from testifying.

d. **Appeal—*Anders* Rule**

On appeal, if counsel genuinely believes that the case lacks merit, she may move to withdraw if she files a brief explaining anything that might arguably support the appeal.

F. RIGHT TO CONFRONT WITNESSES; COMPULSORY PROCESS

1. Confrontation

a. **Constitutional Basis**

The Confrontation Clause of the Sixth Amendment guarantees defendants the right to confront witnesses against them in all criminal prosecutions.

b. **Right of Accused to Be Physically Present**

A defendant has the right to be physically present during his criminal trial unless he voluntarily absents himself from the court or so thoroughly disrupts the proceedings as to waive his right.

c. **Right to Identity of Prosecution Witnesses**

Witnesses who testify against the defendant must reveal their true names and addresses (for purposes of preparing a defense and impeachment), unless pseudonyms are necessary to protect the witnesses or others.

d. **Right to Face-to-Face Encounter**

Generally, a defendant has a right to a face-to-face encounter with the witness, but the right may be denied to serve an ***important public purpose*** (*e.g.*, preventing harm to a child witness) if the reliability of the witness's testimony is otherwise assured.

e. **Right to Cross-Examination**

The Confrontation Clause in the Sixth Amendment also establishes that a defendant has the right to cross-examine witnesses against him and further dictates that limitations on this right are to be closely scrutinized by the courts.

f. **Confrontation Clause and Hearsay Evidence**

Hearsay rules limit the evidentiary use of out-of-court statements. The Confrontation Clause allows a defendant to face his accusers. Thus, the two are quite similar, but they do not necessarily overlap.

(1) **Witness with Lost Memory**

Neither the Confrontation Clause nor the hearsay evidentiary rule is violated by the introduction of a prior identification by a witness who is available for cross-examination at trial, but who is unable, because of memory loss, to testify about the prior identification.

(2) **Prior Testimonial Statement of Unavailable Witness**

If the prosecution offers into evidence a testimonial statement made by a witness at a prior judicial proceeding and the declarant is not available to be cross-examined by the defendant at trial, the statement is inadmissible unless the defendant had ***an opportunity to cross-examine*** the declarant at the time the statement was made. The Supreme Court has not provided a comprehensive definition of the term "testimonial," but it includes, at the least, testimony from a preliminary hearing, grand jury hearing, or former trial.

(a) Police Interrogation

Statements made in response to police interrogation are nontestimonial when made under circumstances indicating that the primary purpose of the interrogation is to enable the police to respond to an ongoing emergency. In contrast, statements are testimonial when there is no ongoing emergency and the primary purpose of the interrogation is to establish or prove past acts.

(b) Scientific Testimony

The Confrontation Clause bars the prosecution from introducing affidavits of lab analysts who tested a substance for drugs because the affidavits contain testimonial statements, unless the analysts who did or observed the testing are available to testify.

(c) Forfeiture by Wrongdoing

A defendant can forfeit her Confrontation Clause objection to a testimonial statement if her wrongful actions were intended to keep the witness who made the statement from testifying.

(d) Three-year-old child's outcry to his teacher about his abuse by accused is not testimonial when the primary purpose of the statement was to seek assistance.

(3) Confessions of a Co-Defendant

The Confrontation Clause is violated when an out-of-court confession of a co-defendant is used at a non-confessing defendant's trial and the co-defendant's confession incriminates the non-confessing defendant. However, if the error is harmless, reversal is not required. Moreover, a confession can be admitted if it can be redacted in a way that does not suggest the non-confessing defendant's participation. Similarly, a confession can be admitted against a non-confessing defendant if the confessing defendant takes the stand at trial and undergoes cross-examination. Finally, note that under the Federal Rules of Evidence (and the rules in many states) out-of-court statements made "in the course of a conspiracy and in furtherance of it" are admissible against any co-conspirators and are nontestimonial.

2. Compulsory Process

The Sixth Amendment provides that a defendant has the right to compulsory process for obtaining witnesses in his favor. Compulsory process is more than the power to subpoena; it includes the right to present a defense, which includes the defendant presenting his own witnesses and his own version of the facts.

G. BURDEN OF PROOF

1. General Standard

Each criminal defendant is presumed to be innocent. The government bears the burden of proving every element of the crime charged beyond a reasonable doubt.

2. Presumptions

A permissive presumption allows the jury to ***infer*** an element of the crime from government proof of the basic fact. The jury may ***reject*** this inference. A mandatory presumption, which requires the jury to accept the element, is unconstitutional.

3. Scientific Evidence in Federal Trials

In federal trials, scientific, technical, and other specialized evidence offered by experts is admissible if it will assist the trier of fact, is beyond the ken of the average juror, and is sufficiently reliable. Such evidence need not have gained general acceptance in the relevant professional community (as is required in states following the *Frye* rule).

Note: Remember to conduct the separate Sixth Amendment Confrontation analysis.

4. Review of Sufficiency of Evidence

When a jury returns a guilty verdict, the court (at trial or on appeal) must decide that there was adequate evidence to justify the verdict.

5. Affirmative Defenses

A defendant may have the burden of proving an affirmative defense (*e.g.*, self-defense, insanity, duress, withdrawal from conspiracy) but not "apparent defenses," which are elements of the crime (*e.g.*, heat of passion "defense" for crime of manslaughter).

H. INSANITY DEFENSE

1. In General

A successful insanity claim is a total defense to all crimes. Nevertheless, a defendant acquitted by reason of insanity may be committed to a mental institution until he has recovered.

2. Tests

Jurisdictions use one or a combination of the following four insanity tests:

a. *M'Naghten* Rule

Because of disease of the mind, defendant did not understand the wrongfulness of his acts.

b. Irresistible Impulse Test

Because of mental illness, defendant lacked capacity for self-control.

c. *Durham* (or Product) Test

Defendant's action was the product of mental disease.

d. Model Penal Code (A.L.I.) Test

This test combines the *M'Naghten* and irresistible impulse tests.

e. No Defense

A minority of states, including Idaho and Kansas, preclude the use of insanity as a defense, except where the accused's mental disease or defect prevents the accused from forming the requisite mens rea for the crime charged. The Supreme Court has found there is no constitutional right to raise the insanity defense.

3. Burden of Proof

In some jurisdictions, the defendant has the burden of proof of insanity by a preponderance of the evidence. Other jurisdictions require the defendant to prove insanity by clear and convincing evidence. In still other jurisdictions, the burden is on the prosecution to show beyond a reasonable doubt that the defendant was sane.

4. Psychiatric Examination

The state must provide a mental health expert for defense preparation if the indigent defendant has shown she probably can use the insanity defense. If the state shows that the defendant is likely to be dangerous in the future, the indigent defendant is entitled to expert examination and testimony in the sentencing proceeding.

5. Post-Acquittal Commitment

After the defendant is acquitted by reason of insanity, some jurisdictions automatically commit the defendant to a mental institution until she recovers. In others, the defendant must be shown to be presently mentally ill or dangerous. A preponderance of the evidence standard on the ***insanity issue*** is sufficient for commitment, and the defendant may be committed until she is sane or is no longer dangerous, even if this is longer than the sentence she would have served if convicted.

6. Diminished Capacity

In some states, a defendant may offer evidence of mental illness (not insanity) to show that the government has not proved the mental state for ***specific intent crimes***. The question is whether the defendant lacked the ability to form the necessary intent due to a mental disorder not amounting to insanity. Other states reject use of diminished capacity evidence.

I. ENTRAPMENT DEFENSE

1. In General

Entrapment is an ***affirmative defense***. In the federal system, it is based on the Supreme Court's interpretation of congressional intent in enacting criminal statutes.

2. Burden of Proof

In the federal system and in many states, if the defendant offers credible evidence of entrapment, the government must disprove the defense beyond a reasonable doubt. In other states, the burden is on the defendant to prove entrapment by a preponderance of the evidence. Entrapment is normally decided by a jury.

3. Basic Test

The majority view focuses on the ***predisposition of the defendant*** to commit the alleged act; the minority view focuses on the conduct of the government agents.

VI. PUNISHMENT

A. GUILTY PLEAS

1. Alternative Pleas

At arraignment, a defendant may plead: (i) ***guilty***, which waives the right to a jury trial; (ii) ***not guilty***; or (iii) in some cases, ***nolo contendere*** (a no contest plea to forgo a trial and accept punishment without admitting guilt).

a. Failure to Plead

If a defendant does not enter a plea, the judge will enter a not guilty plea for the defendant and set a trial date.

2. Entering the Plea

A judge must determine that a defendant's plea is made ***voluntarily and intelligently*** and that there is a ***factual basis*** for the plea. The judge must address the defendant personally, in open court, on the record. However, the judge need not personally explain the elements of each crime to the defendant; defendant's counsel may do so.

3. Plea Bargaining

Frequently used to settle criminal cases, a plea bargain is an agreement by a defendant to plead guilty to one offense in exchange for (i) the dismissal of other pending charges or (ii) a certain sentence recommendation by the prosecutor.

a. Enforcing the Bargain

The state may drive as hard a bargain as the law allows as long as ***no undue influence*** is exerted on the defendant. Once the court has accepted the defendant's guilty plea based on the plea bargain, the defendant and the prosecution have a right to have the bargain enforced (*i.e.,* if one party's terms are not met, the other party can get out of the deal).

4. Collateral Attack After Sentence

Generally, a defendant has ***no*** right to attack a plea on the ground of prior constitutional violations. However, there are certain exceptions (*e.g.*, lack of jurisdiction, ineffective assistance of counsel, failure to keep the bargain).

B. SENTENCING

1. Procedural Rights

Although a defendant is entitled to a lawyer at a sentencing hearing, other procedural requirements are ***less strictly applied*** than at trial. The judge may consider trustworthy evidence beyond the record, and the defendant does not necessarily have the right to cross-examine adverse witnesses.

2. Sentence Imposed

The sentence imposed is normally ***not*** reviewed if it is within statutory limits, unless the sentence is so shocking as to violate the prohibition against ***cruel and unusual punishment*** (*e.g.*, grossly disproportionate sentence, death penalty for crime other than murder, "status" crimes).

Note: A juvenile offender may not be sentenced to life in prison without the possibility of parole, even for homicide offenses.

a. Other Limitations on Sentence

The ***Eighth Amendment*** prohibits excessive penal fines, but this prohibition does not extend to civil fines or even civil forfeitures arising from use of property in the commission of a crime. It also does not violate the Eighth Amendment for a city to impose fines and imprisonment for camping or parking in city parks overnight, even if the law punishes homeless individuals. The ***Equal Protection Clause*** is used to restrict the type of sentence imposed (*e.g.*, sentence of a fine for those able to pay but converting the fine to imprisonment for those who cannot pay is prohibited). Also, ***due process*** requires that a defendant not be punished for appealing her conviction. Thus, a harsher sentence after reconviction may not be imposed unless new information or a subsequent criminal conviction is used at the second sentencing.

b. Sentence Enhancement

If substantive law provides that a sentence may be increased beyond the statutory maximum if additional facts (other than prior conviction) are proved, proof of the facts must be submitted ***to the jury*** and be proved beyond reasonable doubt. The sentencing judge cannot make the determination. The same is true if a fact (such as brandishing or discharging a firearm or whether the defendant engaged in one crime on separate occasions or multiple crimes over a period of days) will increase the statutory minimum sentence for a crime. On the other hand, laws may allow judges to decide whether sentences for multiple crimes are to run consecutively or concurrently.

C. DEATH PENALTY

1. As "Cruel and Unusual" Punishment

Capital punishment is permissible if (i) the sentencing body is permitted to consider, with ***adequate guidelines***, both ***aggravating and mitigating factors*** and (ii) there is a ***procedure for review***.

a. Method of Execution

A method of carrying out a death sentence is not cruel and unusual just because it might cause the condemned person some pain. A method of execution will be found to be cruel and unusual only if the condemned person can prove that: (i) there is a substantial risk of inflicting ***severe pain***; or (ii) an ***alternative procedure*** is feasible, may be readily implemented, and, in fact, significantly reduces substantial risk of severe pain.

2. Particular Statutory Schemes

All statutory rules for imposition of the death penalty must satisfy the strict requirements of the Constitution (*e.g.*, vague or overbroad statutes selectively applied violate the Eighth and Fourteenth Amendments; mandatory death penalty for a broad category of homicides or for a particular category of defendants is invalid; jury must be allowed to consider all mitigating circumstances).

Note: In a jury trial, a trial judge cannot determine whether sufficient aggravating factors justify imposition of a death sentence; a jury must make such a determination.

3. Limitations on Death Penalty

The death penalty may not be imposed for the crime of rape (of an adult or child) or on a person who is intellectually disabled or insane at the time of execution. Neither may it be imposed on murderers who were younger than 18 when they committed the crime. The death penalty may be imposed on a defendant who neither killed nor intended to kill, but who participated in a major way in a felony that resulted in murder, if the defendant acted with reckless indifference to human life.

VII. EX POST FACTO ISSUES

A. APPLICATION

1. Ex Post Facto Defined

The Constitution ***prohibits*** ex post facto laws, *i.e.*, laws increasing punishment beyond what was prescribed when the act was committed. The prohibition applies when the law is ***retrospective*** and ***disadvantages the offender*** affected by it. Specifically, there is a violation if the law:

(i) ***Punishes as a crime*** an act previously committed, which was innocent when committed;

(ii) ***Makes more burdensome*** the punishment for a crime after its commission; or

(iii) ***Deprives a defendant of any defense*** available under the law in effect when the act was committed.

Note: If a law's purpose is civil rather than punitive, it is not an ex post facto law unless its ***effect*** is so ***clearly*** punitive that it negates the legislature's intent.

VIII. POST-CONVICTION ISSUES

A. APPEAL

1. No Constitutional Right to Appeal

While the Supreme Court has never affirmed a constitutional right to an appeal of a criminal conviction, state constitutional provisions and statutes guarantee the right to such appeals.

2. Appellate Review

a. Preservation of Issue for Appeal

For appellate review, claims of error must be preserved at trial, except for plain errors. An error is plain only if, when viewed in context, it undermines the fundamental fairness of the trial and contributes to a miscarriage of justice. The appellate court may reverse a conviction that rests on a plain error even if the error was not properly raised at trial.

b. Standard of Review—Harmless Error

If there is no reasonable possibility that the error contributed to the conviction, the error is "harmless" and the conviction may stand.

c. Automatic Reversal—Structural Error

Denial of the right to counsel at trial (except a short absence of counsel during which only evidence involving co-defendants was introduced) or denial of defendant's choice of retained counsel is never harmless error. A constitutionally deficient reasonable doubt instruction to the jury, denial of a public trial, and exclusion of a member of the accused's race from the grand jury are also structural errors requiring automatic reversal.

3. Indigent Person's Right to Appeal

An indigent defendant has a right to a free transcript on appeal, and the right to appointed counsel in all automatic, but not discretionary, appeals. A presumption of prejudice applies when a lawyer fails to file an appeal as instructed by her client.

4. Retroactivity

Every rule announced by the United States Supreme Court on direct review must be applied retroactively to all other cases currently on direct review.

B. COLLATERAL ATTACK ON CONVICTIONS—HABEAS CORPUS

1. Function of Writ

This constitutionally based writ is designed to release an individual from ***any confinement*** contrary to the Constitution or fundamental law.

2. Procedural Issues

Habeas corpus is a ***civil*** action that is a collateral attack on a criminal conviction, challenging the ***legality of the detention***.

a. Burden of Proof

The burden is on the petitioner to prove, by a preponderance of the evidence, that the detention is unlawful. To prove the detention constitutionally unlawful, the petitioner must prove that the error had ***substantial and injurious effect*** on the verdict, considering the whole context of the case. If there is grave doubt as to the harm caused, the petition must be granted.

b. **No Right to Counsel**

An indigent person has ***no*** right to court-appointed counsel to prepare a writ petition because habeas corpus proceedings are civil matters.

c. **Timeliness**

Under the Antiterrorism and Effective Death Penalty Act ("AEDPA"), habeas petitions generally must be brought within one year. The one-year statute of limitations is not jurisdictional and may be subject to equitable tolling, especially in cases of attorney conduct that impeded a timely filing.

d. **Custody**

To file a petition, the petitioner must be in custody. Custody has been interpreted broadly to include individuals on probation, parole, or out on bail. Custody has even been found where the challenged sentence for the conviction has expired but the petitioner remains in custody on a consecutive sentence or if collateral consequences from the conviction (*e.g.*, loss of voting rights) are still in place.

Note: The definition of custody for habeas corpus purposes is very different from the definition of custody for *Miranda* purposes.

e. **Retroactivity**

New rules of criminal procedure generally may not be announced in habeas corpus proceedings. *Exceptions:* A new rule can be announced if it either:

(1) Places primary individual conduct beyond the power of the criminal lawmaking authority or changes the substantive definition of the crime; or

(2) Is implicit in the concept of ordered liberty.

3. **State Prisoners**

State prisoners may attack the legality of their detention by petitioning the ***state courts*** for the state writ of habeas corpus. Habeas actions may also be brought in ***federal court*** if the detention violates ***federal constitutional rights*** and the prisoner has ***properly exhausted all state remedies***. Additionally, the prisoner must have complied with ***state procedural rules*** (including rules as to appeals). State court findings of fact must be respected.

a. **Statutory Limitation**

The AEDPA prohibits federal courts from granting habeas relief to state prisoners unless the state conviction was "contrary to, or involved unreasonable application of," clearly established federal law as determined by the Supreme Court.

b. **Failure to Comply with State Procedural Rules**

If a state prisoner fails to follow state procedural rules, federal habeas relief will be granted only if the prisoner can show: (i) ***cause*** for the noncompliance and ***actual prejudice*** to the case resulting from the constitutional failure; or (ii) ***actual innocence***.

c. **Grounds Must Be Raised at First Opportunity**

A state prisoner filing a petition for federal habeas corpus relief generally must bring all claims for relief in his first petition. Usually, a successive petition raising issues that were raised in an earlier petition will not be allowed. A successive petition will be permitted to raise new grounds only if: (i) it raises a claim that relies on a new rule of constitutional law that the Supreme Court made retroactive to cases on collateral review; or (ii) new facts have been discovered that clearly establish that a constitutional error led to the conviction of an innocent person.

d. Fourth Amendment Claims Cannot Be Relitigated

Fourth Amendment claims ***cannot*** be relitigated in a federal habeas corpus action where the defendant claimed a search and seizure violation in the original state action. A federal judge can determine only whether the state provided the defendant with a fair opportunity to raise the issue at trial.

4. Federal Prisoners

For a federal prisoner to obtain habeas corpus relief, the prisoner must show actual innocence or show cause for his failure to raise the issue at trial and actual prejudice resulting from the error.

5. Showing Innocence

When seeking habeas relief on grounds of innocence, the petitioner generally must show that it is ***more likely than not*** that but for the constitutional error, no reasonable juror would have found the petitioner guilty.

IX. JUVENILE OFFENDERS

A. INTRODUCTION

Juvenile offenders are treated differently from adult offenders because the state is more interested in rehabilitation than in mere punishment. Although the state proceeds as *parens patriae*, and not as an adversary, due process must still be satisfied.

B. PROCEDURAL PROTECTIONS

1. Constitutional Rights Afforded Juveniles

Many procedural rights are now mandated in federal and state juvenile proceedings. Some of these are:

a. ***Notice of charges*****;**

b. ***Right to counsel*****;**

c. ***Rights of confrontation and cross-examination*****;**

d. ***Privilege against compelled self-incrimination*****;**

e. ***Right to proof beyond a reasonable doubt*****; and**

f. ***Protection against double jeopardy*****.**

2. Limitation—Certain Rights Inapplicable

Some rights available in adult criminal cases do not apply in juvenile matters, allowing more flexibility for government treatment of youthful offenders. Thus, juveniles:

a. ***Have no right to a jury trial*****; and**

b. ***May be held in custody until trial*** if considered a risk to society.

3. Limitation—Search and Seizure

Public school officials may conduct routine, not overly intrusive, searches of students if the officials have reasonable suspicion that a law or school rule has been violated. Probable cause is not required to render such searches reasonable. Schools may also perform random drug tests of students who participate in extracurricular activities.

C. TRANSFER TO ADULT COURT

1. Transfer Hearing

Juveniles alleged to have committed serious crimes can be tried as adults in adult courts but are entitled to a hearing regarding transfer.

2. Limitations on Punishment

A juvenile may not be incarcerated with adults in most jurisdictions. Persons who commit murder when younger than 18 cannot receive the death penalty, and in a non-homicide case, may not receive a sentence of life imprisonment without the possibility of parole.

X. PRISONERS' RIGHTS

A. PAROLE AND PROBATION

1. Right to Parole or Commutation

There is ***no*** constitutional right to parole or commutation. However, if state law creates a right to parole, the fairness requirements of due process apply.

2. Parole and Probation Revocation

There is no automatic right to counsel in revocation cases. However, ***before*** probation or parole may be revoked, a defendant must be notified of the charges and has a right to both: (i) a ***preliminary hearing*** to determine if probable cause exists for revocation, ***and*** (ii) a ***full revocation hearing***.

B. RIGHTS IN DISCIPLINARY SITUATIONS

1. Discipline Resulting in Solitary Confinement or Loss of Good Time

A prisoner may be deprived of earned "good time" or placed in solitary confinement only if the same procedural requirements as required for parole and probation revocation are met. However, a disciplinary action will trigger due process protections only if it constitutes an ***atypical, significant liberty restraint,*** not within the expected range of confinement for the prisoner's sentence.

2. Discipline Resulting in Transfer

There are no procedural due process limitations on an inmate's transfer to another institution. However, a prisoner may not be transferred to a mental hospital without a hearing.

3. Request for Witnesses

If an inmate's request for witnesses at his disciplinary hearing is denied, no reasons for the denial need be given during the hearing. However, reasons must be stated at some time (*e.g.*, at a later judicial proceeding).

C. OTHER RIGHTS OF PRISONERS

1. Access to Courts

Prisoners must have reasonable access to courts and to their lawyers. However, an inmate under investigation for a crime in prison has no right to counsel until adversarial judicial proceedings commence.

a. Access to DNA Testing

A prisoner has no substantive or procedural due process right to DNA test evidence following a conviction affirmed on direct appeal, provided the state gives an adequate procedural mechanism to challenge the conviction in a post-conviction proceeding.

2. First Amendment Rights

Prison officials may generally impose any restriction on prisoners' First Amendment rights that is ***reasonably related to legitimate, penological interests***.

a. Access to the Press

Prison officials may prohibit personal interviews by the press.

b. Censorship of Mail

Incoming mail and ***inmate-to-inmate correspondence*** may be broadly regulated. Prison officials may even open letters from prisoners' attorneys, as long as the prisoner is present and the officials do not read them. ***Outgoing mail*** may be regulated only if the prison officials show the regulation furthers an important government interest, is no more stringent than necessary, and prisoners have adequate opportunity to protest censorship.

c. No Right to Unionize

d. Marriage

Although legitimate security concerns may justify some restrictions on inmates' right to marry, prison officials cannot require prisoners to show a compelling reason to marry.

e. Religion

Under the Constitution, prison regulations reasonably related to legitimate penological interests are valid, even if they interfere with prisoners' ability to practice their religion (*e.g.*, requiring prisoners to work when their religion requires them to pray). However, a federal statute imposes a more stringent standard on any prison receiving federal funding. Under this law, a prison regulation cannot interfere with prisoners' religious practices unless it furthers a compelling government interest and the prison uses the least restrictive means to achieve the governmental goal. The Supreme Court has also held that a prisoner facing execution has a right to have a religious advisor present during the execution.

3. Right to Adequate Medical Care

It is a violation of the Eighth Amendment's cruel and unusual punishment prohibition to deliberately deprive an inmate of necessary medical care.

4. Two Inmates Per Cell

Such housing is not necessarily cruel and unusual punishment.

5. Visitation

Prisoners are not constitutionally guaranteed a right of visitation, but if government regulations or policies explicitly contain mandatory language granting visitation, the prisoners have a protectable right.

6. Place of Incarceration

A prisoner has no constitutional right to avoid transfer or to continued confinement in the general prison population (rather than in administrative segregation) absent an applicable state statute.

7. Fourth Amendment Rights

There is no reasonable expectation of privacy in a cell; thus, a prisoner generally has no protection against searches there.

8. Social Security Benefits

A state may not take a prisoner's Social Security benefits, because federal law exempts such benefits from execution or attachment.

9. Involuntary Treatment with Drugs

A prisoner found to be dangerous to herself or others may be treated against her will with antipsychotic drugs if treatment is deemed to be in her own best interest.

XI. DOUBLE JEOPARDY

A. IN GENERAL

1. Constitutional Basis

The Fifth Amendment establishes the principle that criminal defendants should be subjected to only ***one prosecution*** for a criminal offense. This is also applicable to the states via the Fourteenth Amendment.

a. Civil Actions

The Double Jeopardy Clause prohibits only repetitive ***criminal*** prosecutions. It does not prohibit states from seeking a remedial civil remedy against a defendant who has already been criminally tried for the conduct out of which the civil action arises. The government may also bring a criminal action even though the defendant has already faced a civil trial for the same conduct.

b. Different Sovereigns

One sovereign is not precluded from prosecuting an accused after a different sovereign prosecutes the same defendant. Thus, the federal government may prosecute an accused after she is acquitted by a state, so may an Indian Tribe.

2. When Jeopardy Attaches

Jeopardy attaches in a jury trial upon the swearing in of the jury. In a nonjury trial, it attaches when the first witness is sworn in.

3. An Erroneous Acquittal

An acquittal based on a lack of evidence and insufficient proof bars another prosecution for the same offense, even if the decision to acquit was clearly incorrect.

B. EXCEPTIONS TO DOUBLE JEOPARDY PROHIBITION

1. When Jeopardy Is Not a Bar

a. Mistrials

Jeopardy is not a bar to another prosecution when either the defendant consents (*e.g.*, motion for a mistrial) or justice requires a new proceeding (*e.g.*, hung jury, illness of judge, etc.), which is the concept of manifest necessity.

b. Dismissals

On a ***pretrial*** dismissal, a defendant can be reindicted or the prosecution can appeal. If dismissal occurs ***during trial***, there is no jeopardy bar if the defendant requests the dismissal and the dismissal is ***unrelated*** to the defendant's guilt or innocence. If the dismissal occurs after conviction, the prosecution can attempt to reinstate the conviction.

c. Appeals

(1) Appeal by Defendant

An appeal by a defendant generally constitutes a waiver of the double jeopardy issue. On retrial, however, the defendant cannot be convicted of an offense greater than the offense of his original conviction. Neither can a defendant be retried if the reversal was because of insufficient evidence.

(a) Limitation on Sentencing After Retrial

If a defendant is retried after appeal, double jeopardy generally does ***not*** bar imposition of a more severe sentence on subsequent conviction. However, the Due Process Clause would prohibit a trial judge from imposing a harsher sentence for the subsequent conviction absent a showing of identifiable facts occurring after imposition of the original sentence that constitute a basis for the increased sentence. Also, if a jury in the first trial determined that death is not an appropriate sentence, it cannot be imposed at the second trial.

(b) Appeal After Guilty Plea

A guilty plea usually constitutes a waiver of defenses, including double jeopardy.

(2) Appeal by Prosecution

The prosecution may appeal pretrial orders, convictions set aside by a judge (unless set aside for insufficient evidence), and sentencing orders. Acquittals may ***not*** be appealed.

2. Jeopardy Bars Only the "Same Offense"

Once jeopardy has attached, the defendant normally cannot be prosecuted for the same offense a second time or receive more than one punishment for that same offense.

a. Same Offense Defined

Two crimes are considered the same offense unless ***one crime requires proof of an additional element*** that the other crime does not require—the "*Blockburger*" test. **Blockburger v. United States**, 284 U.S. 299 (1932).

b. Conduct Used as Sentence Enhancer

The Double Jeopardy Clause is not violated when a defendant is indicted for a crime the conduct of which was already used to enhance the defendant's sentence for another crime.

c. Dual Sovereignties

When the same act is a crime under both federal and state law, under Indian Tribal law, or under the laws of two different states, the acquittal or conviction of the defendant in one jurisdiction does ***not*** bar prosecution in the other jurisdiction. *(But note*: Subdivisions of the same jurisdiction—*i.e.,* state and municipality—may not both prosecute the defendant for the same offense.)

C. COLLATERAL ESTOPPEL

In a subsequent prosecution for a different offense arising out of the same criminal act, the prosecution may be estopped to relitigate issues of fact necessarily determined in the defendant's favor in the prior trial.

Exams Strategies

In analyzing any question in Criminal Procedure, use the following basic approach to isolate and identify the legally relevant facts. (For more detailed methods of analyzing specific topics, review the Key Exam Issues section found at the beginning of each chapter.)

1. **Identify the Defendant's Rights**

   Depending on the stage of the criminal proceeding, the defendant will have certain procedural rights. You need to identify the applicable rights and then consider the pertinent case law interpreting the scope of those rights.

2. **Determine Whether the Defendant Has Received Those Rights**

   For each right a defendant may have at a particular stage of the proceeding, you must analyze the facts of the question to determine whether that right was respected by the government (*i.e.*, the police, prosecutor, or court). Again, look to the case law to point out the limits of the government's lawful activities.

3. **Ascertain Whether There Was an Effective Waiver of a Right**

   If you find that the defendant's rights have been violated, consider whether the defendant waived those rights. Be sure that any waiver is both ***voluntary and intelligently made*** and that the defendant is ***competent***. If so, the failure to honor the defendant's rights is excused.

4. **Consider the Effect of a Violation of Defendant's Rights**

   If the defendant's rights have been violated (and not waived), think about what ***remedies*** may be available (*e.g.*, use of the exclusionary rule to bar evidence at trial, reversal of a conviction, etc.). Don't overlook the fact that some violations are considered ***harmless error*** and allow the defendant no practical remedy. Remember, too, that the exclusionary rule does not always apply, even when rights have been breached.

5. **Evaluate Any Rights of Victims**

   In some jurisdictions, the victim may have a statutory—or state constitutional—right to attend proceedings, be advised of charges, or participate in the sentencing procedure.

Introduction

PUBLIC POLICY—INDIVIDUAL'S RIGHTS VS. EFFECTIVE LAW ENFORCEMENT

The study of Criminal Procedure requires a balancing of society's need for law and order against the individual's right to be free from unreasonable searches and seizures, to counsel, to due process and to fundamental fairness in criminal proceedings. This balancing of interests occupies the constant attention of courts, legislatures, scholars, and candidates for public office. Unlike other more esoteric branches of law, the criminal process is the subject of scrutiny by the press and voters in almost every election. Nearly all issues in Criminal Procedure ultimately involve deciding how to balance the need for efficient crime control with society's desire to ensure that no innocent person is swept into the net of the criminal justice system and that basic freedoms are respected.

Beginning in the early 1960s, the United States Supreme Court expressed concern that the real world of crime control bore little relation to the constitutional ideal. Throughout the 1960s, the Warren Court attempted to realign the real and the ideal in a series of decisions substantially expanding the federally protected constitutional rights of state criminal defendants. The Court federalized the criminal process by systematically applying the provisions of the federal Bill of Rights to state criminal cases. As the number of constitutional rights increased, the Court concomitantly increased access of state prisoners to federal courts for the vindication of these newly created rights.

While constitutional status for criminal procedure remains an enduring legacy of the Warren years, the Burger, Rehnquist and Roberts Courts, beginning in the 1970s and continuing through today, reduced both the scope of the state criminal defendant's federally protected rights and a defendant's access to federal courts to overturn state court convictions. It would, nevertheless, be a mistake to see the decisions of the Warren, Burger, Rehnquist or Roberts Courts as uniformly heading in a single direction. In addition to decided cases such as **Miranda v. Arizona** and **Massiah v. United States**, which protected the accused during police interrogations, the Warren Court produced decisions quite favorable to the government, such as those limiting the judicial role in overseeing the conduct of grand juries, permitting investigative detention without probable cause, and denying Fifth Amendment protection to the seizure of incriminatory real or physical evidence. The Burger, Rehnquist and Roberts Courts, while generally accommodating what was perceived as legitimate law enforcement needs, produced real expansions of defendants' rights in decisions mandating selection of juries from pools representing a fair cross-section of the community, requiring appointment of counsel for indigent misdemeanants who receive jail sentences, mandating warrants before police may make a nonemergency arrest of a person in her own home, reaffirming the individual privilege against self-incrimination under the Fifth Amendment, scrutinizing death penalty convictions, and protecting cell phones from warrantless searches.

Even so, some fairly consistent themes emerged from the decisions of the Burger Court since 1970 and have generally continued with the Rehnquist and Roberts Courts:

1. **Hierarchy Among Bill of Rights Provisions**

   The Court created a hierarchy among the provisions of the Bill of Rights. Not all rights receive the same scrutiny at the Supreme Court. The hierarchy is based on a single criterion: How much positive impact does the right in question have on the ultimate mission of the criminal justice system, namely, convicting the guilty and acquitting the innocent? Rights such as the right to counsel and the right to jury trial that have a direct bearing on the guilt-determination process received more favorable attention from the Court than rights such as the Fourth

Amendment right to be free from unreasonable searches and seizures which, when coupled with its remedy of exclusion, may have a negative impact on finding truth at trial.

2. **Accommodation of Law Enforcement Needs**

The Supreme Court has usually sought to accommodate law enforcement investigative needs. Thus, the Court refused to adopt rules or procedures it viewed as unduly restricting effective law enforcement. The Justices refused, for example, to require a *Miranda*-type warning to a person's consent for warrantless searches. Similarly, the Court held that the reasonableness of a police officer's decision to stop a car should be viewed against the whole picture and that an officer's motives for the stop do not matter if the seizure is supported by probable cause or reasonable suspicion, an objective standard.

3. **Limitation of Access to Federal Courts**

The Burger and Rehnquist Courts shifted the power to interpret the meaning of the Constitution in state criminal cases back to the state courts by substantially curtailing the opportunity of state prisoners to relitigate constitutional claims in federal habeas corpus proceedings. The Court also substantially narrowed the access to federal courts for those who fail to assert their constitutional claims in state courts. This theme has continued through current day.

The point is that the Supreme Court in recent years has been generally reluctant to elevate the interest of the individual over that of the state in its oversight of the criminal justice system.

The difference in emphasis between the Courts reflects the diverging approaches that exist on the central issue in Criminal Procedure—how best to protect the rights of the accused while providing for full and effective enforcement of the law.

APPROACH TO SUMMARY

This volume generally follows the chronology of the ordinary model of a criminal case:

1. **Arrest**

Arrest may be with or without a warrant, may or may not involve a search or some questioning, and can arise upon citizen complaint or direct observation by the arresting officer.

2. **Booking; Identification**

This process may include identification procedures, such as fingerprinting and photographing, or even some scientific test performed on the arrestee (*e.g.,* taking blood, urine samples, and a DNA swab). Again, some search may take place.

3. **Initial Appearance**

a. **Felony Cases**

The first appearance is before a judicial officer who sets bail, informs the defendant of their rights, and appoints counsel if the defendant is indigent. Prosecutorial discretion usually begins here.

b. **Misdemeanors**

The initial appearance may be the only appearance; in some cases, trial can be held immediately.

4. **Other Pretrial Procedures**

a. **Preliminary Hearing to Determine Probable Cause to Prosecute**

The preliminary hearing may be waived by the defendant or avoided by the prosecution by securing a grand jury indictment. The defendant is entitled to counsel and, if indigent, to appointed counsel. Both sides may present evidence for the record. Either side may preserve testimony of a witness later unavailable to testify at trial, as long as the other side had a reasonable opportunity to cross-examine the witness.

b. Grand Jury Indictments and Informations

Grand juries are used as a regular part of the charging process in some states and in federal cases unless waived by the defendant. The special or investigative grand jury can initiate a criminal case by indicting someone who is then arrested and held for trial, but indictment prior to arrest is the extraordinary model of the criminal process. In either case, the proceedings of grand juries are secret. The defendant generally has no right to appear or send witnesses. Where the grand jury is not used or is waived by the defendant, the prosecution will charge by information.

c. Motion Hearings

Prior to trial, the defendant will get the opportunity to make certain procedural motions, such as a motion to dismiss, to suppress evidence, or to secure discovery.

d. Arraignment or Plea-Taking

Sometime prior to trial, the defendant will be asked to plead. If the defendant pleads not guilty or remains silent, the judge will set the case for trial. If the defendant pleads guilty (or in some instances nolo contendere), the constitutionally required colloquy between the judge and the defendant as to the voluntariness and intelligence of the plea must take place on the record.

5. Trial

No joinder of issue or responsive pleading is necessary. Some states require the defendant to give the prosecution notice before trial of intent to present either an insanity defense or an alibi, with a list of supporting witnesses. Some affirmative defenses may have to be raised and proved by the defendant. Trial may or may not be by jury.

6. Verdict

The verdict must be unanimous, and the state must prove the defendant guilty beyond a reasonable doubt.

7. Sentence

The defendant has certain rights at sentencing, including the right to counsel and the right to address the court.

8. Appeal

There are tight time limits on appeal. Also important is the relationship between retrial and double jeopardy.

9. Collateral Attack—Petitioning for Writ of Habeas Corpus

Although recently limited in scope, the collateral attack, after direct appeal, is widely used.

Criminal Procedure

Twenty-First Edition

Chapter One

Constitutional Principles

CONTENTS	PAGE

Key Exam Issues

Some of the materials in this chapter are presented principally for their historical value, but are important for understanding other, highly tested legal concepts.

Exams tend to focus on two topics from this Chapter—the ***fruit of the poisonous tree*** doctrine **and *the exclusionary rule***. Remember two key points: (i) evidence obtained as a direct result of police conduct that violates the Fourth, Fifth, or Sixth Amendment is usually subject to exclusion; and (ii) evidence obtained either directly or indirectly as a result of unconstitutionally obtained evidence may also be subject to exclusion, but only if the defense successfully convinces the court that such evidence is closely tied to the initial unconstitutional police activity. Such secondary evidence may be admissible if the prosecution can break the causal chain between the unconstitutional activity and the evidence, such as by the defendant's own voluntary act, independent intervening circumstances, consultation with counsel, and so forth.

A. The Bill of Rights

1. Introduction

The first 10 Amendments to the United States Constitution, commonly known as the Bill of Rights, include a number of provisions limiting the government's power when investigating and prosecuting criminal cases. In particular:

- The ***Fourth Amendment*** provides: "The right of the people to be secure in their persons, houses, papers, and effects, against unreasonable searches and seizures, shall not be violated, and no Warrants shall issue, but upon probable cause, supported by oath or affirmation, and particularly describing the place to be searched, and the persons or things to be seized."
- The ***Fifth Amendment*** provides: "No person shall be held to answer for a capital, or otherwise infamous crime, unless on a presentment or indictment of a Grand Jury, except in cases arising in the land or naval forces . . .; nor shall any person be subject for the same offense to be twice put in jeopardy of life and limb; nor shall be compelled in any criminal case to be a witness against himself, nor be deprived of life, liberty, or property, without due process of law. . . ."
- The ***Sixth Amendment*** provides: "In all criminal prosecutions, the accused shall enjoy the right to a speedy and public trial, by an impartial jury of the state and district wherein the crime shall have been committed and to be informed of the nature and cause of the accusation; to be confronted with the witnesses against him; to have compulsory process for obtaining witnesses in his favor, and to have the assistance of counsel for his defense."
- The ***Eighth Amendment*** provides: "Excessive bail shall not be required, nor excessive fines imposed, nor cruel and unusual punishments inflicted."

2. Selective Incorporation of the Bill of Rights

The Supreme Court has made many of the individual rights guaranteed by the Bill of Rights applicable to the states by reading the rights into the Due Process Clause of the Fourteenth Amendment, a process referred to as "incorporation." However, a Supreme Court majority has never held that the Fourteenth Amendment "totally" incorporates all provisions of the Bill of Rights. Instead, the majority position has been one of "selective" incorporation. In **Duncan v.**

Louisiana, 391 U.S. 145 (1968), the Court proclaimed that those portions of the Bill of Rights "fundamental to our concept of ordered liberty" have been so incorporated.

a. Fourth Amendment

The Supreme Court has incorporated the following Fourth Amendment rights into the Due Process Clause of the Fourteenth Amendment:

(1) ***The prohibition against unreasonable searches and seizures*** [**Wolf v. Colorado**, 338 U.S. 25 (1949)]; and

(2) ***The exclusionary rule***, which prohibits the use of items obtained as a result of an unreasonable search and seizure as evidence against a criminal defendant. [**Mapp v. Ohio**, 367 U.S. 643 (1961)]

b. Fifth Amendment

The Supreme Court has incorporated the following Fifth Amendment rights into the Due Process Clause of the Fourteenth Amendment:

(1) ***The prohibition against double jeopardy*** [**Benton v. Maryland**, 395 U.S. 784 (1969)]; and

(2) ***The privilege against forced self-incrimination*** [**Malloy v. Hogan**, 378 U.S. 1 (1964)]

(3) ***The protections of Miranda v. Arizona***, including the right to remain silent and to have the advice of counsel during custodial police interrogation [**Dickerson v. United States**, 530 U.S. 428 (2000)]. *Note*: Although the Court applies **Miranda** rights to the states, it does not treat **Miranda** violations as direct violations of the constitution, but as violations of a rule intended to protect core Fifth Amendment rights.

c. Sixth Amendment

The Supreme Court has incorporated the following Sixth Amendment rights into the Due Process Clause of the Fourteenth Amendment:

(1) ***The right to a jury trial*** [**Duncan v. Louisiana**, *supra*];

(2) ***The right to a unanimous jury verdict for conviction of a serious crime*** [**Ramos v. Louisiana**, 590 U.S. 83 (2020)];

(3) ***The right to a public trial*** [*In re* **Oliver**, 333 U.S. 257 (1948)];

(4) ***The right to a speedy trial*** [**Klopfer v. North Carolina**, 386 U.S. 213 (1967)];

(5) ***The right to confront witnesses*** [**Pointer v. Texas**, 380 U.S. 400 (1965)];

(6) ***The right to compulsory process to obtain witnesses*** [**Washington v. Texas**, 388 U.S. 14 (1967)];

(7) ***The right to the assistance of an attorney in felony cases*** [**Gideon v. Wainwright**, 372 U.S. 335 (1963)]; and

(8) ***The right to the assistance of an attorney in misdemeanor cases in which a prison term is imposed*** [**Argersinger v. Hamlin**, 407 U.S. 25 (1972); **Scott v. Illinois**, 440 U.S. 367 (1979)]

d. Eighth Amendment

The Supreme Court has held that the Eighth Amendment ***prohibition against cruel and unusual punishment*** has been incorporated into the Due Process Clause of the Fourteenth Amendment. [**Robinson v. California**, 370 U.S. 660 (1962)]

3. Rights Not Incorporated

a. Fifth Amendment Right to Indictment

The Fifth Amendment right to indictment by a grand jury for capital and infamous crimes has been held not binding on the states. [**Hurtado v. California**, 110 U.S. 516 (1884)] ***Many states do not use grand juries as a regular part of the charging process***. Where grand jury indictment is not used or the defendant waives the right to grand jury action, the state charges by ***information***—a formal charging instrument drawn up by the prosecutor.

b. Eighth Amendment Prohibition Against Excessive Bail

The Eighth Amendment prohibition against excessive bail may or may not be binding on the states; this issue has not yet been determined by the Supreme Court. In any case, most state constitutions or statutes prohibit excessive bail.

B. Exclusion of Evidence

1. General Principles of the Exclusionary Rule

To deter government agents from violating the protections provided by the Bill of Rights and the Fourteenth Amendment Due Process Clause, the Supreme Court adopted the "exclusionary rule." Under the rule, evidence obtained by an unconstitutional search or seizure generally is ***not admissible in a criminal proceeding against the victim*** of the search or seizure ***as proof of guilt***. *Rationale*: If the government cannot use evidence obtained from violating a person's constitutional rights, it will be deterred from acting in contravention of those rights. *Note*: Evidence obtained in violation of the constitutional right of A may be introduced into evidence to prove B's guilt. In this case, because only A's rights were violated, B would lack standing to object. The government is also routinely permitted to use illegally obtained evidence to impeach A, if A takes the witness stand. If there is enough separation between the government's illegal conduct and the discovery of the inculpatory evidence, the evidence is sometimes allowed as well. [*See* B.2, *infra*]

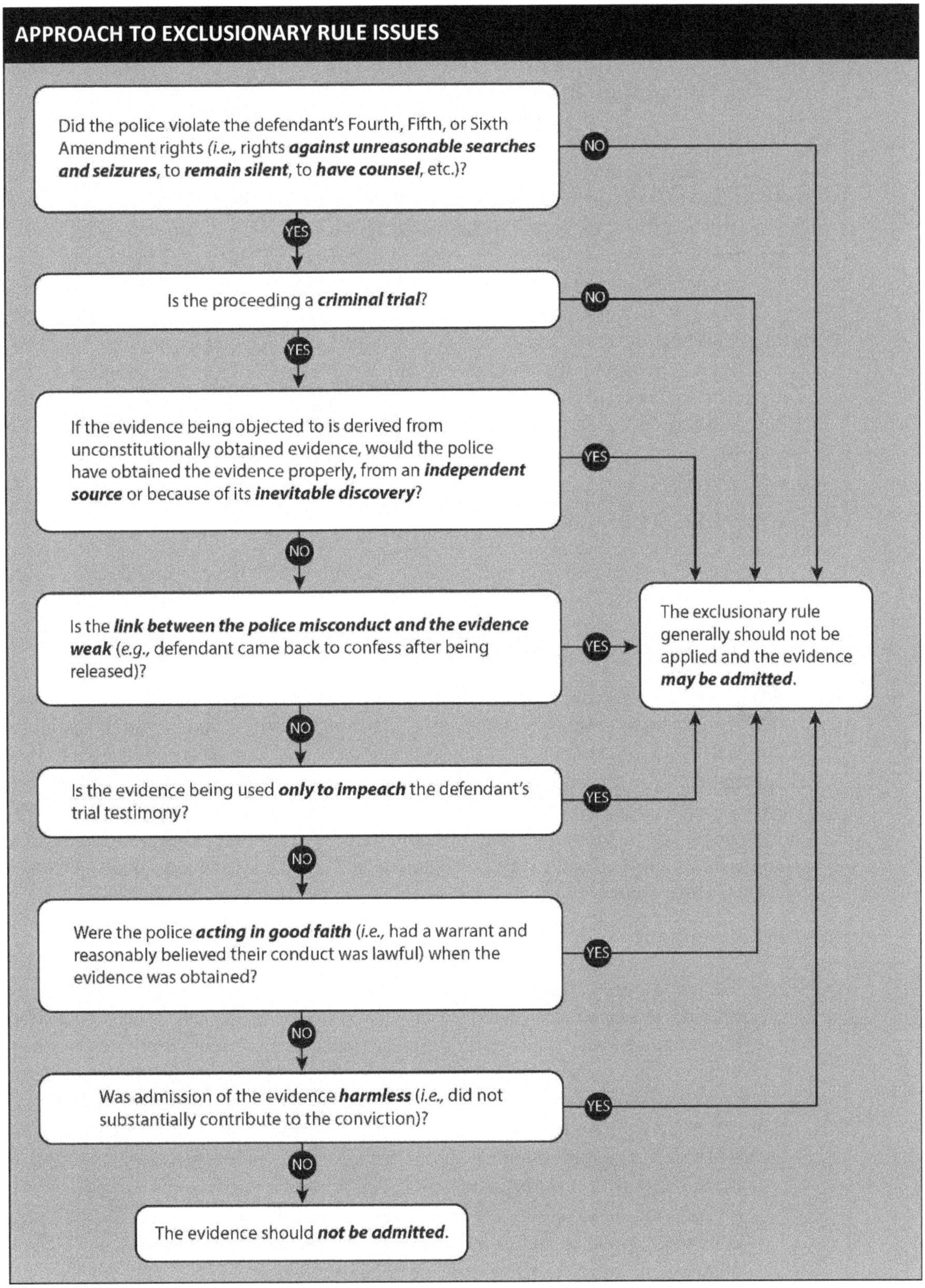

a. Application of Exclusionary Rule

The rule applies in both federal cases [**Weeks v. United States**, 232 U.S. 383 (1914)] ***and*** state cases [**Mapp v. Ohio**, *supra*, p. 3]. The Fourth Amendment limitations apply to any governmental search or seizure. Accordingly, evidence unlawfully obtained by federal officers is inadmissible in state as well as federal cases. Similarly, evidence illegally seized by state officers is inadmissible in federal as well as state cases. [**Elkins v. United States**, 364 U.S. 206 (1960)]

b. Instances Where Rule Does Not Apply

Only the victim of the government's illegal acts may successfully exclude the evidence from trial. [**Rakas v. Illinois,** 439 U.S. 128 (1978); **Byrd v. United States,** 584 U.S. 395 (2018)] Thus, a mere passenger in a car may not successfully exclude evidence uncovered in an illegal search of the car. [**Rakas,** *supra*] Note, however, the driver in lawful possession of a rental car (even if not a driver authorized by the rental agreement) may claim a reasonable expectation of privacy in the rental car for purposes of challenging a search of the car in violation of the Fourth Amendment. [**Byrd,** *supra*] The Supreme Court has also been reluctant to apply the exclusionary rule beyond a criminal trial itself. In determining whether to apply the rule to proceedings other than a criminal trial, the Court weighs the cost of excluding the unconstitutionally obtained evidence (*i.e.,* the likelihood that a guilty person will go free as a result of the exclusion) against the deterrent benefit of extending the rule to a new situation. [**United States v. Calandra,** 414 U.S. 338 (1974)]

(1) Proceedings Beyond Trial

Evidence seized unconstitutionally may be introduced in pretrial proceedings (*e.g.,* during grand jury proceedings, preliminary hearings, and bail hearings). Similarly, unconstitutionally obtained evidence may be considered after a conviction has been entered (*e.g.,* during sentencing or parole hearings).

e.g. **Example:** Witness was called to testify before a grand jury. He refused to answer the grand jury's questions, claiming that they were based on evidence obtained from an unlawful search and seizure. The Supreme Court found that application of the exclusionary rule would impede functioning of the grand jury (whose job is merely to determine whether charges should be brought; *see infra,* p. 13), while any added deterrent effect would be minimal at best, because the unconstitutionally seized evidence could not be used at trial anyway. [**United States v. Calandra**, *supra*]

(a) Comment

The rationale in ***Calandra*** makes sense in cases where the person who is seeking to exclude the evidence is later indicted on the evidence. The police have gained little by presenting the evidence to the grand jury because they cannot later use the illegally seized evidence at trial. However, the rationale is weak in cases where the witness will not be indicted, such as in ***Calandra***, where the witness from whom the evidence had been unconstitutionally seized had been granted immunity from prosecution. In such cases, the police misconduct will never be challenged. The rationale is also weak in cases where defendants plead guilty because the unlawfully obtained evidence may encourage grand jurors to indict the defendant, but after the plea, the illegal conduct will never be subjected to judicial scrutiny.

(2) Civil Suits

The exclusionary rule is not applicable in most civil proceedings. However, it can be applied in civil proceedings that are quasi-criminal in nature, such as in civil forfeiture actions arising from criminal conduct. The exclusionary rule does not apply in deportation actions or tax suits.

2. General Scope

Under the exclusionary rule, evidence must be excluded that has been unconstitutionally obtained. In addition, other evidence acquired, directly or indirectly, as a ***result*** of an unconstitutional search or arrest (called the ***tainted fruit of the poisonous tree***) must be excluded, unless the government can break the link between the unconstitutionally obtained evidence and the discovery of such evidence. [**Nardone v. United States**, 308 U.S. 338 (1939); **Wong Sun v. United States**, 371 U.S. 471 (1963)]

a. Fruit of the Poisonous Tree

In determining whether evidence is tainted fruit of the poisonous tree, courts ask whether the objectionable evidence was obtained through exploitation of the unconstitutionally obtained evidence, or "instead by means sufficiently distinguishable to be purged of the primary taint." [**Wong Sun v. United States**, *supra*]

b. Dissipation of the Taint

Evidence otherwise inadmissible as poisoned fruit may be allowed if the prosecution demonstrates that the taint has been removed. This may be accomplished in three ways:

(1) Inevitable Discovery

If the police would have discovered the evidence regardless of their unconstitutional conduct, it may be admitted under the inevitable discovery exception to the exclusionary rule. [**Nix v. Williams,** 467 U.S. 431 (1984)] The burden is on the government to demonstrate with specific facts and by a preponderance of the evidence that the illegally obtained evidence the prosecution seeks to introduce ultimately would have been discovered by other lawful means. The prosecution is ***not*** required to show that the police acted in good faith; the exception applies even if the police knew that their actions would be unlawful and deliberately chose the unlawful method. [**Nix v. Williams**, *supra*]

e.g. **Example:** Defendant was suspected of murdering a 10-year-old girl. Defendant's attorney advised him to turn himself in. The attorney also advised Defendant not to talk to the police outside the presence of counsel and asked the police not to talk to Defendant without counsel. The police agreed to the attorney's request. During transport to the police station, officers convinced Defendant (by appealing to Defendant's deep religious convictions) that the victim needed a "Christian burial." Defendant confessed and then led the police to the victim's body. The confession was held inadmissible because the police violated Defendant's rights when getting him to lead them to the body. Evidence of the body was, nevertheless, admissible because, given the proximity of search parties to the body, it would have been inevitably found, even if Defendant's confession had not led police to the body. [**Nix v. Williams**, *supra*]

(2) Independent Source

If the police obtained the evidence from an independent source disconnected from the unconstitutional search or seizure, the evidence is admissible. [**United States v. Crews**, 445 U.S. 463 (1980)]

e.g. **Example:** If police initially discover evidence during an unconstitutional search of a warehouse, but subsequently discover the same evidence during a valid search, the evidence is admissible. To avoid the exclusionary rule, the second search must be completely independent of the first, unconstitutional search. [**Murray v. United States**, 487 U.S. 533 (1988)]

(3) Confession

Confessions obtained in violation of a person's Fifth Amendment rights (*e.g.,* the right against compelled self-incrimination) will be excluded from evidence. However, confessions resulting from a seizure of a person in violation of their Fourth Amendment rights (*e.g.,* a warrantless seizure) may be admissible in some circumstances. In such cases, courts look to factors such as whether the defendant was informed of their constitutional rights to remain silent and to the assistance of counsel, the closeness in time between the detention and the confession, the purpose of the government action, and the flagrancy of the official misconduct. [**Brown v. Illinois**, 422 U.S. 590 (1975)] The taint is dissipated if there is a weak link between the illegal police conduct and the challenged evidence. *Rationale*: The exclusionary rule is intended to deter police misconduct (*e.g.,* illegal arrests) by preventing the use of evidence obtained from such misconduct. Courts have reasoned that if the link between the misconduct and the evidence is weak, application of the exclusionary rule serves little police deterrent purpose.

e.g. **Example:** Police had probable cause to arrest Defendant for murder. They went to his home without a warrant and arrested him, which violates the Fourth Amendment. [*see* **Payton v. New York**, 445 U.S. 573 (1980)] Defendant confessed at home, and then the police took him to the police station, where he confessed again. The Supreme Court held that the first confession must be suppressed as fruit of an unconstitutional arrest, but the second confession is admissible. Because the police had probable cause to arrest Defendant, they did not gain anything by the unconstitutional arrest; they could have arrested him the moment he stepped outside of his house and then brought him to the police station for a confession. Thus, Defendant's subsequent statement was not an exploitation of the unconstitutional entry; *i.e.,* it was not fruit of the fact that Defendant was arrested unlawfully within his home, as opposed to someplace else. [**New York v. Harris**, 495 U.S. 14 (1990)]

cf. **Compare:** Defendant was arrested ***without probable cause*** and brought to the police station. The police informed Defendant of his constitutional rights three times and permitted Defendant to see two friends. After six hours at the police station, Defendant confessed. The Court held that the confession must be excluded because it was the direct result of the unconstitutional arrest. If Defendant had not been arrested unconstitutionally, he could not have been in custody and probably would not have confessed. [*See* **Taylor v. Alabama**, 457 U.S. 687 (1982)]

c. Intervening Act of Free Will

A defendant's intervening act of free will can break the causal chain between the confession and the unconstitutional police conduct.

e.g. **Example:** Defendant was released on his own recognizance after an unconstitutional arrest. He later returned to the stationhouse to confess. The confession was admissible because it was not closely related to the illegal arrest. [**Wong Sun v. United States**, *supra*, p. 7]

cf. **Compare:** The fact that the defendant was informed of his constitutional rights alone is insufficient to prove that the confession was the act of free will. [*See* **Taylor v. Alabama**, *supra*]

d. Identification Exception

When the police illegally seize the defendant to assist in the victim's identification of the defendant, courts need not exclude the evidence.

e.g. **Example:** Defendant was unconstitutionally arrested and photographed during his detention. A victim made a positive identification from the photograph at trial. The identification was allowed over Defendant's objection because: (i) the victim was present in court and willing to testify regarding the identity of her attacker based on knowledge independent from the illegal police activity, and (ii) Defendant was physically present at the trial to be viewed by the witness. [**United States v. Crews**, *supra*, p. 7]

e. Witness Statement Exception

In cases where an unconstitutional search helps police locate a witness, the witness's statements will rarely be excluded as the fruit of illegal police conduct. A more direct link is required before exclusion is required. A court considers various factors, including the extent to which the witness is willing to testify and the extent to which excluding the witness would deter future illegal police conduct. The Court has noted that "the degree of free will exercised by the witness is not irrelevant." [**United States v. Ceccolini**, 435 U.S. 268 (1978)]

3. Enforcement of the Exclusionary Rule

a. Suppression Hearing Right

The defendant has a right to a suppression hearing outside the jury's presence at which a judge decides whether evidence or a confession is admissible. [**Jackson v. Denno**, 378 U.S. 368 (1964)] If the judge decides that the evidence or confession is admissible, the jury may consider it. The defendant may present to the jury much of the same evidence presented at the suppression hearing in an attempt to persuade the jury not to believe the confession. [**Lego v. Twomey**, 404 U.S. 477 (1972); **Crane v. Kentucky**, 476 U.S. 683 (1986) (allowing the defense at trial to introduce evidence about the physical and psychological environment in which the confession was made)] Note that the defendant has no right to a specific finding of fact on each factual question. [**La Vallee v. Delle Rose**, 410 U.S. 690 (1973)]

b. Testimony Right

A defendant has a right to testify at a suppression hearing, and if he does, his testimony may not be used against him at trial on the issue of guilt. [**Simmons v. United States**, 390 U.S. 377 (1968)]

c. Government Proof Requirement

The government bears the burden of establishing admissibility of evidence or a confession by a ***preponderance of the evidence***. [**Lego v. Twomey**, *supra*]

4. Exceptions to the Exclusionary Rule

Although historically there is some case support for viewing the exclusionary rule as a constitutional command essential to the protection of fundamental rights, it is currently treated as a judge-made rule intended principally or solely to deter police misconduct. This has enabled the Supreme Court to carve out exceptions to the rule of exclusion when police deterrence would not be adequately served.

a. Impeachment Exception

As discussed above, if evidence is obtained in violation of a defendant's constitutional rights, generally the evidence is inadmissible at trial to help prove the prima facie case of guilt against the defendant. However, if the evidence bears sufficient indicia of reliability, it may be used ***to impeach*** the defendant's credibility if he testifies on his own behalf at trial. [**Harris v. New York**, 401 U.S. 222 (1971)]

(1) Confessions That Violate *Miranda*

Although confessions taken in violation of a defendant's Fifth Amendment rights may not be admitted on the merits to prove his guilt, a defendant's confession may be used to impeach him if he testifies at trial, even though he was not warned of his constitutional rights as required by **Miranda v. Arizona**, *infra* p. 97. [**Harris v. New York**, *supra*; **Oregon v. Hass**, 420 U.S. 714 (1975)]

e.g. **Example:** Police questioned Defendant without informing him of his constitutional rights to remain silent and to have the advice of counsel, and Defendant confessed to selling heroin on two occasions. At trial, Defendant denied making one of the sales. The prosecution was allowed to introduce Defendant's confession, taken in violation of *Miranda*, to impeach his trial testimony. The Supreme Court reasoned that the exclusionary rule should not "be construed to include the right to commit perjury." [**Harris v. New York**, *supra*]

(2) Caveat—Confessions That Violate the Fifth Amendment

A truly involuntary confession (*i.e.,* one that violates the Fifth Amendment because it was coerced from the defendant by force, by threat, or by promises that overcame the defendant's free will) is inherently unreliable and violates long-held principles of fundamental fairness. Therefore, an involuntary confession may not be used even for impeachment purposes. [**Mincey v. Arizona**, 437 U.S. 385 (1978)—police badgered defendant for a confession while he was in the hospital with bullet wounds, partial paralysis, breathing tubes, drugs in his system, etc.]

(3) Caveat—Immunized Testimony

If the prosecution has offered a witness immunity from prosecution in exchange for testimony, the testimony may ***not*** be used for impeachment purposes. [**New Jersey v. Portash**, 440 U.S. 450 (1979)]

(4) Physical Evidence

Illegally obtained real or physical evidence ***may*** be used to impeach the defendant's answers to a prosecutor's cross-examination questions. [**United States v. Havens**, 446 U.S. 620 (1980)]

e.g. **Example:** At Defendant's trial for cocaine smuggling, Defendant testified in his own defense. On cross-examination, Defendant denied cutting patches of cotton from one shirt and sewing them to another shirt to make pockets to conceal cocaine. Furthermore, Defendant denied having a shirt with missing pockets in his luggage when arrested. Over Defendant's objection, such a shirt found in Defendant's luggage during an illegal search was allowed to be introduced at trial for the limited purpose of allowing the jury to assess Defendant's credibility. [**United States v. Havens**, *supra*]

b. Post-Conviction Federal Habeas Corpus Proceeding

As will be discussed *infra* (pp. 208–220), federal habeas corpus is a collateral proceeding that may be brought—after a conviction—by a person seeking relief from confinement. At a habeas proceeding based on a state conviction, the state will seek to show that it provided the defendant with an opportunity for a full and fair hearing of any illegal search and seizure claims. If the state is successful, the defendant may not challenge his state conviction in a later federal habeas corpus proceeding on the ground that evidence used against him was the product of an illegal search. [**Stone v. Powell**, 428 U.S. 465 (1976)]

c. Private Party Search Exception

The Fourth and Fifth Amendments apply only to government action and not to searches and interrogations conducted by private parties. Courts will not exclude evidence illegally obtained by a private party acting ***independently*** of police direction. [**Burdeau v. McDowell**, 256 U.S. 465 (1921)] However, if the police request or encourage a private party to engage in an illegal search, the exclusionary rule ***applies*** because this effectively makes the private party a government actor.

d. Civil Proceedings Exception

The exclusionary rule does not bar the use of evidence illegally seized by an agent of one sovereign in the ***civil*** proceedings of another sovereign. [**United States v. Janis**, 428 U.S. 433 (1976)]

(1) Caveat—Forfeiture Cases

The exclusionary rule does apply to forfeiture proceedings when forfeiture of an article used in the commission of a crime is a penalty for the crime. [**One 1958 Plymouth Sedan v. Pennsylvania**, 380 U.S. 693 (1965)]

e. Police Good Faith Exception

The Supreme Court has carved out an exception to the exclusionary rule for evidence obtained in violation of the Fourth Amendment's search and seizure rules where police officers act based on a facially-valid search warrant and in the objectively reasonable belief that their conduct is not violating the defendant's rights. [**United States v. Leon**, 468 U.S. 897 (1984)] *Rationale*: If the police officer thought she was acting properly, application of the rule would have no deterrent effect. After **Leon**, the exclusionary rule does not apply when the police rely in objective good faith on:

(i) ***Binding appellate precedent*** later overruled by a Supreme Court decision [**Davis v. United States**, 564 U.S. 229 (2011)];

(ii) A ***facially valid statute*** or ordinance as it then exists—even if the law is later declared unconstitutional or changed by court decision [**Michigan v. DeFillippo**, 443 U.S. 31 (1979)], and even if the law purports to authorize a warrantless search which is later held unconstitutional [**Illinois v. Krull**, 480 U.S. 340 (1987)];

(iii) ***A reasonable mistake of law*** when interpreting a state statute [**Heien v. North Carolina**, 574 U.S. 54 (2014)];

e.g. **Example:** It was reasonable (although incorrect) for an officer to interpret a North Carolina statute to mean that a single defective brake light created probable cause for a traffic stop. Thus, the subsequent stop complied with the Fourth Amendment. [**Heien**, *supra*]

(iv) ***A defective search warrant*** [**United States v. Leon**, *supra,* p. 11; **Massachusetts v. Sheppard**, 468 U.S. 981 (1984)—but *see* exceptions p. 12, *infra*];

e.g. **Example:** In a civil action pursuant to 42 U.S.C. § 1983, occupants of a residence asserted that police officers were personally liable for searching a home with a warrant that was unconstitutionally overbroad. Here, the warrant authorized a search for multiple firearms and gang-related materials when evidence supporting probable cause was limited to the use of one, black sawed-off shotgun with a pistol grip—and there was no evidence that the crime under investigation was gang-related. [**Messerschmidt v. Millender**, 565 U.S. 535 (2012)] The Ninth Circuit, sitting *en banc*, denied qualified immunity, finding that a reasonable officer would have "been well aware of th[e] deficiency" in the warrant. The Supreme Court reversed. Citing *Leon*, the Court reiterated that in the ordinary case, an officer "cannot be expected to question the magistrate's probable-cause determination." The Court found that even if the scope of the warrant was overbroad, it was not unreasonable for an officer "to conclude that there was a fair probability that the sawed-off shotgun was not the only firearm" the suspect owned. "The officers' judgment that the scope of the warrant was supported by probable cause may have been mistaken, but it was not 'plainly incompetent.' "

(v) ***Incorrect information*** in a computer database indicating that an outstanding warrant exists for the defendant, whether a court employee is responsible for the error [**Arizona v. Evans**, 514 U.S. 1 (1995)] or law enforcement maintained the database [**Herring v. United States**, 555 U.S. 135 (2009)]

e.g. **Example:** Police arrested Defendant, relying on a warrant clerk's review of a computer database that mistakenly indicated an active arrest warrant for Defendant. Police searched Defendant and his truck pursuant to the supposed warrant and uncovered drugs and a gun. But, there was a mistake. The warrant had been recalled, but the computer record was never updated. The exclusionary sanction was not applied and the drugs and gun were not excluded from evidence. [**Herring v. United States**, *supra*] *Rationale*: To trigger the exclusionary rule, police conduct must be sufficiently deliberate that exclusion can meaningfully deter it. Here, because the recordkeeping error was assumed to be an isolated case of negligence, it did not rise to that level.

e.g. **Example:** Police arrested Defendant and searched the passenger compartment of the car in which he was riding pursuant to binding appellate precedent that permitted such a search incident to arrest. The search uncovered a gun. About two years later, while Defendant's appeal of his motion to suppress the gun was still pending, the Supreme Court ruled that searches incident to arrest like the one in Defendant's case violate the Fourth Amendment. Thus, in hindsight, the police had acted unconstitutionally, but they did so while reasonably believing that binding precedent permitted their actions. Held: The exclusionary sanction did not apply and the gun need not be excluded. *Rationale*: Suppression would not deter police misconduct under these circumstances and would come at a high cost to truth and public safety. [**Davis v. United States**, 564 U.S. 229 (2011)]

(1) Four Exceptions to Good Faith Reliance on a Defective Search Warrant

A police officer cannot get the benefit of the good faith exception if:

(a) The ***affidavit*** on which the warrant was issued was ***so lacking in probable cause*** that no reasonable officer would have relied on it;

(b) The ***warrant is defective on its face*** (*e.g.,* failure of the warrant to state with particularity the place to be searched or the things to be seized);

(c) The ***affiant lied to or misled*** the magistrate; or

(d) The ***magistrate has wholly abandoned his judicial role***. [**United States v. Leon**, *supra*]

f. Grand Jury Exception

Grand jury witnesses may not refuse to answer questions based on unconstitutionally seized evidence. [**United States v. Calandra,** *supra,* p. 6] However, grand jury witnesses ***may*** refuse to answer questions based on evidence obtained in violation of the federal wiretapping statute. [**Gelbard v. United States**, 408 U.S. 41 (1972)]

g. State Law/Agency Rule Exception

If the search does not violate the Constitution and only violates state law or the internal working rules of the searching agency, a defendant is not entitled to exclusion. [**Virginia v. Moore**, 553 U.S. 164 (2008); **United States v. Caceres**, 440 U.S. 741 (1979)]

e.g. **Example:** Police arrested Defendant for driving on a suspended license, searched him, and found cocaine on his person. Under state law, an arrest was not authorized for driving on a suspended license, and Defendant moved to suppress the evidence found during the search. *Held:* Even if Defendant's arrest was not authorized under state law, it may be constitutionally reasonable and the subsequent search incident to arrest may also be reasonable if the police have probable cause to believe Defendant committed a misdemeanor in their presence (*see infra*, p. 23). [*See* **Virginia v. Moore**, *supra*]

e.g. **Example:** Defendant consents to monitoring by the Internal Revenue Service. Defendant challenges the evidence obtained during the monitoring on the ground that the IRS violated its own monitoring regulations. The challenge will fail where the agency made a reasonable, good faith attempt to comply with its rules. [**United States v. Caceres**, *supra*]

h. Parole Revocation Proceeding Exception

The exclusionary rule does not apply in parole revocation proceedings. *Rationale*: Parole revocation proceedings have always been flexible, and unlike a police officer searching for evidence of a crime, a parole officer is less likely to deprive a parolee's constitutional rights because the relationship between a parolee and a parole officer "is more supervisory than adversarial." [**Pennsylvania v. Scott**, 524 U.S. 357 (1998)]

i. Knock and Announce Rule Violations

Exclusion is not an available remedy for violations of the Fourth Amendment's knock and announce rule pertaining to the execution of a warrant. [**Hudson v. Michigan**, 547 U.S. 586 (2006)]

e.g. **Example:** Where officers violate the knock and announce rule (*see infra,* p. 46), the exclusionary rule will not be applied to exclude evidence resulting from the search. *Rationale*: The exclusionary remedy is too attenuated from the purposes of the knock and announce rule of protecting human life and limb, property, privacy, and dignity. Moreover, with the presence of a valid search warrant, the cost of excluding relevant evidence is too high when compared to the deterrence benefit that will be gained. Finally, there are other deterrents to prevent officers from violating the knock and announce rule, such as civil suits and internal police disciplinary sanctions. [**Hudson v. Michigan**, *supra, p. 13*]

EXAM TIP

In an exam fact pattern, whenever the government is seeking to introduce evidence against a defendant, consider whether the evidence has been obtained in violation of the defendant's Fourth, Fifth, or Sixth Amendment rights. If it has, you must discuss the exclusionary rule. Remember that the rule is, at once, both ***more expansive and more restrictive*** than it seems. It expands to require exclusion not only of the unconstitutionally obtained evidence, but also ***evidence derived*** solely from the unconstitutionally obtained evidence. On the other hand, its application generally is restricted to criminal trial settings. Even there: (1) it will not be applied if application will ***not further the rule's mission*** of deterring the police from trampling a defendant's constitutional rights, for example, if police relied on a facially valid search warrant; (2) it will not be applied if the police violated only the "knock and announce rule"; and (3) it may not be applied if the court deems the police illegality merely isolated negligence and not willful, reckless, or part of a pattern of police misconduct.

5. Effect of Exclusionary Rule Violation

a. General Rule—Reversal

If the defendant has made a timely motion to suppress, it constitutes error for a court to admit unconstitutionally obtained evidence. Such an error requires reversal ***unless*** the error is determined to be "harmless." [**Chapman v. California**, 386 U.S. 18 (1967)]

(1) Waiver

Unless certain procedural requirements are met, the defendant waives her objection to the use of unconstitutionally obtained evidence. If the defendant fails to object or move to suppress the unconstitutionally obtained evidence, the failure will usually bar subsequent consideration of the issue at trial or on appeal. [**Wainwright v. Sykes**, 433 U.S. 72 (1977)]

b. Establishing Harmless Error

To establish harmless error and avoid reversal, the prosecution must show beyond a reasonable doubt that admission of the evidence, which should have been excluded, did not contribute to the conviction. [**Chapman v. California**, *supra*]

(1) Trial Rulings—Harmless Error Test Applies

In determining whether the admission of unconstitutionally obtained evidence substantially influenced the jury's verdict, a reviewing court may assess the error in the context of all other evidence presented. Once the defendant has established constitutional error, the burden shifts to the government to prove beyond a reasonable doubt that the error was harmless. If there is overwhelming evidence of guilt apart from the erroneously admitted material, the error may be ruled harmless. [**Milton v. Wainwright**, 407 U.S. 371 (1972)]

(a) Application

The harmless error test has been applied in the following circumstances:

1) Jury instructions misstating an element of the crime charged [**Pope v. Illinois**, 481 U.S. 497 (1987)];

2) Denial of the defendant's right to be present at trial [**Rushen v. Spain**, 464 U.S. 114 (1983)];

3) Denial of confrontation rights upon admission of the confession of a non-testifying codefendant [**Harrington v. California**, 395 U.S. 250 (1969)];

4) Admission of an involuntary confession [**Arizona v. Fulminante**, 499 U.S. 279 (1991)]; and

5) Comment on the failure of the accused to testify [**Chapman v. California**, 386 U.S. 18 (1967).

(2) Judge's Pretrial Violation of Rule 11, Fed. R. Crim. P.—Harmless Error Test Applies

The harmless error analysis applies when a magistrate judge violates Rule 11, Fed. R. Crim. P., governing pleas, by participating in plea discussions and urging a defendant to plead guilty in direct defiance of the rule. [**United States v. Davila**, 569 U.S. 597 (2013)]

(3) Structural Errors—Automatic Reversal

Harmless error analysis ***does not apply*** to constitutional defects in the structure of a criminal prosecution. Such defects include adjudication by a biased judge, deprivation of the right to counsel, deprivation of the defendant's choice of counsel, allowing defense counsel in a death penalty case to concede guilt, as a strategy to save the defendant's life, over the defendant's objection, and denial of the right to a public trial. Such errors result in automatic reversals. [**Holloway v. Arkansas**, 435 U.S. 475 (1978); **United States v. Gonzalez-Lopez**, 548 U.S. 140 (2006); **Waller v. Georgia**, 467 U.S. 39 (1984); **McCoy v. Louisiana**, 584 U.S. 414 (2018)] But *see* **Woods v. Donald**, 575 U.S. 312 (2015), an attorney's brief absence from trial during testimony concerning an accused's codefendants is not necessarily a structural error. Neither is wrongly restricting the accused's closing argument. [**Glebe v. Frost**, 574 U.S. 21 (2014)]

6. Retroactivity

Supreme Court decisions interpreting or delineating constitutional rights will be applied ***retroactively to all convictions*** that are ***not yet final*** or that are ***pending on direct review***. This rule ensures that similarly situated defendants are treated similarly and prevents judicial review from becoming a mere lottery in which one defendant's conviction is reversed but others' are not. The retroactivity rule applies even if the Court's decision is a clear break from past precedent. [**Griffith v. Kentucky**, 479 U.S. 314 (1987); **Teague v. Lane**, 489 U.S. 288 (1989)]

Chapter Two

The Fourth Amendment

CONTENTS | PAGE

Key Exam Issues

In almost every Criminal Procedure course you will see Fourth Amendment issues on your exam. The questions normally break down into a small group dealing with arrest and a large section dealing with search and seizure. The following are useful approaches to these issues:

1. Arrest

The preliminary question is whether the defendant has, in fact, been arrested. The chief issue is whether the defendant has been isolated and taken ***into custody*** by law enforcement officers ***against her will***. At a minimum, an arrest requires a ***physical application of force*** by a police officer with the intent to restrain or a ***submission to an officer's show of authority***. *Note*: Routine investigatory stops are not arrests, even when a person is "seized" and not free to leave (for example, during many traffic stops). Also *note*: Whether an officer intended to restrain a person is evaluated by an objective standard (*i.e.*, whether an officer objectively manifests an intent to restrain). Consider, for instance, a police officer pursuing a fleeing suspect riding a bike, and the officer bumps the suspect's bike with the pursuing police car. The suspect is probably seized because the objective facts demonstrate that the officer intended to restrain the suspect.

Next consider whether the arrest was valid. To make a valid arrest, the police must have ***probable cause*** to believe that a crime is being (or has been) committed. Remember that most arrests do not require a warrant (*e.g.*, if the arrest takes place in a public area).

2. Search and Seizure

Search and seizure is usually a large part of the exam. To analyze the issues, focus your attention on four key questions:

a. Was There Government Conduct?

The Constitution, and specifically the Fourth and Fourteenth Amendments, simply do not apply to actions taken by private individuals—unless such individuals are closely associated with, or acting at the direction of, state or federal officials.

b. Did the Government Search or Seize?

(1) Did the Government Conduct a Search?

A search occurs when the government infringes a reasonable expectation of privacy or the government physically trespasses on private houses, papers, or effects to obtain information.

(2) Did the Government Conduct a Seizure?

(a) Of a Person

(b) Of a House, Papers, or an Effect?

The core of the search and seizure provision is the protection of privacy, and the courts will consider the ***totality of the circumstances*** in determining whether privacy interests exist. Watch for cases in which the defendant may have voluntarily given up privacy interests, such as by leaving items in plain view, abandoning them, etc. Also remember that the defendant's mere presence on the premises when a search takes place does not establish a privacy interest. The question is whether the defendant's personal privacy interest was invaded by the challenged government conduct. Until 2012, the Court focused singularly on the defendant's subjective and reasonable expectation of privacy.

But since 2012 and the decision in **United States v. Jones,** 565 U.S. 400 (2012), physical intrusions on private property and effects are increasingly relevant.

c. Was There a Warrant?

Consider whether the search or seizure was pursuant to a warrant based on probable cause.

(1) If So, Was the Warrant Valid?

To establish the validity of the warrant, there must be an affidavit establishing ***probable cause***, considering the totality of circumstances. The warrant must also be issued by a ***neutral magistrate***, and it must ***describe with reasonable particularity*** the place or person to be searched and the items to be seized.

(2) If the Warrant Was Not Valid

If the warrant was not valid, consider the good faith "exception." The evidence will not be excluded if the police officers ***reasonably and in good faith*** relied on the warrant.

d. If There Is No Warrant, Did an Exception to the Warrant Requirement Apply?

This is an important area in most Criminal Procedure exams, because there are numerous warrant exceptions that may apply in routine criminal investigations.

(1) No warrant is needed for searches ***incident to a constitutionally valid arrest***, carried out at the time and place of that arrest. *Note*: The scope of a search incident to a lawful arrest is a separate issue to be considered. The scope differs in a home, a car, and on a person.

(2) ***Automobile searches*** typically do not require warrants due to the mobility of the vehicle and the lesser expectation of privacy persons are thought to have while in their automobiles. Police must have ***probable cause*** to conduct the search, or at least reasonable suspicion (when the search is limited to a search for weapons). A search of an automobile under the exception for lawful arrests (above) is a different warrant exception with a different scope.

(3) ***Items in plain view*** are normally not subject to the warrant requirement because an owner has no expectation of privacy in items in plain view. But police must be lawfully entitled to their vantage (*i.e.*, standing on a public sidewalk) to establish that such items were found in plain view. Other searches that require physical intrusion affecting a person's house, papers, and "effects"—for example, placing a GPS tracking device on a car—may require a warrant. *Note*: Plain view also includes plain smell or plain hearing, assuming that police used their senses.

(4) Police officers may conduct a ***limited stop*** of a suspect for investigatory purposes without probable cause or a warrant. They need only an ***articulable, reasonable suspicion*** that the person may be involved in a crime. If the police also reasonably think the suspect is armed, they may ***frisk*** the suspect for weapons and seize anything, which by its plain feel, they reasonably believe to be a weapon or contraband. The Supreme Court has created a further exception involving searches of ***public schoolchildren by school officials***. In these cases, no warrant is needed, and no probable cause determination is required. If officials have ***reasonable suspicion*** that they will find evidence that laws or school rules have been broken, a search can be conducted.

(5) All suspects may ***consent*** to a search or seizure, eliminating the need for a warrant or probable cause, as long as the consent is ***voluntarily given***.

(6) Police officers benefit from a ***limited emergency exception*** (sometimes called the "exigent circumstances" or "community caretaker" exception) to the warrant requirement concerning ***hot pursuit, evanescent evidence,*** and other special emergencies. *Note*: The metabolization of alcohol in the human body does not

necessarily constitute an emergency based on the destruction of evidence. Those cases must be analyzed on the specific facts.

A. Arrests and Other Detentions

1. Introduction

The Fourth Amendment prohibits the government from conducting unreasonable searches and seizures.

a. "Search"

A search can be defined as any governmental **intrusion upon a person's reasonable and justifiable expectation of privacy or the government physically intruding on private property (houses, papers, or effects) to obtain information.** (This topic will be covered in detail *infra*, pp. 33 *et seq.*)

b. "Seizure"

A seizure can be defined as the ***exercise of control*** by the government over a person, house, papers, or effects. Seizures of houses, papers, and effects will be discussed in greater detail along with the material on searches, *infra*. Seizures of the person—arrests and other detentions—will be discussed in this section.

c. Reasonableness

Whether a seizure of a person is reasonable under the Fourth Amendment depends on the scope of the seizure (*e.g.,* is it an arrest or merely an investigatory stop), including the length of the seizure, the amount of force applied, if any, to accomplish it, and the strength of the suspicion prompting the seizure (*e.g.,* an arrest requires probable cause, *see infra,* p. 22, whereas an investigatory stop requires only reasonable suspicion, *see infra,* p. 26).

2. Arrests

Because an arrest is a seizure, all arrests must satisfy the requirements of the Fourth Amendment.

a. What Constitutes an Arrest

For an arrest, the police must take a person into custody through intentionally applied means, against the person's will, for purposes of criminal investigation, prosecution, or interrogation. This requires the ***physical application of force*** by a police officer with the objective intent to restrain the person or a ***submission of a person to an officer's show of authority***. [**Torres v. Madrid**, 592 U.S. 306 (2021); **California v. Hodari D.**, 499 U.S. 621 (1991)] The arrestee must not be free to leave of her own volition. It is not relevant whether the act is termed an arrest under state law [**Dunaway v. New York**, 442 U.S. 200 (1970)], and mere words (*e.g.,* "Stop in the name of the law!") do not normally constitute an arrest [**California v. Hodari D.**, *supra*] especially in cases where suspects do not obey the command.

e.g. **Example:** No "arrest" or "seizure" occurs when an officer simply approaches a person in a public place and asks her if she is willing to answer questions—as long as the person is not involuntarily detained. [**Florida v. Royer**, 460 U.S. 491 (1983)]

e.g. **Example:** A police officer's pursuit of an individual constitutes a "seizure" only when a reasonable person would have believed that she was not free to leave and she submits to police authority. For example, there was no arrest where Defendant started running after seeing a squad car, and officers in the car accelerated "to see where he was going." Although the investigatory pursuit of Defendant may have been intimidating, this was not a seizure because the officers did not block Defendant, activate their siren or flashers, display any weapons, or ask Defendant to stop. [**Michigan v. Chesternut**, 486 U.S. 567 (1988)]

e.g. **Example:** There is not necessarily a "seizure" when officers board a bus shortly before its departure and ask individuals for identification or for consent to search their luggage. The test is whether, under the totality of the circumstances, a reasonable person would feel free to refuse the officers' requests or otherwise terminate the encounter. [**Florida v. Bostick**, 501 U.S. 429 (1991)] *Note*: Officers conducting such a search need not tell the bus occupants that they are free to refuse consent. [**United States v. Drayton**, 536 U.S. 194 (2002)]

e.g. **Example:** A high speed pursuit of a suspect terminating when the police accidentally run over and kill the suspect does not amount to a seizure. A seizure occurs only when termination of the suspect's freedom of movement occurs through *intentionally applied means*. [**Sacramento v. Lewis**, 523 U.S. 833 (1998)] But *see* **Torres v. Madrid**, 592 U.S. 306 (2021) (holding that police seize a person when they shoot her multiple times, applying force to her body, with the intent to restrain her, even if she does not yield to police and is not subdued).

cf. **Compare:** Kaupp, age 17, and his friend were brought to the police station for questioning concerning the disappearance of the friend's half-sister. Kaupp was cooperative, passed a lie detector test, and was allowed to leave. Kaupp's friend failed three lie detector tests and eventually confessed to stabbing his half-sister to death and implicated Kaupp in the crime. Police sought a warrant to bring Kaupp in for questioning, but were denied a warrant for lack of evidence against Kaupp. Nevertheless, at around 3 a.m., six police officers went to Kaupp's home and were admitted by Kaupp's father. At least three officers entered Kaupp's room, woke him, and told him that they wanted him to "go and talk." Kaupp replied, "Okay" and was handcuffed and taken out of his house, shoeless and dressed only in his underwear. Kaupp was taken to the police station, where he confessed to playing a minor role in the crime. Kaupp's attorney sought to have Kaupp's confession suppressed as the fruit of an illegal arrest, but the trial court ruled that Kaupp was not arrested until after his confession, on the rationale that he consented to going to the police station by saying, "Okay," and was handcuffed only pursuant to a policy adopted to protect officers when transporting persons in their squad cars. Kaupp was convicted and sentenced to 55 years' imprisonment. The Supreme Court overturned the conviction on appeal, finding that Kaupp's "Okay" was merely an assent to the exercise of police authority, that a reasonable person would not know that the handcuffs were merely for the protection of the officers, and that it cannot seriously be suggested that under the circumstances a reasonable person would feel free to tell the officers when questioning started that he wanted to go home and go back to bed. [**Kaupp v. Texas**, 538 U.S. 626 (2003)]

EXAM TIP

The question of whether police action constitutes an arrest often appears on law school exams. Remember the basics: There must be a ***physical application of force*** by the police with an objectively manifested intent to restrain (not all physical touching suffices) or ***submission by the suspect to an officer's show of authority***. Also, be ready to distinguish a brief investigatory stop (sometimes called a Terry stop, which is still a seizure) from a full-fledged, more intrusive arrest.

b. Probable Cause Requirement

The Constitution requires that an arrest (with or without an arrest warrant) be based on ***probable cause***. This requirement is satisfied when, at the time of arrest, the facts and circumstances within the officers' knowledge, which must be based upon reasonably trustworthy information, ***are sufficient to warrant a prudent person in believing that the suspect had committed or was committing an offense***. [**Beck v. Ohio**, 379 U.S. 89 (1964)] Thus, officers lawfully arrest someone if they mistakenly, but reasonably, believe that person is committing (or has committed) a crime based on the totality of the circumstances. [**District of Columbia v. Wesby,** 583 U.S. 48 (2018)] *Note*: Probable cause can rest on officers' collective knowledge, even if the arresting officer does not have personal knowledge of each pertinent fact. [**United States v. Harris**, 585 F.3d 394 (7th Cir. 2009)] The idea is that the probable cause for arrest is present if the arresting officer is reasonably acting at the direction of others who together have sufficient information for probable cause.

e.g. **Example:** At 3:16 a.m., a police officer stopped a car occupied by three men for speeding. The driver consented to a search of the car. The officer found $763 in rolled-up cash in the glove compartment in front of where Pringle was sitting and five baggies of cocaine between the back-seat arm rest and the back seat. None of the men admitted ownership of the cocaine or the money. Under these circumstances, the officer had probable cause to believe that Pringle, alone or jointly with the other occupants, committed the crime of possession of cocaine. [**Maryland v. Pringle**, 540 U.S. 366 (2003)]

e.g. **Example:** A purely anonymous note claimed that a couple was selling drugs from their home in Illinois and that the wife drove a car to Florida periodically, where she left it for the husband to fly to Florida, acquire the drugs, and drive the drugs back in the trunk of the car. The husband was tracked flying from Chicago to West Palm Beach, where the couple was observed staying in a hotel for only one night before driving a car registered in their names. Their route was "northbound on an interstate frequently used by travelers to the Chicago area." Held, the police had probable cause for a search warrant to search the couple's home and car. [**Illinois v. Gates**, 462 U.S. 213 (1983)]

c. Effect of Invalid Arrest

Although an arrest can be more intrusive than a search, an unlawful arrest ***by itself*** has no impact on a subsequent criminal prosecution. An invalid arrest is ***not*** a defense to being convicted of the offense charged. [**Frisbie v. Collins**, 342 U.S. 519 (1952)] Of course, evidence found during a search incident to an unconstitutional arrest will be suppressed (*see supra*, p. 7), and this suppression may affect the prosecution's case. A confession obtained as a result of an unlawful arrest may also be suppressed. [**Brown v. Illinois**, *supra*, p. 8]

(1) Civil Ramifications

If an arrest is made as the result of an unreasonable mistake, the arresting officer may be liable under 42 U.S.C. § 1983 for violating the arrestee's Fourth Amendment rights. [**Albright v. Oliver**, 510 U.S. 266 (1994)] A § 1983 claim for malicious prosecution is not precluded when police charge a person with multiple crimes, and probable cause is lacking for each charge. [**Chiaverini v. City of Napoleon**, 602 U.S. 556 (2024)] However, an arrest is not constitutionally invalid merely because the grounds stated for the arrest at the time it was made are erroneous [**Devenpeck v. Alford**, 543 U.S. 146 (2005)], or even if state law does not provide for arrest under the circumstances [**Virginia v. Moore**, *supra*, p. 13], as long as the police had probable cause to make the arrest.

e.g. **Example:** Police officers pulled Alford over on suspicion that he was impersonating an officer because his car had police-type "wig-wag" lights. The officers also found Alford's answers to their questioning evasive. Upon discovering that Alford was taping their conversation, Officer Devenpeck arrested Alford, ***erroneously*** thinking that the taping violated a state privacy law. The erroneous charges were later dropped, and Alford sued for civil damages, claiming that the arrest violated his Fourth Amendment rights. *Held:* If the officers had probable cause to arrest Alford for impersonating an officer, the arrest was valid; it does not matter that they lacked probable cause for the "offense" they stated at the time of the arrest. [**Devenpeck v. Alford**, *supra,* p. 22]

e.g. **Example:** There was no Fourth Amendment violation when police arrested a defendant on probable cause to believe the defendant was driving on a suspended license, even though state law did not provide for arrest for such a crime. Because the police had probable cause to believe a misdemeanor was committed, the arrest was constitutional under the Fourth Amendment. [**Virginia v. Moore**, *supra,* pp. 13, 22]

d. Arrest Warrant Not Required Except for Home Arrests

The Fourth Amendment requirement that searches and seizures be reasonable does not mean that a warrant must be obtained before making every arrest. [*See* **United States v. Watson**, 423 U.S. 411 (1976)—police need ***not*** obtain a warrant before arresting a person in a ***public place*** even though there was time and opportunity to do so] In fact, most arrests are made without a warrant.

(1) Arrests in Public Places

Under the common law, arrests may be made without a warrant under the following circumstances:

(a) Felonies

A police officer may arrest a person in a public place without a warrant when the officer has reasonable grounds to believe that a felony has been committed and that the person committed the offense. Such authority has been codified for various federal agents. [*See, e.g.,* 18 U.S.C. § 3052—FBI agents; 18 U.S.C. § 3053—United States marshals; 18 U.S.C. § 3056(c)—secret service agents; 18 U.S.C. § 3061(a)—postal inspectors]

(b) Misdemeanors

A police officer may arrest a person in a public place without a warrant for a misdemeanor committed in the presence of the officer. A crime is committed in an officer's "presence" if the officer is aware of it through any of their senses.

1) Note

If a police officer has probable cause to make an arrest, the Fourth Amendment does not forbid a warrantless arrest, even if the crime is minor, does not involve breach of the peace, and is punishable only by a fine, even when the arrest is prohibited under state law. [**Atwater v. Lago Vista**, 532 U.S. 318 (2001); **Virginia v. Moore**, *supra*]

(2) Arrests in the Home

The Supreme Court's approach to in-home arrests is quite different from its approach to arrests in public places. The Court imposes a presumption that warrantless, in-home arrests are unreasonable and, therefore, invalid under the Fourth Amendment, unless exigent circumstances (*i.e.,* emergencies) are present or the arrestee consents. For minor offenses, the presumption is difficult to overcome. [**Payton v. New York**, 445 U.S. 573 (1980)] The government bears the burden of demonstrating exigent circumstances. [**Welsh v. Wisconsin**, 466 U.S. 740 (1984)] *Note*: If the police illegally arrest a defendant at home without a warrant, they may maintain custody over him if they had probable cause for the arrest. [*See* **New York v. Harris**, 495 U.S. 14 (1990); *see supra*, p. 22]

(a) Exception—Hot Pursuit

If police officers have probable cause to arrest a person, and the person retreats into his home, a warrantless entry into the person's home is permissible if it is necessary for the police to act quickly to prevent the suspect's escape or the destruction of evidence. [**United States v. Santana**, 427 U.S. 38 (1976); *and see infra*, p. 64]

(b) Exception—Emergency Assistance

Police may enter a home without a warrant to render emergency aid to an injured occupant or to protect an occupant from imminent injury. This is often referred to as the community caretaker exception. Officers may also enter if they reasonably believe that immediate entry is necessary to protect themselves from serious harm. [**Brigham City v. Stuart**, 547 U.S. 398 (2006); **Michigan v. Fisher**, 558 U.S. 45 (2009); **Ryburn v. Huff**, 565 U.S. 469 (2012) (per curiam)]

(c) Announcement Requirement

A police officer ***must usually announce her authority and purpose before using force to enter a home to make an arrest or execute a search warrant.*** This requirement is called the knock and announce requirement. Generally, failure to make such an announcement renders the entry unlawful, although most jurisdictions recognize exceptions to this requirement (*e.g.,* the officer's reasonable belief that an announcement would endanger her or prompt the suspect's escape or permit the destruction of evidence). An announcement allows the occupants of the home to prepare for the entry and to avoid unnecessary property destruction. [**Richards v. Wisconsin**, 520 U.S. 385 (1997)—overruling Wisconsin Supreme Court's bright line rule that officers may always make a "no-knock" entry when executing warrants in felony drug investigations]

1) Exclusionary Rule Not Applicable

Although failure to announce might be "unlawful," the Supreme Court has held that exclusion is not an available remedy for violations of the knock and announce rule. [**Hudson v. Michigan**, 547 U.S. 586 (2006)] *Rationale*: The exclusionary remedy is too attenuated from the purposes of the knock and announce rule of protecting human life and limb, property, privacy, and dignity. Moreover, the cost of excluding relevant evidence—when police have a search warrant—because of knock and announce violations—is too high when compared to the deterrence benefit gained. Finally, other deterrents prevent officers from violating the rule, such as civil suits and internal police disciplinary sanctions. [**Hudson v. Michigan**, *supra*]

(d) Scope of Search

A warrant to arrest someone in the home does not authorize a full search of the home. Police may enter to look for the suspect and must stop the search upon locating her. To conduct a search for evidence or contraband, police need to obtain a search warrant. *Note*: Police may conduct a cursory, protective sweep of premises incident to an in-home arrest to ensure the safety of officers and others during execution of the warrant. Such a quick search is allowed when police have a reasonable belief (reasonable suspicion) that others in the home pose a danger to the officers. [**Maryland v. Buie**, 494 U.S. 325 (1990)] This search is not for evidence; it is for people.

(e) Third-Party Premises

Absent exigent circumstances, police officers executing an arrest warrant may ***not*** search for the person named in the warrant in the ***home of a third party*** without first obtaining a separate search warrant for the third-party premises. [**Steagald v. United States**, 451 U.S. 204 (1981)] *Note*, however, that an arrestee found on premises owned by a third person and illegally searched by the police might lack standing to challenge the search. (*See infra*, p. 36.)

EXAM TIP

Be sure to remember the general standards for arrests on your exam: An officer can arrest a person in a public place without a warrant if: (i) the officer has reasonable grounds (*i.e.*, probable cause) to believe that the arrestee has committed a felony; or (ii) the arrestee committed a misdemeanor in the officer's presence. However, an officer generally may not arrest a person at home without an arrest warrant supported by probable cause. If there is an in-home arrest with probable cause but no warrant, consider whether the government can justify the lack of warrant with some rationale, such as exigent circumstances.

EXAM TIP

Remember, a warrant to arrest in the home does not authorize a full search of the home. Police may enter to look for the suspect they seek to arrest, but must stop searching upon locating her. To search for evidence or contraband, the police need to obtain a search warrant supported by probable cause. Nevertheless, evidence observed in plain view while looking for the suspect may be admissible. (*See infra*, p. 44, 47.)

(3) Obtaining Warrant

To obtain an arrest warrant, a complaint must set forth facts showing the ***commission*** of an offense and the ***accused's responsibility*** for the act. [Fed. R. Crim. P. 4(a)] Generally, the complaint is in the form of an affidavit (*i.e.*, a sworn written statement by a police officer). The sufficiency of the complaint is determined by federal constitutional standards; *i.e.*, probable cause must be demonstrated before a valid arrest warrant may be issued by a judicial officer. [**Giordenello v. United States**, 357 U.S. 480 (1958)]

3. Deadly Force

There is a Fourth Amendment "seizure" when a police officer uses deadly force to apprehend a suspect. An officer may not use deadly force unless it is ***reasonable*** to do so under the circumstances. [**Scott v. Harris**, 550 U.S. 372 (2007)] Whether the force used is reasonable is determined under a totality of the circumstances test and is highly fact dependent and context sensitive. [**Barnes v. Felix**, 605 U.S. 73 (2025)]

e.g. **Example:** It was reasonable for an officer to end a chase by bumping a suspect's car (which ultimately resulted in the suspect's becoming a paraplegic) where the suspect was driving at high speeds and weaving in and out of traffic. Under such circumstances, the suspect's conduct posed an immediate threat to his own life and to the lives of innocent bystanders. [**Scott v. Harris**, *supra*]

cf. **Compare:** It was unreasonable to shoot a fleeing suspect who refused to stop when ordered to do so when there was no evidence that the suspect was armed or posed any threat to the police or others, even though the police had probable cause to believe that the suspect had committed a burglary. [**Tennessee v. Garner**, 471 U.S. 1 (1985)]

4. Stops and Other Detentions

The Supreme Court has recognized that not all seizures must be supported by full probable cause; limited stops and brief detentions may be justified on a lesser showing of reasonable suspicion. Indeed, in certain cases when ***special needs*** are involved, even suspicionless stops may be reasonable (*see infra,* pp. 30–31). All Fourth Amendment seizures are governed by the reasonableness of the stop.

a. Limited Detention—Stop and Frisk

(1) Stop

Police have the authority to stop (seize) a person and detain them briefly for questioning even without probable cause to believe that the person has committed a crime. Such an investigatory stop does not constitute an arrest and is permissible when prompted by three factors: (i) ***observation of unusual conduct***, (ii) leading to a **"*reasonable suspicion*"** that criminal activity may be afoot, and (iii) the ***ability to point to specific and articulable facts*** to justify that suspicion. [**Terry v. Ohio**, 392 U.S. 1 (1968)] The *Terry* Court ruled that the government interests in effective crime prevention and detection as well as ensuring officer safety outweigh the severe, but brief, intrusion of the stop.

(a) "Reasonable Suspicion"

There is no bright line test to determine whether reasonable suspicion exists. "Reasonable suspicion" involves ***something less than probable cause*** but requires ***something more than a vague suspicion.*** An officer must be able to "articulate more than an inchoate and unparticularized suspicion or 'hunch' of criminal activity." The suspicion must be based on ***objective, articulable facts***. [**Illinois v. Wardlow**, 528 U.S. 119 (2000); **United States v. Sokolow**, 490 U.S. 1 (1989)] Nevertheless, reasonable suspicion requires "a showing ***considerably less than preponderance of the evidence***[.]" Circumstances suggesting reasonable suspicion may include the high incidence of crime in the area coupled with the defendant's "suspicious looks." [**Brown v. Texas**, 443 U.S. 47 (1979)] While presence in a high drug crime area alone is insufficient for reasonable suspicion, when coupled with unprovoked flight from police, there is probably reasonable suspicion. [**Wardlow**, *supra*] The Supreme Court has stated that the ***totality of the circumstances*** must be taken into account. The detaining officers must have a ***particularized, objective basis for suspecting the particular person stopped*** of criminal activity. [**United States v. Cortez**, 449 U.S. 411 (1981)] Mere association with suspected criminals, by itself, is insufficient for reasonable suspicion. [**Sibron v. New York**, 392 U.S. 40 (1968)]

Example: The Court has upheld a stop based on a drug courier profile—*i.e.,* a list developed by the Drug Enforcement Agency of traits frequently exhibited by drug couriers. [**United States v. Sokolow**, *supra*] *Note*: The Court did ***not*** base its decision on the fact that the defendant matched the drug courier profile, but rather it undertook an independent review of whether the facts objectively known by the police raised a reasonable suspicion. The defendant had purchased two round-trip airline tickets from Hawaii to Miami with $2,100 in cash. The defendant's scheduled return trip was within 48 hours of arrival, and the defendant checked no luggage. Also, the defendant gave the ticket agent a phone number that was listed under another name and appeared nervous during the trip. The Court found that these factors raised a reasonable suspicion.

Example: An officer acted with reasonable suspicion when he initiated a traffic stop of a driver after processing a car tag and learning that the owner's driver's license was revoked. In the absence of contrary information, the officer was reasonable in believing that the person driving was the owner of the car with the revoked license. The Court noted, "Although a mere 'hunch' does not create reasonable suspicion, the level of suspicion the standard requires is considerably less than proof of wrongdoing by a preponderance of the evidence and obviously less than is necessary for probable cause." [**Kansas v. Glover**, 589 U.S. 376 (2020)]

Compare: The Court reversed a conviction under a state statute requiring an individual to comply with an officer's request for identification. The officers saw the defendant and another man walking away from each other in an alley in a high-crime neighborhood and stopped the defendant. The stop was ruled unconstitutional because the officers could not point to objective facts to show that criminal activity was afoot or that the defendant was armed. [**Brown v. Texas**, *supra,* p. 26] Similarly, the Court has held that an anonymous tip that a person is wearing certain clothing and carrying a gun, by itself, is insufficient to justify a stop and frisk. [**Florida v. J.L.**, 529 U.S. 266 (2000)]

1) Officer's Knowledge Relevant

In determining whether there is reasonable suspicion under the totality of the circumstances, an officer may assess "the situation in light of his specialized training and familiarity with the customs of the area's inhabitants." [**United States v. Arvizu**, 534 U.S. 266 (2002)]

Example: A border patrol officer had reasonable suspicion to stop a vehicle that he observed on routine patrol in a remote part of Arizona when: (i) the defendant dramatically slowed his vehicle at the sight of the officer but failed to acknowledge him and appeared stiff; (ii) children in the back seat of the defendant's car waved oddly to the officer and had their knees up as if resting on something; (iii) the defendant was driving on a dirt road often traveled by smugglers, in a minivan (which is often the vehicle of choice for smugglers in the area) that was registered to a residence in an area "notorious for alien and narcotics smuggling," at a time when the border patrol's shifts normally change, and on a route that makes little sense for normal traffic. [**United States v. Arvizu**, *supra*]

(b) Scope and Duration

An investigatory stop must be ***temporary*** and ***no longer than necessary*** to effectuate its purpose—to confirm or dispel the officer's suspicion [**Florida v. Royer**, *supra*, p. 20—when police remove without his consent from a public area in an airport to a police room in the airport while keeping his license and airline ticket, the detainee is "seized"; **Rodriguez v. United States,** 575 U.S. 348 (2015)—prolonging a traffic stop by seven or eight minutes to allow a police dog to sniff for contraband is not a de minimis intrusion and violates the Fourth Amendment]

(c) Property Seizures on Reasonable Suspicion

If the police have a reasonable suspicion (the standard for making a "stop") that a person's luggage contains narcotics, they may detain the unopened luggage ***temporarily*** to investigate the circumstances. Although this is a "seizure" within the meaning of the Fourth Amendment, the strong government interest outweighs the minimal intrusion. Like other stops, however, the seizure must be for no longer than necessary. [**United States v. Place**, 462 U.S. 696 (1983)—90-minute detention of luggage ***unreasonable*** under the circumstances]

(2) Frisk

Even if the stop is reasonable, a police officer may only "frisk" a person (*i.e.,* conduct a limited pat down of a person's outer clothing for weapons) if the officer reasonably suspects that the person is armed and dangerous. [**Terry v. Ohio**, *supra,* p. 26]

EXAM TIP

Although you often hear "stop and frisk" as if it is one thing, remember to analyze each—the seizure (stop) and the search (frisk)—separately. A ***stop*** is not an arrest, but it is a seizure, so an officer need not have probable cause. However, she must have a reason to believe that criminal activity is afoot—*i.e.,* reasonable suspicion based on specific and articulable facts. Thus, seeing a person pace repeatedly in front of a jewelry store might justify a stop. However, a ***frisk*** will be justified only if the officer also reasonably thinks the suspect has a weapon.

(a) Frisk Applied to Automobiles

If the police have lawfully detained an automobile and have an "articulable suspicion" that an occupant may gain immediate control of a weapon from the car, they may, before the suspect reenters the automobile, search those parts of the passenger area that may contain a weapon. [**Michigan v. Long**, 463 U.S. 1032 (1983)]

e.g. **Example:** Officers noticed that Defendant's car was being driven erratically and eventually was driven into a ditch. Defendant met the officers at the back of his car but left his driver's door open. The officers immediately noticed that Defendant appeared drunk and asked him for his license and registration. Defendant returned to the passenger compartment of the car. The officers accompanied Defendant and immediately noticed a hunting knife on the floor in the car. The officers then searched the car, ostensibly to ensure that no other weapons were present. They found a pouch of marijuana. Given the circumstances (observance of the hunting knife, Defendant's intoxicated state, the time and rural location of the search), the

Court upheld the search, finding it reasonable for the officers to fear that another weapon might be present in the car. [**Michigan v. Long**, *supra*]

(3) Stop and Identify Statutes

A criminal statute requiring persons who loiter or wander on the streets to provide a "credible and reliable" identification when stopped by police, but which fails to clarify what will satisfy the identification requirement, is unconstitutional under the Due Process Clause of the Constitution because it is vague. [**Kolender v. Lawson**, 461 U.S. 352 (1983)] Due process prohibits regulations that fail to give reasonable notice of what is prohibited—*i.e.,* the ***void for vagueness*** doctrine.

Example: The Court has held a statute void for vagueness that allowed the police to order persons to disburse from loitering even though the statute (i) defined loitering (remaining in one place with no apparent purpose) and (ii) could be invoked only if the officer reasonably believed at least one of the loitering persons to be a criminal street gang member. *Rationale*: The statute is too vague to give officers sufficient guidelines and violates the Due Process Clause because of the great potential for arbitrary police enforcement. [**Chicago v. Morales**, 527 U.S. 41 (1999)]

The Court upheld a stop and identify statute where the stop was based on reasonable suspicion sufficient to satisfy ***Terry*** (*supra,* p. 26) and a Nevada statute had been interpreted to require only that the suspect disclose his name. [**Hiibel v. Sixth Judicial District Court**, 542 U.S. 177 (2004)] (But *see* **Brown v. Texas**, 443 U.S. 47 (1979)) (reversing a conviction for defendant's failure to identify himself in violation of a Texas statute, when police lacked reasonable suspicion to stop the defendant in the first place). *Note*: The Fourth Amendment only imposes obligations on the government; it "cannot require a suspect to answer questions." [**Hiibel**, *supra*] The duty to provide information, such as a name, rests on other sources of law, such as a state statute.

b. Automobile Stops

The Supreme Court has held that police officers may not stop a vehicle for the sole purpose of checking the driver's license and the vehicle's registration unless the officers have at least a reasonable and articulable suspicion as required by ***Terry***, *supra* (*e.g.,* a reasonable belief that a traffic law has been violated). [**Delaware v. Prouse**, 440 U.S. 648 (1979)—unconstitutional for officer to ***randomly*** stop defendant's car to check registration; such "unbridled discretion" opens the door for police abuse and is the "kind of standardless and unconstrained discretion" the Fourth Amendment is designed to prevent]

(1) Pretextual Stops

If a police officer has probable cause to believe that a traffic law has been violated, the officer may stop the suspect's car, even if the officer's actual motive is to investigate whether some ***other law***—for which the officer lacks reasonable suspicion—is being violated. [**Whren v. United States**, 517 U.S. 806 (1996)—police in a high drug area stopped Defendant's car after observing Defendant pause a long time at an intersection, abruptly turn without signaling, and depart at an unreasonable speed] As long as the stop was lawful (based on reasonable suspicion or probable cause), the police may detain the suspect by asking for permission to search the car, even after a warning or traffic citation has been given and the suspect's license has been returned. [**Ohio v. Robinette**, 519 U.S. 33 (1997); but *see* **Knowles v. Iowa**, 525 U.S. 113 (1998)—stopping a motorist for speeding, but issuing the motorist a citation, rather than arresting the motorist, did not authorize the officer to conduct a search of the vehicle, even though the officer had probable cause to make a full custodial arrest and *see* **Rodriguez v. United States**, 575 U.S. 348 (2015)—engaging a dog to sniff a car after police complete a traffic stop is unlawful when use of the dog prolongs the time reasonably required to complete the mission of issuing a ticket]

(2) Seizure of Occupants

An automobile stop constitutes a seizure not only of the automobile's driver, but also of any passengers in the car. *Rationale*: Such a stop curtails the travel of the passengers as well as the driver, and a reasonable passenger in a stopped vehicle would not feel free to leave the scene without police permission. [**Brendlin v. California**, 551 U.S. 249 (2007)]

e.g. **Example:** Officer pulled Driver's car over for, admittedly, no valid reason. Upon approaching Driver's car and asking Driver for her license, Officer noticed that Passenger resembled a person wanted for a parole violation. Officer confirmed his suspicion via radio and arrested Passenger. Upon searching Passenger, Officer discovered drug paraphernalia. *Held:* Passenger may challenge the admissibility of the drug paraphernalia as the fruit of an unlawful seizure. [**Brendlin v. California**, *supra*]

(3) Roadblocks

Stopping a person at a roadblock is a seizure for purposes of the Fourth Amendment. [**Brower v. Inyo County**, 489 U.S. 593 (1989)] However, the Court has upheld roadblock searches made ***without individualized suspicion*** that the driver has violated a law under certain conditions: First, the roadblock must stop cars on the basis of some ***neutral, articulable standard*** (*e.g.,* every car or every fifth car) to negate unconstrained police discretion and its potential for discriminatory abuse. [*See* **Delaware v. Prouse**, *supra*—suggesting that stopping every car that passes to verify drivers' licenses and registrations would be permissible] Relatedly, the stops must be made pursuant to guidelines, not left to the discretion of individual officers. Such guidelines reduce the "standardless and unconstrained discretion" that the Fourth Amendment prohibits. [*See* **Michigan Department of State Police v. Sitz**, 496 U.S. 444 (1990)] Second, the roadblock must be designed to serve purposes ***closely related to a particular problem related to automobiles*** and/or their mobility. [*See* **Indianapolis v. Edmond**, 531 U.S. 32 (2000)] Roadblock stops may also be used to gather information and ask vehicle occupants for their help. [**Illinois v. Lidster**, 540 U.S. 419 (2004) (allowing police highway checkpoint to gather information about a hit-and-run accident in the same location one week earlier)]

(a) Search for Undocumented Immigrants

Because of the difficulty of discerning whether an automobile near the border is transporting immigrants into the country without the permission of the Attorney General, as required to make entry legal, roadblocks near the border in which every car passing the roadblock is stopped to search for undocumented persons are valid. The government interest in stopping the illegal influx of persons unauthorized to be in the United States outweighs the minimal intrusion into the privacy of passersby. [**United States v. Martinez-Fuerte**, 428 U.S. 543 (1976)] However, it is unconstitutional to stop a motorist near the Mexico border based solely on the occupants' apparent ancestry. [**United States v. Brignoni-Ponce**, 422 U.S. 873 (1975)]

(b) Sobriety Checkpoints

Because of the gravity of the drunk driving problem and the magnitude of the government's interest in removing drunk drivers from the roads, the Court has upheld the use of roadblocks to check the sobriety of all drivers passing by. [**Michigan Department of State Police v. Sitz**, 496 U.S. 444 (1990)] The Court found that the intrusion into privacy was slight and was outweighed by the government's interest in preventing drunk driving.

(c) Distinguish—Interdiction Checkpoints

The Court has held that checkpoints set up to search cars for illegal drugs are unconstitutional seizures. In determining whether individualized suspicion is required for a seizure, the Court considers the nature of the interests threatened and their connection to the law enforcement practices at issue. The purpose of a drug interdiction checkpoint is to detect evidence of "ordinary criminal wrongdoing." The checkpoints are unrelated to highway safety, as in ***Sitz***, *supra*. A general interest in detecting crime does not justify a suspicionless seizure; neither does the "intractable nature of the drug problem." If an exception were carved out for such general law enforcement interests, nearly all suspicionless seizures would be justified. [**Indianapolis v. Edmond**, *supra*, p. 30]

1) Distinguish—Informational Roadblock

Unlike the roadblock in *Edmond*, a roadblock set up to ask drivers if they had information regarding a deadly hit-and-run that occurred a week earlier in the same area, was held to be constitutional. The police were not seeking incriminating information about the drivers stopped, but rather were asking for help in solving a crime. [**Illinois v. Lidster**, 540 U.S. 419 (2004)—roadblock unsuccessfully challenged by driver who was arrested for driving under the influence of alcohol after nearly running over one of the officers at the roadblock]

EXAM TIP

Roadblock scenarios can make an interesting topic on an exam. If you see a roadblock question, remember that roadblocks looking for ***undocumented immigrants*** or ***drunk drivers*** have been upheld, while roadblocks looking for drivers carrying drugs have been found unconstitutional. The difference in result relies on the difference in purpose. Rooting out drunk drivers and undocumented immigrants within the United States is distinguishable from the ordinary purpose of detecting criminal wrongdoing. Drunk driving is a problem directly related to the safety of the automobile, and the mobility and speed of automobiles makes protecting the borders difficult. However, the Court has found no special relationship between the automobile and illegal drugs. In any case, remember that even a roadblock to detect drunk drivers or immigrants entering without authorization will be found ***unconstitutional if the police have discretion*** regarding who they will stop. Instead, some neutral basis established by guidelines for stopping cars (*e.g.*, stopping every fifth car) must be used.

(4) Ordering Persons out of Vehicle

If a police officer has lawfully detained a vehicle for a traffic violation, the officer may order the occupants out of the vehicle (*i.e.*, the driver ***and*** the passengers) without any additional suspicion that the occupants are dangerous. *Rationale*: Because the occupants of the vehicle have already been detained, the added intrusion of forcing them to get out of the car is minimal (de minimis), while the potential danger is significant to the police officer in allowing the occupants to remain in the car is great. [**Pennsylvania v. Mimms**, 434 U.S. 106 (1978); **Maryland v. Wilson**, 519 U.S. 408 (1997)]

(5) Distinguish—Boats

The Fourth Amendment does not prohibit the "suspicionless" boarding of a sailboat in a channel leading to the open sea by United States Customs agents for the purpose of examining the vessel's documentation, even though such boarding is no less "random" than the highway stops condemned in *Prouse, supra,* p. 29. This is due to the waterborne setting, which precludes the use of fixed checkpoints or roadblocks and permits access to the open sea. [**United States v. Villamonte-Marquez**, 462 U.S. 579 (1983)]

c. Detention During Lawful Search Permissible

When executing a search warrant, the police may detain those persons who are present on the premises while the search is conducted. [**Michigan v. Summers**, 452 U.S. 692 (1981); ***and*** *see* **Muehler v. Mena**, 544 U.S. 93 (2005)—upholding the handcuffing and questioning of an occupant for two to three hours during a search for weapons in a house believed to belong to gang members] This is based on the legitimate law enforcement interest of preventing flight of occupants if incriminating evidence is found; it serves to make the search easier to complete and helps ensure the safety of the officers conducting the search. Nevertheless, police may not detain persons "beyond the immediate vicinity of the premises being searched," even if police observe those people leave the place subject to the search warrant. [**Bailey v. United States**, 568 U.S. 186 (2013)—holding that the categorical authority to detain incident to the execution of a search warrant is limited to the immediate vicinity of the premises to be searched, and a detention one mile away was outside the immediate vicinity]

(1) Authority to Pat Down Detained Persons

Although the police may detain persons on the premises when executing a search warrant, their authority to pat down (search) the occupants is limited. They may not conduct a frisk unless they have a reasonable and articulable suspicion that criminal activity is afoot and that the detainees are armed. [**Ybarra v. Illinois**, 444 U.S. 85 (1979)—holding that police violated the Fourth Amendment when they searched a patron in a public bar with only probable cause to believe that the bartender was violating the law, and *see infra*, p. 46]

(2) No Authority to Detain Persons Beyond "Immediate Vicinity"

Although the police may readily detain persons on or immediately outside the premises of a lawfully executed search warrant, that authority does not extend to areas beyond the immediate vicinity of the premises covered in the warrant. [**Bailey v. United States**, *supra*] There, before officers executed a search of an apartment with a warrant, the defendant and a companion left the home in a car and drove about a mile before they were stopped by police, detained, and searched. The Court held that detentions of this kind are limited to the immediate vicinity of the premises to be searched, and the defendant had been detained "at a point beyond any reasonable understanding of the immediate vicinity of the premises in question[.]"

d. Police Station Investigations

Police officers ***must have probable cause*** to bring a suspect to the police station for questioning [**Dunaway v. New York**, *supra*, p. 20], or for fingerprinting [**Hayes v.**

Florida, 470 U.S. 811 (1985)]. When police arrest someone for a serious crime, and the arrest is supported by the requisite probable cause, police may also take and analyze a cheek swab of the arrestee for DNA as part of a routine booking procedure. [**Maryland v. King**, 569 U.S. 435 (2013)] The Court has also suggested that under certain, limited circumstances (*e.g.*, where police schedule a suspect to come in for fingerprinting at a convenient time, do not question the suspect, and do not use the procedure to harass the suspect), it might be permissible to require a person to go to the police station for investigatory purposes without probable cause for arrest. [**Davis v. Mississippi**, 394 U.S. 721 (1969)] The Court has also suggested in dicta that the Fourth Amendment would permit fingerprinting if police had reasonable suspicion that a suspect committed a crime, and there is a reasonable basis to believe that fingerprinting would "establish or negate the suspect's connection with that crime[,]" provided fingerprinting was completed "with dispatch." [**Hayes v. Florida**, *infra* p. 32]

5. Grand Jury Subpoena Exception

The Fourth Amendment requirement that searches and seizures be reasonable does not protect a person from being compelled by subpoena to appear before a grand jury. Even if a person is asked to give handwriting or voice samples in addition to testifying, the subpoena does ***not have to be based on probable cause or objective suspicion***. [**United States v. Dionisio**, 410 U.S. 1 (1973)]

a. Caveat—Overbroad Subpoena

The Supreme Court has suggested that a grand jury subpoena could be unreasonable if it is extremely broad and sweeping or is being used for harassment. [**United States v. Mara**, 410 U.S. 19 (1973)]

B. Evidentiary Search and Seizure

1. Introduction

Like arrests, evidentiary searches and seizures are covered by the Fourth Amendment. The Fourth Amendment prohibits the government from conducting ***unreasonable*** searches (intrusions upon a person's privacy or protected property) and seizures (meaningful interference with a thing (effect), the application of force to a person with intent to restrain, or a show of police authority to which a person submits). Reasonableness here usually requires that a ***warrant be obtained*** before a search is commenced (*compare* arrests, *supra*, pp. 23, where a warrant generally is not required).

a. Scope of Items Subject to Search and Seizure

Provided that the search is reasonable, the police may search for, and seize, the following [**Warden v. Hayden**, 387 U.S. 294 (1967)]:

(1) ***The instrumentalities of crime*** (such as burglar's tools);

(2) ***The fruits of crime*** (such as stolen goods);

(3) ***Contraband*** (such as illegal drugs); and

(4) ***Mere evidence of crime***, as long as probable cause exists to believe that the item is connected to criminal activity (such as suspect's clothing worn during the crime).

2. Governmental Conduct Requirement

The Fourth Amendment protects ***only against governmental conduct***—not against searches by private persons. [**Burdeau v. McDowell**, 256 U.S. 465 (1921)] Government agents include publicly paid police, private persons acting at police direction, privately paid police (such as security guards) ***who are deputized members of the public police force***, and public school officials. Note that privately paid police whose primary function is law enforcement do not qualify as government agents unless deputized.

3. Reasonable Expectation of Privacy Requirement

The Supreme Court originally applied the Fourth Amendment to searches almost entirely on the basis of whether the place searched was a place identified in, and protected by, the Fourth Amendment (*e.g.,* a person's house or private papers). In 1967, the Court departed from this property-based approach, holding that the "Fourth Amendment protects people, not places." [**Katz v. United States**, 389 U.S. 347 (1967)] In 2012, the Supreme Court resuscitated the long dormant property-based approach while keeping the *Katz* approach. The Court held that a search falls within the protections of the Fourth Amendment when government action physically intrudes on a constitutionally protected area (including "houses, papers, and effects"), to obtain information [**United States v. Jones**, 565 U.S. 400 (2012)] or the government infringes an area where a person has a reasonable and legitimate expectation of privacy. [**Katz**, *supra*; **Grady v. North Carolina**, 575 U.S. 306 (2015), full-time satellite-based monitoring of a sex offender is a "search" subject to Fourth Amendment reasonableness]

The *Katz* approach does not expand Fourth Amendment protection as greatly as it might first appear. There can be no reasonable and justifiable expectation of privacy in things exposed to the public, so searches of such items are not within the scope of Fourth Amendment protection. Also, the Supreme Court limits the scope of Fourth Amendment protection by requiring **standing**—*i.e.*, only a person with an expectation of privacy in the place searched or the item seized may challenge the search.

a. Standing

To have standing to challenge a search under the Fourth Amendment, a person must have a ***legitimate expectation of privacy***. [**Rakas v. Illinois**, 439 U.S. 128 (1978); **Byrd v. United States**, 584 U.S. 395 (2018)] Whether a person has standing is determined on a case-by-case basis, assessing the claimant's reasonable expectation of privacy under the ***totality of the circumstances***. The Supreme Court has held that a person has standing to raise a Fourth Amendment claim any time:

(i) ***The person owned or had a right to possess*** the place searched (including the right to exclude others);

(ii) ***The place searched was in fact the person's home*** whether or not the person owned or had a right to possess it (*e.g.,* a grandson living in the house owned by his grandmother); or

(iii) ***The person was an overnight guest*** of the owner or otherwise had a genuine privacy interest in the place searched and could exclude others [**Minnesota v. Olson**, 495 U.S. 91 (1990)]

APPROACH TO SEARCH AND SEIZURE QUESTIONS

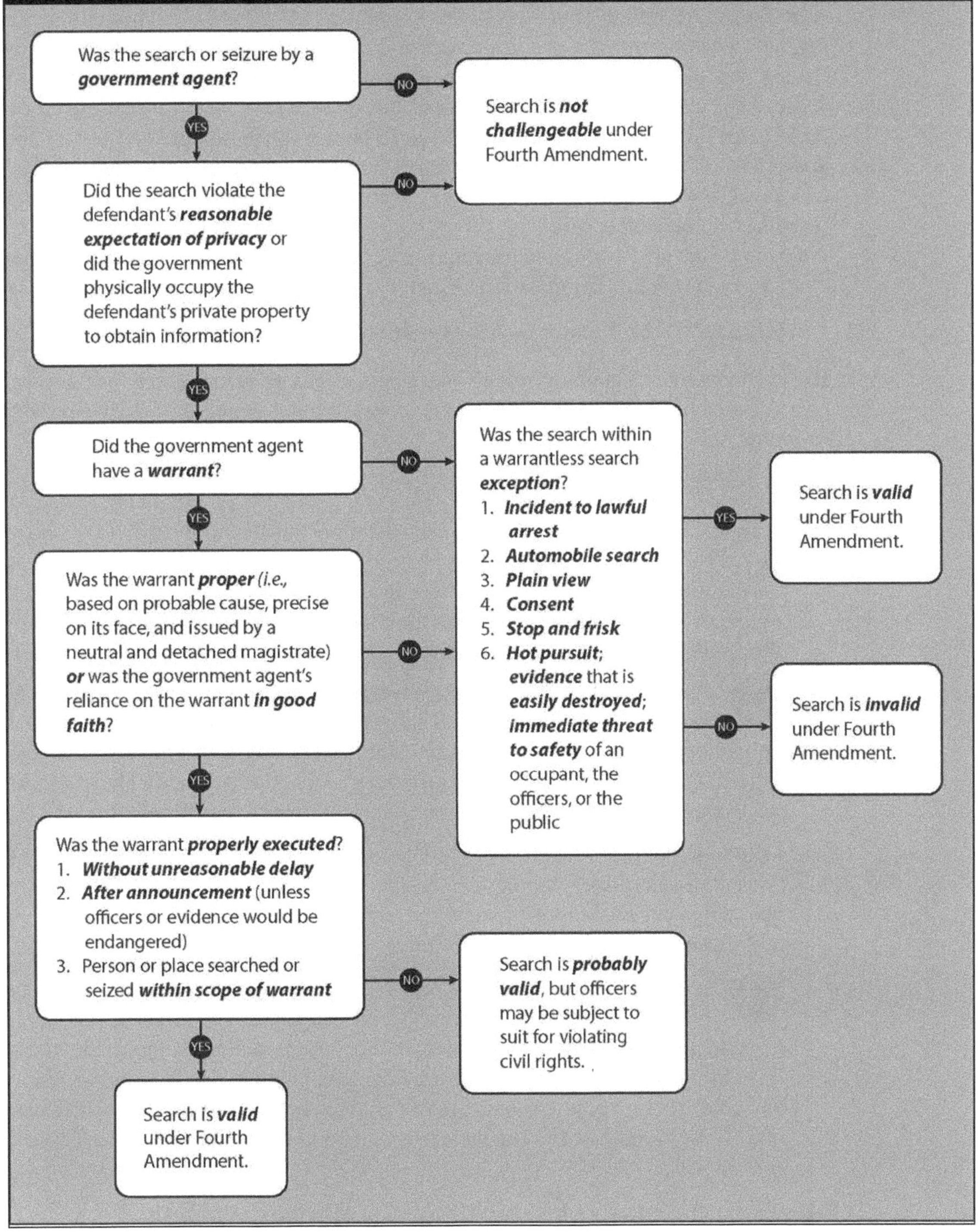

e.g. **Example:** A police officer peered through the closed window blind of Lessee's apartment and observed Lessee and defendants bagging cocaine.

When defendants left the apartment, the officer followed them to their car and arrested them. The car and apartment were searched, and cocaine and a weapon were found. At trial, defendants moved to suppress all evidence, claiming that the officer's peeking through the window blind constituted an illegal search. It was determined that defendants had spent little time in Lessee's apartment and had come there solely to conduct a business transaction (*i.e.,* bagging the cocaine). *Held:* The defendants did not have a sufficient expectation of privacy in the apartment. They were there for only a few hours and were not overnight guests. Moreover, they were there for business purposes rather than social purposes, and there is a lesser expectation of privacy in commercial settings. Therefore, the defendants had no Fourth Amendment protections in the apartment and could not challenge the search. [**Minnesota v. Carter**, 525 U.S. 83 (1999)]

(1) "Legitimately" on Premises Alone—Insufficient

It is not enough for "standing" merely that a person was harmed through introduction of evidence obtained from an allegedly unconstitutional search of a ***third person's property***.

(a) Application to Automobiles

Anyone who is in an automobile that is stopped unconstitutionally (*see supra,* pp. 29–31) may challenge the stop. However, if an automobile is constitutionally stopped, a passenger in the automobile may not challenge a search of the automobile merely because the passenger was legitimately within the automobile. [**Rakas v. Illinois**, *supra* p. 34]

e.g. **Example:** Police stopped Driver's car based on probable cause to believe that it was involved in a robbery. Upon searching the car, the police found a sawed-off shotgun and some shells. None of the passengers in Driver's car claimed ownership of the gun or shells. *Held:* None of the passengers may challenge the search of the car. [**Rakas v. Illinois**, *supra*]

Unlike a mere passenger in a car, the driver of a rental car, who is not listed as an authorized driver in the car rental agreement, does generally have a reasonable expectation of privacy, *i.e.*, standing, to challenge an illegal search of the rental car. [**Byrd v. United States**, *supra*, p. 34]

e.g. **Example:** Police stopped a rental car driven by Byrd. Byrd was the only person in the car but was not listed as an authorized driver in the rental agreement. Police searched the car without consent, including the trunk where Byrd had stored his belongings. *Held*: Someone in otherwise lawful possession and control of a rental car has a reasonable expectation of privacy in the car, even if she is not listed in the rental agreement as an authorized driver. [**Byrd**, *supra*]

(2) Mere Ownership of Property Seized—Insufficient

Ownership of the property seized is not necessarily enough for standing. An evaluation of the ***totality of the circumstances*** must be made to determine whether an individual had a reasonable expectation of privacy, considering the location of the property at the time of the search in addition to ownership of the property seized. [**Rawlings v. Kentucky**, 448 U.S. 98 (1980)]

e.g. **Example:** Defendant had placed drugs in his friend's purse. The friend was required to empty the contents of her purse onto a table. When the drugs fell out, she turned to Defendant and said, "Take what's yours." Defendant took the drugs, which were introduced against him in a drug possession prosecution. Defendant claimed standing based on his ownership of the property seized—the drugs. The Supreme Court held that mere ownership of the seized property is not dispositive of a citizen's reasonable expectation of privacy, but is only a factor to be considered in an overall case-by-case inquiry. [**Rawlings v. Kentucky**, *supra*, p. 36]

(3) Ownership in Possessory Crime—No Automatic Standing

At one time, the Supreme Court held that in cases where possession of the item seized during a search is an element of the crime charged (such as in drug possession cases), it would be unfair to require the defendant to claim an ownership interest in the item seized to show the requisite legitimate expectation of privacy needed for standing to challenge the search and seizure. The defendant would be forced to choose between: (i) admitting an element of the crime and challenging the search, or (ii) forgoing a challenge to the search to avoid admitting an element of the crime. The Court imposed a rule that in such a case, the defendant would automatically have standing to challenge the search. [**Jones v. United States**, 362 U.S. 257 (1960)] Later cases found that such admissions could not be used to prove the defendant's guilt. As a consequence, this automatic standing rule—that a person has standing to object to the legality of a search and seizure any time the evidence obtained was introduced against him for a possessory offense—has been abolished. [**United States v. Salvucci**, 448 U.S. 83 (1980)]

e.g. **Example:** Mere possession of stolen mail does not give "automatic standing" to challenge the search of the stolen mail. [**United States v. Salvucci**, *supra*] Defendants can challenge the admissibility of the fruits of a search only if the search violated their ***own*** Fourth Amendment rights.

(4) Conspirator—No Automatic Standing

That a conspirator may be aggrieved by the introduction of damaging evidence seized from a co-conspirator does not give the conspirator automatic standing to challenge seizure of the evidence. The conspirator must show that his own expectation of privacy was violated. [**United States v. Padilla**, 508 U.S. 77 (1993)]

e.g. **Example:** Police stopped the vehicle that Defendant was driving and found over 500 pounds of cocaine in the vehicle's trunk. Defendant told the police that he was involved in a drug distribution conspiracy with three other people. The three others were eventually arrested and, at their trial, sought to challenge the search of the car. The Supreme Court held that the mere fact that they were involved in a conspiracy with Defendant did not give them standing to challenge the search of the car. [**United States v. Padilla**, *supra*]

(5) Contraband—No Legitimate Privacy Interest and No Standing

Governmental intrusions that only reveal possession of controlled substances (*e.g.,* "sniff tests" by trained narcotics detection dogs [**United States v. Place**, *supra*, p. 28], or cocaine field tests [**United States v. Jacobsen**, 466 U.S. 109 (1984)]) do not invade any ***legitimate*** interest in privacy; therefore, the defendant has no standing to assert a Fourth Amendment violation. But *see* **Florida v. Jardines**, 569 U.S. 1 (2013) (holding that using a drug-sniffing dog on a homeowner's porch to investigate contents within the home is a search).

(6) Facial Challenges to a Statute Are Permitted

Although standing is required, "facial challenges under the Fourth Amendment are not categorically barred or especially disfavored." [**Los Angeles v. Patel**, 576 U.S. 409 (2015)]

e.g. **Example:** Hotel operators in Los Angeles challenged a city statute requiring them to keep specific information on their guests for 90 days, including name, address, car make and model, license plate number, dates of arrival and departure, etc. The statute further required the operators to provide the recorded information to police upon request. Failure to comply with the statute was punishable as a misdemeanor. The Court allowed the operators to challenge the statute's constitutionality and held that it violated the Fourth Amendment because it did not afford hotel operators an opportunity to have a neutral decision maker review an officer's demand for records. [**Patel**, *supra*]

b. Items Exposed to the Public

(1) In General

A person does ***not have a reasonable expectation of privacy*** in objects held out to the public. Examples of items exposed to the public include the following:

(a) ***A person's handwriting*** [**United States v. Mara**, *supra*, p. 33];

(b) ***The sound of a person's voice*** [**United States v. Dionisio**, *supra,* p. 33];

(c) ***Telephone numbers dialed***—"pen registers" [**Smith v. Maryland**, 442 U.S. 735 (1979)] (although a telephone conversation itself is statutorily protected by Title III of the Omnibus Crime Control and Safe Streets Act of 1968 [18 U.S.C. §§ 2510–2522]);

(d) ***Bank records*** [**Fisher v. United States**, 425 U.S. 391 (1976)];

(e) ***Paint on the outside of a car*** [**Cardwell v. Lewis**, 417 U.S. 583 (1974)], and the movement of one's car on public roads and the arrival at a private residence, even if detection of such movement requires the use of an electronic beeper, provided the beeper reveals only movements that could have been seen with visual surveillance. [**United States v. Knotts**, 460 U.S. 276 (1983)];

cf. **Compare:** The government's warrantless use of an electronic beeper to obtain information inside a home that it could not have observed from outside the home's curtilage—is a warrantless search. [**United States v. Karo**, 468 U.S. 705 (1984)]

cf. **Compare:** The government's attachment of a Global-Positioning-System (GPS) tracking device to a suspect's sport utility vehicle and subsequent use to monitor its movements on public streets for 28 days is a search. Although property rights are not the sole measure of Fourth Amendment violations, the reasonable expectation of privacy test was "*added to*, not *substituted for*, the common-law trespassory test." [**United States v. Jones**, supra, p. 37]

cf. **Compare:** The government conducts a search when it accesses historical cell phone data maintained by private wireless providers that collectively provide a comprehensive picture of a cellphone's previous physical locations and movements. "Much like GPS tracking of a vehicle, cellphone location information is detailed, encyclopedic, and effortlessly compiled." "Given the unique nature of cell phone location records, the fact that the information is held by a third party does not by itself overcome the user's

Fourth Amendment protection." [**Carpenter v. United States**, 585 U.S. 296 (2018)]

cf. **Compare:** The government's warrantless use of a drug-detection dog on the front porch, *i.e.*, the curtilage, of a home to detect odors of drugs inside the home is a "search" protected by the Fourth Amendment. [**Florida v. Jardines**, 569 U.S. 1 (2013)] Officers in **Jardines** gathered information by physically entering and occupying the area immediately surrounding the home without invitation.

(f) ***Magazines offered for sale*** [**Maryland v. Macon**, 472 U.S. 463 (1985)]; and

(g) ***The smell of one's luggage or automobile*** (*i.e.,* a sniff test by a drug-sniffing dog is not generally a search) [**United States v. Place**, *supra,* p. 37; **Illinois v. Caballes**, 543 U.S. 405 (2005)]

cf. **Compare:** An officer's physical manipulation of a bus passenger's carry-on luggage positioned in an overhead storage space intrudes on the passenger's reasonable expectation of privacy because the passenger expects that other passengers and bus employees may move the bag but not "feel the bag in an exploratory manner." [**Bond v. United States**, 529 U.S. 334 (2000)]

(2) Open Fields Doctrine

Under the "open fields doctrine," privately-owned areas outside the home and outside the curtilage (the area immediately surrounding and associated with the home and its intimate activities) are subject to police investigation without violating the Fourth Amendment. Thus, plants growing in an area a significant distance from a home, even if protected by no trespassing signs, woods, fences, and embankments, may be deemed in an open field lacking Fourth Amendment protection. [**Oliver v. United States**, 466 U.S. 170 (1984)] Similarly, garbage left for collection beyond the curtilage may be searched without implicating the Fourth Amendment's protections, even if such placement of garbage cans is required by local ordinance. [**California v. Greenwood**, 486 U.S. 35 (1988)] But, the porch of a home is part of the curtilage, which "enjoys protection as part of the home itself." [**Jardines**, *supra*; *see* also **Collins v. Virginia**, 584 U.S. 586 (2018) (holding that police violated the Fourth Amendment when they trespassed without a warrant onto the curtilage of the suspect's property to access a motorcycle believed to be stolen)] The Court has yet to decide whether police may knock on any door accessible to visitors (as opposed to only the front door) when seeking to talk with occupants of a home without a warrant or other exception to the Fourth Amendment. [**Carroll v. Carman**, 574 U.S. 13 (2014)]

(a) Outbuildings

Not all outbuildings are within the curtilage. The Court has stated that it will consider four factors: (i) proximity of the home to the area claimed to be curtilage; (ii) whether the area is included within an enclosure that surrounds the home; (iii) the nature of the uses to which the area is put; and (iv) the steps taken by the resident to protect the area from observation. The ultimate question, however, is whether the outbuilding in question is ***"so intimately tied to the home"*** that it should warrant Fourth Amendment protection. [**United States v. Dunn**, 480 U.S. 294 (1987)]

e.g. **Example:** A barn was held not to be within the curtilage of a home because it was 60 yards from the home and 50 yards outside the fence surrounding the home, it was used to manufacture drugs rather than to carry on intimate activities of the home, and it was protected only by low fences designed to corral livestock rather than to prevent viewing. [**United States v. Dunn**, *supra,* p. 39]

(b) Flyovers and Aerial Surveillance

Flyovers are treated differently from on-the-ground physical invasions of the curtilage. Police may observe private property from the air, if they are in airspace where the general public is legitimately allowed to fly. In these cases, the Court has deferred to air traffic regulations to determine navigable airspace. *Rationale*: There can be no legitimate expectation of privacy in things that may be observed by the public while flying in public airspace.

e.g. **Example:** Based on a tip that defendant was growing marijuana in his backyard, police rented a plane and flew 1,000 feet over defendant's house (within navigable airspace). They observed and photographed the marijuana. The search was upheld despite the fact that defendant tried to protect his yard from view by erecting a 10-foot fence around it. [**California v. Ciraolo**, 476 U.S. 207 (1986)] Similarly, the Court upheld a 400-foot flyover by a helicopter, where police observed marijuana growing in defendant's greenhouse, even though the defendant had taken steps to obscure the aerial view by partially covering the roof. The helicopter was in legitimate airspace. [**Florida v. Riley**, 488 U.S. 445 (1989)]

1) Vision Enhancing Cameras

The Court has allowed the use of powerful cameras to take photographs from the air, as long as the cameras are generally available to the public, and the plane is in legitimate airspace. [**Dow Chemical Co. v. United States**, 476 U.S. 227 (1986)]

a) Distinguish—Technologically Enhanced Searches of the Home

The Supreme Court has held that because of the strong expectation of privacy within one's home, using sense enhancing technology to obtain information regarding the interior of a home—that could not otherwise have been obtained without physical intrusion—constitutes a search, at least where the technology is not in general public use. [**Kyllo v. United States**, 533 U.S. 27 (2001)—use of thermal imager on defendant's home to detect the presence of high intensity lamps commonly used to grow marijuana constitutes a search] Nevertheless, lower federal courts have allowed the government to use cameras placed on public property to observe a private residence for an extended period, finding that the cameras only capture the outside of the home and that the homeowner "knowingly expose[s] the areas captured by the . . . cameras." [**United States v. Tuggle**, 4 F.4th 505 (7th Cir. 2021)]

EXAM TIP

Watch out for questions involving searches conducted with high tech equipment. On your exam, you can explain that there is no search when police view premises from a place an ordinary person could be (*e.g.*, from a tree across the street or from legal airspace). Police also can use common technological aids, such as binoculars and high-powered cameras with telephoto lenses. Things get "iffy" when police use high tech equipment that an ordinary person would not likely have (*e.g.*, a thermal imager). ***Police may not use such high tech equipment to invade the privacy of one's home and obtain information that they could not otherwise obtain***

without physically intruding on a constitutionally protected area. Whether and how they may use such gear to invade the privacy of a business has not been decided and is complicated by rapidly advancing technology (*e.g.*, drones). Given the Court's focus in **Kyllo** on the sanctity of the home, it is possible that such warrantless searches of businesses would be permitted. Also, given the Supreme Court's ruling in **Jones**, *supra*, p. 37, the government now conducts a search, and you should analyze the reasonableness of that search, whenever the government invades someone's property, papers, or effects to obtain information. Similarly, when smart phones and information from them are at issue, the Court has shown a willingness to treat them differently than other "containers," finding a reasonable expectation for data stored on them or data transmitted by them (*e.g.*, the owner's location).

(3) Contraband

As noted above, a person does not have a legitimate expectation of privacy in contraband. Therefore, no (unconstitutional) search occurs when contraband in luggage is sniffed out by a narcotics detection dog. [**United States v. Place**, *supra,* p. 37—submitting luggage to a dog sniff does not constitute a search because unlike a typical "search," general contents of the container are not disclosed to police; however, warrantless detention of luggage for an unreasonable time (90 minutes) before the luggage is submitted for a dog sniff does render the seizure unreasonable]

(a) Dog Sniffs at Traffic Stops

As long as the police have constitutionally stopped a car and do not extend the stop beyond the time necessary to issue a ticket and conduct ordinary inquiries incidental to such a stop, a dog sniff of the car does not implicate the Fourth Amendment. [**Illinois v. Caballes**, *supra*, p. 39—Fourth Amendment was not violated when, during a routine traffic stop, a police officer walked a narcotics detection dog around defendant's car, and the dog alerted to the presence of drugs, even though before the dog alerted, the officer did not have a reasonable and articulable suspicion that would justify a search] But, extending a traffic stop after its completion for seven or eight additional minutes to conduct a dog sniff without consent or reasonable suspicion violates the Fourth Amendment. *See* **Rodriguez**, *supra*, p. 28.

4. Searches Conducted Pursuant to a Warrant

a. Warrant Requirement

Generally, a warrant is required before a search or seizure may be conducted. This requirement is central to the Fourth Amendment's protection against unreasonable searches and seizures. ***Searches conducted without a warrant are unconstitutional*** unless they qualify under one of the six ***exceptions*** to the warrant requirement (*see infra*, pp. 48 *et seq.*). [**Marshall v. Barlow's, Inc.**, 436 U.S. 307 (1978); **Michigan v. Tyler**, 436 U.S. 499 (1978); **United States v. Ross**, 456 U.S. 798 (1982); **Arizona v. Hicks**, 480 U.S. 321 (1987)]

(1) General Warrant Requirements

If and when a warrant is issued, it must:

(a) Be based on ***"probable cause"***;

(b) Be "***supported by oath or affirmation***";

(c) ***Particularly describe what is to be searched or seized***; and

(d) Be issued by a ***neutral magistrate***.

b. Probable Cause Requirement

A warrant must be based on an adequate showing of probable cause.

(1) What Constitutes Probable Cause

Officers must present to a magistrate sufficient underlying facts and circumstances such that a reasonable person would conclude that seizable evidence would be found on the premises or person to be searched. [**Carroll v. United States**, 267 U.S. 132 (1925)]

(a) May Be Anticipatory

It is sufficient that there is a fair probability that seizable evidence will be found on the premises on a specific future date; there need not be probable cause to believe that there is seizable material on the premises at the time the warrant is issued. [**United States v. Grubbs**, 547 U.S. 90 (2006)—warrant was properly issued when it "predicted" that seizable material would be found in defendant's home after police, as part of a sting operation, delivered to defendant's home pornographic material that he had ordered] *Note*: Two probability showings must be satisfied for a lawful anticipatory warrant: 1) If the triggering condition occurs, there is probable cause to believe that contraband or evidence will be on the premises; and 2) there is probable cause to believe that the triggering condition will happen. [**Grubbs**, *supra*]

(2) What Constitutes Adequate Showing

Information is provided to the magistrate by affidavit or sworn testimony. This information must enable the magistrate to make an independent evaluation of whether probable cause is present. [**United States v. Ventresca**, 380 U.S. 102 (1965)] Affidavits or sworn testimony must allege facts, not mere conclusions. [**Aguilar v. Texas**, 378 U.S. 108 (1964)]

e.g. **Example:** An unsupported allegation that the suspect is a "known gambler" is conclusory. Without specific facts, such an allegation should be afforded no weight in determining probable cause. [**Spinelli v. United States**, 393 U.S. 410 (1969)]

e.g. **Example:** An affidavit is conclusory and lacks sufficient facts if it says, "Affiants have received reliable information from a credible person and do believe that" drugs are being kept on the described premises to be searched. [**Aguilar**, *supra*]

(3) Affidavits Based on Hearsay—Totality of the Circumstances

A warrant may issue based on affidavits that include hearsay (*e.g.,* police officer swears to facts reported to her by victim of crime, witnesses, or police informants). The affidavit must show by a ***totality of the circumstances*** that there is a fair probability that contraband or evidence of crime will be found in a particular place. Among the considerations are whether the ***affidavit shows*** that (i) the information comes from a ***reliable informant*** and (ii) the informant had a sound ***basis of knowledge*** for the information. [**Illinois v. Gates**, 462 U.S. 213 (1983)]

(a) Rules Governing Informants

The validity of a warrant based on an informant's tip is determined by a "totality of the circumstances" test. It is not fatal to the issuance of a valid warrant based on such a tip that the reliability and credibility of the informant cannot be established. All that is required of an affidavit based in part on an informant's tip is that all the allegations in the affidavit, taken together, permit the magistrate to make a commonsense evaluation of probable cause. [**Illinois v. Gates**, *supra,* p. 42]

e.g. **Example:** Police received an anonymous tip that named Defendants as drug dealers and specified that D1 would drive to Florida on a particular day and D2 would fly down shortly thereafter to drive the car back loaded with drugs. Police confirmed that D2 had made a reservation to fly to Florida as indicated in the tip. After D2 arrived in Florida, police saw him go to a hotel room registered to Dl. Police then sought a warrant to search the car and Defendants' home, presenting the above information to the magistrate. Although there was nothing in the affidavit regarding the informant's reliability or the basis of the informant's knowledge, the Supreme Court found that given the totality of the circumstances, there was probable cause to issue the warrant. [**Illinois v. Gates**, *supra*]

(b) Identity of Informant

Generally, the informant's identity does ***not*** have to be revealed. [**McCray v. Illinois**, 386 U.S. 300 (1967)]

1) Exception—Percipient Witness

If the informant was a percipient witness to the crime (*e.g.,* an eyewitness) and the testimony may be material to determining the accused's guilt or innocence, the identity of the informant must be revealed at or before trial. [**Roviaro v. United States**, 353 U.S. 53 (1957)]

(c) Reliable Informant

Generally, an allegation in the affidavit that the informant has provided credible information on several prior occasions is sufficient to establish the informant's credibility. [*See* **McCray v. Illinois**, *supra*]

(4) Affidavits Based on Criminal Record

Although a person's criminal record typically is inadmissible at trial (for fear that the person will be convicted because of his past conduct rather than for committing the present crime), it may be used to support probable cause in an affidavit for a search warrant. [*See* **United States v. Harris**, 403 U.S. 573 (1971)]

(5) Challenging the Warrant

A defendant may challenge the validity of a search warrant by contesting any assertion in the affidavit upon which the warrant was issued. A search warrant is invalid if a defendant makes a "substantial showing" by a "preponderance of the evidence" of ***all*** of the following facts:

(i) ***A false statement was included*** in the affidavit by the affiant;

(ii) ***The false statement was necessary*** to find probable cause; and

(iii) ***The affiant knowingly or recklessly included*** that false statement.

[**Franks v. Delaware**, 438 U.S. 154 (1978)] *Note*: The truthfulness of the informant's statement is not directly subject to challenge. Only statements made by the law enforcement affiant may be challenged. Even if the police included a knowingly false statement in the affidavit, the defendant is only entitled to a hearing to determine whether probable cause would still exist if the false statement was removed.

EXAM TIP

The mere fact that an affiant (police officer) included a false statement in an affidavit for a search warrant does not automatically invalidate the search warrant. This happens if the affiant was acting in good faith (*i.e.*, did not know that the statement was untrue). The test for invalidating an affidavit is very restrictive—***all three requirements for invalidity*** (falsehood, intentionally or recklessly included, and material to probable cause) ***must be met***. Thus, if the affiant believed the lie, the affidavit is valid. Even when a police affiant intentionally includes lies, if there is still sufficient support for probable cause excluding the police lies, the affidavit is valid. A defendant is rarely successful in challenging the affidavit.

(6) Effect of Lack of Probable Cause

A finding that the warrant was invalid because it was not supported by probable cause does not necessarily entitle a defendant to exclude the evidence obtained with the warrant. Evidence obtained by police in ***objectively reasonable reliance*** on a facially valid warrant may be used by the prosecution, despite an ultimate finding that the warrant lacked probable cause. [**United States v. Leon**, 468 U.S. 897 (1984)]

c. Precision Requirement

A warrant must describe ***with particularity (reasonable certainty)*** the ***place*** to be searched and the ***items*** (or person) to be seized. If it does not, the warrant is unconstitutional even if an underlying affidavit gives such detail. [**Groh v. Ramirez**, 540 U.S. 551 (2004)]

e.g. **Example:** In cases where the warrant authorizes a search of only one apartment in a multi-apartment structure, the warrant must specify the apartment itself (*e.g.*, "Apartment 204"). Listing only the address of the apartment building is not sufficiently precise. However, if police reasonably believe there is only one apartment on the floor of a building, they may obtain a warrant to search the "third floor apartment." This is true even if during the course of the search they discover that there are, in fact, two apartments on the third floor. [**Maryland v. Garrison**, 480 U.S. 79 (1987)]

e.g. **Example:** Defendant was suspected of having committed criminal fraud regarding certain complex real estate transactions. A search warrant was issued authorizing the search for various described documents and "other fruits, instrumentalities, and evidence of the crime at this time unknown." This warrant was sufficiently precise given the complex nature of the crime and the difficulty of predicting precisely what form the evidence of guilt would take. [**Andresen v. Maryland**, 427 U.S. 463 (1976)]

(1) Exception—Plain View

An item not described in a warrant may be seized if it is immediately apparent that it is incriminating evidence or contraband. [**Coolidge v. New Hampshire**, 403 U.S. 443 (1971); *see infra*, p. 56] The discovery of the evidence need not be inadvertent. [**Horton v. California**, 496 U.S. 128 (1990)] Before police may seize an item under the plain view theory, there must be probable cause to believe that the item is, in fact, contraband or evidence of a crime. [**Arizona v. Hicks**, 480 U.S. 321 (1987)]

d. Disinterested Magistrate Requirement

A warrant must be issued by a ***"neutral and detached" magistrate*** (*i.e.,* judicial officer). It is sometimes easier to determine who is ***not*** "neutral and detached," as illustrated in the following examples:

Example: A magistrate who ***receives a fee when she issues a warrant,*** but not when she denies one, is not neutral and detached. [**Connally v. Georgia**, 429 U.S. 245 (1977)]

Example: The state's ***chief investigator and prosecutor*** (state attorney general) is not neutral and detached from "the often competitive business of law enforcement." [**Coolidge v. New Hampshire**, *supra,* p. 44]

Example: A ***magistrate who participates in the search to determine its scope*** lacks the requisite neutrality and detachment. [**Lo-Ji Sales, Inc. v. New York,** 442 U.S. 319 (1979)]

Example: The ***United States Attorney General*** may not authorize domestic security surveillance without judicial approval. [**United States v. United States District Court**, 407 U.S. 297 (1972)]

Compare—Minor Offenses: A court clerk may issue arrest warrants for violations of city ordinances (such as traffic violations). [**Shadwick v. City of Tampa**, 407 U.S. 345 (1972)]

e. Third-Party Premises May Be Searched

Searches of property belonging to persons not suspected of a crime are permissible as long as probable cause exists to believe that evidence of someone's guilt (or other items subject to seizure) will be found.

Example: A demonstration occurs in which police officers are hurt. The police cannot identify the attackers, but they know a newspaper staff photographer took photographs of the demonstration. The police may get a warrant to search the newspaper's offices provided that probable cause exists that evidence of someone's guilt may be found. [**Zurcher v. Stanford Daily**, 436 U.S. 547 (1978)]

f. Rules Governing Warrant Execution

(1) Police Execution Requirement

Only the police may execute a warrant. Private citizens may not. Moreover, when executing a warrant ***in a home***, the police may not be accompanied by a member of the media or any other third party, unless the third party is there to aid in executing the warrant (*e.g.,* to identify stolen property that might be found in the home). [**Wilson v. Layne**, 526 U.S. 603 (1999)—unreasonable to allow newspaper reporter and photographer to accompany police during execution of an arrest warrant in plaintiff's home] *Rationale*: To be reasonable, police action pursuant to a warrant must be related to the objectives of the warrant. Thus, the presence of reporters or other third parties not aiding in the execution of the warrant renders the search unreasonable. *Note*: While the First Amendment prohibition against abridging freedom of the press is an important right, it does not supersede the very important Fourth Amendment right of persons to be free of unreasonable searches.

(2) Announcement Requirement

Generally, an officer executing a search warrant must knock and announce her authority and purpose and wait a reasonable time before using force to enter the place to be searched. However, no announcement need be made if the officer has reasonable suspicion, based on facts specific to this particular entry, that knocking and announcing would be ***dangerous or futile*** or that it would ***inhibit the investigation****, e.g.,* because it would lead to the destruction of evidence. [**Richards v. Wisconsin**, 520 U.S. 385 (1997)] In any event, recall that the exclusionary rule does ***not*** apply to violations of the knock and announce rule. [**Hudson v. Michigan**, *supra,* p. 24] *Note*: If officers lack a warrant but knock and announce "police," and the announcement gives officers probable cause to believe that evidence is being destroyed within, officers may enter without a warrant to save the evidence. [*See* **Kentucky v. King**, 563 U.S. 452 (2011)] In addition, some jurisdictions permit courts to issue no-knock warrants on a case-by-case basis.

(3) Search Specification Requirement

A search warrant does ***not*** authorize the police to search persons found on the premises who are not named in the warrant. [**Ybarra v. Illinois**, *supra,* p. 32] The Court reasoned that "a person's mere [proximity] to others . . . does not, without more, give rise to probable cause to search that person."

(a) Distinguish—Probable Cause to Arrest

If officers have probable cause to ***arrest*** a person found at the place to be searched, the person may be searched incident to their lawful arrest.

(b) Distinguish—Probable Cause Based on Evidence of a "Common Enterprise"

Although mere association with others in a public place does not give rise to probable cause, [**Sibron v. New York**, 392 U.S. 40 (1968)], under the "common enterprise" theory, probable cause may exist when multiple occupants travel together in a small passenger car and drugs and money are found. [**Maryland v. Pringle**, 540 U.S. 366 (2003)]

(4) Detention During Search Permissible

When executing a search warrant, the police may detain those persons who are present on the premises to be searched while the search is conducted, but the authority does not extend to areas beyond the immediate vicinity of the premises covered by the warrant [**Michigan v. Summers**, 452 U.S. 692 (1981), *supra*, p. 32; **Bailey v. United States**, 568 U.S. 186 (2013), *supra*, p. 32] Detention of persons serves the government interests in preventing flight, ensuring officer safety, and facilitating the orderly completion of the search.

(a) Detention to Obtain Warrant

The Supreme Court found no Fourth Amendment violation when police had probable cause to believe that a suspect had hidden drugs in his home and for the two hours it took to obtain a search warrant, the police prevented the suspect from going unaccompanied into the home. [**Illinois v. McArthur**, 531 U.S. 326 (2001)] The Court found the restriction reasonable because: (i) immediately upon exiting the suspect's trailer, the suspect's wife told police, who were at the scene, that she just saw the suspect "slide dope" underneath the couch; (ii) the police had good reason to believe that if the suspect were not restrained, he would destroy the drugs before they could return with a warrant; (iii) the police neither arrested the suspect nor searched the home before a warrant was obtained; they merely prohibited the suspect from entering unaccompanied and stood just inside the door to observe the suspect when he reentered the home a few times to get cigarettes and make phone calls; and (iv) the restraint was imposed for no longer than necessary to obtain a warrant.

(5) Time of Service Requirement

A ***search*** warrant should be executed without unreasonable delay. Furthermore, statutes often require that search warrants be executed during daylight hours unless night searches are specifically authorized. For example, the Federal Rules of Criminal Procedure require search warrants to be executed in the daytime, which is defined as between 6 a.m. and 10 p.m., unless reasonable cause is shown and the issuing magistrate authorizes otherwise. [Fed. R. Crim. P. 41(e)(2), (f)]

(a) Distinguish—Arrest Warrants

Generally, arrest warrants are valid indefinitely.

(6) Scope of Search

The scope of the search may not exceed the ***premises described*** in the warrant, and the search is limited to locating the ***items described*** in the warrant. [**Marron v. United States**, 275 U.S. 192 (1927)]

(a) Caveat—Seizure of Items Not Described in Warrant

When executing a warrant, the police generally may seize any contraband or fruits or instrumentalities of crime that they discover—whether or not specified in the warrant. *Note*: Police need probable cause to believe that the item seized is, in fact, evidence of a crime before they seize items not identified in the warrant. [**Arizona v. Hicks**, 480 U.S. 321 (1987)]

(b) Caveat—Objectively Reasonable Mistake

If police officers make an objectively reasonable mistake when executing a warrant, the evidence obtained is still admissible. For example, if police have a warrant to search one apartment but mistakenly search an adjoining apartment and discover evidence of criminal activity, the evidence is admissible despite the error. As long as the mistake is ***objectively reasonable***, the evidence will not be excluded. [**Maryland v. Garrison**, *supra,* p. 44]

(7) Search of Third-Party Premises to Execute Arrest Warrants

Generally, absent consent or exigent circumstances, a search warrant is required before police may enter a third party's home to seize a person named in an arrest warrant. [**Steagald v. United States**, *supra*, p. 25]

g. Caveat—Evidence May Be Admissible Even if Warrant Is Invalid

Remember that evidence obtained by the police in objectively reasonable reliance on a defective search warrant will not be excluded. [*See* **United States v. Leon**; **Massachusetts v. Sheppard**, 468 U.S. 981 (1984), *supra*, pp. 11–12, 44] *Rationale*: Excluding evidence in such circumstances would not deter officers from misconduct because the officers have acted reasonably—they obtained a warrant, and the defect in the warrant was the fault of the issuing magistrate, not the officers.

e.g. **Example—Unreliable Informant:** A warrant was issued based in part upon the testimony of an informant of unproven reliability. Evidence seized pursuant to the warrant was admissible. [**United States v. Leon**, *supra,* p. 11–12]

e.g. **Example—Technical Error:** A warrant to search for evidence of a homicide was issued on a form for a search for narcotics and did not incorporate the accompanying affidavit for the search warrant. Evidence seized pursuant to the technically invalid warrant was admissible because the judge told law enforcement that the warrant was valid. [**Massachusetts v. Sheppard**, *supra,* p. 11–12]

5. Exceptions to the Warrant Requirement

While all searches must be reasonable, the Supreme Court has recognized that reasonableness does not require the police to obtain a search warrant before conducting every search. "When faced with special law enforcement needs, diminished expectations of privacy, minimal intrusions, or the like" [**Illinois v. McArthur**, *supra,* p. 46], the Court has carved out exceptions to the warrant requirement. For a warrantless search to be valid, it must satisfy all the requirements of at least one of the following six exceptions to the warrant requirement.

CHECKLIST OF EXCEPTIONS TO THE WARRANT REQUIREMENT
WARRANTLESS EVIDENTIARY SEARCHES ARE PERMITTED:
☑ ***Incident to any constitutional arrest***
☑ Of ***automobiles***, when police have probable cause to believe that the vehicle contains fruits or instrumentalities of crime, evidence of crime, or contraband
☑ Of evidence in ***plain view*** when police are legitimately on the premises and police have probable cause to believe the item to be contraband or fruits or instrumentalities of crime
☑ If police have an articulable suspicion that a person is involved in criminal activity (a ***"Terry stop"***) and reasonably believe the stopped person is armed and dangerous—police may ***frisk*** the person
☑ To the extent the police have ***consent*** to search, given by a person with actual or apparent authority to consent
☑ In certain ***emergencies*** (*e.g.*, when police are in "hot pursuit" of a suspect, if the evidence is likely to disappear before a warrant can be obtained, if there is reason to believe someone may be in imminent physical danger—sometimes called the community caretaker exception)

a. Search Incident to a Constitutional Arrest

A search may be conducted without a warrant if it is incident to a ***constitutional*** arrest.

(1) Any Lawful Arrest Sufficient

The police may conduct a search incident to arrest whenever they lawfully arrest a person (*i.e.,* based on probable cause and with a valid warrant, if required). Although the rationale for the search is to protect the arresting officer and to preserve evidence, the police need not actually fear for their safety or believe that they will find evidence of a crime, as long as the suspect is placed under lawful arrest. The search incident to a lawful arrest is a full search of the suspect, containers on the suspect, such as a cigarette pack in the suspect's shirt pocket, and areas within the suspect's wingspan. [**United States v. Robinson**, 414 U.S. 218 (1973)]

(a) Issuance of Traffic Citation Insufficient Basis

For traffic violations, if the suspect is not arrested, there can be no search incident to arrest, even if state law gives the officer the option of arresting a suspect or issuing a citation. [**Knowles v. Iowa**, *supra,* p. 29—nonconsensual automobile search conducted after the suspect was issued a citation for driving 43 m.p.h. in a 25 m.p.h. zone was unconstitutional, and contraband found during the search was excluded from evidence] *Rationale*: When a citation is issued, there is less of a threat to the officer's safety than there is during an arrest, and the only evidence that needs to be preserved in such a case (*e.g.,* the suspect's speeding or other illegal conduct) has already been found.

(2) Arrest Must Be Constitutional

Most Supreme Court cases dealing with searches incident to arrest have indicated that the search must be "lawful," which the Court has found to mean "constitutional." [*See* **Virginia v. Moore**, *supra*, p. 22] To be constitutional, an arrest must be made ***pursuant to a warrant*** based on probable cause or the police must have had ***probable cause*** to make the arrest when no warrant is required (for example, when a person is arrested in a public place).

(a) Caveat—Arrest Under Unconstitutional Law

If an officer makes an arrest for violation of a statute that the officer believes in good faith to be constitutional, a later ruling that the law is unconstitutional does not render the arrest unlawful. [**Michigan v. DeFillippo**, 443 U.S. 31 (1979)]

(b) Arrest in Violation of State Law

The constitutionality/lawfulness of an arrest does not depend on whether the arrest was authorized by state law, but on whether the police had probable cause and, if required, a warrant to arrest. [**Virginia v. Moore**, *supra*—no Fourth Amendment violation where police arrested defendant on probable cause to believe that defendant was driving on a suspended license even though the arrest violated state law]

(3) Scope of Search

At the time of an arrest, the police may generally conduct a full search of the person arrested ***and*** the areas within the person's immediate reach (or "wingspan"). [**Chimel v. California**, 395 U.S. 752 (1969)] Such a search prevents (i) concealment or destruction of evidence by the arrestee and (ii) the arrestee from seizing a weapon to resist arrest or assist in escape. A search incident to a lawful arrest generally allows police to search a person's pockets, wallet, under their clothing, and in containers on or near the person, but police must generally secure a warrant before searching a cell phone on the person for digital information. In **Riley v. California**, 573 U.S. 373 (2014), the Court distinguished cell phones from other containers, noting that "[m]odern cell phones . . . implicate privacy concerns far beyond those implicated by the search of a cigarette pack, a wallet, or a purse." Officers may, however, "examine the physical aspects of a phone to ensure that it will not be used as a weapon" against them. *See* search incident to arrest involving automobiles, *infra*.

(a) Protective Sweep

The police may perform a "protective sweep" of the areas immediately adjoining the place of arrest from which an attack by accomplices could be launched (*e.g.*, adjoining closets). The protective sweep can expand to areas outside the immediate area of arrest if the police have a reasonable and articulable suspicion that accomplices who might pose a threat to the police may be present (*e.g.*, if police were told that two armed suspects were in a house, they could search the house for the second person after arresting the first). The sweep must be limited to places where the persons could be found. [**Maryland v. Buie**, 494 U.S. 325 (1990)]

EXAM TIP

On your exam, be sure to remember that a search incident to arrest justifies a full search, not only of the arrestee's immediate person, but also of any area the arrestee may reach. If the police have a ***reasonable and articulable suspicion*** that accomplices might be present who could pose a threat to the police, the police may perform a ***protective sweep*** by looking in areas where accomplices could be hiding. Because the protective sweep is not a search for evidence, but only a cursory look to determine if people are present who pose a threat, the reasonable scope includes only places where someone could hide.

1) Evidence Seen During Protective Sweep

Evidence found in "plain view" during a protective sweep after the suspect has been apprehended may be lawfully seized.

(b) Entering Arrestee's Dwelling

If an arrest is made outside the arrestee's home, the police may not search the home incident to the arrest. However, if the police allow the arrestee to briefly enter the home, they may enter with the arrestee. Once inside the arrestee's home, the police may search any area within the arrestee's wingspan as he moves through the home, and may seize any contraband discovered in plain view. [**Washington v. Chrisman**, 455 U.S. 1 (1982)]

(c) Automobile Occupants

Contemporaneous with the arrest of an automobile occupant (or recent occupant), a police officer may conduct a warrantless search of the passenger compartment of the automobile (including its contents) if the arrestee is unsecured and police reasonably believe that the arrestee may access the vehicle ***to obtain immediate control of a weapon, or*** if it is reasonable to believe that ***evidence of the offense of arrest might be found*** in the automobile. [**Arizona v. Gant**, 556 U.S. 332 (2009)] **Gant** effectively overturned an earlier decision permitting a search incident to arrest of the entire interior of an automobile whenever the person arrested had recently been in the car. [**New York v. Belton**, 453 U.S. 454 (1981)] After **Gant**, if an auto's occupant is arrested for a typical traffic violation, there should be no reasonable basis for a search for evidence relevant to the offense of arrest, and if the occupant is secured away from the car and cannot access the car's interior, a search of the interior is not allowed.

e.g. **Example:** A police officer stopped a vehicle for speeding. Upon approaching the vehicle, he smelled burnt marijuana and saw an envelope on the floor marked with the street name of a certain type of marijuana. He ordered the four occupants out of the vehicle and arrested them for unlawful possession of marijuana. Having only one pair of handcuffs and no assistance, he could not secure the arrestees. He directed them to stand apart from each other and searched the passenger compartment of the vehicle. During the search, the officer discovered cocaine in a jacket in the vehicle. The search was a valid search incident to arrest either because an "unsecured" arrestee easily could have gained access to the vehicle, or because the officer could reasonably believe that the vehicle contained evidence of the drug charge for which he arrested the occupants. [**New York v. Belton**, *supra,* p. 50]

cf. **Compare:** The police arrested defendant for driving on a suspended license shortly after he stepped out of his car. Defendant was handcuffed and placed in a squad car. The police then searched the passenger compartment of the defendant's car and found cocaine in a jacket in the car. The search was an ***invalid*** search incident to arrest. Because defendant was handcuffed and locked in a squad car, he could not likely gain access to the interior of the car. Nor did the police have any reason to believe that the car contained any evidence relevant to the charge of driving on a suspended license. [**Arizona v. Gant**, *supra*]

1) Other Exceptions Not Affected

Note that **Gant** does not affect (or involve) the automobile exception to the warrant requirement. (*See infra*, pp. 53–55.) Police may still search an automobile if they have probable cause to believe that it contains contraband or fruits, instrumentalities, or evidence of a crime (under the automobile exception to the warrant requirement). Also, **Gant** does not affect an officer's ability to search an automobile for weapons, if the officer makes a stop and reasonably believes the detainee is armed and dangerous. (*See supra*, p. 28.) All of these exceptions involve automobiles, but the parameters of each are different.

2) Searches Conducted Before Decision in *Gant*

Evidence obtained in searches conducted by police after **Belton**, which most lower courts had interpreted to allow a full search of the interior of a vehicle whenever a recent occupant was arrested, will not be excluded as long as police relied in good faith on appellate precedent that, although erroneous, held such searches constitutional. [**Davis v. United States**, 564 U.S. 229 (2011)]

(d) Distinguish—*Terry* Search

A *Terry* search only authorizes a pat down of the outer clothing for weapons or evidence of an immediately incriminating nature. A search incident to arrest includes all clothing, pockets, under clothing, and any containers found on or near the person (*i.e.*, within their wingspan). However, it does not authorize a body cavity search.

(4) Search Must Be Contemporaneous to Arrest

A search incident to an arrest must be contemporaneous in time and place with the arrest. [**Preston v. United States**, 376 U.S. 364 (1964)—search of car after suspects were arrested and incarcerated and after car was towed to garage is not incident to arrest; **United States v. Chadwick**, 433 U.S. 1 (1977)—search of a suspect's footlocker more than an hour after both the suspect's arrest and the government's gaining control over the footlocker was not incident to arrest]

(a) Exception—Valid Reason for Delay

A search may be deemed incident to an arrest even if the search is conducted later than the time of arrest if there is a valid reason for the delay.

e.g. **Example:** A search of clothing was allowed the morning following an evening arrest when no substitute clothing was available at the time of booking. [**United States v. Edwards**, 415 U.S. 800 (1974)]

(b) Exception—Station House Inventory Search

When an arrested person is taken to the police station, the police may make a full inventory search of his person and all property in his possession before he is jailed. However, the search must be done pursuant to established procedures. This is "reasonable" to protect the suspect's property, to protect the police against false claims of theft of the arrestee's property, to discover dangerous objects, and to assist in identifying the suspect. [**Illinois v. Lafayette**, 459 U.S. 986 (1983)] *Note*: Having established administrative procedures is a key to the legality of such searches, which are administrative and must not provide the police with unfettered discretion to fish around for new evidence.

1) Inventory Search of Closed Containers in Impounded Vehicles

For similar reasons, the police may make an inventory search of lawfully impounded automobiles pursuant to established procedures, and they may generally open containers within the autos to ensure against claims of lost, stolen, or vandalized property and to guard against danger. [**Colorado v. Bertine**, 479 U.S. 367 (1987)] Incriminating evidence found during an inventory search is admissible under the plain view doctrine. Moreover, if an inventory search gives rise to probable cause to search the vehicle for additional evidence, no warrant is needed for the further search. [**Michigan v. Thomas**, 458 U.S. 259 (1982)]

EXAM TIP

If your exam raises an issue of an inventory search, be sure to determine whether the search was conducted *pursuant to an established procedure*. If there is no established procedure, the search is likely unconstitutional because it provides the police with unbridled discretion unsupported by sufficient cause, *i.e.,* reasonable suspicion or probable cause.

2) Search Pursuant to Jail Procedures

Based on a lawful arrest alone, jail personnel may subject an arrested person who is held in jail to a close visual inspection while the arrestee is undressed. No evidence of whether the arrestee is dangerous or that she possesses contraband need be shown.

e.g. **Example:** Albert Florence was arrested based on an incorrect computer entry showing a warrant for failure to appear at a hearing to enforce a fine. At the county jail, Florence was required to shower with a delousing agent, and officers inspected his naked body for scars, marks, tattoos and contraband. The jail's policy was to visually inspect every detainee regardless of the circumstances of the arrest, the seriousness of the suspected offense, or the detainee's behavior or criminal history. The

Court held that the Fourth Amendment was not violated. [**Florence v. Board of Chosen Freeholders of County of Burlington**, 566 U.S. 318 (2012)]

(5) Taking DNA as Part of Booking

As part of the normal booking procedure for serious offenses, police may take an arrestee's DNA using a swab to the inside of her cheeks. [**Maryland v. King**, 569 U.S. 435 (2013)] The fact of a felony arrest makes this search reasonable, provided it is conducted as part of the routine procedure of booking.

b. Automobile Exception

The second exception to the warrant requirement concerns searches of automobiles.

(1) Probable Cause Requirement

Before beginning any search pursuant to the automobile exception, the police must have probable cause to believe that a moving vehicle, or a vehicle that has temporarily stopped, contains the fruits or instrumentalities of crime, evidence of crime, or contraband. [**Carroll v. United States**, *supra*, p. 42]

(a) Probable Cause to Search May Develop as a Result of Observations After Stopping Vehicle

As long as the stop (seizure) of the automobile was lawful, police observations can "ripen" into probable cause to believe that the car contains the evidence of a crime to justify the full warrantless search of the vehicle.

Example: The police lawfully stopped Motorist's automobile to give him a speeding ticket. While writing out the citation, the officer observed that (i) Motorist and his companion fit a broadcast description of persons involved in theft of auto parts, and (ii) there were wrenches, lug nuts, and similar items in the back seat, suggesting tools for stealing parts. The Court held that the officer's observations gave him probable cause to justify a warrantless search under the automobile exception to the warrant requirement because, had a magistrate been present while Motorist's car was stopped, the police officer could have obtained a warrant with the information. [**Colorado v. Bannister**, 449 U.S. 1 (1980)]

(b) Probable Cause to Search May Develop as a Result of a Well-Trained Dog Sniff

Probable cause to search may develop as a result of a well-trained dog sniff, even if the dog's alert turns out to be incorrect. [**Florida v. Harris**, 568 U.S. 237 (2013)] Probable cause "is not reducible to 'precise definition or quantification.' " It requires assessment of the totality of the circumstances.

Example: An officer stopped defendant's truck for an expired license plate. The defendant was visibly nervous, so the officer asked for permission to search the truck. When defendant refused, the officer walked his trained drug detection dog around the truck. The dog signaled that there were drugs hidden near the driver's side door handle. The search turned up evidence of a crime, but not the type of contraband the dog was trained to detect. After a significant break in time, the same dog was used by the same officer to detect drugs in the same truck. Again, the dog alerted. This time, no evidence of wrongdoing was found. Defendant challenged probable cause based on poor performance of the dog in the field, especially when dealing with the defendant's vehicle. The Supreme Court found that the dog's first alert provided probable cause for the officer's search. In addition to the false positives in the field, the dog had a record of significant training in narcotics detection during which he was rated, "really good." [**Harris**, *supra,* p. 53] *See* also **Rodriguez**, *supra*, p. 28 (noting that police violate the Fourth Amendment when they extend a traffic stop for seven or eight minutes to conduct a dog sniff).

(c) Probable Cause That Car Is Contraband

If the police have probable cause to believe that the car itself is contraband, it may be seized from a public place without a warrant. [**Florida v. White**, 526 U.S. 559 (1999)]

e.g. **Example:** On three occasions, the police observed Defendant selling cocaine from his car, giving the police probable cause to believe that Defendant's car was used to transport cocaine. Under state law, a car used to transport cocaine is contraband subject to forfeiture. Several months later, the police arrest Defendant on unrelated drug charges while he was at work and, based on their prior observations, seized his car from the parking lot without a warrant. While inventorying the contents of the car, the police found cocaine and pursued drug charges against Defendant. The cocaine was admissible as evidence. Even though the police did not have probable cause to believe that the car contained cocaine when it was seized, they did have probable cause to believe that the car was contraband and therefore seizable, and inventory searches of seized items are lawful (*see supra,* p. 52). [**Florida v. White**, *supra*]

(2) Mobility Requirement

The inherent exigency created by an automobile's ready mobility excuses the officers' failure to secure a warrant and justifies the warrantless search of the ***entire automobile*** (interior compartment and trunk), provided probable cause extends to the whole car. [**Carroll v. United States**, *supra,* p. 53; **United States v. Ross**, 456 U.S. 798 (1982)]

(3) Lower Expectation of Privacy Requirement

The automobile exception **applies only to automobiles, mobile recreational vehicles** (*e.g.*, motor homes), **boats, and airplanes**, as to which the Supreme Court has held that **citizens have a lesser expectation of privacy**. **[California v. Carney**, 471 U.S. 386 (1985)] The exception does not apply to homes, offices, and personal property (*e.g.*, a locked footlocker carried by a suspect). [**United States v. Chadwick**, *supra*, p. 51]

(a) Containers Found in Vehicles

When the police have probable cause to justify a warrantless search of an automobile, they may search the entire car and open any packages or luggage found there that could ***reasonably contain the items*** for which they have probable cause to search. [**United States v. Ross**, *supra*]

(b) Containers Placed in Vehicles

Police can also search, without a warrant, any container that they have probable cause to search after it is placed in a car. [**California v. Acevedo**, 500 U.S. 565 (1991)] The majority in ***Acevedo*** emphasized that the police may not search the rest of the car unless they have probable cause to search that area as well. "The scope of a warrantless search based on probable cause is no narrower—and no broader—than the scope of a search authorized by a warrant supported by probable cause."

EXAM TIP

Police have broad authority to search a vehicle depending on what they are looking for. If there is probable cause to believe that contraband is hidden somewhere within the vehicle, police can search the entire car and anything in it that *might contain* the contraband that they have probable cause to look for, whether the item is owned by the driver or a passenger. Thus, if they are looking for evidence of illegal drugs, they can look almost anywhere in the car, but if they are looking for undocumented immigrants, they cannot look inside a small suitcase or in the glove box, where people will not fit. Likewise, if police only have probable cause to believe that evidence will be found inside a specific container (*e.g.*, a gun case), they must confine their search to the container for which they have probable cause.

1) Passenger's Belongings

The search may extend to packages belonging to a passenger and is not limited to the driver's belongings. [**Wyoming v. Houghten**, 526 U.S. 295 (1999)—search of passenger's purse upheld after officer noticed driver had syringe in his pocket] *Rationale*: Like a driver, a passenger has a reduced expectation of privacy in a car.

(c) Technological Aids

Generally, a person traveling in a car on public thoroughfares has no "reasonable expectation of privacy" in his movements; therefore, visual surveillance by the police from a public area does not constitute a "search," even if police use a beeper to help track the car. [**United States v. Knotts**, *supra*, p. 38] But as technology continues to develop, it is less clear whether police can use all forms of sensory-enhancing surveillance technology to "search." Both Justice Alito and Justice Sotomayor have said that long-term GPS monitoring of private activities may impinge on reasonable expectations of privacy, *see* ***Jones***, *supra*, p. 37 *see also* **Grady v. Carolina**, 575 U.S. 306 (2015) (holding that full-time satellite-based monitoring of a sex offender constitutes a search). It is also now clear that when police physically occupy constitutionally protected property to gather information, they have "searched" for Fourth Amendment purposes. [*See* **Jones**, *supra*]

(4) Search Need Not Be Contemporaneous to Stop

If the police could have conducted a warrantless search of a vehicle based on probable cause when the vehicle was stopped, the vehicle may be towed to the police station and searched. [**Chambers v. Maroney**, 399 U.S. 42 (1970); **United States v. Johns**, 469 U.S. 478 (1985)] Similarly, packages removed from a lawfully searched vehicle may be taken to a remote location and searched later without obtaining a warrant.

(5) Special Circumstances

Warrantless searches of vehicles may be deemed reasonable in special circumstances where the police believe it necessary for the safety of the general public.

e.g. **Example:** A search of a car involved in a traffic accident was reasonable where the hospitalized driver was a police officer believed to be carrying a revolver. [**Cady v. Dombrowski**, 413 U.S. 433 (1973); *see* also **Caniglia v. Strom**,

593 U.S. 194 (2021) (noting the difference between vehicles and homes when evaluating reasonableness for a "caretaking" search)]

c. Plain View Exception

The third exception to the warrant requirement concerns seizures of certain objects in plain view.

(1) Requirements

Warrantless seizures by the police are justified when:

(i) The police are ***legitimately on the premises***;

(ii) They discover objects that they have ***probable cause*** to believe are ***contraband or fruits or instrumentalities*** of crime; and

(iii) They observe such evidence ***in plain view***.

[**Coolidge v. New Hampshire**, *supra*, p. 44; **Arizona v. Hicks**, 480 U.S. 321 (1987)]

e.g. **Example:** Police may seize *items not described in a valid warrant* that are observed by the police while executing the warrant. Thus, if the police enter a house pursuant to a valid search warrant to look for a gun used in a robbery, and while in the house, they observe marijuana plants in pots on the kitchen counter, the plants may be seized under the plain view exception.

EXAM TIP

For the "plain view" exception, be sure the police officer is *legitimately on the premises* (for Fourth Amendment purposes), such as on a public sidewalk, in a home executing a warrant, or in a home because of exigent circumstances. If she is, anything the officer sees (or smells, hears, etc.) in plain view is seizable, if the officer has probable cause to believe the item is evidence of a crime or contraband. Thus, while executing a search warrant for a handgun, an officer who opens a small drawer where the gun could be and sees heroin, may lawfully seize the heroin. The heroin was in plain view, the officer was executing a lawful search, and there was probable cause to believe the heroin is contraband. This is true even though the heroin was not the subject of the search and was not listed in the search warrant. *Note*: Even if police trespass on private property, if they remain in an "open field," they may observe evidence in plain view, provided they do not intrude on curtilage.

e.g. **Example:** ***If the police enter a house in hot pursuit*** of a fleeing felon, they may seize items in plain view in the house as long as they have probable cause to believe such items are contraband or evidence. [**Warden v. Hayden**, 387 U.S. 294 (1967)]

e.g. **Example:** Officers entering an apartment to find a shooter, after a bullet fired through the floor injured a man in the room below, may record the serial numbers of the expensive stereo equipment found in the apartment. *But note*: ***When the officers move the stereo*** equipment to better view the serial numbers, ***an additional "search" has occurred***, for which probable cause is required. [**Arizona v. Hicks**, *supra*]

(2) Inadvertence Not Required

Evidence may constitutionally be seized under the plain view exception even if its discovery is not inadvertent. [**Horton v. California**, 496 U.S. 128 (1990)]

Example: Police had probable cause to believe that Defendant had committed an armed robbery and that the proceeds and weapons were likely to be found at his home. They obtained a warrant for the money. During the scope of their search for the money, they discovered the weapons. The seizure of the weapons is permissible under the plain view exception despite the fact that the police expected to find the weapons. [**Horton v. California**, *supra,* p. 56]

Example: Evidence seen from an airplane in a "flyover" directed at a suspect's house or yard is admissible if viewed from public airspace with equipment available to the general public. [**California v. Ciraolo,** *supra*, p. 40; **Dow Chemical Co. v. United States**, *supra*, p. 40]

(3) Prior Justification for Intrusion

A police officer does not normally have a right to seize evidence on private property merely because it is in plain view. There must be some prior justification for the officer's presence on the property.

Example: If a police officer is walking on a public sidewalk and sees an object through the window of someone's home, the officer cannot cross the threshold of the home to seize the object. He must obtain a warrant, or there must be an exigency that allows him immediate entry.

Compare: When the police are in the process of ***investigating a loud party complaint*** and Defendant opens the door, the police may seize contraband lying in plain view on a table inside the dwelling.

(a) Note

Even when police illegally enter private property, evidence initially discovered during that illegal entry may be admissible if it later is discovered during a valid search that is wholly unrelated to the illegal entry. For example, if police officers illegally enter a warehouse and discover bales of marijuana, the marijuana would still be admissible if the officers later search the warehouse pursuant to a warrant based on information not obtained during the illegal entry. [**Murray v. United States**, 487 U.S. 533 (1988)]

(4) Sufficiency of Belief

Certain knowledge that incriminating evidence is involved is ***not*** necessary. For example, evidence was admissible where an officer saw, in plain view, a tied-off, opaque balloon which he suspected, based on his experience and knowledge, contained illegal drugs. [**Texas v. Brown**, 460 U.S. 730 (1983)]

Compare—Insufficient Knowledge: The presence of expensive stereo equipment in an otherwise poorly furnished apartment does not give rise to probable cause to believe that the equipment was stolen. [**Arizona v. Hicks**, *supra,* p. 57]

(5) Other Senses

The plain view doctrine does not require an officer to actually "see" the incriminating evidence.

(a) Plain Smell

If a police officer can smell the presence of marijuana outside the door of a residence, that plain smell could give rise to probable cause to search that residence. [**State v. Kosman**, 892 P.2d 207 (Ariz. 1995)] But, police engage in a Fourth Amendment "search" subject to a reasonableness inquiry when they use a police dog on the front porch of a home to sniff for drugs, because although the public has a license (implied by the property laws and habits in our country) to approach the door using the common walkway, that license does not extend to such intrusive searches using drug detection police dogs. [**Florida v. Jardines**, 569 U.S. 1 (2013)]

(b) Plain Hear

If a police officer, lawfully positioned, overhears a conversation in an adjacent room, that evidence would be admissible. [**United States v. Mankani**, 738 F.2d 538 (2d Cir. 1984)]

d. Stop and Frisk Exception

The fourth exception to the warrant requirement allows the police to stop (seize) a suspect and frisk (limited search) that person for weapons.

(1) Reasonable Suspicion Required

As noted *supra* (p. 26), when the police have an ***articulable, reasonable suspicion*** that someone may be engaged in criminal activity, they may stop (forcibly seize) the person even though they do not have probable cause. If the police reasonably believe that the suspect may be ***armed and dangerous***, they may also conduct a protective frisk (search) of the person for weapons limited to a pat down of the exterior of the suspect's clothing. [**Terry v. Ohio**, *supra*, p. 26]

(a) Reasonable Suspicion Need Not Be Based on Personal Knowledge

A stop is permissible to investigate a suspect of a completed crime. Reasonable suspicion may be based on a "wanted" flyer or bulletin. However, for the stop to be valid, the flyer or bulletin must have been issued based on probable cause. [**United States v. Hensley**, 469 U.S. 221 (1985)]

(2) Totality of Circumstances Considered

In making their decision as to whether to stop and frisk a person, the police may consider the totality of the circumstances—*i.e.,* the whole picture. [**United States v. Cortez**, 449 U.S. 411 (1981)]

e.g. **Example:** Experienced border patrol officers consistently noticed a distinctive V-shaped shoeprint and other shoeprints along a well-defined path leading from the border of Mexico to a nearby U.S. highway. The officers reasoned that the person with the distinctive shoeprint was guiding undocumented immigrants into the United States and, further, that a pickup truck-type vehicle would be capable of transporting the immigrants without arousing suspicion. Knowing these and other facts, the officers stopped a pickup truck and observed a passenger wearing shoes with soles matching the distinctive design. Based on the "whole picture" in this case, the officers could reasonably believe Defendant's vehicle was engaged in criminal activity. [**United States v. Cortez**, *supra*]

Example: Police received an anonymous 911 call reporting that the driver of a pick-up truck forced the 911 caller off the road. The report was relayed to police within five minutes of the incident. Caller gave a specific physical description of the truck. Although the police followed the truck and observed only safe driving, given the totality of the circumstances, police had reasonable suspicion to stop the truck. "By reporting that she had been run off the road by a specific vehicle—a silver Ford F-150 pickup, license plate 8D94925—the caller necessarily claimed eyewitness knowledge of the alleged dangerous driving. That basis of knowledge lends significant support to the tip's reliability." [**Navarette v. California**, 572 U.S. 393 (2014)]

(a) Flight

The Supreme Court has ruled that a person's unprovoked flight after seeing a marked police car passing through a high crime area provided officers with reasonable suspicion to conduct a ***Terry*** stop of the runner. [**Illinois v. Wardlow**, 528 U.S. 119 (2000)] The Supreme Court rejected a per se rule that an individual's flight always provides reasonable suspicion to conduct a ***Terry*** stop, but the opinion strongly suggests that reasonable suspicion will almost always exist when an individual's flight occurs in a high crime area.

(3) Scope Limited

(a) Frisk

The scope of a frisk is generally limited to a ***pat down of the outer clothing***. [**Terry v. Ohio**, *supra*]

1) Caveat—Specific Information Supplied by an Informant

An officer may reach into an area of a person's clothing, such as a belt, without a preliminary frisk, when the officer has specific information that a weapon is hidden there. The source of this information may even be an unnamed informant's tip, if the tip has some indicia of reliability. The tip need not have sufficient reliability to support a warrant to justify the seizure. [**Adams v. Williams**, 407 U.S. 143 (1972)]

2) Stop for Traffic Violation

Once a police officer has lawfully stopped a vehicle for a traffic violation, he may "frisk" the passenger compartment of the vehicle for weapons if he reasonably believes that the passenger compartment contains a weapon and the occupant may grab it. The scope of the search is limited to the areas in which a weapon may be hidden. [**Michigan v. Long**, *supra*, p. 28] Because of the potential danger to police officers in conducting a traffic stop, the police may also order the occupants out of the vehicle (*i.e.,* driver and passengers), even without suspecting criminal activity. If the officer reasonably suspects that someone is armed and dangerous, the officer may conduct a frisk of that person. [**Pennsylvania v. Mimms**, *supra,* p. 32; **Maryland v. Wilson**, *supra*, p. 32; **Terry v. Ohio**, *supra*, p. 26]

APPROACH TO ADMISSIBILITY OF EVIDENCE FOUND DURING A PAT DOWN

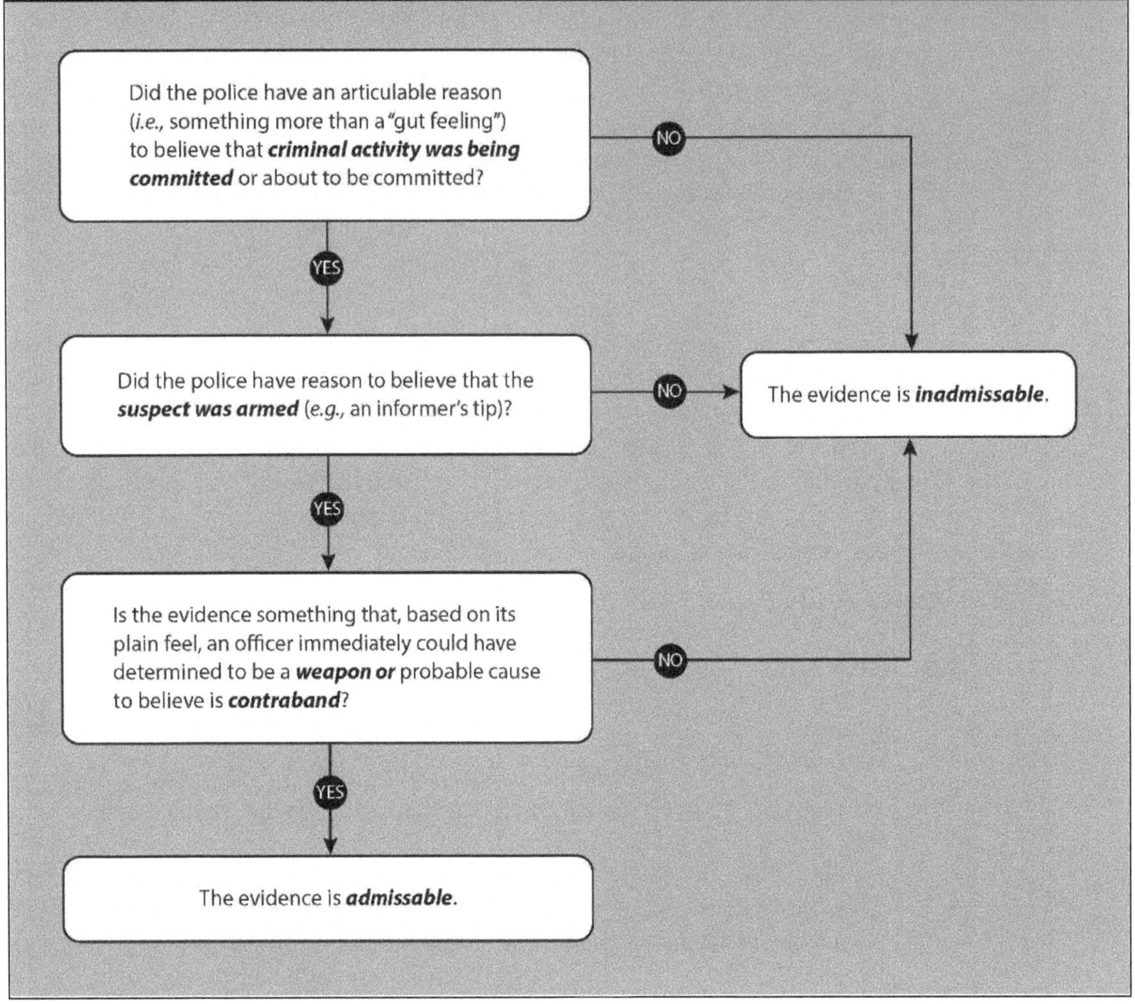

(b) Stop (Seizure)

A seizure occurs when the police conduct is such that a reasonable person would believe that he is not free to leave and the person yields to police authority, or police apply physical force to a person with intent to restrain her. [**Michigan v. Chesternut**, *supra,* p. 21; **Torres v. Madrid**, *supra*, p. 21] There is ***no rigid time limit for*** the length of an investigative stop. To determine whether the length of a seizure is permissible, the Court considers: (i) the purpose of the stop, (ii) the reasonableness of the time in effectuating the purpose, and (iii) the reasonableness of the means of investigation. [**United States v. Sharpe**, 470 U.S. 675 (1985)] If a *Terry* seizure is unreasonably long or intrusive, it will be treated as an arrest, which is invalid without probable cause.

Example: A 20-minute stop was held to be reasonable where two officers split up because the narcotics suspects they were following split up. One officer stopped Defendant and detained him for 15 minutes, waiting for the additional officer to arrive. The other officer stopped the second suspect and waited for additional officers to arrive to detain them. The officer who stopped Defendant felt that he could not properly conduct an investigation himself because he: (i) had joined the chase late and was not aware of all the facts that might justify an investigation; and (ii) lacked the other officer's narcotics investigation experience. Once the other officer arrived, he conducted a five-minute investigation of Defendant and his truck and found marijuana. The Supreme Court found this to be a ***Terry*** stop rather than an arrest because the officers had not unreasonably detained Defendant; rather, they acted "in a diligent and reasonable manner." [**United States v. Sharpe**, *supra*, p. 60]

cf. **Compare:** Police stopped Defendant in an airport to question him because he matched a drug courier profile. They became suspicious of his answers and removed him to a small room 40 feet off the main concourse. Defendant was then detained for 15 minutes while his luggage was retrieved. The police asked Defendant for permission to open his luggage; he consented, and drugs were found. The Court held the police conduct to be unreasonable under ***Terry***. Any suspicion justifying the initial stop was insufficient to justify Defendant's removal from the concourse into a small room and 15 minute detention therein. It would have been less intrusive to simply submit the luggage to a dog sniff. Thus, the evidence was held to be inadmissible as the fruit of an illegal arrest, lacking probable cause. [**Florida v. Royer**, 460 U.S. 491 (1983)]

(4) Evidence Admissibility Standards

If a police officer conducts a patdown within the bounds of ***Terry*** and feels a suspicious item, the officer may reach into the suspect's clothing and seize the item, if based on its "plain feel," the officer reasonably believes it is a ***weapon***, or the officer has probable cause to believe the item is ***contraband***. For example, if during a patdown the officer feels a baseball-size rock of crack cocaine, and he can tell immediately by feel that it is contraband, the officer may lawfully seize it. [But *see* **Minnesota v. Dickerson**, 508 U.S. 366 (1993)—excluding from evidence cocaine that officer found during lawful patdown because officer had to manipulate the item (an additional search) before deciding that it likely was drugs]

(5) Stop and Identify Statutes

The Supreme Court has held that if the police have the reasonable suspicion required to make a ***Terry*** stop (*supra,* p. 26), they may require the detainee to identify himself, and the detainee may be arrested for failing to comply. [**Hiibel v. Sixth Judicial District Court**, *supra*, p. 29] *Note*: In **Hiibel**, the identification requirement originated with state law and not the Fourth Amendment. The Fourth Amendment does not impose obligations on citizens; it restricts only government actors.

e. Consent Exception

The fifth exception to the warrant requirement is consent.

(1) Valid Consent

A search may be conducted without a warrant and without probable cause or reasonable suspicion if ***voluntary*** consent is given. [**Schneckloth v. Bustamonte**, 412 U.S. 218 (1973)] Considering the totality of the circumstances, the consent must not be obtained by duress or coercion.

(a) Knowledge of Right Not Required

Knowledge of the right to withhold consent is ***not*** a prerequisite to proving that voluntary consent was given. It is one factor to be considered. Accordingly, the police do not have to warn a person of their right to withhold consent. [**Schneckloth v. Bustamonte**, *supra*]

e.g. **Example:** After Deputy stopped Defendant for speeding, gave him a verbal warning, and returned his license, Deputy asked Defendant if he was carrying any drugs in the car. Defendant answered "no" and consented to a search of his car, which uncovered drugs. Defendant argued that his consent was invalid because he was not told that he was free to go after his license was returned. The Supreme Court, applying the principles of ***Shneckloth***, found that no such warning was necessary. Voluntariness is to be determined from all of the circumstances, and knowledge of the right to refuse consent is just one factor in determining voluntariness. [**Ohio v. Robinette**, 519 U.S. 33 (1996)]

(b) Police Announcement Limitation

When the police claim to have a valid search warrant and it later turns out that they did not, consent is not voluntarily given because police claimed a legal right to search with or without consent. [**Bumper v. North Carolina**, 391 U.S. 543 (1968)]

(2) Scope of Consent Search

The scope of a consent search is limited by the scope of the consent (*e.g.,* consent to search for a stolen television would not justify a warrantless search of jewelry boxes). The permissible scope of a search is evaluated objectively. Consent to search extends to any object or container that a reasonable officer would understand to fall within the scope of the consent. *Note*: Consent may be ***revoked***, in which case, the search must stop, unless there is a rationale beyond consent to continue to search.

e.g. **Example:** A police officer stopped Defendant for a traffic infraction after observing Defendant participating in what appeared to be a drug transaction. The officer told Defendant that he suspected that Defendant was carrying cocaine and asked Defendant for permission to search the car. Defendant consented. The officer found a bag on the floorboard, opened it, and found cocaine. The officer arrested Defendant. At trial, Defendant objected to introduction of the cocaine, claiming that his consent did not extend to the closed container. The Supreme Court held that because Defendant did not place any restrictions on his consent and knew that the officer was searching for drugs, it was reasonable for the officer to assume that he could search the bag. [**Florida v. Jimeno**, 500 U.S. 248 (1991)]

(3) Capacity to Consent

Any person with an equal right to use or occupy property ("common authority") may consent to a search of the property, and any evidence found may be used against all owners or occupants. The government has the burden of proving that the consenting individual has joint access or control of the premises. This burden may be satisfied by circumstantial evidence. [**United States v. Matlock**, 415 U.S. 164 (1974)]

e.g. **Example:** Where two persons share an apartment, either person can consent in the other's absence to a search of common areas (such as a living area or bathroom), but not as to areas reserved to only the other occupant (such as a locked closet in a private bedroom). [**United States v. Matlock**, *supra*]

e.g. **Example:** Officers asked the joint user of a duffel bag for consent to search the bag. The joint user consented, and clothing inside the bag implicated Defendant. The joint user's consent was valid against Defendant. [**Frazier v. Cupp**, 394 U.S. 731 (1969)]

cf. **Compare:** Generally, a landlord does not have authority to give effective consent to a search of a tenant's premises. Similarly, a hotel clerk may not consent to the search of a guest's room. [**Stoner v. California**, 376 U.S. 483 (1964)]

(a) Limitation—Where Party Is Present and Objects

The police may not act on consent from one occupant if a co-occupant is present and objects to the search. [**Georgia v. Randolph**, 547 U.S. 103 (2006)] *Note*: Evidence found during such a search may be used only against the consenting co-occupant. Nevertheless, after police have removed a physically-present and objecting co-occupant, for an objectively reasonable purpose (*i.e.*, a lawful arrest based on probable cause), the remaining occupant may give lawful consent to search the shared premises. [**Fernandez v. California**, 571 U.S. 292 (2014)]

(b) Lack of Authority to Consent

Even if a person has no actual authority to consent to a search of property, consent is valid if the ***police reasonably believe*** that the person giving consent has an equal right to use or occupy the searched premises. It does not matter that the person does not actually have common authority. Thus, the Supreme Court upheld a consent search where Defendant's girlfriend agreed to a search of Defendant's apartment, when police erroneously, but reasonably, believed that the girlfriend lived in the apartment. It was significant that she had a key to the apartment and referred to it as "our apartment," although she was actually an infrequent visitor to the apartment. [**Illinois v. Rodriguez**, 497 U.S. 177 (1990)] *Rationale*: The Fourth Amendment protects only against unreasonable searches, and it was not unreasonable for the police to believe that consent was obtained from an authorized co-occupant.

EXAM TIP

Exam questions on the validity of warrantless searches often suggest consent as a choice, especially the consent of someone other than the defendant. Be careful to check whether the person has either ***actual authority*** **to consent** (as a co-occupant with common authority) or **reasonably apparent authority to consent**. For example, a homeowner/parent can consent to a search of the home's kitchen, and probably to a search of her son's room, *unless* the facts strongly indicate that the parent does not have a right to go in the room (*e.g.*, always locked, only defendant has a key). Even when there is no actual authority to consent, be sure to consider whether there is apparent consent (an officer is reasonable under the totality of the circumstances, in believing that the consenting party is a co-occupant with actual authority).

f. Emergency Exceptions

The sixth exception to the warrant requirement concerns certain "emergency" situations (sometimes referred to as the "***exigent circumstances***" exception).

(1) Threat of Immediate Physical Danger

The police may conduct a search without a warrant if they reasonably believe there is an immediate threat to their physical safety, the public, a minor, or another adult. [**Brigham City v. Stewart**, 547 U.S. 398 (2006); **Ryburn v. Huff**, 565 U.S. 469 (2012)] Whether an emergency exists is determined objectively, from the officer's point of view. [**Michigan v. Fisher**, 558 U.S. 45 (2009)] *Note*: Some states refer to this exception as the ***community caretaker exception***.

Example: Police responded to a domestic disturbance call at a home. Upon arriving, they found blood on the hood of a pickup truck and windows broken out of the home. Through an open window, they saw defendant screaming and with a cut on his hand. An officer asked if medical attention was needed, and defendant used an expletive and told the officer to get a warrant. The officer then opened the house door partway, and defendant pointed a gun at the officer. Evidence of the gun need not be suppressed as the fruit of an unlawful entry. The officer could have objectively believed that the defendant was attacking a spouse or child who needed aid or that the defendant was in danger himself. [**Michigan v. Fisher**, *supra*]

Example: The Court has noted that a warrant would not be required to search a container reasonably believed to contain explosives that might be detonated imminently. [**United States v. Chadwick**, 433 U.S. 1 (1977)]

Example: Where police have information that a child is being abused and is in immediate danger, they may enter a home without a warrant. [**State v. Hunt**, 406 P.2d 208 (Ariz. 1965)—house cleaner informed police that she found her employer's child beaten and bloodied, tied up, and locked in a furnace room; evidence of criminal child abuse obtained while retrieving child from house without a warrant was admissible]

Example: A warrantless entry into a home was proper when, while responding to a complaint about a loud party, police officers saw through a screen door an altercation between four adults and a juvenile and observed the juvenile punch one of the adults hard enough to make him spit blood into the sink. [**Brigham City v. Stewart**, *supra*, p. 63]

(2) Hot Pursuit

The police may make a warrantless search and seizure when they are in "hot pursuit" of a dangerous suspect. The scope of such a search may be as extensive as reasonably necessary to prevent the suspect from resisting or escaping. [**Warden v. Hayden**, *supra*, p. 56] When the police have probable cause and attempt to make a warrantless arrest in a "public place," they may pursue the suspect into a private dwelling. [**United States v. Santana**, *supra*, p. 24]

Example: After their taxi company was robbed at gunpoint, taxi drivers followed Defendant to a house and immediately summoned the police. The police arrived within minutes and entered the house. The officers found incriminating clothing in the washing machine, a shotgun, a pistol, and Defendant. The Supreme Court held that clothing found in the washing machine was admissible evidence. *Rationale*: "Speed here was essential, and only a thorough search of the house for persons and weapons could have ensured that Defendant was the only man present and that the police had control of all weapons that could be used against them or to effect an escape." [**Warden v. Hayden**, *supra*]

(a) Minor Offenses May Not Justify Entry

While **United States v. Santana**, *supra*, p. 24, and **Warden v. Hayden**, *supra*, allowed an officer's warrantless entry while in hot pursuit of a felony suspect, the holding in these cases was not expressly limited to felonies. Whether an officer in hot pursuit of a misdemeanant may enter a home without a warrant sharply divides the lower courts. [**Stanton v. Sims**, 571 U.S. 3 (2013)] The Supreme Court in **Welsh v. Wisconsin**, 466 U.S. 740 (1984), excluded evidence where Defendant was suspected of drunk driving, and police entered his home to obtain a blood sample, noting that under applicable state law, Defendant's offense was only a civil, non-jailable traffic violation, not a criminal offense. *Note*: **Welsh** was not a hot pursuit case. Thus, the Court did not reach the issue. In **Lange v. California**, 594 U.S. 295 (2021), the Court held that exigencies arising from misdemeanants' flight must be assessed on a case-by-case basis. According to the Court, "[w]hen the totality of circumstances shows an emergency—such as imminent harm to others, a threat to the officer himself, destruction of evidence, or escape from the home—the police may act without waiting. . . . But the need to pursue a misdemeanant does not trigger a categorical rule allowing home entry, even absent a law enforcement emergency."

(3) Destruction of Evidence

Under the exigent circumstances exception to the warrant requirement, the police may make a warrantless entry to prevent the imminent destruction of evidence. Police action that does not violate or threaten to violate the Fourth Amendment, such as knocking loudly and yelling "police," does not make a warrantless entry into a home unreasonable. Even if the police create the exigency by causing occupants within the home to begin destroying evidence, warrantless entry is still reasonable. [**Kentucky v. King**, *supra*, p. 46]

e.g. **Example:** Police officers followed a suspected drug dealer on foot into an apartment complex, but the suspect entered one of the apartments and disappeared. Officers were unsure which apartment the suspect entered, but they smelled marijuana emanating from one of the apartments. The officers then knocked on that apartment door and announced their presence. When they heard noises inside, they announced their presence again and kicked in the door. The entry was not unlawful, even if the exigency (destroying evidence) was caused by the police knocking and yelling and even if the police mistakenly believed that the suspect was inside, provided the officers did not violate or threaten to violate the Fourth Amendment before entering the apartment. [**Kentucky v. King**, *supra*]

(4) Evanescent Evidence

The police may make a warrantless seizure of evidence that is likely to disappear before a warrant can be obtained. One example of evanescent evidence is fingernail scrapings. [**Cupp v. Murphy**, 412 U.S. 291 (1973)] A blood sample suspected to contain evidence of driving under the influence of alcohol may or may not qualify, depending on the circumstances. [**Schmerber v. California**, 384 U.S. 757 (1966) (officer reasonably believed that he was confronted with emergency need to have suspect's blood drawn before alcohol dissipated); **Missouri v. McNeely**, 569 U.S. 141 (2013) (natural dissipation of alcohol from the bloodstream, without more, did not give police exigency to have blood drawn for testing; dissipation, alone, is not a per se exigency); **Mitchell v. Wisconsin**, 588 U.S. 840 (2019) (plurality decision) (holding that exigent circumstances almost always exist to allow law enforcement to obtain a blood test of suspected drunk driver without a warrant when the driver is unconscious and no breath test can be obtained)]

Incident to a lawful arrest, police may also require someone suspected of drunk driving to submit to a breath test because "breath tests do not implicate significant privacy concerns." But blood tests are different because they pierce the skin—a significant bodily intrusion. [**Birchfield v. North Dakota**, 579 U.S. 438 (2016)]

(5) Special Emergencies

Warrantless searches and seizures are permissible in certain other emergencies. For example, firefighters may enter burning buildings to investigate the source of the fire, even for a short period (*e.g.*, a few hours) after the fire has been extinguished. [**Michigan v. Tyler**, *supra*, p. 41] Similarly, inspectors can enter a business suspected of harboring contaminated foods. [**North American Cold Storage Co. v. City of Chicago**, 211 U.S. 306 (1908)]

cf. **Compare—Testing Pregnant Women for Cocaine Use:** Special needs do not justify a warrantless and nonconsensual urinalysis test to determine whether a pregnant woman has been using cocaine. [**Ferguson v. Charleston**, 532 U.S. 67 (2001); *and see infra*, p. 75]

SUMMARY OF VALID WARRANTLESS SEARCHES

Type of Search	Need Probable Cause?	Contemporaneousness Required?	Other Limitations?
1. ***Search Incident to Lawful*** (*i.e.*, Constitutional) ***Arrest***	Yes (for arrest)	Yes	Arrest based on probable cause
• **Search Incident to Incarceration** (Inventory Search)	No	No	Established procedures
2. ***"Automobile" Exception***	Yes	No	Containers—limited to those that could contain the evidence sought
3. ***Plain View***	Yes (to believe item is evidence, contraband, etc.)	Yes	Police lawfully on premises; evidence in plain view
4. ***Stop and Frisk***			
• ***Stop***	No	Yes	Reasonable and articulable suspicion of criminal activity
• ***Frisk***	No	Yes	Reasonable belief that person is armed; limited to pat down of outer clothing
5. ***Consent***	No	Yes	Voluntary consent given; actual or apparent authority to consent; can be revoked

6. Emergencies, Hot Pursuit	No	Yes	Emergency situation—no time to get warrant

(6) Limitation

Note, there is ***no general "emergency" exception***. Thus, a warrant is required to: search a burned building for evidence of arson several days after the fire has been extinguished [**Michigan v. Tyler**, *supra*, p. 66], search a murder scene several days after the murder [**Flippo v. West Virginia**, 528 U.S. 11 (1999); **Mincey v. Arizona**, 437 U.S. 385 (1978)], or check for occupational safety violations [**Marshall v. Barlow's, Inc.**, *supra*, p. 41]

6. Electronic Surveillance

Any form of electronic surveillance, including wiretapping, that violates a person's ***reasonable expectation of privacy*** constitutes a search; actual physical trespass is not required for a search, although a physical trespass on houses, papers, or effects for the purpose of gathering information is a search. [**Katz v. United States**, 389 U.S. 347 (1967); **United States v. Jones**, 565 U.S. 400 (2012)]

a. Warrant Requirements

To be constitutionally valid, a warrant authorizing any form of electronic surveillance, including wiretapping, must satisfy the following requirements [**Berger v. New York**, 388 U.S. 41 (1967)]:

(1) ***The warrant must describe with particularity*** the conversations to be intercepted;

(2) ***A showing of probable cause*** to believe that a specific crime has been or is being committed;

(3) ***The wiretapping must be for a limited period of time*** (although extensions may be obtained upon an adequate showing);

(4) ***The suspects*** whose conversations are to be overheard ***must be named***;

(5) ***A return must be made to court***, showing what conversations were intercepted; and

(6) The wiretapping must ***terminate when the desired information has been obtained***.

b. Disinterested Magistrate Authorization Requirement

A neutral, detached judge must determine whether a warrant should issue authorizing electronic surveillance. The President may not order such surveillance without prior judicial approval. [**United States v. United States District Court**, *supra*, p. 45]

c. Title III Compliance Requirement

All electronic surveillance must comply with the requirements of Title III of the 1968 Omnibus Crime Control and Safe Streets Act. [18 U.S.C. §§ 2510–2522] This statute requires more than the constitutional minimum, including, for example, that a U.S. district court or U.S. court of appeals judge approve the surveillance.

(1) Equipment Installation

If the surveillance satisfies the requirements of Title III, the police may covertly enter a place for the purpose of installing electronic surveillance devices without prior judicial approval. A separate warrant authorizing the covert entry is not required. [**Dalia v. United States**, 441 U.S. 238 (1979)]

(2) Title III Warrant Requirements

Under Title III, a warrant must include:

(i) The identity of the applicant;

(ii) Details of the offense;

(iii) Particular descriptions of the facilities to be used, the types of communication to be intercepted, and the identity of the person whose conversation is to be intercepted;

(iv) A description of other law enforcement techniques used to obtain the information and a description of why those efforts failed or would likely fail;

(v) The time period of the surveillance; and

(vi) Previous applications made for the same surveillance. [18 U.S.C. § 2518(1)]

(3) Video Surveillance

Title III does not specifically extend to video surveillance, although circuit courts have applied it to video surveillance by analogy. [*See* **United States v. Torres**, 751 F.2d 875 (7th Cir. 1984)] In any case, the Fourth Amendment may apply. [**United States v. Mesa-Rincon**, 911 F.2d 1433 (10th Cir. 1990)]

d. Pen Registers

Pen registers record the numbers dialed from a particular telephone. The Fourth Amendment does ***not*** require prior judicial approval for installation and use of pen registers. [**Smith v. Maryland**, *supra*, p. 38] Similarly, no such approval is mandated by Title III, because Title III applies only when the ***contents*** of electronic communications are intercepted. Nevertheless, by statute [18 U.S.C. §§ 3121 *et seq.*] police must obtain a court order finding pen register information relevant to an ongoing investigation before using a pen register. Information obtained in violation of the statute will not necessarily be excluded from evidence in a criminal trial; the statute merely provides for a criminal penalty.

e. Patriot Act of 2001

Six weeks after the September 11, 2001, attacks on the World Trade Center and Pentagon, Congress adopted the Patriot Act, which included hundreds of amendments to federal law. It extended the pen register provisions to the Internet and provided for roving wiretaps under the Foreign Intelligence Surveillance Act ("FISA"), as well as subjected United States citizens to surveillance under FISA under specified conditions.

f. "Uninvited Ear" Exception

The defendant may not argue that his Fourth Amendment rights have been violated if he did not attempt to keep his communications private. [**Katz v. United States**, *supra*, p. 67] This applies to conversations conducted in a reckless fashion with disregard for whomever might be listening.

e.g. **Example:** Defendant makes several incriminating statements while using a public telephone. Several persons overheard these remarks, because Defendant was speaking loudly and making no attempt to keep his conversation private. Defendant may not object to the use of the statements against him, because he did not attempt to safeguard his conversation from others nearby.

g. "Unreliable Ear" Exception

The defendant assumes the risk that the person with whom he is speaking is "unreliable"—*i.e.*, will consent to the government monitoring their conversation. If the person turns out to be a police informer who is wired for recording, the defendant's Fourth Amendment rights are not violated by the recording or transmitting. [**United States v. White**, 401 U.S. 745 (1971)]

e.g. **Example:** A wired government informer hears defendants on the eve of trial planning to bribe jurors. The statements are admissible in a subsequent trial for attempting to bribe jurors. [**Hoffa v. United States**, 385 U.S. 293 (1966)]

7. Searches in Foreign Countries or at the Border

a. Searches in Foreign Countries

The Fourth Amendment does not apply to searches and seizures by United States officials in foreign countries and involving foreign citizens, at least when the foreign citizen does not have a substantial connection to the United States. Thus, for example, the Fourth Amendment was held not to bar the use of evidence obtained in a warrantless search of a foreign citizen's home in Mexico. [**United States v. Verdugo-Urquidez**, 494 U.S. 259 (1990)]

b. Border Searches—General Rule

Routine searches by government agents (typically Immigration and Customs Enforcement agents) at an international border or its "functional equivalent" (*e.g.*, international airports or locations near a border where several routes leading to the border intersect) may be conducted ***without a warrant or probable cause***. [**Almeida-Sanchez v. United States**, 413 U.S. 266 (1973)] The border search authority is based on the concept of national sovereignty.

e.g. **Example:** Defendant was detained at the Los Angeles airport because she was suspected of smuggling contraband in her alimentary canal. She had a swelling in her abdomen, was wearing two plastic underpants, carried $5,000 in cash, spoke no English, and had recently made numerous trips to Los Angeles and Miami but knew no one in the United States. Her 16-hour detention was permissible because it was based on a reasonable suspicion of her illegal activities. [**United States v. Montoya de Hernandez**, 473 U.S. 531 (1985)]

(1) Note—Extends to Laptop Computers

The border search rationale has been used to uphold searches of the contents of laptop computers at the border of the United States, but federal courts are split on the particulars of such searches. [**United States v. Cotterman**, 709 F.3d 952 (9th Cir. 2013)] The Fourth Circuit Court of Appeals has held a forensic search of a digital phone to fall outside the reach of the routine border search because of the extensive private information on such phones. [**United States v. Aigbekaen**, 943 F.3d 713 (4th Cir. 2019), but *see* **United States v. Touset**, 890 F.3d 1227 (11th Cir. 2018) (allowing forensic searching of electronic devices at borders)] Such border searches have uncovered evidence of child pornography and identity fraud. [**United States v. Arnold**, 533 F.3d 1003 (9th Cir. 2008); **United States v. Ickes**, 393 F.3d 501 (4th Cir. 2005)]

c. Rules Governing Permanent Checkpoints

It is permissible for border officials to ***stop*** vehicles at reasonably located, fixed (permanent) checkpoints to question occupants of the vehicles, even without reasonable suspicion that the vehicles contain undocumented immigrants. [**United States v. Martinez-Fuerte**, 428 U.S. 543 (1976)] Officials may disassemble stopped vehicles at such checkpoints, even without reasonable suspicion. [**United States v. Flores-Montano**, 541 U.S. 149 (2004)—search of vehicle at border, including removal of vehicle's fuel tank, was valid even without reasonable suspicion] *Rationale*: The government's inherent authority to protect its territorial integrity against entry by unwanted persons and their effects "is at its zenith at the international border," and such searches "are reasonable simply by virtue of the fact that they occur at the border." Moreover, a person has a lower expectation of privacy at the border than in the interior of the United States. Nevertheless, the Court has suggested that non-routine, personal searches at the border (*e.g.,* strip searches or body-cavity searches) may require probable cause.

(1) Note

The Supreme Court approves fixed checkpoints more readily than roving checkpoints because fixed checkpoints involve less police discretion and, consequently, provide less opportunity for police abuse. This rationale has been used by courts to uphold fixed checkpoints in other contexts. [*See, e.g.,* **Michigan Dept. of State Police v. Sitz**, 496 U.S. 444 (1990), *supra*, p. 30 (brief suspicionless stop at fixed checkpoint to combat drunk driving is constitutional); **United States v. Moore**, 952 F.3d 186 (4th Cir. 2020)—drivers' license and proof of insurance checkpoint upheld; but *see* **City of Indianapolis v. Edmund**, 531 U.S. 32 (2000), supra, p. 30—finding unconstitutional a fixed checkpoint with a primary purpose to detect evidence of ordinary criminal wrongdoing—for example, looking for illegal drugs]

d. Rules Governing Roving Patrols

(1) Stops

A roving patrol near the border may ***stop*** (seize) vehicles for questioning if the officers reasonably suspect that the vehicle contains undocumented immigrants. But *note*: The fact that persons inside the vehicle appear to be of Mexican descent is insufficient to constitute reasonable suspicion. [**United States v. Brignoni-Ponce**, *supra,* p. 30]

(2) Searches

Roving patrols near the border may not conduct a ***search*** without a warrant unless such a search qualifies as one of the exceptions to the warrant requirement. For example, border patrol officials may search a vehicle if the driver consents to it. [**Almeida-Sanchez v. United States**, *supra*]

e. Rules Governing Inspection of International Mail

The border search rules permit the opening of international mail at its place of entry into the country when postal authorities have ***reasonable cause*** to suspect that the mail contains contraband. However, postal regulations prohibit the officials from reading any correspondence inside. [**United States v. Ramsey**, 431 U.S. 606 (1977)—no Fourth Amendment violation for postal authorities to open, without a warrant, a heavy package from a known narcotics source country]

(1) Note

Once a package has lawfully been determined to contain contraband, its subsequent reopening by customs agents after delivery to the defendant is ***not*** a search within the meaning of the Fourth Amendment unless there is a substantial likelihood that the container's contents have been changed during any gap in surveillance. [**Illinois v. Andreas**, 463 U.S. 765 (1983)]

f. Rules Governing Immigration Actions

The Supreme Court held that the Immigration and Naturalization Service ("I.N.S."), which in 2003 became Immigration and Customs Enforcement (ICE), ***may*** conduct a "factory survey" of the entire workforce in a factory to determine citizenship of each employee, without implicating Fourth Amendment issues. The "factory survey" is not a "detention" or a "seizure" under the Fourth Amendment. [**Immigration & Naturalization Service v. Delgado**, 466 U.S. 210 (1984)] Furthermore, evidence illegally obtained in violation of the Fourth Amendment may be used in a civil deportation hearing. [**Immigration & Naturalization Service v. Lopez-Mendoza**, 468 U.S. 1032 (1984)]

8. Administrative Searches

a. Probable Cause Standard Relaxed

Government inspectors who perform administrative searches must have a warrant to search private residences and commercial buildings. [**Camara v. Municipal Court**, 387 U.S. 523 (1967)] However, the traditional probable cause standard is relaxed. Thus, a valid administrative inspection warrant does not require a showing of specific violations of laws or of particular conditions of particular buildings; ***a showing of a general and neutral enforcement plan justifies issuance of a warrant***. Also, probable cause may be based on factors such as the passage of time, the nature of the building, or conditions in the same geographic area. Random, periodic area inspections are then permitted. The real purpose of an administrative search warrant is to guard against selective enforcement of these common health and safety regulations. For that reason, blanket area inspection warrants are allowed without a showing of probable cause. [**Marshall v. Barlow's, Inc.**, *supra*, p. 67]

(1) Balancing

In deciding that traditional probable cause should not be required to obtain a warrant for an administrative search, the Court in ***Camara*** balanced the interests at stake. It found that the government had a strong regulatory interest in preventing the types of dangerous conditions that such searches uncover and that the government's interest outweighed any individual interest in avoiding the intrusion. Indeed, the Court found the individual interest weak because: (i) there is a long history of public acceptance of such searches, and (ii) the searches are not personal or terribly intrusive in nature, and are not aimed at the discovery of crimes.

b. Airport Exception

Searches of airline passengers before boarding are permissible. Such searches are based on an administrative inspection or consent rationale. [**Corbett v. Transp. Sec. Admin.**, 767 F.3d 1171 (11th Cir. 2014)] Some courts have held that passengers may avoid such a search by agreeing not to board the plane.

c. Welfare Inspections

The Supreme Court upheld a state law permitting welfare case workers to enter a residence without a warrant. The Court reasoned that the Fourth Amendment did not apply because there was no criminal sanction involved, merely a potential termination of welfare benefits. [**Wyman v. James**, 400 U.S. 309 (1971)]

d. Contaminated Food Exception

Inspectors do not need a warrant before seizing spoiled or contaminated food. [**North American Cold Storage Co. v. City of Chicago**, *supra*, p. 66]

e. Highly Regulated Industries Exception

A warrant is not required for searches of businesses in highly regulated industries. This exception is based on two theories: (i) the urgent public interest involved, and (ii) the implied consent of businesses entering such industries. Furthermore, such regulatory violations are often easily hidden, and a business owner could thwart government regulation unless warrantless searches were permitted. [**United States v. Biswell**, 406 U.S. 311 (1972)]

(1) Illustrations of Such Industries

(a) ***Liquor*** [**Colonnade Catering Corp. v. United States**, 397 U.S. 72 (1970)];

(b) ***Guns*** [**United States v. Biswell**, 406 U.S. 311 (1972)];

(c) ***Strip mining*** [**Donovan v. Dewey**, 452 U.S. 594 (1981)];

(d) ***Automobile junkyards*** [**New York v. Burger**, 479 U.S. 812 (1987)]; and

(e) ***Railroads*** [**Skinner v. Railway Labor Executives' Association**, 489 U.S. 602 (1989)]

(2) Caveat—Industries Not Included

Certain other industries, although regulated, are ***not*** included in the highly regulated industry exception category—*e.g.,* car leasing [**G.M. Leasing Corp. v. United States**, 429 U.S. 338 (1977)], general manufacturing [**Marshall v. Barlow's, Inc.**, supra, p. 71], and the hotel industry [**City of Los Angeles v. Patel**, 576 U.S. 409 (2015)]

f. Public School Exception

Public school officials do not need a warrant or probable cause before conducting a search at school. They need only ***reasonable grounds*** for the search. This exception is justified because of the nature of the school environment—public school officials have a duty to protect students both from other students and from themselves. [**New Jersey v. T.L.O.**, 469 U.S. 325 (1985)] Reasonable grounds will exist if the school official reasonably believes that the search will turn up evidence that the student has violated a school rule or the law. The scope of the search must be reasonably related to the circumstances that justified the search in the first place.

e.g. **Example:** A teacher discovered a 14-year-old student smoking in the girls' washroom and reported the incident to the vice principal. The vice principal asked the student about the incident, and when the student denied ever smoking, the principal looked in her purse and found cigarettes and rolling papers. He then searched the purse more thoroughly and found marijuana and a list of "people who owe me money." Next, he found two letters in the purse which he read and which implicated the student in drug dealing. Because the teacher's report gave the vice principal sufficient suspicion to believe that the purse contained cigarettes, the initial search of the purse was reasonable. Discovery of rolling papers made closer inspection of the purse reasonable. Discovery of the marijuana and the list supported the inference that the student was dealing drugs, thus justifying the reading of the letters. As a result, all the evidence was admissible in the delinquency proceeding against the student. [**New Jersey v. T.L.O.**, *supra*]

e.g. **Example:** A 13-year-old female middle school student was subjected to a search of her body, beneath her bra and underpants. Based on information from another student, an assistant principal suspected the searched student of distributing over-the-counter pills in school. Because there were no reasons to suspect the drugs presented a danger or were concealed in the student's underwear, and because the scope of the search was invasive and beyond anything routine, the search violated the Fourth Amendment. [**Safford Unified School District No. 1 v. Redding**, 557 U.S. 364 (2009)]

EXAM TIP

On your exam, it is important to remember that searches of public-school students by public school officials are not the same as other searches. Because of the nature of the school environment, a school official may search a student or a student's locker if the official has ***reasonable grounds*** to believe that the search will turn up evidence that the student violated ***school rules or any law***. ***Probable cause is not required***. What if the search is performed by police officers at the request of school officials? The Supreme Court has not yet decided the issue, but a strong argument can be made that the result would not change—if a school official could have performed the search in question, but because of safety concerns asked the police to perform the search, the student is in no worse position than if the official performed the search and turned over evidence to the police. On the other hand, it could be argued that the public school exception should not apply here, because when a public school official conducts such a search, his main concern is school safety, but when a police officer conducts such a search, her main concern is law enforcement.

(1) Drug Testing of Students

A school district may randomly conduct urinalysis drug testing, monitored by an adult of the same sex as the student, of any student participating in ***any extracurricular activity*** and may suspend students who test positive. [**Board of Education v. Earls**, 536 U.S. 822 (2002)] *Note*: Under the program in ***Earls***, positive test results could not be given to the police; it is unclear whether a program that allowed positive test results to be given to the police would be constitutional. *Note also*: The rationale in ***Earls***—that such testing furthers the school's safety interest in its students—could support a school-wide drug testing program (*i.e.*, a program not limited to students participating in extracurricular activities). However, ***Earls*** was a 5–4 decision, and the Justice casting the fifth vote for the majority expressed discomfort with such an expansive rule.

g. Probationers' Homes Exceptions

(1) Search by Probation Officer

Probation officers do not need a warrant to search a probationer's home if a state statute authorizes warrantless searches and there are reasonable grounds to believe that contraband is present in the probationer's home. Because probation entails limitations on the probationer's liberties, full probable cause and a judicially approved warrant are not required to search. [**Griffin v. Wisconsin**, 479 U.S. 1053 (1987)] Furthermore, the Court reasoned that the rehabilitative and preventative goals of probation would be disserved by a warrant requirement.

(2) Search by the Police

The Court has upheld a warrantless search of a probationer's home on reasonable suspicion by a ***police officer investigating criminal activity***. [**United States v. Knights**, 534 U.S. 112 (2001)] In ***Knights***, the defendant had agreed that as a condition of probation, he would submit to searches by any probation officer or law enforcement officer at any time, with or without a search warrant or reasonable suspicion. The Court did not decide whether the defendant's acceptance of this condition constituted a consent to search, but rather ruled that under the totality of circumstances, the search was reasonable under the Fourth Amendment because the defendant had a diminished expectation of privacy based on the parole condition, and the government has a heightened need to search probationers' homes because they are less likely than the general population to be law abiding.

h. Search of Parolee

The Supreme Court has upheld a warrantless search of a parolee by a police officer without reasonable suspicion under a statute similar to the statute involved in ***Knights***. [**Samson v. California**, 547 U.S. 843 (2006)]

i. Government Employees' Exceptions

(1) Desk

A warrantless search of a government employee's desk and file cabinet is permissible under the Fourth Amendment if the search is reasonable in scope and justified at its inception by a non-investigatory, work-related need or a ***reasonable suspicion*** of work-related misconduct. Probable cause is not required. [**O'Connor v. Ortega**, 480 U.S. 709 (1987)—doctor in public hospital suspected of work-related misconduct] The Court noted that the delay involved in obtaining a warrant would cause an unreasonable hardship on employers and might jeopardize the agency's work and the public good.

(2) Pager

A city's warrantless review of transcripts of an employee's text messages sent and received on a city-issued pager was reasonable because the review was motivated by the city's legitimate work-related purpose of determining whether a cap on the number of texts was sufficient to meet the city's work needs. [**City of Ontario v. Quon**, 560 U.S. 746 (2010)]

j. Drug Testing Exception

The Court has relaxed the Fourth Amendment with regard to employee drug testing. Such testing constitutes a search when administered by the government or a government agent, but the Court has upheld drug testing without a warrant and without probable cause (indeed, without even individualized suspicion). [**Skinner v. Railway Labor Executives' Association**, 489 U.S. 602 (1989); **National Treasury Employees Union v. Von Raab**, 489 U.S. 656 (1989)] The Court's rationale in these cases seems to be similar to its rationale for warrantless searches of highly regulated industries—*i.e.,* urgent public interest.

(1) Railroad Accidents

The Court upheld a regulation requiring any railroad employee who is involved in an accident or suspected of violating certain rules to submit to a blood or breath test for alcohol or drugs. [**Skinner v. Railway Labor Executives' Association**, *supra*] *Rationale*: The railroad is a highly regulated industry, and the government has a legitimate interest in taking all steps necessary to prevent hazardous conduct on the railroads. Because of the secretive nature of drug use, it is reasonable and necessary for the government to administer such tests to employees engaged in safety sensitive tasks.

(2) Customs Position Involving Drugs or Weapons

The Court approved a requirement of the United States Customs agency that anyone who applies for, or seeks promotion to, a customs position connected with drug interdiction, the use of weapons, or access to classified material be tested for drug use. [**National Treasury Employees Union v. Von Raab**, *supra*, p. 74] *Rationale*: It is reasonable for the government to require testing here because of the government's need to prevent promotion of drug users to positions that might endanger national borders or the safety of citizens.

(3) Students in Extracurricular Activities

The Court upheld a school district rule requiring students who participate in extracurricular activities to submit to drug testing. [**Board of Education v. Earls**, *supra*, p. 73]

(4) Tests for Sobriety of Drivers—Not Administrative

When police suspect drunk driving, they may compel the driver to submit to a warrantless breath test incident to a lawful arrest of the driver, but may not, without an exigency, require the driver to submit to a blood draw to determine sobriety. Breath tests "do not implicate significant privacy concerns." They don't pierce the skin, and they entail minimum inconvenience. In contrast, blood tests pierce the skin, "extract a part of the subject's body[,]" and "place in the hands of law enforcement authorities a sample that can be preserved and from which it is possible to extract information beyond a simple BAC reading." [**Missouri v. McNeely**, 569 U.S. 141 (2013); **Birchfield v. North Dakota**, 579 U.S. 438 (2016)]

(5) Power Not Limitless

The Court has indicated that the government's drug testing power is not without limit. A Georgia law required candidates for a number of state offices to certify that within 30 days prior to qualifying for nomination or election, they had taken a drug test and that the result was negative. The Supreme Court found this unreasonable under the Fourth Amendment. The Court explained that ordinarily searches must be based on individualized suspicion absent ***"special need."*** No special need was shown here. There was no indication that there is a suspicion of drug use by state officials. Moreover, the testing was not likely to deter drug use, because the time of testing was selected by the candidate. [**Chandler v. Miller**, 520 U.S. 305 (1997)] The Court distinguished **Von Raab**, *supra,* a case in which there also was little evidence of abuse. Elected officials are not like the employees in ***Von Raab,*** who were working in drug interdiction, had ready access to large quantities of drugs, and were not subject to the day-to-day scrutiny to which an elected official is subject.

e.g. **Example:** To stem the rise in cocaine use by pregnant women, a state hospital, in cooperation with local police, developed a program in which they would test pregnant women's urine for drug use and turn over positive tests to the police. The Court held that the balancing test employed in ***Skinner*** and ***Von Raab,*** *supra*—weighing the intrusion into the individual's privacy interest against the special needs that supported the drug testing programs in each case—was not appropriate here. In those cases, the special need was divorced from the state's general interest in law enforcement. Here, the central purpose of the testing program was to generate evidence that may be used by law enforcement personnel to coerce women into drug programs. Warrantless, suspicionless, nonconsensual searches cannot be justified on these grounds. [**Ferguson v. Charleston**, *supra,* p. 66]

9. General Evidence-Gathering Limitations

Due process of law requires that state criminal prosecutions not be conducted in an unfair manner. Accordingly, ***evidence*** that has been obtained by means that "shock the conscience" will ***not*** be admissible, even though no specific rule has been violated. Furthermore, if the ***actions of government officials*** encourage the commission of a crime in a way that "shocks the conscience," any subsequent conviction for the crime violates due process.

e.g. **Example:** Defendant was restrained while a heroin capsule was removed from his stomach at the hospital by a stomach pump. The action of the police in obtaining the capsule "shocks the conscience." [**Rochin v. California**, 342 U.S. 165 (1952)]

a. Compelled Surgery

To determine whether surgery is necessary to remove evidence of a crime, the individual's interest in privacy must be weighed against the state's need for the evidence. [**Winston v. Lee**, 470 U.S. 753 (1985)]

e.g. **Example:** A robbery victim shot his robber. Defendant was arrested and charged with the robbery. The state sought to remove a bullet lodged in Defendant's collarbone to prove that it was fired from the victim's gun. The state's need for the evidence was not great, because the victim had identified Defendant as the robber. Moreover, there was testimony that the bullet might not be useful because it might have corroded. On the other hand, there was testimony that the surgery could last two hours, would require general anesthetic, and would cause some damage to Defendant's nerves, vessels, and tissue. Under these circumstances, the Court prohibited the operation, finding that Defendant's interests in privacy and bodily integrity outweighed the state's need for the evidence. [**Winston v. Lee**, *supra*]

Chapter Three

Fifth Amendment Privilege Against Self-Incrimination

CONTENTS	PAGE

Key Exam Issues

The Fifth Amendment privilege against self-incrimination is an important part of most Criminal Procedure courses. There are a few things you need to remember. The privilege can be applied ***only if***:

(i) The prosecutor seeks to admit the ***defendant's own statements*** (*i.e.*, not statements made by other people);

(ii) The defendant's statements are ***testimonial*** in nature (*i.e.*, not blood samples, fingerprints, etc.);

(ii) The statements might be ***incriminating*** (*i.e.*, could provide a ***link*** to a crime); and

(iii) The statements ***may be used against the defendant*** (*i.e.*, if the defendant is wholly immunized or if the statute of limitations on the offense has run, the privilege cannot be invoked).

Keep in mind that no penalty can be attached for the defendant's assertion of the privilege (*i.e.*, a prosecutor may not comment on a defendant's failure to testify at trial).

Let's turn our attention to the Fifth Amendment topic most tested on by law professors: ***confessions***. Here, the issue is whether the defendant's confession can be admitted into evidence over defense objection. Under these circumstances, the defendant may make three distinct constitutional challenges:

1. **Due Process Approach**

   Under the Due Process Clause, confession issues involve the ***voluntariness*** of the statement: Was the defendant freely speaking at the time she confessed? A Due Process approach requires a case-by-case totality of the circumstances analysis involving careful review of all relevant facts (*i.e.*, the actions and behavior of the law enforcement officers and the suspect's knowledge, age, experience, etc.). A Due Process objection can be raised to confessions obtained ***before*** formal adversarial proceedings have been initiated against the suspect. However, the defense will need compelling facts to convince a court that a confession was involuntary. In addition, even if the defendant can prove on appeal that the jury mistakenly heard an involuntary confession, this will not necessarily result in a reversal of the conviction, because the harmless error test applies.

2. **Right to Counsel Approach**

   A confession can also be excluded if it violates the Sixth Amendment right to counsel. After the right has attached, ***interrogation*** (whether or not covert) ***cannot take place*** unless the defendant is told that she may have her attorney present. The critical limitation here is that the right to counsel ***does not attach until after the initiation of adversary judicial proceedings*** (*i.e.*, indictment by a grand jury, a preliminary hearing or arraignment, or any other proceeding where a suspect is formally charged with a crime) against the defendant.

3. **Self-Incrimination Approach**

   The self-incrimination approach covers the largest amount of doctrine in this area, with the primary focus on **Miranda v. Arizona.** While defendants' ***Miranda*** rights have been significantly narrowed over time, the case remains good law and is heavily considered in courts throughout the country. Like the Due Process approach, ***Miranda*** objections can be raised to confessions obtained ***before*** formal adversarial proceedings have been initiated against the suspect. The critical limitation here is that ***Miranda*** only precludes the prosecutor from using statements made ***in response to custodial interrogation by a government official*** as part of their case-in-chief. The four key ***Miranda*** questions that continue to be litigated are:

a. Were Warnings Properly Given?

You've probably watched enough police shows on television to know the warnings. Note that the four warnings need not be given in any particular order or with precise wording, but the gist of these points must be accurately conveyed to the defendant.

b. Was the Defendant in Custody?

Miranda applies only if the defendant was in custody. This means that investigatory questioning does not require ***Miranda*** warnings unless the suspect has been arrested or her ***freedom of movement has been significantly limited*** by the police. For example, routine traffic stops or voluntary appearances at the police station are not custody for ***Miranda*** purposes. Even a prisoner interrogated within a prison facility may not be "in custody" for ***Miranda*** purposes.

c. Were Defendant's Statements Made in Response to Interrogation?

Purely voluntary statements by suspects are not within the reach of the Fifth Amendment. So, the important question is whether the defendant's statements were made in response to interrogation. Because interrogation is not limited to traditional questioning by the police, you must carefully evaluate the facts. The issue is whether the police officers ***reasonably should have known*** that their words and actions would elicit an incriminating response.

Questions about whether a defendant was responding to interrogation may arise if she received warnings and, after deciding not to speak with the police, invoked her *Miranda* right to remain silent. Under these circumstances, if the suspect invoked only her ***right to silence***, a law enforcement officer could wait, re-warn, and reinterrogate the suspect. If the suspect has changed her mind and decided to waive her *Miranda* rights, the waiver would be effective because ***Miranda*** was not violated. In contrast, if a different defendant, instead invoked his ***right to an attorney***, the interrogation cannot resume unless either: (1) the attorney was present; or (2) the suspect himself initiated communication with the police on a topic related to the investigation. A suspect's invocation of their right to counsel remains effective for 14 days.

As with all other forms of waiver, the validity of a defendant's waiver of ***Miranda*** rights requires consideration of the ***totality of circumstances*** to decide whether the defendant made a knowing and voluntary decision to respond to law enforcement interrogation.

d. Can a Confession Obtained in Violation of *Miranda* Be Used by the Prosecutor?

Miranda only prevents the prosecutor from using confessions to prove the defendant's guilt as part of the case-in-chief. This means that prosecutors can still use confessions that violate ***Miranda*** for other purposes. They can be used in the grand jury. Because the "Fruit of the Poisonous Tree Doctrine" does not apply to such confessions, derivative physical evidence will not be excluded. They are also admissible for impeachment, if a defendant testifies in a manner inconsistent with the confession.

You should remember that statements that violate ***Miranda*** are treated differently from statements that directly violate the constitution. Statements that result from a direct violation (*i.e.*, involuntary statements) may not be used at trial for any purpose and derivative evidence resulting from such statements that do not fit an exception (*e.g.*, inevitable discovery) should be excluded as well.

A. Privilege Against Self-Incrimination

1. Constitutional Basis

The Fifth Amendment guarantees that "no person shall be compelled in any criminal case to be a witness against himself." This privilege against [compulsory] self-incrimination was made applicable to the states in **Malloy v. Hogan**, *supra,* p. 3.

2. Purpose of the Privilege Against Self-Incrimination

The privilege against self-incrimination has a three-fold purpose:

a. Reliability

Compelled testimony that is self-incriminating is often the product of coercion and not a product of the defendant's free will. For this reason, compelled testimony may be unreliable evidence. Confessions obtained by coercion are often made by an accused simply to end the interrogation. Extensive valid empirical evidence has demonstrated that, especially under the threat of physical pain or terror, an innocent person might confess to a crime they did not commit.

b. Avoidance of Coercion

The bar against compelled self-incrimination also provides a safeguard against the use of coercion or torture by government agents in efforts to secure confessions. *Rationale*: If evidence obtained through coercive methods will be excluded at trial, and as a result a guilty person might go free, government agents should avoid such methods.

c. Conformance with Adversarial System

The privilege against self-incrimination reflects the fact that our legal system is adversarial, not inquisitorial, in nature. The accused is not expected to prove innocence; instead, the government must shoulder the burden of proving the defendant's guilt with relevant and reliable evidence obtained without torture or coercion.

3. Who May Assert the Privilege

Only ***natural persons*** may assert the privilege against self-incrimination—not corporations, associations, or partnerships. [**United States v. White**, 322 U.S. 694 (1944); *and see* **Bellis v. United States**, 417 U.S. 85 (1974)] The privilege is ***personal*** and can be asserted by a party only when her testimony will be self-incriminating. The Fifth Amendment does not preclude the admission of testimony that will incriminate another person or testimony from another person that will incriminate the defendant. Although the privilege is personal, an attorney may assert the privilege for the benefit of a client. [**Fisher v. United States**, *supra,* p. 38]

4. When the Privilege Against Self-Incrimination May Be Asserted

The privilege can be ***asserted at any proceeding*** (*e.g.,* criminal, civil, administrative) at which the government ***might compel incriminating testimony*** from the person asserting the privilege ***for use in a later criminal prosecution***. The privilege can be asserted ***at any stage of the proceeding*** (*e.g.,* pretrial proceedings, grand jury investigations, custodial interrogations). The privilege can be asserted, even if the witness claims innocence, as long as the ***witness***

reasonably fears that her testimony could lead to prosecution. [**Ohio v. Reiner**, 532 U.S. 17 (2001)(babysitter, who claimed to have had nothing to do with baby's death, could properly assert the privilege at baby's father's trial for murder because father's experts had testified that baby's fatal injuries could have been caused by babysitter). *See also* **Wallace v. Branker**, 354 F. App'x 807, 824 (4th Cir. 2009) (the Privilege Against Self-Incrimination extends to a witness's answers that "would furnish a link in the chain of evidence needed to prosecute.")]

a. Assertion Required

An individual must claim the privilege against self-incrimination at the time of questioning. Otherwise, her testimony may later be used against her in a criminal prosecution. The individual cannot answer a question voluntarily and later claim the privilege prohibits the use of her answer. Similarly, an individual cannot merely remain silent when questioned. The privilege must be asserted to protect the witness from contempt for failing to answer.

b. Method for Asserting the Privilege

A criminal defendant has a right not to take the witness stand at trial. Other witnesses must rely on the privilege to avoid answering questions that could subject them to prosecution.

(1) Presumed Assertion During Questioning

Under ***Miranda***, which governs custodial police interrogations [*see infra,* p. 78], the privilege against self-incrimination is automatically asserted. Thus, statements made in response to custodial police interrogation are generally not admissible to prove the defendant's guilt unless the defendant affirmatively (although not necessarily expressly, *see infra,* p. 108) waived her ***Miranda*** rights.

5. Scope of the Privilege Against Self-Incrimination

a. What Testimony Is Incriminating

The Fifth Amendment bars only compulsory "self-incriminating" testimony, but the Supreme Court has held that the word "incriminating" must be broadly construed. In a longstanding and often cited case, the Court held that a witness may refuse to answer any question if the answer might furnish a "link in the chain of evidence needed to prosecute." [**Hoffman v. United States**, 341 U.S. 479 (1951)]

e.g. **Example:** In ***Hoffman,*** the defendant, a known criminal underworld figure, refused to answer questions about his present occupation or about whether he had seen a friend who was a fugitive witness. The Court held that the defendant had validly asserted the privilege and was not required to respond.

cf. **Compare:** Merely being required to furnish one's name after a ***Terry*** stop (*see supra*, pp. 26–29, 58–59) generally does not violate the Fifth Amendment because the disclosure of one's name typically poses no danger of self-incrimination. [**Hiibel v. Sixth Judicial District Court**, *supra*, p. 24] However, the ***Hiibel*** Court left open the possibility that the compelled revelation of one's name might be incriminating if it provided the police with a link in the chain of evidence needed to convict the defendant of some crime.

(1) Foreign Prosecutions

A foreign prosecution is not considered a "criminal case" under the Fifth Amendment. Thus a person has no self-incrimination privilege to refuse to answer a question based on the fear that the answer could be used against him in a criminal prosecution by a foreign government. [**United States v. Balsys**, 524 U.S. 666 (1998)—no privilege for person who refused to answer question about wartime activities between 1940 and 1944, because U.S. criminal statute of limitations had run, even though foreign governments could use answers against defendant in foreign prosecutions]

(2) Overruling the Claim

Once a witness asserts the privilege by claiming that the response to a question would be self-incriminating, the judge can overrule the witness if the prosecutor has made it "perfectly clear" that the answer cannot tend to incriminate the witness. [**Hoffman v. United States**, *supra,* p. 81] Usually, courts err on the side of supporting the individual's privilege claim, because the state can compel the witness to respond by granting immunity. (*See infra,* p. 87.)

b. Only Testimonial Incrimination Covered

The seizure of "real or physical" incriminating evidence from a defendant implicates no Fifth Amendment rights; the privilege bars only compelled ***testimony***. Thus, the Fifth Amendment does not apply to real or physical evidence. The state ***may*** compel blood samples and voice and handwriting exemplars without violating the privilege against compulsory self-incrimination. [**Schmerber v. California**, *supra*, p. 65—blood samples; **Gilbert v. California**, 388 U.S. 263 (1967)—writing samples; **United States v. Wade**, 388 U.S. 218 (1967)—voice exemplars] The state can also require a defendant to produce a fingerprint, stand in a lineup, or submit to the taking of a photograph without violating the privilege. [**United States v. Wade**, *supra*]

(1) Distinguish—Custodial Interrogation and Lie Detector Tests

The state ***cannot*** compel a person to undergo custodial police interrogation or to take a lie detector (*i.e.*, polygraph) test without violating Fifth Amendment rights. [**Miranda v. Arizona**, *infra,* p. 78]

(2) Refusals to Submit to Blood Tests

The Fifth Amendment does ***not*** prevent the prosecution from introducing into evidence an alleged drunk driver's refusal to submit to a blood alcohol test even though he was not warned that his refusal might be used against him. [**South Dakota v. Neville**, 459 U.S. 553 (1983)]

(3) Execution of Consent Forms Is Not Testimonial Incrimination

The Fifth Amendment is not violated when the government compels a suspect to sign consent forms directing foreign banks to release records of accounts controlled by the suspect. According to the Supreme Court, forcing the suspect to sign consent forms is not testimonial, because a signature does not relate a factual assertion or disclose information. As long as the forms do not refer to a specific account or require the suspect to acknowledge the existence of any account, the signing of the forms is not testimonial. [**Doe v. United States**, 487 U.S. 201 (1988)]

EXAM TIP

If an exam question presents a person pleading "the Fifth," keep in mind that ***only testimonial evidence*** is protected by the Fifth Amendment proscription against compelled self-incrimination. Non-testimonial evidence, such as pictures, blood samples, voice samples, handwriting samples, consent forms, and the like are ***not*** protected. Requiring individuals to provide their names to law enforcement is also not protected.

c. Books, Papers, and Documents

Fifth Amendment protection for books and papers is very limited. The compelled production of documents and other records, even if the evidence tends to incriminate the producer, does ***not*** involve testimonial self-incrimination and thus is generally outside the scope of the privilege.

e.g. **Example:** A custodian of corporate records may not resist a subpoena for such records on the ground that the production would incriminate him in violation of the Fifth Amendment. The production of the records by the custodian is not considered a personal act, but an act of the corporation, which possesses no privilege against self-incrimination. [**Braswell v. United States**, 487 U.S. 99 (1988)]

e.g. **Example:** Defendant argued that compliance with a subpoena for accountant's records that Defendant had given his attorney violated his privilege against self-incrimination. The Court rejected Defendant's argument, noting that the papers had been voluntarily prepared and, as such, the subpoena had not compelled the creation of the incriminating information contained in the sought documents. [**Fisher v. United States**, *supra*, p. 38]

(1) And Note

The Supreme Court later ruled that the seizure of papers from a petitioner's office did not implicate the Fifth Amendment because the seizure was of real or physical evidence. [**Andresen v. Maryland**, *supra,* p. 44]

d. When Does a Violation Occur?

A violation of the Self-incrimination Clause does not occur until a person's compelled statements are used against him in a criminal case. [**Chavez v. Martinez**, 538 U.S. 760 (2003)]

e.g. **Example:** While Martinez was being treated for a gunshot wound that he received in an altercation with the police, he was interrogated by an officer without having been given ***Miranda*** warnings (*see infra,* pp. 78 *et seq.*). Although Martinez admitted to using heroin and that he had taken an officer's gun during the incident in which he was shot, he was never charged with a crime. Nevertheless, Martinez sued police officers for violating his Fifth Amendment right against compelled self-incrimination.

Held: Because Martinez had not been charged with a crime, there was no Fifth Amendment violation, as the statements were never introduced against him in a criminal proceeding. [**Chavez v. Martinez**, *supra*]

6. Compulsion Requirement

The Fifth Amendment only bars the use of ***compelled*** self-incriminating testimony. The issue of whether testimony is compelled often arises where statutes require reporting or registration. Generally, courts presume that sufficient compulsion flows from any governmental questioning. The Supreme Court has held, however, that certain situations lack sufficient compulsion to trigger the Fifth Amendment:

a. Notice Requirement for Affirmative Defense

Under the criminal procedure codes of many states, a defendant who seeks to raise an alibi defense must first provide notice to the prosecution. The Supreme Court has ruled that this notice requirement is not unconstitutional compulsion, because there is no requirement that a defendant raise an alibi defense. [**Williams v. Florida**, 399 U.S. 78 (1970)]

b. Reporting—Required Records Test

When a law requires that certain records be kept and such records relate to a lawful administrative purpose, and not to the enforcement of criminal laws, the compulsory maintenance and/or production of such records is ***not*** protected by the Fifth Amendment. Thus, any self-incriminating information an individual reports in those records can be used against him in a criminal prosecution. [**Shapiro v. United States**, 335 U.S. 1 (1948)]

(1) Tax Returns

The Fifth Amendment does not protect an individual who fails to file a tax return even if the individual's income is illegal. A taxpayer may leave blanks on the income tax return if the required information would tend to incriminate them, but may not fail to file a return. [**United States v. Sullivan**, 274 U.S. 259 (1927)]

e.g. **Example:** Where Defendant had reported his occupation as "professional gambler" and substantial income from "gambling" or "wagering" on his federal tax return, the introduction of the return into evidence to support his conviction for "fixing" sporting events did not violate his privilege because he voluntarily supplied the incriminating information. Defendant could have asserted his privilege against self-incrimination in filling out his returns, but did not choose to do so. Because he completed his tax return at his leisure in private, his incriminating responses were not compelled and introduction of them into evidence to support his conviction violated no Fifth Amendment right. [**Garner v. United States**, 424 U.S. 648 (1976)]

(2) Blood Testing

When a person suspected of drunk driving refused to submit to a blood-alcohol test after having been informed that he could either consent to the test or refuse and have his license suspended, there was no compulsion, and the police could testify to the suspect's refusal to take the blood-alcohol test. [**South Dakota v. Neville**, *supra*, p. 82]

(3) Abused Child

The state can require a person civilly charged with being an unfit mother to produce her child. [**Baltimore City Department of Social Services v. Bouknight**, 493 U.S. 549 (1990)] *Rationale*: Although producing the child may be testimonial, the matter is civil in nature rather than punitive (the state is trying to enforce important civil policy—protecting children from abuse—not punish the mother). Therefore, the production is not protected by the Fifth Amendment.

(4) Prison Sexual Abuse Treatment Program

The Supreme Court has held that compelling a prisoner to disclose all prior sexual activities, including activities constituting uncharged criminal offenses, to enter a sexual abuse treatment program does not raise privilege concerns. The Fifth Amendment does not apply, even if the prisoner who refuses to comply will be transferred from a medium security facility to a maximum security facility and deprived of visitation rights, prison work and earnings opportunities, and other privileges. [**McKune v. Lile**, 536 U.S. 24 (2002)]

c. Registration Requirements

The Fifth Amendment prohibits statutory registration schemes only when three factors are present: (i) the registration statute is ***directed at a specific group***; (ii) the group is ***inherently suspect*** of criminal activity; and (iii) the inquiry is into an ***area of law permeated with criminal statutes***. This three-part test was first applied to strike down provisions of the Subversive Activities Control Act, which required Communists to register with the government. [**Albertson v. Subversive Activities Control Board**, 382 U.S. 70 (1965)]

(1) Other Applications

The three-part test of ***Albertson*** has been applied to invalidate, on Fifth Amendment grounds, a registration and tax for gamblers [**Marchetti v. United States**, 390 U.S. 39 (1968)]; a firearms registration tax [**Haynes v. United States**, 390 U.S. 85 (1968)]; a federal excise tax on wagering [**Grosso v. United States**, 390 U.S. 62 (1968)]; and reporting provisions of the Marijuana Tax Act [**Leary v. United States**, 395 U.S. 6 (1969)]

(2) "Hit and Run" Statute Upheld

In **California v. Byers**, 402 U.S. 424 (1971), the Supreme Court applied the *Albertson* criteria to ***uphold*** a California law that required motorists involved in accidents to leave their names at the scene of an accident. A plurality of the Court found that the statutory reporting requirement did not entail a "substantial risk of self-incrimination."

d. No Protection for False Statements

An individual who is required to register or report information may not avoid self-incrimination by making false statements but must instead invoke the privilege.

e. Mental Illness

A defendant's confession or self-incriminating statements are not "compelled" simply because they were prompted by a mental illness that impedes the defendant's ability to exercise free will. Some ***official compulsion or coercion*** (*i.e.*, from law enforcement) must be present for a statement to be inadmissible under the Fifth Amendment. [**Colorado v. Connelly**, 479 U.S. 157 (1986)—Defendant, a schizophrenic, confessed to a murder after the "voice of God" told him to lead police to the scene of the killing; confession should not be suppressed because the Court found no police overreaching]

f. Use of Compelled Testimony

Testimony compelled in violation of a defendant's rights may be used against the defendant in a subsequent proceeding ***for perjury***. [**Butterfield v. State**, 992 S.W.2d 448 (Tex. 1999); *and see* **United States v. Wong**, 431 U.S. 174 (1977)—testimony obtained after an ineffective warning regarding the privilege against self-incrimination may be admissible in a subsequent perjury case]

EXAM TIP

For exam purposes, two of the most important things to remember about the privilege against self-incrimination are:

- Only ***testimonial*** evidence is protected. Therefore, a defendant cannot raise a Fifth Amendment self-incrimination objection to the admission of a lineup or other identification procedure—even if he is asked to say certain words (*e.g.*, "Your money or your life!"). Such procedures typically do not involve testimonial evidence because words are used solely for identification purposes.
- Only ***compelled*** testimonial evidence is privileged. Thus, if defendant produced a writing of his own free will (*e.g.*, took incriminating notes of a meeting), the police may seize this writing, or the defendant may be compelled to produce it by subpoena, because he was not compelled to make the statement originally.

7. Efforts to Burden Assertion of the Privilege Against Self-Incrimination

The state may not chill the exercise of the privilege by penalizing those who invoke it.

a. Penalties for Failure to Testify

The state may not fire police officers for invoking the privilege during an investigation. [**Garrity v. New Jersey**, 385 U.S. 493 (1967)] Nor may the state invalidate preexisting state contracts or prohibit a person from holding a party office for exercising the privilege. [**Lefkowitz v. Turley**, 414 U.S. 70 (1973)—contracts; **Lefkowitz v. Cunningham**, 431 U.S. 801 (1977)—party office]

b. Comments on Defendant's Silence

At trial, a prosecutor may not mention or question the defendant regarding her ***silence after receiving Miranda warnings*** (*see infra,* pp. 97 *et seq.*). The warnings carry an implicit guarantee that silence will carry no penalty. [**Doyle v. Ohio**, 426 U.S. 610 (1976)] A prosecutor may, however, comment on a defendant's silence in response to police questions, if such silence occurred before the defendant was in custody and ***before Miranda warnings*** were given. [**Salinas v. Texas**, 570 U.S. 178 (2013)]

(1) Insanity Defense

A prosecutor may not use the defendant's silence after receiving the ***Miranda*** warnings to rebut the defendant's claim of insanity. [**Wainwright v. Greenfield**, 474 U.S. 284 (1986)]

(2) Harmless Error

However, a single improper question by a prosecutor regarding the defendant's silence after receiving the warnings is not ground for reversal if the trial court sustained an objection to the question and instructed the jury to disregard the question. [**Greer v. Miller**, 483 U.S. 756 (1987)]

c. Comments on Defendant's Failure to Testify

A prosecutor may not comment on the defendant's ***failure to testify at trial***. [**Griffin v. California**, 380 U.S. 609 (1965)] A defendant, upon timely request, is also entitled to have the trial judge ***instruct the jury members*** that they are to draw ***no adverse inference*** from the defendant's failure to testify. [**Carter v. Kentucky**, 450 U.S. 288 (1981)]

The Supreme Court has yet to decide whether such admonition is necessary during the penalty phase of a case. [**White v. Woodall**, 572 U.S. 415 (2014)] At trial, the "no adverse inference" instruction may be given over the defendant's objection without violating the Fifth Amendment privilege. [**Lakeside v. Oregon**, 435 U.S. 333 (1978)—defendant argued that the instruction called the jury's attention to the failure to testify]

(1) Harmless Error

The "harmless error" test should be applied where the prosecutor commented on the defendant's failure to rebut the victim's testimony, if there exists overwhelming evidence of the defendant's guilt and the defendant's evidence was scanty and inconsistent. [**United States v. Hasting**, 461 U.S. 499 (1983)]

(2) Exception

The prosecutor ***may*** comment on the defendant's failure to take the stand if the comment is in response to defense counsel's assertion that the defendant was not allowed to explain his side of the story. [**United States v. Robinson**, 485 U.S. 25 (1988)]

8. Eliminating the Privilege

As previously discussed, the privilege can be asserted only when the government seeks to ***compel*** someone to ***incriminate*** themselves using their own ***testimony***. The privilege does not apply when there is no possibility of incrimination because: (1) the defendant has been granted immunity; (2) the statute of limitations has run; or (3) the privilege has been waived. In these situations, a witness can be compelled to testify on pain of contempt.

a. Immunity

When an individual is granted immunity, she can be compelled to testify because immunity, by promising that a prosecution will not occur, eliminates the possibility of self-incrimination. Thus, failure to testify post-immunity may lead to civil or criminal contempt of court.

(1) Types of Immunity

Two types of immunity exist. The first, which is narrower, is ***use*** and ***derivative use immunity***, barring use of any immunized testimony and any evidence derived from immunized testimony. The second, which is more expansive, is ***transactional immunity***, which protects the witness from being prosecuted for any activity mentioned in the immunized testimony.

(a) Use and Derivative Use Immunity Sufficient

The Supreme Court has held that prosecutors need only grant use and derivative use immunity to compel an unwilling individual to testify. The Court held that this type of immunity is coextensive with the privilege against self-incrimination, even though such immunity does not guarantee that the witness will not be prosecuted. Use and derivative use immunity only ensures that her testimony and evidence derived from that testimony will not be used against her. [**Kastigar v. United States**, 406 U.S. 441 (1972)]

1) Burden of Proof

When prosecuting a previously immunized witness, the government must show by a preponderance of the evidence that the evidence used in the prosecution is independent of the immunized testimony. [**Kastigar v. United States**, *supra*] Some courts have held that such proof requires a thorough review of the record to ensure that no immunized testimony was improperly used. [**United States v. Slough**, 641 F.3d 544 (D.C. Cir. 2011); **United States v. North**, 910 F.2d 843 (D.C. Cir.), ***reversed in part on other grounds***, 920 F.2d 940 (D.C. Cir. 1990)]

(2) Use of Testimony by Another Sovereign Impermissible

The privilege prohibits a state from compelling testimony under a grant of immunity if such testimony might be used by a federal prosecutor. Therefore, federal prosecutors may not use evidence obtained as a result of a state grant of immunity, and vice versa. [**Murphy v. Waterfront Commission**, 378 U.S. 52 (1964), ***but see*** **United States v. Balsys**, 524 U.S. 666, 687–88 (1998) (noting that ***Murphy*** partially rests on unsound historical assumptions)]

(3) Immunized Testimony Cannot be Used for Impeachment

A state cannot use immunized testimony to impeach a defendant. In **New Jersey v. Portash**, *supra,* p. 10, the Supreme Court held that immunized testimony is of its very essence coerced, because once immunity is granted the witness must answer questions and does not have the option to remain silent. Thus, use of the immunized testimony against the defendant either as part of the state's case-in-chief or to impeach violates the privilege.

(a) Distinguish—Prosecution for Perjury

Immunized testimony may be used against a defendant in a prosecution for perjury. [**United States v. Apfelbaum**, 445 U.S. 115 (1980)]

b. Statute of Limitations

If the relevant statute of limitations has expired there is no possibility of prosecution and the individual can be compelled to testify. [*See, e.g.,* **United States v. Balsys**, *supra*, p. 82—no privilege for person who refused to answer questions about wartime activities between 1940 and 1944 because statute of limitations had run]

c. Waiver

The privilege bars only ***coerced*** testimony. An individual may expressly waive the protection of the privilege. In some situations, the Supreme Court has held that such waivers need not be express.

(1) Waiver by Defendant

A defendant who waives the privilege to provide direct testimony opens herself to cross-examination on the matters relevant to the substance of her testimony or designed to impeach her credibility. [**Brown v. United States**, 356 U.S. 148 (1958)]

(2) Waiver by Witness Other than Defendant

An admission by a nondefendant witness of a self-incriminating fact is a waiver of the privilege with respect to the details of that admission. [**Rogers v. United States**, 340 U.S. 367 (1951)] But a witness cannot be compelled to provide further information if it will increase the risk of the witness's conviction or create a risk of their conviction for a different offense.

e.g. **Example:** Witness appeared before a grand jury concerning her relationship with the Communist Party (an illegal activity at the time). On questioning, she admitted that she previously had party documents in her possession. When asked to whom she had given the documents, Witness invoked her privilege and refused to answer. Witness was then found guilty of contempt for her refusal to answer and the conviction was upheld. *Rationale*: Witness had voluntarily subjected herself to criminal penalty from her admission, so her admission of the details did not present a real danger of further incrimination. In contrast, allowing her to protect the details would distort the evidence, thwarting the judicial need for reliable evidence. [**Rogers v. United States**, *supra*]

B. Confessions

1. Due Process "Voluntariness" Approach

Before a confession of guilt will be admitted into evidence, the trial judge must find that it was ***voluntarily made***, as required by the Due Process Clauses of the Fifth and Fourteenth Amendments. The test for voluntariness is whether "the confession [was] the product of an essentially free and unconstrained choice by its maker." [**Culombe v. Connecticut**, 367 U.S. 568 (1961)]

APPROACH TO ADMISSIBILITY OF DEFENDANT'S CONFESSION

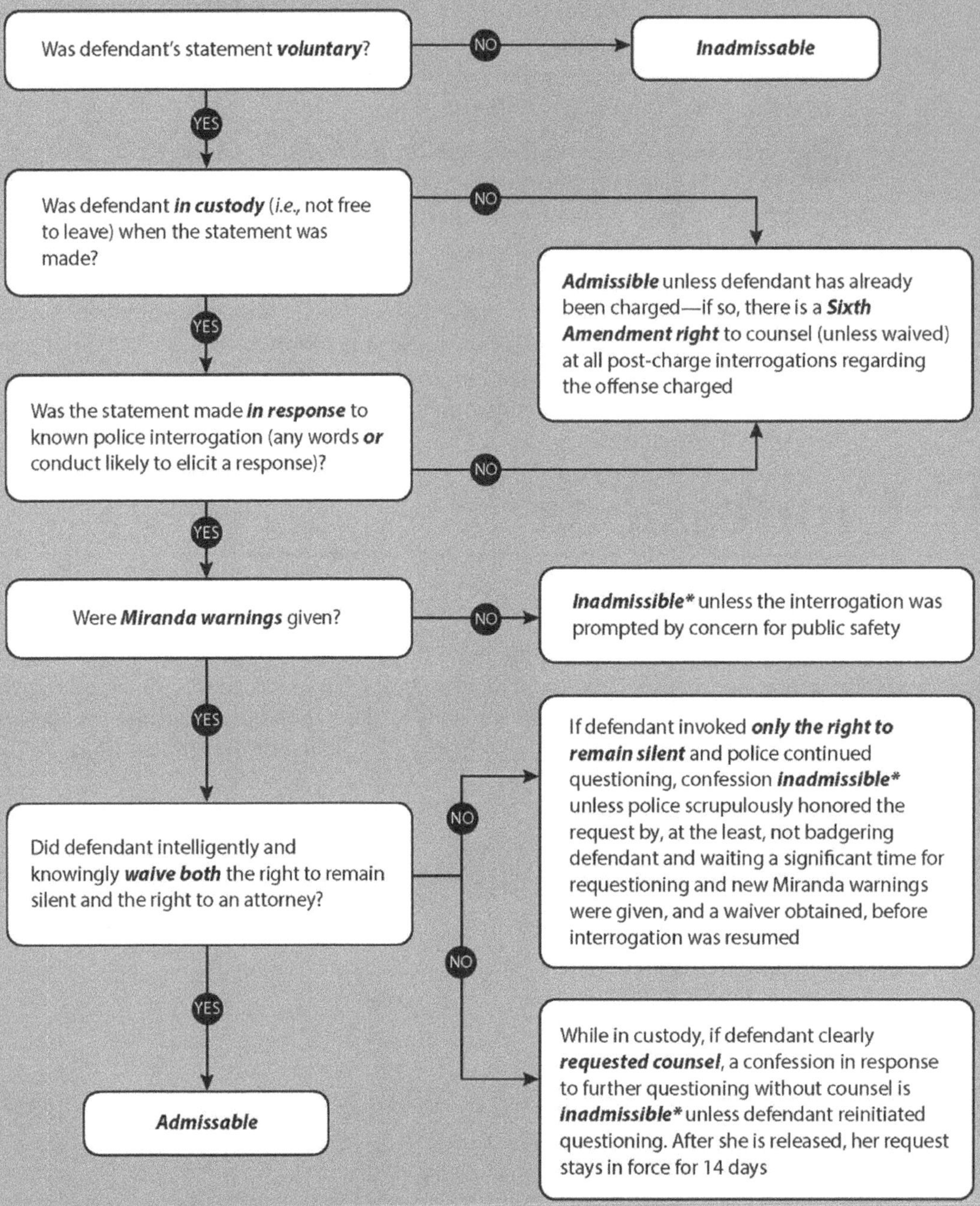

*These statements are indamissible at trial to prove guilt, but can be used in the grand jury, during cross-examination of the defendant, and any derivative evidence is admissible.

Note: Confessions obtained in violation of *Miranda* are admissible to ***impeach*** defendant's trial testimony.

And note: If inadmissible confessions are erroneously admitted into evidence, a resulting conviction need not be reversed if there is other overwhelming evidence of guilt (the "harmless error" test).

a. Purposes Served by Requirement

Three distinct purposes are served by requiring a confession to have been voluntarily made: (i) the interest in ***trustworthy evidence***, (ii) the preservation of ***individual freedom***

of choice, and (iii) the ***deterrence of unlawful police conduct***. [**Lego v. Twomey**, *supra,* p. 9]

b. Mere Reliability Insufficient

Proof that a compelled confession was reliable should not make it admissible. Even confessions that have some indicia of reliability should be excluded based on a finding of unlawful police conduct in violation of Due Process.

c. Application

(1) Procedure

Before the jury can hear a confession, the judge must determine that the confession was voluntarily given; this determination is made under a preponderance of the evidence standard. [**Jackson v. Denno**, *supra,* p. 9; **Lego v. Twomey**, *supra,* p. 9]

(a) Habeas Corpus Procedure

The voluntariness of a confession is an issue of law which the federal courts must evaluate independently in a federal habeas corpus proceeding. [**Miller v. Fenton**, 474 U.S. 104 (1986)]

(2) Factors

Whether a confession was voluntarily made is to be judged on a ***subjective*** basis considering the ***totality of the circumstances***. Thus, the question is not whether the will of a reasonable person would have been overborne by law enforcement under the circumstances, but ***whether defense counsel can prove that the defendant's will was actually overborne***, considering factors such as the following:

(i) The defendant's ***personal characteristics*** (*e.g.,* age, education, intelligence, experience, physical and mental health, etc.);

(ii) The ***nature of the detention*** (delays in arraignment, whether the defendant was advised of constitutional rights, the defendant's access to counsel and the outside world, conditions of confinement, etc.);

(iii) The ***manner of interrogation*** (length and number of sessions, number of interrogators, conditions of interrogation); [**United States v. Pena**, 115 F.4th 1254 (10th Cir. 2024) confession not coerced despite three officers questioning Defendant for almost four hours, implying that Defendant's children might commit suicide because of Defendant's actions, informing Defendant that his children had talked about committing suicide, exhorting Defendant to confess almost 100 times with phrases like "be honest" and "tell the truth," deceiving Defendant by telling him he was not a suspect, threatening jail time, implying Defendant could earn leniency by confessing]; and

(iv) The ***use of force, threats, promises, or deceptions***.

e.g. **Example:** Defendant, a Black man, was a suspect in the murder of a White farmer. To obtain a confession, the authorities beat Defendant severely and hanged him twice from a tree. Other Black suspects were jailed and repeatedly beaten until they also confessed. Based solely on these coerced confessions, Defendant was convicted and sentenced to death on the second day of the trial. The Court held that the admission into evidence of such a ***coerced*** confession is a due process violation. [**Brown v. Mississippi**, 297 U.S. 278 (1936)]

(a) Threats

Certain threats by law enforcement may render a suspect's statement involuntary, such as threats: (i) of physical violence; (ii) of refusal to provide necessary medication; (iii) to remove a defendant's spouse or children [*see, e.g.,* **Rogers v. Richmond**, 365 U.S. 534 (1961)]; (iv) to arrest or prosecute friends or relatives; and (v) of harsher consequences if a confession is not given [*see, e.g.,* **Lynumn v. Illinois**, 372 U.S. 528 (1963)—defendant's incriminating statements, made after defendant was told that cooperation would lead to leniency and that failure to cooperate could lead to loss of welfare benefits and custody of her children, were found to be coerced]

(b) Promises

Improper promises or inducements may also cause a confession to be considered involuntary. This occurs when a promised benefit is impossible, improper, or illusory (*e.g.,* promises by officers not to arrest or harass family and friends, or to grant a lenient sentence are generally prohibited).

1) Minority Position—Leniency and Collateral Benefits

Under traditional standards, promises of leniency would likely yield inadmissible statements. However, some states hold that offering collateral benefits that do not deal directly with the criminal charge or severity of the sentence do not make a statement involuntary. For example, promises to not arrest others, or to keep the defendant out of a certain prison, might not render a statement involuntary.

(c) Length of Interrogation

An unduly long interrogation may cause a confession to be considered involuntary.

e.g. **Example:** Police arrested Defendant and subjected him to questioning nonstop for 36 hours. Defendant confessed, but the confession was found to be involuntary. [**Ashcraft v. Tennessee**, 322 U.S. 143 (1944); *and see* **Chambers v. Florida**, 309 U.S. 227 (1940)—Defendant refused to confess during four days of interrogation but finally broke down on the fifth day after all-night interrogation session]

(d) Plea Bargain Confessions

Traditionally, statements obtained as a result of plea bargains or offers of immunity were inadmissible against the maker. However, the Supreme Court has declared that such statements are inadmissible ***only if they were required*** by the conditions of the plea. [**Hutto v. Ross**, 429 U.S. 28 (1976)] Therefore, even if a defendant subjectively believes that a confession is necessary to guarantee the plea, if a confession is not an ***explicit*** condition of the plea agreement, the confession will be admissible at trial.

1) Note

In proceedings on the merits, the Federal Rules of Evidence bar use of ***all*** confessions obtained in the course of plea discussions. [Fed. R. Evid. 410] However, such confessions may be used ***for impeachment purposes*** unless they are found to be involuntary.

2) **And Note**

If a defendant initiates the plea negotiation by offering a confession in return for some benefit, the defendant cannot later claim that the statement was involuntary.

(e) **Police Deception**

Statements obtained through deceit are generally admissible as long as the deceit does not nullify ***Miranda*** warnings (*see infra,* p. 107–108), circumvent the right to counsel, overbear the individual's will, falsely describe judicial proceedings, or call into question the reliability of the statement.

e.g. **Example:** If a defendant confesses after being falsely informed that there is an eyewitness to the crime, his confession is probably voluntary unless the defendant has already requested counsel.

1) **But Note**

Some courts have emphasized the difference between verbal falsehoods, which are usually permitted, and falsehoods included in documentation manufactured for the purpose of deceiving a defendant, which are more suspect. [**Gray v. Commonwealth**, 480 S.W.3d 253 (Ky. 2016)] False documentation can include false scientific evidence. [**State v. Cayward**, 552 So. 2d 971 (Fla.App.1989) (distinguishing deception generally from police-created false lab reports linking the suspect to the crime)]

2) **And Note**

Some courts distinguish between ***intrinsic lies*** (*e.g.,* those regarding strength of evidence, witnesses, etc.) and ***extrinsic falsehoods*** (*e.g.,* promises of favorable treatment, lies concerning the legal process, etc.). Intrinsic falsehoods will not necessarily invalidate a resulting confession, but extrinsic falsehoods should be "regarded as coercive per se." [*See, e.g.,* **State v. Kelekolio**, 849 P.2d 58 (Haw. 1993)]

e.g. **Example:** In **State v. Ritter**, 485 S.E.2d 492 (Ga. 1997), the court struck down Defendant's confession when it was based on "an implied promise that [he] could not be charged with murder if he gave a statement to the police, but could only be charged with aggravated assault."

(f) **Minors**

Statements made by minors are not presumed to be involuntary but the age and understanding of the individuals involved must be considered. In some states a minor must have the opportunity to consult with a parent or guardian prior to making a statement. Age is also a factor in whether a suspect is "in custody" for purposes of ***Miranda*** (*see infra*, pp. 101–102).

e.g. **Example:** Police questioned Defendant, a 15-year-old boy, from midnight until 5 a.m., when he confessed. The Supreme Court found the confession involuntary considering Defendant Defendant's age and the length and time of the interrogation. [**Haley v. Ohio**, 332 U.S. 596 (1948)]

(g) Mental Impairment

A person's mental impairment alone does not make a statement inadmissible, but it may be considered a factor in determining voluntariness. "All the circumstances attendant upon the confession must be taken into account." [**Reck v. Pate**, 367 U.S. 433 (1961)]

(h) Intoxication

The use of drugs or proof of addiction does not render a statement made under the influence inadmissible. However, other factors such as withdrawal symptoms may contribute to a decision that the statement was involuntary. [**State v. Granskie**, 77 A.3d 505 (N.J. Super. 2013)]

(3) Right to Challenge Court Determination

If the judge rules a confession voluntary, the defendant may still challenge the reliability of the confession by introducing proof of coercion to the jury. A judge's decision barring the defendant from introducing testimony about the environment in which the police secured the confession denies the defendant a meaningful opportunity to challenge the reliability of the confession and, therefore, denies the defendant due process. [**Crane v. Kentucky**, 476 U.S. 683 (1986)]

d. *McNabb-Mallory* Rule

In a series of cases decided before many of the recent major confession cases, the Supreme Court held that persons arrested in federal jurisdictions must be brought before a judicial officer "as soon as possible," so that the authorities would not hold an accused merely in hope of extracting a confession. The ***McNabb-Mallory*** rule provided that if law enforcement did not promptly take an arrestee to a judicial officer, any statement obtained from that person during the delay could not be admitted at trial. [**McNabb v. United States**, 318 U.S. 332 (1943); **Mallory v. United States**, 354 U.S. 449 (1957)]

In **Corley v. United States**, 556 U.S. 303 (2009), the Supreme Court explained the rule as follows: "In a world without ***McNabb-Mallory***, federal agents would be free to question suspects for extended periods before bringing them out into the open, and we have always known what custodial secrecy leads to. No one with any smattering of the history of 20th century dictatorships needs a lecture on the subject, and we understand the need even within our own system to take care against going too far. Custodial police interrogation, by its very nature, isolates and pressures the individual."

The ***McNabb-Mallory*** rule has been modified by a federal statute [18 U.S.C. § 3501(c)], providing that a confession "shall not be inadmissible solely because of delay in bringing such person before a magistrate," if the confession was made within six hours after arrest (or longer if the delay is reasonably attributable to transporting the defendant). [**United States v. Bin Laden**, 132 F. Supp. 2d 198, 207 n.12 (S.D.N.Y. 2001) ("section 3501 legislatively overruled the McNabb-Mallory rule only to the extent of (1) unreasonable pre-arraignment, pre-confession delays of less than six hours and (2) reasonable delays in excess of six hours.")]

e. Harmless Error Test Applies

In dicta, a majority of the Supreme Court agreed that the harmless error test should be applied to determine whether a conviction must be overturned because of the erroneous admission of a coerced confession. [**Arizona v. Fulminante**, 499 U.S. 279 (1991)—***not harmless error*** to admit Defendant's confession given to police-informer cellmate who had offered to protect Defendant from other prisoners in exchange for "the truth," because conviction appeared to be based on confession]

2. Sixth Amendment Right to Counsel Approach

Even if a statement is admissible under the voluntariness test, it may still be excluded from trial if the taking of the statement violated the defendant's Sixth Amendment right to counsel. The right is violated if, after adversary judicial proceedings have begun (*e.g.,* after indictment), the police question the defendant ***outside the presence of counsel or without a defendant's valid waiver of the right to counsel.*** [**Massiah v. United States**, 377 U.S. 201 (1964)—conversations overheard by law enforcement officers through a bug placed in defendant's car were inadmissible because the government had ***intentionally*** elicited incriminating evidence ***after indictment*** and in the ***absence of counsel***]

EXAM TIP

Note that there can be no violation of the Sixth Amendment right to counsel before formal proceedings have begun. Thus, a defendant who is ***arrested but not yet charged*** does not have a Sixth Amendment right to counsel. *But note*: He has a Fifth Amendment right to counsel under *Miranda* if he is being interrogated while in custody. (See *infra*, pp. 97 *et seq.*)

a. When Defendant Not Explicitly Questioned

The Sixth Amendment right to counsel can be violated even if the defendant is not explicitly questioned, when incriminating information was ***actively secured*** by government agents from the defendant without the presence of counsel. [*See* **United States v. Henry**, 447 U.S. 264 (1980)—cellmate initiated conversations with incarcerated defendant] The test is whether the government obtained incriminating statements by knowingly circumventing the accused's right to have counsel present in a confrontation between the accused and a government agent. [**Maine v. Moulton**, 474 U.S. 159 (1985)] The key question is whether the government officers or agents "deliberately elicited" the incriminating statement from the suspect. [**Fellers v. United States**, 540 U.S. 519 (2004)]

e.g. **Example:** The defendant's Sixth Amendment right to counsel was violated when the police arranged to record conversations between the defendant and a co-defendant (who was a government informant) at a meeting during which both defendants, without counsel, planned to discuss defense strategy. [**Maine v. Moulton**, *supra*]

cf. **Compare—Passive Listening:** It is not a violation merely to place an informer in a defendant's cell—the informer must take some action designed deliberately to elicit incriminating remarks beyond mere listening. [**Kuhlman v. Wilson**, 477 U.S. 436 (1986)] It is unclear when behavior becomes deliberate elicitation. For instance, an informant who starts a conversation may not be engaged in deliberate elicitation. Because state action is required, a prisoner who deliberately elicits information ***before*** becoming an informant cannot violate the accused's right to counsel.

b. When Defendant's Lawyer Is Not Present at Interrogation

The courts look carefully at confessions obtained from defendants who have retained lawyers when the police do not allow the lawyer to assist their client during interrogation. In such cases, the courts are more likely to find that the right to counsel has been violated.

e.g. **Example:** Defendant, an escapee from a mental hospital, was suspected of murdering a 10-year-old girl. On advice of counsel, Defendant turned himself in to police. The police promised Defendant and his attorney that they would not question Defendant until he had a chance to talk with his attorney. While transporting Defendant to a police station across the state, one of the detectives, who knew that Defendant was deeply religious, informed Defendant (in what became known as the "Christian burial speech") that they were predicting snow that night, that he thought Defendant was the only person who knew where the victim's body was located, that once it snowed Defendant might not be able to find the place again, and that "the parents of this little girl should be entitled to a Christian burial for the little girl who was snatched away from them on Christmas Eve and murdered." *Held:* The defendant's resulting statement was inadmissible, as Defendant had clearly invoked his right to counsel and the police ignored Defendant's invocation. [**Brewer v. Williams**, 430 U.S. 387 (1977)]

c. Offense Specific

The Sixth Amendment right to counsel is "offense specific." Only statements relating to the crime charged will be inadmissible. Statements about ***other crimes for which the right has not attached*** (*i.e.,* for which charges have not yet been filed) are fully admissible. Thus, if a defendant makes a Sixth Amendment request for counsel for one charge, he must make another request if he is subsequently charged with a separate related or unrelated crime and desires counsel for the second charge. Similarly, even though a defendant's Sixth Amendment right to counsel has attached regarding one charge, he may be questioned without counsel concerning an unrelated charge. [**Illinois v. Perkins**, 496 U.S. 292 (1990)]

e.g. **Example:** Defendant was in jail on a battery charge. Because the police suspected Defendant of an unrelated murder, they placed an undercover officer in Defendant's cell. The officer elicited a damaging confession from Defendant regarding the murder. The interrogation did not violate the Sixth Amendment because, at the time, Defendant had not yet been charged with the murder. [**Illinois v. Perkins**, *supra*] Neither did the interrogation violate Defendant's Fifth Amendment right to counsel under ***Miranda***. (*See infra,* pp. 101–102)

(1) Test for "Different Offenses"

The Sixth Amendment right to counsel does not apply to an uncharged offense merely because it is factually intertwined with a charged offense for which the defendant's right to counsel has attached. The right extends only to the charged offense(s) and lesser included offenses.

The test for determining whether there are two different offenses under the Sixth Amendment is the ***Blockburger*** test (which is the double jeopardy test *see infra,* p. 248). Under ***Blockburger***, two crimes are considered different offenses if ***each*** requires proof of an ***additional element*** that the other crime does not require. [**Texas v. Cobb**, 532 U.S. 162 (2001)—because burglary and murder are different crimes under ***Blockburger***, Defendant's confession to murder was not obtained in violation of the Sixth Amendment because, although Defendant had received appointed counsel on the burglary charge, police had questioned Defendant without his attorney present about persons missing from the burglarized premises]

d. When Defendant Is Focus of Investigation

In the famous ***Escobedo*** case, the Supreme Court held that a confession obtained from the defendant was inadmissible when: the investigation had focused on the suspect, he had been taken into custody, he had requested and been denied an opportunity to consult with his lawyer, and the lawyer was present and available to consult with him—even though the defendant had not yet been charged (*i.e.*, there had been no prior adversarial judicial proceeding). [**Escobedo v. Illinois**, 378 U.S. 478 (1964)] However, the very narrow holding in ***Escobedo*** is principally of historical interest today because of **Miranda v. Arizona**, *infra.*

e. Impeachment

A statement obtained in violation of a defendant's Sixth Amendment right to counsel, while not admissible in the prosecution's case-in-chief, may be used to impeach the defendant's inconsistent trial testimony. [**Kansas v. Ventris**, 556 U.S. 586 (2009)] This rule is similar to the rule that applies to statements resulting from ***Miranda*** violations. (*See infra*, pp. 108–109.)

Example: After Defendant was charged with murder and arrested for aggravated robbery, police placed an informant in his cell, telling the informant to keep his ears open. The informant told Defendant that he looked like he had something serious on his mind (which probably was sufficient to violate Defendant's Sixth Amendment right to counsel). Defendant responded that he had just shot a man in his head and taken his money. At trial, Defendant testified that an accomplice had shot and robbed the victim. The informant then testified as to what Defendant had told him. *Held:* The informant's testimony was admissible for impeachment purposes. [**Kansas v. Ventris**, *supra*]

3. Privilege Against Self-Incrimination Approach

As stated *supra,* the privilege against self-incrimination provides that "no person shall be compelled in any criminal case to be a witness against himself." In **Miranda v. Arizona**, 384 U.S. 436 (1966), the Supreme Court established the privilege against self-incrimination as a basis for determining the admissibility of a pre-trial confession in both state and federal prosecutions. The core of the ***Miranda*** decision was the Court's conclusion that custodial police interrogation is ***inherently coercive***. To combat this coerciveness, the Court ruled that when a ***law enforcement officer interrogates a suspect in custody***, the officer must inform the suspect of his rights, warn him of the consequences of waiving those rights, and obtain a waiver; otherwise, any confession made by the suspect is ***inadmissible at trial to prove the suspect's guilt.***

Although the decision in ***Miranda*** appeared to demand exclusion of any statement taken in violation of its directives, the U.S. Supreme Court has often described the decision as merely "prophylactic" (*i.e.*, not required by the Fifth Amendment). As a result, despite the Court's recognition in **Dickerson v. United States**, 530 U.S. 428 (2000), that ***Miranda*** is a "constitutional rule," members of the Court continue to disagree about ***Miranda***'s constitutional bona fides and to recognize new exceptions. [*See*, *e.g.*, **New York v. Quarles** and **Missouri v. Seibert**, *infra*]

Most recently, in **Vega v. Tekoh**, 597 U.S. 134 (2022), the Supreme Court held that a violation of ***Miranda*** cannot provide the basis for a claim under 42 U.S.C. § 1983. To reach this conclusion, the Court reiterated its view that ***Miranda*** warnings are merely "additional procedural protections" for core Fifth Amendment rights.

As the ***Tekoh*** Court explained, "In *Miranda*, the Court concluded that additional procedural protections were necessary to prevent the violation of this important right when suspects who are in custody are interrogated by the police. To afford this protection, the Court required that custodial interrogation be preceded by the now-familiar warnings . . . and it directed that statements obtained in violation of these new rules may not be used by the prosecution in its case-in-chief. *Miranda* itself and our subsequent cases make clear that *Miranda* imposed a set of prophylactic rules. Those rules, to be sure, are 'constitutionally based,' ***Dickerson***, 530 U.S. at 440, 120 S. Ct. 2326, but they are prophylactic rules nonetheless.

. . .

[I]n the words of the *Dickerson* Court, the *Miranda* rules are 'constitutionally based' and have "constitutional underpinnings." But the obvious point of these formulations was to avoid saying that a *Miranda* violation is the same as a violation of the Fifth Amendment right.

. . .

After *Miranda* was handed down, the Court engaged in the process of charting the dimensions of these new prophylactic rules. As the Court would later spell out, this process entailed a weighing of the benefits and costs of any clarification of the rules' scope. *See* ***Shatzer***, 559 U.S., at 106 ('A judicially crafted rule is 'justified only by reference to its prophylactic purpose,' . . . and applies only where its benefits outweigh its costs')."

a. Warnings

Under Miranda, the defendant must be informed, prior to custodial interrogation, that:

(i) He has the ***right to remain silent***;

(ii) ***Anything he says can be used against him*** at trial;

(iii) He has the ***right to the assistance of a lawyer***; and

(iv) ***If he cannot afford a lawyer; the government will provide him*** with one.

EXAM TIP

It is extremely likely that a *Miranda* issue will show up on your Criminal Procedure exam. If you can remember the basics, you will likely do well. In *Miranda*, the Supreme Court held that to offset the inherently coercive nature of *custodial police interrogation*, and to assure that confessions are *voluntary*, detainees must be (i) *informed* of their rights to remain silent and to an attorney, (ii) *warned* that any statements they make can be used against them in court (*i.e.,* the same *Miranda* warnings known to everyone who regularly watches television or movies), and (iii) that police must obtain a voluntary waiver from the suspect before initiating custodial interrogation.

---

(1) Application

Most police departments direct officers to provide the warnings as given above. In some cases, inexact warnings may still comply with *Miranda* if the defendant is given adequate information with respect to the right to have an attorney present and the right to remain silent. However, to adequately convey a suspect's rights, police must touch all of the bases of **Miranda**. [**California v. Prysock**, 453 U.S. 355 (1981); **Florida v. Powell**, 559 U.S. 50 (2010)] *Miranda* also does not require that the suspect be told of the particular crime being investigated. [**Colorado v. Spring**, 479 U.S. 564 (1987)]

e.g. **Example:** *Miranda* warnings are not invalid if a police officer tells a suspect that an attorney would be appointed "if and when you go to court." [**Duckworth v. Eagan**, 492 U.S. 195 (1989) language suggesting that defendants are entitled to appointed counsel only "if and when" they go to court is a de minimis variation from the classic *Miranda* warnings]

(2) Failure to Give Warnings

The exclusionary rule is applied to statements obtained in violation of ***Miranda*** as a deterrent to coercive police practices. If the warnings are not given, generally any statement obtained from interrogating the defendant will ***not be admissible to prove guilt***—even if the defendant's Sixth Amendment right to counsel was not violated and even if the confession was voluntarily given (*i.e.*, the defendant's Due Process rights were not violated). However, the Court has been willing to dispense with the *Miranda* warnings when other factors, such as public safety, outweigh their perceived benefits.

(a) Exception—Concern for Public Safety

The Supreme Court has carved out a "public safety" exception to the requirement that *Miranda* warnings be given before a suspect's answers may be admitted into evidence. The Court held that concern for public safety must be paramount to adherence to the literal language of *Miranda*. Thus, when police officers ask questions reasonably prompted by their concern for public safety, the defendant's responses need not be suppressed, even though the defendant was in police custody when the statements were made and *Miranda* warnings were not provided prior to limited interrogation**.** [**New York v. Quarles**, 467 U.S. 649 (1984)]

e.g. **Example:** Police were told that Defendant entered a supermarket with a gun. Four officers entered the supermarket late at night with their guns drawn, spotted Defendant, ordered him to stop, subdued him, frisked him, and found that he was wearing an empty shoulder holster. The officers handcuffed Defendant and immediately (*i.e.,* without *Miranda* warnings) asked him where the gun was. Defendant pointed to some empty cartons. The officers then retrieved the gun, placed Defendant under arrest, and read him *Miranda* warnings. The trial and appellate courts held that the gun was inadmissible evidence because Defendant was clearly in custody when he was asked about the gun. However, the Supreme Court held that the warnings should give way to concerns for public safety here. As long as the whereabouts of the gun were unknown, it posed a danger to the public that outweighed the benefits of the warnings. [**New York v. Quarles**, *supra*] *Note*: There was some testimony showing that the officer who asked about the gun's whereabouts was not concerned about safety at the time. The Court avoided this problem by holding that their new public safety exception should be judged by an ***objective standard*** (*i.e.*, whether a reasonable officer under the circumstances would think there is a public danger).

(b) Warnings After Unwarned Custodial Interrogation and Confession

If the police obtain a confession from a defendant without first giving *Miranda* warnings and then give the defendant the warnings and obtain a subsequent confession, the subsequent confession will be inadmissible if the police used this "question first, warn later" to reduce the effect of the *Miranda* warnings. [**Missouri v. Seibert**, 542 U.S. 600 (2004) confession excluded because police were trained to use question first scheme to circumvent *Miranda*]

e.g. **Example:** Defendant was arrested for her suspected involvement in a fire at her trailer in which an 18-year-old, mentally ill man was killed. The police questioned Defendant for 30 to 40 minutes at the police station. She confessed that she had feared that she would be charged with neglect in connection with the death of one of her sons, who was afflicted with cerebral palsy. She also admitted that she was present when her other sons and their friends planned to set the fire to cover up the death. The police then took a 20-minute break, and upon returning, gave Defendant *Miranda* warnings for the first time. After confronting Defendant with her earlier statement, she re-confessed. Defendant moved to have both confessions suppressed. The questioning officer testified that he made a conscious decision to withhold *Miranda* warnings during the initial questioning period. The Supreme Court held that this type of "question first, warn later" scheme violates ***Miranda***. [**Missouri v. Seibert**, *supra*]

cf. **Compare:** In **Oregon v. Elstad**, 470 U.S. 298 (1985), the police went to Defendant's home and arrested him in connection with the burglary of a neighbor's house. He was not given *Miranda* warnings. While one officer was in the kitchen with Defendant's mother, explaining why they were arresting her son, another sat in the living room with Defendant and struck up a conversation, asking if Defendant knew why he was being arrested and whether he knew the victims of the crime alleged. The officer then told Defendant that he thought that Defendant was involved in the burglary. Defendant admitted his involvement and was taken to the police station. At the station, Defendant was first given *Miranda* warnings and then he re-confessed. Defendant's confession was found to be valid. *Note*: The *Seibert* Court found that *Elstad* was not relevant, because the officer's brief questioning at Defendant's home in *Elstad* seemed unplanned and removed from the questioning at the police station.

In **Bobby v. Dixon**, 565 U.S. 23 (2011), the Court did not find the *Seibert* "question first, warn later" scheme. Defendant was interrogated three times. The first occurred during a "chance encounter," when Defendant was not in custody. He was issued *Miranda* warnings and refused to answer questions without his lawyer present. The second occurred five days later, when Defendant was interrogated while in post-arrest custody and without warnings. During this interrogation, Defendant admitted engaging in forgery but denied any involvement in murder. The third occurred later that day, when Defendant was *Mirandized* and inculpated himself in a murder. In distinguishing *Seibert*, the per curiam decision stressed that during Defendant's first unwarned interrogation, he denied involvement in the murder. This was distinct from *Seibert* in which the "suspect's first, unwarned interrogation left 'little, if anything, of incriminating potential left unsaid,' making it 'unnatural' not to 'repeat at the second stage'" of interrogation. The *Dixon* Court also found no nexus between the unwarned admission to forgery and the later, warned admission of murder. There was also a break in time and circumstances between the unwarned and warned interrogations.

b. Governmental Involvement

The *Miranda* warnings are intended to offset the inherently coercive nature of police-dominated interrogation. Therefore, no *Miranda* warnings are needed when a suspect is interrogated by someone whom she does not know to be a police officer. [**Illinois v. Perkins**, *supra,* p. 96—*Miranda* warnings need not precede questioning by a cellmate covertly working for the police]

(1) Rationale

If the defendant does not know that he is being interrogated by the police, there is no coercive atmosphere to offset.

(2) But Note

Questioning by a cellmate can violate the defendant's Sixth Amendment right to counsel if the defendant has been formally charged with a crime. (*See supra,* pp. 95–96.)

EXAM TIP

Be sure to remember that if a detainee does not know that the person questioning him is a police officer, *Miranda* warnings ***need not be given.*** This is because *Miranda* warnings are intended to offset the coercive effect that arises when a person is questioned by someone they know to be a police officer.

c. Custody

A person is in custody if his ***freedom of movement has been limited by the police***. There must be either a formal arrest or restraint on freedom of movement of the degree associated with a formal arrest. [**California v. Beheler**, 463 U.S. 1121 (1983)]

(1) Test Is Objective

The determination of whether a person was in custody during interrogation depends on the ***objective circumstances of the interrogation*** and not on the subjective views of the person being questioned or those of the officers conducting the questioning. A person will be found to be in custody if a ***reasonable person under the circumstances*** would feel that ***their freedom of action was denied in a significant way*** (*e.g.,* she would not feel free to leave). Although this is an objective test, courts must consider circumstances that would affect how a reasonable person in the suspect's position would perceive her freedom to leave. Thus, the age of a minor suspect may impact whether the minor is "in custody" for purposes of *Miranda.* [**J.D.B. v. North Carolina**, 564 U.S. 261 (2011)]

e.g. **Example:** A 13-year-old, seventh grade student was removed from class and questioned for 30–35 minutes by two police officers in the presence of two school administrators. No ***Miranda*** warnings were given. The student confessed to stealing. The Court ruled that the age of the student, if known or readily apparent to the officers, was a proper consideration in determining whether the student was "in custody." [**J.D.B. v. North Carolina**, *supra*]

e.g. **Example:** At 4 a.m., four officers entered Defendant's house, went to his bedroom, awakened Defendant, and began to question him about a murder. Under these circumstances, a reasonable person would be in custody because they would not feel free to leave. [*See* **Orozoco v. Texas**, 394 U.S. 324 (1969)]

e.g. **Example:** Defendant was in jail on a state charge. An I.R.S. agent came to the jail and began questioning Defendant regarding a federal criminal tax matter. Because Defendant clearly was not free to go, he was in custody and ***Miranda*** warnings should have been given. It does not matter that the charges were unrelated. [**Mathis v. United States**, 391 U.S. 1 (1968)]

cf. **Compare:** A police officer left Defendant, a parolee, a note asking Defendant to call so that they could "discuss something." When Defendant called, the officer asked Defendant to come to a police station near Defendant's apartment. When Defendant arrived, the officer assured Defendant that he was not under arrest but asked Defendant to step into an office. Once inside, the officer told

Defendant that he was suspected of committing a burglary. Within five minutes of entering the room, Defendant confessed. Only then was he given *Miranda* warnings. After he confessed, Defendant was permitted to leave the police station. *Held:* The fact that the interview took place at a police station was not enough to make this a custodial interrogation, because Defendant had understood that he was free to leave. [**Oregon v. Mathiason**, 429 U.S. 492 (1977)]

In **Howes v. Fields**, 565 U.S. 499 (2012), Defendant (a prisoner in a state jail) was escorted by corrections officers to a conference room within the jail where two sheriff's deputies questioned Defendant for between five and seven hours about his criminal conduct outside of jail. Before the interview, Defendant was told that he was free to leave and return to his cell. He was not handcuffed during the interview. Although Defendant never asked to return to his cell, he did tell the deputies several times that he "no longer wanted to talk" to them. During the interview, Defendant confessed. *Held*: A prisoner is not always in custody for purposes of *Miranda* even when isolated from the general prison population and questioned. "The determination of custody should focus on all of the features of the interrogation."

(2) Focus of Investigation

The mere fact that an investigation has focused on the defendant does not make an interrogation custodial unless a reasonable person would believe that he is unable to leave. [**Beckwith v. United States**, 425 U.S. 341 (1976)]

e.g. **Example:** I.R.S. agents came to Defendant's home at 8:00 a.m. to question him because they suspected Defendant had committed tax fraud. They interviewed Defendant for three hours, during which time he made some incriminating statements. Despite the fact that the investigation was focused on Defendant, the interrogation was found to be noncustodial. [**Beckwith v. United States**, *supra*]

(3) *Terry* Stops

Stops conducted pursuant to the rule announced in **Terry v. Ohio** (*supra,* p. 26) present special problems. In their original and limited form, ***Terry*** stops were significantly less intrusive than arrests and thus were rarely custodial within the meaning of *Miranda*. However, in practice *Terry* stops have become more expansive and longer, so their potential constitutional impact has changed. Today a *Terry* stop of sufficient scope and duration may result in custody under *Miranda*.

(4) Traffic Stops

An ordinary traffic stop does not constitute custody; thus, *Miranda* warnings need not be given after a motorist is stopped. [**Berkemer v. McCarty**, 468 U.S. 420 (1984)]

EXAM TIP

Whether a person is in custody for the purpose of *Miranda* often is an important exam issue and is resolved by determining whether a ***reasonable person under the circumstances*** would feel that ***his freedom of action was denied in a significant way***. A person who voluntarily accompanies police is not in custody, neither is a person briefly detained for a traffic violation (although the traffic detainee is technically not "free to leave"). What constitutes custody? A traditional arrest, being ordered (as opposed to asked) to sit in a squad car, and similar restrictive detentions are considered custodial for *Miranda* purposes.

d. Interrogation

A defendant's statement is subject to *Miranda* only if it is given in response to interrogation. Volunteered statements (spontaneous remarks not made in response to questioning) are not covered. Interrogation, however, is not limited to any particular type of questioning. The inquiry is whether police officers should know that their actions, whether direct questions or their functional equivalent, are ***reasonably likely to elicit an incriminating response*** from the suspect. [**Rhode Island v. Innis**, 446 U.S. 291 (1980)]

e.g. **Example:** Interrogation occurs when the police officers, knowing of the defendant's religious interest, make remarks designed to appeal to the defendant's religious interest and thus have him confess. [**Brewer v. Williams**, *supra,* p. 96]

cf. **Compare:** Defendant was arrested for a murder which took place near a school for handicapped children. While transporting Defendant to the police station, one officer mentioned to the other officer that he hoped that none of the children came upon the weapon with shells in it because they might hurt themselves. Upon hearing this, Defendant told the officers that he could show them where the weapon was. The Court found that this was not interrogation describing the conversation as "nothing more than a dialogue between the two officers to which no response from [Defendant] was invited." Distinguishing *Brewer, supra,* (a case with similar facts decided on Sixth Amendment right to counsel grounds) the Court found nothing to suggest that the officers knew that Defendant was peculiarly susceptible to an appeal to his conscience concerning the safety of handicapped children. [**Rhode Island v. Innis**, *supra*] Interrogation also does not occur when the police allow a suspect's wife to talk to the suspect in the presence of police officers who are taping the conversation with the suspect's knowledge. [**Arizona v. Mauro**, 481 U.S. 520 (1987)]

EXAM TIP

On your exam, be sure to remember that while police conduct reasonably likely to elicit an incriminating response constitutes interrogation, *merely informing* a suspect that he is under arrest is *not enough* to constitute interrogation. For example, if an officer approaches a suspect, tells the suspect that he is under arrest, and the suspect immediately makes an incriminating remark, such as "I didn't kill Victim," *Miranda* is not violated because there was no interrogation.

(1) Psychiatric Examination

Examination of the defendant by a state psychiatrist to determine the defendant's competency to stand trial is custodial interrogation for purposes of *Miranda*. [**Estelle v. Smith**, 451 U.S. 454 (1981)] The admission of such evidence, however, may constitute harmless error. [**Satterwhite v. Texas**, 486 U.S. 249 (1988)]

(2) Grand Jury Investigation

Answers given to questioning during a grand jury investigation are *not* statements in response to custodial interrogation. Because the setting is wholly different from custodial police interrogation, *Miranda* warnings are not required. [**United States v. Mandujano**, 425 U.S. 564 (1976)] Witnesses who give false testimony before grand juries may be convicted of perjury even if no ***Miranda*** warnings were given. [**United States v. Wong**, 431 U.S. 174 (1977)]

e. Resumption of Questioning

After being given *Miranda* warnings, the suspect may choose to say nothing to the police. Two very different rules govern whether the government can resume questioning.

(1) If Defendant Wishes to Remain Silent

If the defendant clearly tells the police that she wishes to remain silent, this request must be ***scrupulously honored***. In the leading case, the Supreme Court found the request scrupulously honored where questioning was resumed when the police:

(i) ***Immediately ceased*** the interrogation ***when the defendant indicated his desire to remain silent***;

(ii) Questioning was resumed only ***after passage of a significant period of time*** (two hours);

(iii) ***New Miranda warnings*** were given before questioning was resumed; and

(iv) The later interrogation was restricted to a ***crime that was not the subject of the first interrogation***.

[**Michigan v. Mosley**, 423 U.S. 96 (1975)] Lower courts are divided over the issue of whether the later interrogation must be about a different crime.

[*Compare* **United States v. Sawyer**, 588 F.3d 548 (8th Cir. 2009), abrogated on other grounds, **United States v. Reddick**, 910 F.3d 358 (8th Cir. 2018), *with* **Stock v. State**, 191 P.3d 153 (Alaska App. 2008)]

(a) Invocation Must Be Explicit, Unambiguous, and Unequivocal

An invocation of the right to remain silent must be explicit, unambiguous, and unequivocal (*e.g.,* the detainee's failure to answer does not constitute an invocation of the right). If the detainee does not respond to *Miranda* warnings or does so in an ambiguous fashion, the police may continue to question the detainee. [*See* **Berghuis v. Thompkins**, 560 U.S. 370 (2010)]

(2) If Defendant Wishes to Consult Attorney

If, after receiving ***Miranda*** warnings, the defendant clearly informs the officers that he wishes to speak with his attorney, he may not be subjected to further interrogation while in custody until his attorney has been made available to him, unless he initiates discussions with the police. [**Edwards v. Arizona**, 451 U.S. 477 (1981)] After he is released from custody, his request for counsel remains in effect for 14 days. [**Maryland v. Shatzer**, 559 U.S. 98 (2010)]

(a) Note

For a period, the Supreme Court applied *Edwards* if an attorney was appointed to a defendant at a pretrial arraignment. [*See* **Michigan v. Jackson**, 475 U.S. 625 (1986)] However, **Michigan v. Jackson** has been overruled. In **Montejo v. Louisiana**, 556 U.S. 778 (2009), the Court overruled **Jackson** holding that a defendant's waiver of the **Miranda** right to counsel is not presumptively invalid (*i.e.*, **Edwards** does not apply) simply because, at the time of such waiver, the defendant was represented by counsel.

e.g. **Example:** Defendant was arrested, given ***Miranda*** warnings, and confessed to a murder. He was then brought before a judge, who appointed counsel under state procedures that did not depend on a defendant's request. Later that day, police officers went to Defendant's cell and asked him to help them find the weapon he used to commit the murder. The police gave Defendant a fresh set of ***Miranda*** warnings and convinced him to write a letter apologizing to his victim's widow. Later, the appointed attorney met with Defendant. At trial, Defendant's attorney argued that the letter was taken in violation of Defendant's Sixth Amendment right to counsel under ***Jackson***. *Held:* ***Jackson*** was improvidently decided and is now overruled. Because Defendant had not requested the appointment of an attorney, his right to an attorney was not violated. [**Montejo v. Louisiana**, *supra*]

(b) Questioning on Unrelated Offense

Once a suspect cuts off questioning by invoking his right to counsel under the Fifth Amendment, the suspect may ***not*** be questioned about ***any offense***, including one wholly unrelated to the subject of the initial interrogation. [**Arizona v. Roberson**, 486 U.S. 675 (1988)] Thus, unlike the Sixth Amendment right to counsel, the **Miranda** right to counsel is not offense specific.

(c) Questioning After Conference with Counsel

Once counsel is requested, interrogation must cease whether or not the defendant consults counsel. Similarly, once the right is asserted, the mere fact that a suspect has earlier consulted with counsel is irrelevant; the attorney must actually be present during interrogation. Thus, the Fifth Amendment right to counsel is violated where the defendant requests counsel, is given an opportunity to confer with counsel, and is then forced to talk to the police without counsel present. [**Minnick v. Mississippi**, 498 U.S. 146 (1991)]

(d) Ambiguities in Request

Once the suspect has clearly expressed an unequivocal desire to receive counsel, all questioning of the accused must cease, and no *subsequent* questions or responses may be used to cast doubt on the request. In contrast, if the request is ambiguous, police may continue to interrogate the suspect until an unambiguous request for counsel has been made. The test is whether the suspect's request was sufficiently clear that a reasonable police officer in the same situation would understand the statement to be a request for counsel. For example, the statement "Maybe I should talk to a lawyer," is not sufficiently clear to invoke the right to counsel. [**Davis v. United States**, 512 U.S. 452 (1994)] The request must be explicit. (*See supra,* p. 104–105.)

(e) Distinguish—Defendant Initiates Further Contact with the Police

Interrogation can continue if the suspect, who has requested counsel, subsequently initiates a conversation with the police. Questions incidental to custody (*e.g.*, requests for water or the bathroom) do not initiate a conversation. However, a suspect who has invoked his right to counsel and then asks the interrogating officer, "What is going to happen to me now?" and is rewarned of his *Miranda* rights before taking a polygraph examination and making a confession, has made a valid waiver of his rights under *Miranda.* [**Oregon v. Bradshaw**, 462 U.S. 1039 (1983)]

(f) Duration of Prohibition

The prohibition against questioning a suspect after he requests an attorney lasts the entire time that the suspect is in custody for interrogation purposes, plus 14 more days after the suspect returns to his normal life. After that point, the suspect can be questioned regarding the same matter upon receiving a fresh set of *Miranda* warnings and making a waiver. [**Maryland v. Shatzer**, *supra,* p. 104—while in prison for a different crime, suspect was questioned about alleged sexual abuse, invoked his right to counsel, and was released back into the general prison population (his normal life); police could reinitiate questioning after 14 days without first providing counsel]

EXAM TIP

Note the difference here depending on what the defendant says. If the defendant clearly indicates that he wishes to ***remain silent***, the police may probably reinitiate interrogation after a break, if fresh warnings are administered and a waiver obtained. If the defendant clearly ***requests counsel***, the police may **not** resume interrogating the defendant while he is in custody until counsel has been provided. However, interrogation may result if the defendant initiates communication with the police and fresh warnings are administered and a waiver obtained. In addition, a defendant's request for counsel stays in force for 14 days.

f. Waiver

A defendant may ***give up*** his *Miranda* rights and choose to talk to the police without a lawyer present. Dicta in *Miranda* explained that a heavy burden rests on the government to demonstrate that a waiver was ***knowing and intelligent***. The Court also stated that waiver will not be presumed simply from the silence of the accused after warnings are given or simply from the fact that a confession was obtained. However, the Supreme Court has consistently found for the government when the validity of a *Miranda* waiver is in issue.

(1) Burden—Preponderance of the Evidence

After *Miranda,* the Supreme Court reiterated its position that the government has a heavy burden in proving waiver. [**Tague v. Louisiana**, 444 U.S. 469 (1980)—overturning state court decision placing burden on the defendant] However, the Court subsequently held that the government can meet this burden by showing a waiver by a preponderance of the evidence. [**Colorado v. Connelly**, 479 U.S. 157 (1986)]

(2) Knowing and Intelligent

In *Miranda* the Court did not specify what evidence could demonstrate that a confession was knowing and intelligent. The Court has subsequently held that it will look at the ***totality of the circumstances***, considering factors such as the suspect's intelligence, physical and mental condition, and the circumstances surrounding the waiver. [**Fare v. Michael C.**, 442 U.S. 707 (1979)] Cases applying the waiver test have been satisfied with proof that a defendant said he ***understood the Miranda warnings*** (*see supra,* pp. 91–94). The differences in the burdens of proof should be noted. For the defendant, proof of an invocation of the right to remain silent or the right to counsel must be explicit, unambiguous, and unequivocal (*e.g.*, the detainee's failure to answer does not constitute an invocation of the right to silence and statements like "a lawyer could be helpful" do not constitute an invocation of the right to counsel). In contrast, the government can prove that a suspect "understood" their **Miranda** rights simply be showing that the suspect could read or speak the language used by the police. If the detainee can read a portion of the warnings out loud, even if they do not waive and do not respond to warnings (or do so only in an ambiguous fashion), the police may continue to interrogate the custodial detainee. [*See* **Berghuis v. Thompkins**, 560 U.S. 370 (2010)]

(a) Suspect's Understanding of the Warnings

Once warnings are given, the government will generally have little difficulty in proving that a defendant understood the rights.

e.g. **Example:** Defendant was arrested and given *Miranda* warnings. He refused to give the police any written statements but told them he had no problem talking with them. Although the Court recognized that Defendant's actions may have been illogical, it found the waiver to be valid. [**Connecticut v. Barrett**, 479 U.S. 523 (1987)]

e.g. **Example:** Defendant was arrested in his home and questioned without first being given *Miranda* warnings. He made incriminating statements and was taken to the police station. At the police station, Defendant was given *Miranda* warnings and he signed a written confession. The Oregon Supreme Court held that Defendant's written confession was inadmissible because Defendant likely assumed that he had "let the cat out of the bag." In other words, Defendant believed that the first confession could be used against him, so there was no reason not to confess again. The Supreme Court reversed, finding that the second confession was pursuant to a voluntary and informed waiver. [**Oregon v. Elstad**, *supra*, p. 100; *compare* **Missouri v. Seibert**, *supra,* p. 99—where the first confession resulted from a police question-first-warn-later scheme designed to negate the effectiveness of *Miranda*, defendant's waiver before a subsequent confession will not be effective]

(b) Suspect's Knowledge

The government need not show that the defendant understands the nature or extent of the crimes the police will be investigating during the interrogation.

e.g. **Example:** Defendant was arrested on weapons charges, was given *Miranda* warnings, and waived his rights. Police then questioned Defendant about a murder. The Supreme Court found that the failure of the police to inform Defendant that they would also question him about a murder did not invalidate his waiver. [**Colorado v. Spring**, 479 U.S. 654 (1987)]

1) Trickery

Police trickery generally will not invalidate a waiver unless it affects the likely charge or the contents of the warning (*e.g.,* trickery could invalidate a waiver if the police convince the defendant that he really has no right to remain silent despite the warnings).

e.g. **Example:** Defendant was arrested on burglary charges but was also suspected of committing a murder. Defendant's sister obtained a lawyer for Defendant, who called the police and said that she would represent Defendant during any questioning. When the lawyer called the police, they falsely told her that they would not be questioning Defendant or putting him in any lineup until the following day. They also failed to tell the lawyer that Defendant was also a murder suspect. The police never told Defendant that his sister had obtained a lawyer for him and that the lawyer had contacted the police on his behalf. Instead, the police read Defendant *Miranda* warnings, he signed a waiver, and then he confessed to the murder. The waiver was upheld. The fact that the police kept Defendant in the dark about the attorney and that they kept the attorney in the dark about Defendant has no bearing on the validity of Defendant's waiver. [**Moran v. Burbine**, 475 U.S. 412 (1986)]

(c) Suspect's Sanity

The fact that a person may be suffering from a mental health condition that causes delusions will not necessarily render a *Miranda* waiver invalid.

e.g. **Example:** Defendant appeared at a police station and said that he wanted to talk about a murder. The police read Defendant *Miranda* warnings, and Defendant continued to talk about the crime. Later psychiatric evaluations showed that Defendant was likely suffering from mental delusions when he made his statements, because he later told a psychiatrist that he approached the police because the voice of God had ordered him to confess or commit suicide. The Supreme Court found Defendant's waiver valid under these circumstances because the police had done nothing to coerce the confession. [**Colorado v. Connelly**, *supra,* p. 106]

(3) Form of the Waiver

(a) Express or Implied

The clearest form of waiver is for the suspect to expressly affirm that she understands her rights, does not desire to have an attorney present, and wishes to make a statement. However, such an explicit waiver is not required. All that is required is a ***course of conduct indicating a knowing and voluntary waiver***. Thus, waivers need not be express and can be implied from a defendant's conduct. [**North Carolina v. Butler**, 441 U.S. 369 (1979); *and see* **Berghuis v. Thompkins**, *supra,* p. 104—suspect scarcely said anything after receiving ***Miranda*** warnings, but was held to have voluntarily waived his right to remain silent when he responded "yes" to a single incriminating question posed nearly three hours into his interrogation]

(b) In Counsel's Presence

The presence of the suspect's attorney at an interrogation is very persuasive evidence that a waiver was made and was valid.

g. Impeachment

Confessions that are ***involuntary*** under the Due Process Clause (*e.g.,* confessions obtained through torture, through depriving a defendant of food, drink, or sleep, etc.) ***may not be used for any purpose***. If the jury hears an involuntary confession, the conviction must be reversed unless the error was harmless. [**Arizona v. Fulminante**, *supra,* p. 94] However, a confession that is merely obtained ***in violation of Miranda may be used to impeach*** the defendant's testimony—if the defendant takes the stand at trial and contradicts the confession. The jury should be instructed that the confession may not be considered as evidence of guilt but may be considered solely on the issue of whether the defendant is telling the truth at trial. [**Harris v. New York**, *supra,* p. 10] However, a confession obtained in violation of *Miranda* may not be used to impeach the in-court testimony of other witnesses. [**James v. Illinois**, 493 U.S. 307 (1990)]

(1) Post-Arrest Silence

The post-arrest silence of the defendant may not be admitted [**Doyle v. Ohio**, 426 U.S. 610 (1976)], unless the defendant's decision to remain silent was made without reliance on *Miranda* warnings [**Fletcher v. Weir**, 455 U.S. 603 (1982)]. Recall, however, that a single improper question regarding a defendant's post-*Miranda* silence is subject to harmless error analysis. [**Greer v. Miller**, *supra,* p. 86]

(a) Distinguish—Pre-Arrest Silence

The silence of the defendant before arrest ***may*** be used against the defendant at trial. This is because prior to arrest, the defendant is not relying on the *Miranda* warnings. [**Jenkins v. Anderson**, 447 U.S. 231 (1980)]

h. Nontestimonial Fruits of an Unwarned Confession

If the police fail to give *Miranda* warnings and during interrogation a suspect provides information that leads to nontestimonial evidence, the nontestimonial evidence should not be suppressed as the fruit of an unlawful interrogation. Although there was no majority opinion on this point, five Justices have held that suppression was not necessary under these circumstances. [**United States v. Patane**, 542 U.S. 630 (2004)—three-Justice plurality with two Justices concurring in the result]

e.g. **Example:** The police went to Defendant's home to arrest him for violating a temporary restraining order. They had received a tip that he had a pistol. When they arrested Defendant, they began to give him *Miranda* warnings, but Defendant interrupted, saying that he knew his rights. The officers then asked Defendant about the pistol, and he told them where to find it. Defendant was indicted for possession of a firearm by a convicted felon. He moved to suppress the pistol as the fruit of an unwarned statement. Five Justices agreed that because the pistol is nontestimonial evidence, its admission could not violate Defendant's Fifth Amendment rights under *Miranda.* [**United States v. Patane**, *supra*]

Chapter Four

Pretrial Proceedings

CONTENTS	PAGE

Key Exam Issues

The topic in this chapter most likely to be tested is ***identification procedures***. Your analysis of the problem should center on three constitutional issues:

1. **Privilege Against Self-Incrimination**

   Remember that a defendant's Fifth Amendment privilege is ***not*** violated by simply requiring him to participate in a proceeding that identifies him (*e.g.*, a lineup).

2. **Right to Counsel**

   At a routine lineup, the suspect has a right to have his attorney present. But there are two important limitations here: (i) there is no right to counsel if the lineup occurs ***prior to the commencement of an adversary judicial proceeding*** (*e.g.*, an indictment, preliminary hearing, or charging); and (ii) there is no right to counsel at any time ***unless the defendant is personally confronted*** by the witness (*i.e.*, there is no right to counsel if the police display photographs of the suspect to a witness or victim).

3. **Due Process**

   Consider here whether the procedure used, ***under all the circumstances***, was likely to result in an ***unreliable identification***. If so, due process is violated. *But note*: There are two important ***limitations*** on a defendant's ability to respond to an identification taken in violation of her due process rights: (i) ***in-court testimony*** can be used (despite the prior unlawful identification) as long as the in-court identification has a source independent from the tainted pretrial identification; and (ii) on appeal, a violation of the defendant's due process rights during an identification will not result in reversal if it is found to be a ***harmless error***.

The other topics in this chapter are less emphasized. Indeed, in a typical law school class, little attention is paid to matters such as speedy trial, disclosure, and competency, although you should review those topics briefly.

More importantly, you should be familiar with the three principal charging methods and with bail proceedings:

1. **Charging Methods**

   The three main methods that states use to formally charge a defendant are:

   a. The defendant can be informed of the charges in a complaint at a ***preliminary hearing***. During this hearing, a judge determines if there is probable cause to prosecute.

   b. A prosecutor can present a grand jury comprised of ordinary citizens with evidence. If the grand jury determines that there is probable cause, it can issue an ***indictment*** (return a "true bill").

   c. A prosecutor can charge a defendant in an ***information***, although probable cause determinations would be linked to a preliminary hearing as well.

2. **Bail**

   Excessive bail is prohibited by the Eighth Amendment, and a hearing must be conducted to determine if bail provisions are reasonable and will assure the defendant's appearance at trial.

A. Identification Procedures

1. Introduction

The police use a variety of identification procedures to verify that the government has a factual evidence-based belief that the suspect taken into custody perpetrated the crime. Identification procedures have the dual function of solving crimes and providing evidence for trial. Three important constitutional provisions are considered in connection with identification procedures: the privilege against compelled self-incrimination, the right to counsel, and the Due Process Clause.

2. Privilege Against Self-Incrimination

It does not violate a defendant's Fifth Amendment privilege against compelled self-incrimination to compel her to stand in a lineup, to utter specified words when asked to do so, or to put on some item of clothing. These acts have been deemed "nontestimonial" and thus not within the privilege, which protects a person against serving as "a witness against himself." [**United States v. Wade**, 388 U.S. 218 (1967)]

a. Spelling

While handwriting samples do not raise constitutional concerns, some lower courts have held that spelling is protected by the Fifth Amendment privilege. *Rationale*: Spelling "is the result of the operation of a person's mind, the expression of which generally falls within the Fifth Amendment's protection." [**United States v. Matos**, 990 F. Supp. 141 (E.D.N.Y. 1998); **SPV-LS, LLC v. Herbst, No. 16-MC-197 (PART ONE),** 2016 U.S. Dist. LEXIS 73897, at *4 (S.D.N.Y. June 3, 2016)]

3. Right to Counsel

The Sixth Amendment gives the defendant a right to have a lawyer present during certain identification proceedings to ensure the fairness of the trial process. [**United States v. Wade**, *supra*] The function of the lawyer is not, however, clear. Some jurisdictions allow the attorney to participate only by observing the proceedings, while other jurisdictions allow direct involvement by defense counsel. The rationale for extending the right to counsel to some post-indictment identification procedures is to permit the defendant, with the help of counsel, to recreate for the jury the circumstances of the identification to demonstrate the suggestiveness of the procedure and to allow for effective cross-examination.

a. Pre-Complaint Lineups

The right to counsel attaches ***only after the initiation of an adversary criminal proceeding*** against the accused, such as a formal charge, indictment, or preliminary hearing. [**Moore v. Illinois**, 434 U.S. 220 (1977)] There is ***no right*** to assistance of counsel at police lineups conducted ***prior*** to the time the accused is indicted, arraigned, or otherwise formally charged with the crime. [**Kirby v. Illinois**, 406 U.S. 682 (1972)]

(1) "Adversarial Criminal Proceeding"

Of course, the question may be what constitutes an adversarial criminal proceeding or confrontation. This may ***not*** require an arraignment or the like. Some courts have held that if the accused is ***taken into custody*** under an ***arrest warrant***, this is tantamount to a "formal charge" (because an arrest warrant can be issued by a magistrate only on a showing of probable cause). Other states, by statute, have determined that the ***issuance of the arrest warrant*** is the initiation of adversarial judicial proceedings under *Kirby*.

(a) But Note

Some states, under appropriate state constitutional provisions, wholly reject the *Kirby* post-indictment stage restriction and ***require counsel at all lineups***. [*See, e.g.,* **Blue v. Alaska**, 558 P.2d 636 (Alaska 1977)]

b. Post-Complaint Lineups

A police lineup or other "face-to-face" confrontation conducted ***after*** the accused has been formally charged with the crime is considered a "critical stage" of the proceedings, and the accused has a ***right to have counsel present***. [**United States v. Wade**, *supra*] A critical stage of the proceeding is defined as a time when the defendant's rights can be compromised, and having an attorney for the defendant might avoid the compromise of rights.

(1) "Nonadversarial Confrontation"

The defendant is entitled to counsel at pretrial identification proceedings only when she is physically present in a trial-like adversary confrontation. Thus, the defendant has no right to counsel during a photo identification procedure. [**United States v. Ash**, 413 U.S. 300 (1973)] In *Ash*, the Court reasoned that a "trained observer" was not necessary at a photo display because, although defense counsel was not present, counsel could effectively reconstruct the photo identification procedure at trial for cross-examination.

c. In-Court Identifications

If a defendant is identified by a witness at a pretrial procedure, and the defendant's right to counsel was violated there, testimony concerning that tainted identification procedure cannot be admitted at trial. However, an unlawful pretrial procedure does not automatically exclude the testimony of a witness who identified the defendant during such procedure. If ***at trial*** the witness can identify the defendant—without having to rely on the earlier pretrial identification—the in-court identification is admissible. [**Gilbert v. California**, 388 U.S. 263 (1967), *supra*, p. 82] To decide whether such in-court identification testimony is admissible, the judge must conclude that the witness's identification testimony is "purged of the primary taint" created by the unlawful pretrial procedure. [**Wong Sun v. United States**, 371 U.S. 471 (1963), *supra,* p. 7]

(1) Independent Source

The question is whether the in-court identification has a source independent of the illegal pretrial lineup. For example, the source may be independent if the witness's initial description of the defendant was precise and later corroborated, or if the witness had a particularly good view of the defendant at the time of the crime.

Factors affecting the independent source determination are:

(i) The witness's opportunity to view the defendant during the criminal act;

(ii) Any discrepancy between a pre-lineup description and the defendant's actual appearance;

(iii) Any identification by the witness of another person prior to the lineup;

(iv) Any photo identification by the witness before the lineup; and

(v) the witness's failure to identify the defendant on a prior occasion.

[**United States v. Wade**, *supra*]

(2) Eye-Witness Identification

Congress sought to ensure the admissibility of eye witness identification evidence after *Wade*, *supra*, with 18 U.S.C. § 3502 ("The testimony of a witness that he saw the accused commit . . . the crime . . . shall be admissible in evidence in a criminal prosecution. . . .")

d. Harmless Error Test May Apply

When the right to counsel ***at trial*** is violated, the denial is usually reversible error per se, not subject to harmless error analysis. [*See, e.g.,* **Holloway v. Arkansas**, 435 U.S. 475 (1978)—conflict of interest reversible error], but not always [**Woods v. Donald**, 575 U.S. 312 (2015)—no per se reversal when accused's attorney was briefly absent during trial testimony concerning only other defendants]

Note that in ***nontrial settings***, such as at a lineup, errors are much more likely to be deemed harmless. [**United States v. Wade**, *supra*]

EXAM TIP

Be sure to remember this important distinction: While denial of the right to counsel ***at trial is almost always*** a ***"structural," automatic reversible error***, when the denial occurs at a ***lineup*** or other identification proceeding, it may be ***harmless error***. If results of the improper identification are erroneously admitted into evidence and the defendant is convicted, the conviction will not be overturned if the government shows beyond a reasonable doubt that in light of the other evidence, the defendant would have been convicted even without the identification.

4. Due Process Clause

Quite apart from the right to counsel, a pretrial confrontation for identification purposes may be so unreliable as to infringe upon the defendant's right to due process of law. [*See* **Stovall v. Denno**, 388 U.S. 293 (1967)]

a. Depends on Totality of Circumstances

In determining the constitutionality of identification procedures, the courts consider ***all of the circumstances*** leading to the identification. A due process violation will be found only if, in the light of such circumstances, police used an unnecessarily suggestive identification procedure. However, the Supreme Court has refused to find a due process violation in circumstances where the identification was suggestive, but was ***not arranged by law enforcement officers***. [**Perry v. New Hampshire**, 565 U.S. 228 (2012)] Even a clearly unnecessarily suggestive identification procedure, such as a one photo "show up," does not violate due process if the identification is deemed ***reliable***. [**Manson v. Brathwaite**, 432 U.S. 98 (1977)—identification admissible where police officer-witness purchased drugs from individual, returned to station house and described individual, and was shown one picture of defendant, which he identified as being the individual who sold him drugs]

(1) Factors Affecting Reliability

To resolve the ultimate issue in the due process question—whether the identification was reliable—the courts consider the totality of the circumstances, namely:

(i) The witness's ***opportunity to view the defendant*** at the time of the crime;

(ii) The witness's ***degree of attention*** at that time;

(iii) The ***accuracy of any prior description*** given by the witness;

(iv) The ***level of certainty demonstrated by the witness*** at the identification; and

(v) The ***length of time between the crime and the identification***.

[**Manson v. Brathwaite**, *supra*]

(a) Note

While ***suggestiveness in the identification procedure*** will not per se disqualify an identification, it has traditionally been met with judicial disapproval and will be considered a part of the "totality of the circumstances." [**Manson v. Brathwaite**, *supra*] A higher degree of suggestiveness in the identification procedure will be tolerated if the procedure is considered necessary (*i.e.*, exigent circumstances exist). [**Simmons v. United States**, 390 U.S. 377 (1968) (no due process violation when suggestive photo lineup was used to apprehend bank robber still at large; **Davis v. Smith**, 145 S.Ct. 93, 95 (2025) (an identification is excludable only if the testimony poses "a very substantial likelihood of irreparable misidentification" and identifications with "sufficient aspects of reliability" should be admitted)]

e.g. **Example:** There was no constitutional violation where the witness identified the defendant's photo six months after the robbery, as the witness had earlier had a good view of the assailant, the area was well lit, and the witness had seen the assailant for a relatively lengthy period of time. [**Hudson v. Blackburn**, 601 F.2d 785 (5th Cir. 1979)]

cf. **Compare:** There was a due process violation where the only persons in the lineup other than the defendant were five to six inches shorter, the witness was initially not sure that the defendant was the robber, and the defendant was only positively identified by the witness at a second lineup in which the defendant was the only person who had appeared in the first lineup. [**Foster v. California**, 394 U.S. 440 (1969)]

5. Refusal to Cooperate

The trial judge may jail a defendant who refuses to comply with a court order to participate in an identification procedure. Also, the prosecution may comment to the jury on the defendant's unwillingness to participate in the identification procedure. [**South Dakota v. Neville**, 459 U.S. 553 (1983), *supra*, p. 82]

B. Preliminary Hearing

1. Introduction

A preliminary hearing is a judicial proceeding that occurs between the suspect's arrest and trial. Generally, a preliminary hearing may serve one of three purposes: (1) to determine whether ***probable cause*** for an arrest and detention exists; (2) to ***set bail*** or some other condition for pretrial release; and (3) to ***review the prosecutor's decision*** to charge the accused. A preliminary hearing may also allow the accused an initial opportunity to discover the prosecutor's case.

2. Probable Cause to Detain

The first purpose of the preliminary hearing is to determine whether the arrest and detention of the accused is based on probable cause. Because the probable cause determination is sometimes made by a judge or a grand jury at an earlier stage, this purpose may already have been achieved. Thus, when a ***grand jury indictment*** is obtained prior to arrest, or when an arrest is made pursuant to an ***arrest warrant***, probable cause to detain has already been established and need not be addressed during a hearing. However, when a person who has not been charged is arrested without a warrant, she has a constitutional right (pursuant to the Fourth Amendment) to a judicial determination (typically in the form of a hearing, often referred to as a "Gerstein Hearing") of probable cause. [**Gerstein v. Pugh**, 420 U.S. 103 (1975)]

a. Characteristics of the *Gerstein* Hearing

The probable cause to detain hearing must be held within a reasonably short period of time following arrest. A 48-hour delay has been held to be presumptively reasonable and a delay of more than 48 hours is presumptively unreasonable. Fewer than 48 hours could also be unreasonable depending on the circumstances. [**Riverside County v. McLaughlin**, 500 U.S. 44 (1991)]

b. Remedy for *Gerstein* Violation

The failure to hold a ***Gerstein*** hearing (or holding the hearing late) will not invalidate a subsequent conviction. However, in federal court, if law enforcement obtain statements or consent to a search from a defendant during an unreasonably long pre-hearing delay, the statements and other fruits of the search could be excluded if the statements or consent resulted from the unconstitutional delay. [**Powell v. Nevada**, 511 U.S. 79 (1994)]

3. Initial Appearance to Set Bail

All defendants should be brought before a judicial officer within 24 to 72 hours of arrest for what is often called an "initial appearance." At this initial appearance, the judicial officer will: (1) inform a defendant of her rights; (2) set bail or other conditions of pretrial release; and (3) appoint counsel if the defendant is indigent. The initial appearance, like an indictment, begins adversarial judicial criminal proceedings triggering the Sixth Amendment right to counsel. At this point, the government's relationship to the defendant "has become solidly adversarial" because this "signals a sufficient commitment to prosecute. . . ." [**Rothgery v. Gillespie County**, 554 U.S. 191 (2008)] The right to counsel attaches whether or not a prosecutor is involved or present.

4. Bindover Hearing

A bindover hearing (or probable cause to prosecute hearing) reviews the prosecutor's decision to charge the defendant. The defendant is entitled to counsel and, if indigent, counsel should be appointed. [**Coleman v. Alabama**, 399 U.S. 1 (1970); **Rothgery v. Gillespie County**, *supra*] Both sides may swear witnesses and present evidence. In most jurisdictions, the prosecution must prove that there is competent evidence supporting each element of the charged offense. Generally, the accused must be given an opportunity to present defenses. At preliminary hearings, either side may preserve the testimony of witnesses who may later be unavailable to testify at trial. For the prosecution to use such testimony at trial, the

Confrontation Clause of the Sixth Amendment requires that the defense must have an opportunity to cross-examine. [**Crawford v. Washington**, 541 U.S. 36 (2004)]

a. Right to Counsel—Rationale

In extending the right to counsel to a preliminary hearing to determine probable cause to prosecute, the Court reasoned that a lawyer can help an indigent defendant expose weaknesses in the government's case, impeach witnesses for use at trial, preserve favorable testimony for trial, and make effective arguments to secure bail or an early psychiatric examination. [**Coleman v. Alabama**, *supra*]

SUMMARY OF PRELIMINARY HEARINGS

	GERSTEIN HEARING	INITIAL APPEARANCE	BINDOVER HEARING
PURPOSE	Quick check to determine whether there is probable cause	Set bail, appoint counsel	Review prosecutor's decision to charge
TIMING	Immediately after or within 48 hours of arrest if there is a significant restraint on defendant's liberty and no indictment or warrant was issued	As set by statute; may be combined with *Gerstein* hearing if held within 48 hours	As set by statute, usually well after arrest
CONSTITUTIONALLY REQUIRED?	Yes, by Fourth Amendment	No, unless combined with *Gerstein* hearing	No, may be waived by defendant or by grand jury indictment
ADVERSARIAL?	No	Yes	Yes

5. Limitations

a. Grand Jury Indictment

In federal court cases in which a grand jury has returned an indictment, no preliminary hearing is required (*see infra*, pp. 121–124). The grand jury ***indictment constitutes a determination that probable cause exists*** with respect to the charges against the accused. Generally, this also applies in states that use grand juries.

b. Misdemeanors

In most jurisdictions, no preliminary hearing is required in misdemeanor cases.

c. Waiver

An accused may waive the right to a preliminary hearing.

C. Bail

1. Constitutional Basis

Bail is a sum of money or property that is exchanged for the release of an arrested person from custody as a guarantee of that person's appearance for trial. Typically, bail is returned after the criminal court proceedings are complete, but failure to appear in court as directed can result in forfeiture. The Eighth Amendment guarantees that "excessive bail shall not be required."

Note that this is not a guarantee of a right to bail, only a prohibition against excessive bail when bail is granted. It has not been determined whether the prohibition is binding on the states. [But *see* **Timbs v. Indiana**, 586 U.S. 146 (2019) (finding the Excessive Fines Clause incorporated to the states and suggesting that the excessive bail prohibition may be too)] Most state constitutions explicitly grant a right to bail and prohibit excessive bail.

2. Function of Bail

The main function of bail is to assure the presence of the accused at trial. [**Stack v. Boyle**, 342 U.S. 1 (1951)] Bail is usually set by a judicial officer at the initial appearance of the defendant after arrest. Bail is also intended to ***prevent the infliction of punishment before conviction***, thereby giving meaning to the ***presumption of innocence*** that underlies our criminal justice system. Release on bail also ***permits an accused to assist in the preparation of her defense***. If a defendant's presence in the community is necessary for her attorney to secure and interview witnesses, denial of bail may give rise to a claim of ineffective assistance of counsel.

3. What Constitutes "Excessive Bail"

The Supreme Court has held that the function of bail is to assure the presence of the accused at trial. Thus, bail is excessive if it is set higher than an amount ***reasonably calculated to assure the presence*** of the accused at trial.

a. Case-by-Case Determination

Some state courts use "bail schedules," which set the amount of bail based only on the offense committed. However, the Supreme Court has suggested that bail should be set on a case-by-case basis to ensure the presence of the defendant. [**Stack v. Boyle**, *supra*]

4. Denial of Bail—Capital Cases

No right to bail exists in capital cases. The rationale for this exception is that someone accused of a crime for which she might lose her life is highly unlikely to return for trial no matter how high the bail.

5. Denial of Bail—Preventive Detention

Many states (and Congress) have adopted preventive detention provisions that permit courts to deny bail to defendants who are alleged to be dangerous to society. Preventive detention is designed to ensure that ***dangerous individuals*** are not released from custody into society, where they might engage in additional criminal activities pending trial.

a. State Provisions

Opponents argue that a system of preventive detention denies an accused the right to bail and requires courts to make speculative and often inaccurate predictions of future dangerousness. In Tennessee, the state constitution guarantees every defendant a right to pretrial release (although that right can be forfeited through subsequent criminal behavior while released on bail.) [**Tennessee v. Burgins**, 464 S.W.3d 298 (Tenn. 2015)] Nevertheless, preventive detention schemes have increased and have usually been upheld by courts when tied to expedited docket positions for detained defendants. Because preventively detained defendants must be brought to trial more quickly than others, prosecutors in some jurisdictions are reluctant to invoke preventive detention.

b. Federal Provision

Federal courts have the authority under the Bail Reform Act of 1984 to detain an arrestee when a judge determines, after a hearing, that no condition of release would "reasonably" assure the appearance of the person and "the safety of . . . the community." At the bail hearing, the defendant has the right to testify, the right to present other evidence, the right to counsel, and the right to cross-examine witnesses. The court's decision to detain an arrestee must be based on ***clear and convincing evidence***, and if detention is ordered, the defendant is entitled to an expedited review of the decision. The Supreme Court upheld these preventive detention provisions, reasoning that pretrial detention is "regulatory, not penal," and that the liberty interests implicated are outweighed by the government's "overwhelming" interest in community safety. [**United States v. Salerno**, 479 U.S. 1026 (1987); *and see* **Schall v. Martin**, 467 U.S. 253 (1984)—upholding the constitutionality of a New York statute authorizing preventive detention of dangerous juveniles]

(1) Prompt Hearing Requirement

The hearing must be held at the first appearance in front of a judicial officer, or within five days after that appearance if the government seeks a continuance. [**United States v. Montalvo-Murillo**, 495 U.S. 711 (1990)] In *Montalvo-Murillo*, the Court found failure to abide by the prompt hearing requirement to be harmless error, at least where the person is subsequently found eligible for detention.

(2) Preventive Detention Presumptively Required for Some Offenses

The federal bail provisions explicitly presume that no conditions of release will reasonably assure the appearance of persons charged with crimes of violence or many controlled substance offenses. [18 U.S.C. § 3142(e), (f)(1)]

6. Appellate Review

Appealability of an order pertaining to bail varies from jurisdiction to jurisdiction. In some states, a decision denying bail is considered a final order and thus appealable. In other states, the order is considered interlocutory and is appealable only if authorized by statute. If not immediately appealable, the denial of bail can be the subject of a ***petition for the writ of habeas corpus***.

a. Timeliness of Claim

Denial of bail can be raised at ***any*** stage of the proceedings against an accused.

b. Standard of Review

Setting bail is a matter within the discretion of the trial court. A bail decision by the trial court will be reversed or reduced only if a ***gross abuse of discretion*** is indicated.

(1) Distinguish—Denial of Bail

Federal law provides that defendants who are denied bail are entitled to an expedited review of the decision, and denial of bail must be supported by ***clear and convincing evidence***. [**United States v. Salerno**, *supra*]

7. Bail During Appeal

While an appeal is pending, even a convicted individual may be entitled to bail in the federal system and in many states. [18 U.S.C. § 3143; Fed. R. Crim. P. 46(c)] However, bail will be denied if the court finds that the appeal is frivolous or taken solely to delay imposition of sentence.

a. Standards

A federal defendant requesting bail while appealing her conviction must overcome a presumption against bail. This can only be done with clear and convincing evidence that the defendant is unlikely to flee, does not pose a danger to the community, and that the appeal raises a substantial question of law or fact likely to result in reversal, a new trial, a sentence that does not include a term of imprisonment, or a reduced sentence to a term of imprisonment less than the total time already served plus the expected duration of the appeal. [18 U.S.C. § 3143(b)]

8. Types of Bail

The predominant system of pretrial release is the money bail system. The premise of the system is that risk of a high financial loss will deter the accused from fleeing and will assure her presence at trial. An accused can either post the security herself, or she can obtain a bond from a bail bondsperson by paying a fee (usually 10% of the face value of the bond).

a. Criticism

The money bail system has been criticized as inequitable because those with access to money are released, while the poor must remain in jail pending trial or appeal.

b. Reform Movement

Dissatisfaction with the money bail system has led to changes in bail procedures. These changes include releasing defendants on their own recognizance, unsecured appearance bonds, surety bonds, and property bonds. Some jurisdictions have promised not to seek bail for lesser crimes, such as prostitution. Others have adopted programs placing various conditions on the released defendant to assure her presence at trial. These conditions might include an agreement not to commit any crimes while on release, to remain in the custody of a designated person, to maintain employment, to maintain a curfew, or to avoid contact with certain persons, etc. [*See* 18 U.S.C. § 3142(c)] Some courts offer alternative methods of pretrial detention, such as house arrest.

D. Indictment

1. Introduction

An indictment is a written accusation submitted to a grand jury by a prosecutor that charges a person with a crime, typically a felony. A grand jury will endorse this "bill of indictment" with the words "A True Bill" if the grand jurors believe, after hearing evidence presented by the prosecutor, that there is probable cause to believe that the person has committed a crime.

Alternatively, a grand jury may decide that the person should not be prosecuted. In this case, the bill of indictment will be marked "No True Bill" and be dismissed.

a. Note

If a grand jury refuses to indict, there is no federal constitutional barrier to a prosecutor subsequently presenting the same indictment before a second grand jury. If the grand jury indicts, the finding of probable cause is determinative. The defendant does not have a right to challenge that finding in a preliminary hearing. [**Kaley v. United States**, 571 U.S. 320 (2014)] Double Jeopardy does not apply to Grand Jury proceedings.

2. Use of Indictments

a. Federal Felony Cases

A person has a Fifth Amendment right to a grand jury indictment in all federal felony prosecutions. Misdemeanors, however, can be tried by information or indictment.

b. Not Required in State Cases

There is no constitutional right to a grand jury indictment in state criminal prosecutions. [**Hurtado v. California**, 110 U.S. 516 (1884), *supra*, p. 4] Many states, pursuant to their state constitutions or statutes, require grand jury indictments in felony prosecutions.

3. Proceedings

a. Grand Jury

(1) Secrecy

Grand jury proceedings are secret. A defendant has ***no right*** to appear, to present evidence, to have their counsel appear, or send defense witnesses. However, the Supreme Court has held that when the desire for grand jury secrecy conflicts with a witness's First Amendment rights, the latter may prevail.

e.g. **Example:** The First Amendment prohibits banning a grand jury witness from recounting the gist of his testimony after the grand jury term has ended. [**Butterworth v. Smith**, 494 U.S. 624 (1990)]

(a) Federal Grand Juries

A federal rule allows the disclosure of grand jury proceedings to other attorneys for the government and other personnel who assist the prosecutor appearing before the grand jury. [Fed. R. Crim. P. 6(e)(3)(A)] The court may also authorize disclosure of grand jury proceedings, at the defendant's request, if disclosure could provide grounds to dismiss the indictment. [Fed. R. Crim. P. 6(e)(3)(E)]

(2) Sufficiency of Evidence

A grand jury indictment cannot be challenged on the ground that the grand jury relied upon incompetent or inadequate evidence. [**United States v. Calandra**, 414 U.S. 338 (1974), *supra*, p. 13] Similarly, an indictment may be based on ***illegally obtained evidence*** which subsequently will be excluded at trial. [**Calandra**, *supra*] An indictment can also be based entirely on ***hearsay evidence.*** [**Costello v. United States**, 350 U.S. 359 (1956)]

(a) Exculpatory Evidence

An indictment may not be dismissed by a federal court for a prosecutor's failure to present exculpatory evidence to the grand jury, unless the prosecutor's conduct violates a preexisting constitutional, legislative, or procedural rule. [**United States v. Williams**, 504 U.S. 36 (1992)]

(b) Challenges for Duplicity and Multiplicity

Indictments may be challenged on due process grounds based on the way the offenses are charged. An indictment may not charge a defendant with the same offense in multiple counts because that would be a duplicitous count. If challenged, the government must elect which offense it wishes to charge. In addition, one count of an indictment may not contain several different offenses because this raises the problem of multiplicity. If challenged, the government must consolidate the offenses or eliminate the repeated counts. Both practices violate due process by increasing the chances that a person will be convicted based on the manner the offenses are charged.

(3) Content Specificity

The indictment must contain the elements of the offense. Generally an indictment that "tracks" or duplicates the language of the statute is sufficient, so long as the statute fully and clearly sets forth all the elements of the offense. [**Hamling v. United States**, 418 U.S. 87 (1974); but *see* **Russell v. United States**, 369 U.S. 749 (1962)—reversing conviction for refusing to answer certain questions before a congressional subcommittee because an indictment that merely tracked the language of the statute insufficiently set forth the elements of the offense charged] The indictment must also be specific enough to enable the defendant to plead an acquittal or conviction barring future prosecution for the same offense. [**Hamling v. United States**, *supra*]

(4) No Unanimity Requirement

Grand jurors need not be unanimous to issue an indictment. A federal grand jury, for example, consists of between 16 and 23 persons, 12 of whom must concur to indict. [Fed. R. Crim. P. 6(a), (f)]

EXAM TIP

Note that the grand jury's job is quite different from that of the trial (petit) jury. The grand jury's only job is to determine ***whether there is probable cause*** to believe that a particular person has committed a crime. It does ***not*** determine guilt and/or punishment. Thus, keep in mind that in making its determination, the grand jury can hear evidence that would be inadmissible at trial, including illegally-obtained evidence and hearsay testimony.

b. After Indictment

(1) Prosecutorial Discretion

Once a grand jury has returned an indictment, the prosecutor retains discretion to prosecute, or not to prosecute, the accused.

(2) Grand Jury Determination Is Binding

An indicted criminal defendant has no right to contest a grand jury's determination of probable cause to challenge a pretrial order ensuring the availability of property for forfeiture proceedings. [**Kaley**, *supra*, p. 121]

(3) Court Amendment of Indictment

When an indicted person is brought to trial, a judge may amend the indictment based on the evidence presented at the trial. *But note*: If the judicial amendment increases the maximum authorized punishment that the accused can receive, the indictment must be returned to the grand jury.

(4) Variance in Proof

If the proof presented at trial varies from the proof presented in the indictment, there is no violation of the right to a grand jury as long as the trial proof is ***clearly within*** the allegations of the indictment. [**United States v. Miller**, 471 U.S. 130 (1985)] To challenge a conviction based on a variance, the defendant must prove that the variance prejudiced the defendant at trial. [**Berger v. United States**, 295 U.S. 78 (1935)]

4. Waiver

An accused can waive a grand jury indictment in federal court in all but capital cases. [Fed. R. Crim. P. 7(a), (b)] In cases where waiver is permitted, prosecution of the offense will be authorized by an information, in lieu of a grand jury indictment (*see* below). Some states do not permit such a waiver by the accused.

5. Special or Investigative Grand Jury Indictments

An indictment may also originate from a grand jury's own investigation of criminal activity. This represents the extraordinary model of the criminal justice system, as most criminal proceedings begin by information (*infra*). Such special or investigative grand juries typically operate in cases involving organized crime or political corruption.

E. Information

1. Introduction

An information is a written accusation prepared by a prosecutor in the name of the government charging a person with the commission of a crime. An information is used to charge persons with criminal offenses in cases in which a grand jury indictment is not required or has been waived by the accused. In the federal system, an information is used for misdemeanors.

In modern practice, ***the information is used more frequently than the indictment***. As mentioned *supra*, p. 122, accused persons have a constitutional right to be indicted by a grand jury in federal felony cases. In federal misdemeanor cases, a prosecutor has the option to proceed by indictment or information. [Fed. R. Crim. P. 7(a)(2)] Similarly, most states permit prosecution by information or indictment at the prosecutor's option.

2. Limitations on Filing an Information

a. Prior Preliminary Examination

Before a prosecutor can file an information, most states require that the accused have a preliminary examination before a magistrate.

(1) Caveat—Not a Constitutional Right

Some federal courts have held, and the Supreme Court has implied [**Gerstein v. Pugh**, *supra*, p. 117], that the Constitution does ***not require*** a preliminary judicial hearing to determine whether there is probable cause for the prosecutor to file an information.

b. Content Specificity

The information must "reasonably apprise the accused of the charges against him so that he may have the opportunity to prepare and present his defense." This requirement is generally satisfied if the charges are expressed in the words of the statute defining the offense. Frequently, the information also states the date, time, and place that the offense was committed, but generally these elements are not essential.

3. Magistrate's Findings Not Always Binding

Some jurisdictions allow a prosecutor to charge the accused in the information only with the offenses for which a magistrate determined there was probable cause. In other jurisdictions, the information can include the crime for which probable cause was found at the preliminary examination, as well as other crimes supported by the evidence at the preliminary hearing. Still other states allow an information to charge a person with all crimes related to the same facts adduced at the preliminary hearing. Finally, in most states, a finding of no probable cause by one magistrate does not preclude a prosecutor from presenting the case to another magistrate.

4. Joinder of Offenses and Defendants

According to the Federal Rules and many state rules, an information or indictment can charge two or more offenses that are connected in their commission or are of the same or similar character. [*See* Fed. R. Crim. P. 8(a); Ark. R. Crim. R 21.1; Colo. R. Crim. P. 8; Conn. Gen. Stat. Ann. § 54–57; D.C. Code § 23–311] Also, two or more defendants may be charged in the same information or indictment if they participated in the same transaction or series of transactions charged. [Fed. R. Crim. P. 8(b); Ark. R. Crim. P. 21.2; Colo. R. Crim. P. 8; D.C. Code § 23–311]

F. Right to a Speedy Trial

1. Constitutional Basis

The Sixth Amendment, applicable to federal courts and incorporated to apply in state cases, provides that "in all criminal prosecutions the accused shall enjoy the right to a speedy . . . trial." [**Klopfer v. North Carolina**, 386 U.S. 213 (1967), *supra,* p. 3]

a. Purposes

The purposes of the constitutional guarantee of a speedy trial are twofold:

(i) ***To relieve the defendant of unnecessary consequences of being accused*** of a crime, such as oppressive pretrial incarceration (with resulting disruption of employment, drain on financial resources, etc.), subjection to public scorn, personal anxiety, and impairment of the defense.

(ii) ***To promote society's interest in promptly disposing of charges*** to enhance the proper administration of justice.

[**Barker v. Wingo**, 407 U.S. 514 (1972)]

b. Remedy

The sole remedy for violation of the right to a speedy trial is ***dismissal*** of the charge. [**Strunk v. United States**, 412 U.S. 434 (1973)] This dismissal bars all future prosecutions for the offense. Courts are, therefore, reluctant to find violations of the right. The Supreme Court has held that the dismissal remedy should be used sparingly. Even when courts find a violation, they often dismiss ***without*** prejudice. The Court will often overturn a lower court's decision to dismiss ***with*** prejudice, especially if based only on a claim of a "nonchalant government attitude." [**United States v. Taylor**, 487 U.S. 326 (1988)]

2. When Right to Speedy Trial Attaches

The right to a speedy trial attaches only after a person has become an "accused"—i.e., after indictment, information, or actual restraint imposed by arrest. [**Doggett v. United States**, 505 U.S. 647 (1992)] Hence, the right is ***not*** violated by a delay in filing charges, although such delay may violate other rights (*see* below). Once arrested, however, a person is deemed an "accused" and is entitled to a speedy trial, even if he is released thereafter and not indicted for a substantial period of time. [**Dillingham v. United States**, 423 U.S. 64 (1975)] The Speedy Trial Clause is ***not*** violated by a delay between dismissal of charges and reindictment for the same offense. [**United States v. MacDonald**, 456 U.S. 1 (1982)]

a. Knowledge of Charges Unnecessary

The Speedy Trial Clause attaches even if the defendant does not know about the charges against him and is thus not restrained in any way. [**Doggett v. United States**, *supra*]

b. "Pre-Accusation Delay"

As stated above, delay in arresting or charging a person with a crime does not violate the constitutional right to a speedy trial, because the right attaches only when the person has become an "accused." However, ***a person is protected by the Due Process Clauses of the Fifth and Fourteenth Amendments against unnecessary pre-accusation delay that causes substantial prejudice to a fair trial.*** In each case, the reasons for the delay and the impact on the trial (*i.e.,* any prejudice to the defendant that may have resulted) must be considered. [**United States v. Lovasco**, 431 U.S. 783 (1977)—reversing dismissal when indictment charging firearms offenses was filed over 18 months after the last alleged criminal act and after two material witnesses died during the delay; *and see* **United States v. Marion**, 404 U.S. 307 (1971)—dismissal of indictment not constitutionally required merely because defendant was indicted for fraud three years after the latest act alleged without a showing by the defendant of actual prejudice]

3. Determining Unreasonableness of Delay

Whether a case must be dismissed for lack of a speedy trial requires a ***balancing test***. The conduct of both the prosecution and the defendant is weighed, and factors including the length of delay, reason for the delay, defendant's assertion or nonassertion of right, and prejudice to the defendant are considered. [**Barker v. Wingo**, *supra*]

a. Length of Delay

The length of delay alone does not establish a violation of the right to a speedy trial. However, unless there is a delay of sufficient length to be arguably prejudicial, courts will not investigate the other relevant factors in the balancing test.

(1) Distinguish—Statutes

Various statutes impose specific time limits within which an accused must be brought to trial (*see* below). Under these statutes, delay alone may require a dismissal.

b. Reason for Delay

(1) Delay by Prosecution

A deliberate attempt by the prosecution to delay the trial to receive an advantage may violate the defendant's right to speedy trial. However, a justifiable reason for prosecution delay (*e.g.*, missing witness, illness of parties) may result in a finding of no constitutional violation. [**Barker v. Wingo**, *supra*]

(2) Delay by Accused

If the delay is attributable to ***willful*** delay tactics by the accused, she is deemed to have ***waived*** her right to a speedy trial. [**Strunk v. United States**, *supra*] The mere fact that the accused is ***serving a jail sentence in another jurisdiction*** does not justify the delay of her trial on a pending charge. The prosecution must attempt to have the other jurisdiction temporarily cede custody for purposes of trial on the pending charge. [**Smith v. Hooey**, 393 U.S. 374 (1969)—forum that wishes to prosecute a prisoner, incarcerated in another jurisdiction, for a crime committed in the forum has a constitutional duty to make a diligent, good-faith effort to bring the accused into the forum for trial]

(3) Delays Caused by Assigned Counsel

Delays caused by court-appointed defense counsel should ordinarily be attributed to the defendant and not to the government. [**Vermont. v. Brillon**, 556 U.S. 81 (2009)]

c. Detainers

A detainer is a request by one jurisdiction to another jurisdiction to advise the incarcerated defendant of the right to demand a speedy trial on unresolved charges in the requesting jurisdiction. Forty-eight states, the District of Columbia, and the federal government have signed the Interstate Agreement on Detainers ("IAD"). The IAD applies to transfers of prisoners for unrelated trials between two states, from the federal government to a state, and from a state to the federal government. The IAD requires trial in the detainer requesting jurisdiction within 180 days after the date the defendant demands a speedy trial and within 120 days after arriving in that jurisdiction. [18 U.S.C.A. App. § 2]

(1) **Waiver**

A defendant can waive the right to a speedy trial under the IAD. The Supreme Court has ruled that defense counsel's agreement to a trial date outside the IAD time limits waives the defendant's speedy trial rights under the IAD, even without express consent of the defendant. [**New York v. Hill**, 528 U.S. 110 (2000)]

d. **Defendant's Assertion or Non-Assertion of Right**

The defendant may raise the speedy trial issue at trial, even if no pretrial motion was made. The failure to assert the right, however, is heavily weighed by the courts. [**Barker v. Wingo**, *supra*]

e. **Prejudice**

The nature and amount of prejudice resulting from trial delay must be considered in light of the consequences the right is designed to prevent—*e.g.,* oppressive incarceration, loss of evidence, inaccuracy of witness testimony, anxiety to accused, etc. A showing of prejudice is strongly considered in the speedy trial analysis. [**Barker v. Wingo**, *supra*]

e.g. **Example:** A defendant who was arrested 8½ years after his federal indictment due solely to the government's neglect and who promptly asserted his right to a speedy trial claim was ***presumptively prejudiced*** so that an actual showing of prejudice was not necessary. [**Doggett v. United States**, *supra*]

4. Statutory Provisions

The Federal Speedy Trial Act [18 U.S.C. § 3161] sets out ***specific time limits*** for the prosecution of federal criminal cases and remedies for violations of the Act. For example, the Act provides that in any case in which the defendant pleads not guilty, the trial "shall commence within seventy days." The Act provides specific periods of delay that are excluded from the 70-day calculation, such as delay to assess the defendant's mental competency, delay resulting from an interlocutory appeal, etc. Many states also have statutes that deal with speedy trial issues in substantial detail, with fixed time periods for prosecution. Many state statutes vary the time periods depending on whether the defendant is incarcerated prior to trial.

EXAM TIP

Don't be fooled by an exam question that sets up a long delay in bringing charges. Such a delay is irrelevant to the right to a speedy trial. The right applies ***only after*** a person has been indicted, charged by information, or arrested. Even then there is no bright line test for determining how much delay is too much. You should consider the conduct of the parties, the reason for the delay, whether the defendant asserted the right to speedy trial, and whether the defendant has been prejudiced by the delay. Note that under state speedy trial statutes, there may be very specific time limits.

G. Government's Obligation to Disclose Information and Notice of Defenses

1. Constitutional Provisions

The Sixth Amendment to the Constitution provides that in "all criminal prosecutions, the accused shall . . . be informed of the nature and cause of the accusation." This provision has been applied in a very limited way and requires only that the indictment or other charging document give the defendant ***sufficient detail*** so that he will be prepared to present an adequate defense. [**Russell v. United States**, 369 U.S. 749 (1962)] The principal requirement for the disclosure of information by the government emanates from the Due Process Clause.

a. Affirmative Obligation to Avoid Use of False Evidence

The government has an affirmative obligation to avoid the knowing use of false evidence or testimony. [**Alcorta v. Texas**, 355 U.S. 28 (1957)] A due process violation will be found if prosecutors ***knowingly*** allow false testimony to go uncorrected—even if the testimony is unsolicited and relates only to the credibility of witnesses. [**Napue v. Illinois**, 360 U.S. 264 (1959)]

(1) Result—Reversal

A conviction based on knowingly false evidence must always be reversed. [**Napue v. Illinois**, *supra*]

2. Duty to Disclose Favorable Evidence

The government has a duty to disclose material, exculpatory evidence to the defendant. Failure to disclose such evidence violates the Due Process Clause. This doctrine is referred to as the "*Brady* rule." [**Brady v. Maryland**, 373 U.S. 83 (1963)]

a. The *Agurs* Tests of Materiality

Brady left open several questions, including what exculpatory evidence will be considered material. The Supreme Court first answered this question in **United States v. Agurs**, 427 U.S. 97 (1976), by dividing cases into three situations:

(1) When the prosecutor relies on ***perjured testimony***, the conviction must be overturned if there is ***any reasonable likelihood*** that the false testimony could have affected the judgment of the jury;

(2) When the prosecutor ***fails to disclose specifically requested information***, the Court applied substantially the same test as for perjured testimony; and

(3) When the prosecutor ***fails to disclose unrequested information*** (which includes responses to nonspecific requests such as requests for "all *Brady* material"), the conviction must be overturned if such evidence creates ***reasonable doubt*** in the mind of the trial judge as to the defendant's guilt.

b. The *Bagley* Test of Materiality

The Court revisited the ***Brady*** issue and the ***Agurs*** holding in **United States v. Bagley**, 473 U.S. 667 (1985). In ***Bagley***, the Court eliminated the ***Agurs*** difference in treatment between "specifically requested" and "nonrequested or generally requested" situations. The *Bagley* Court ruled, instead, that whenever the prosecutor fails to disclose exculpatory information, the conviction must be overturned whenever "there is a ***reasonable probability that, had the evidence been disclosed to the defense, the result of the proceeding would have been different***."

c. The *Kyles* Refinements

In **Kyles v. Whitley**, 514 U.S. 419 (1995), the Supreme Court further illuminated the ***Bagley*** materiality test by clarifying four aspects of the test:

(1) The *Bagley* test is ***not a preponderance test***; the question is not whether the defendant would, more likely than not, have received a different verdict but whether, in absence of the exculpatory evidence, he received a fair trial;

(2) The *Bagley* test is ***not a sufficiency of evidence test***—the defendant need not show that, after discounting the inculpatory evidence in light of the exculpatory evidence, there would not have been sufficient evidence to convict the defendant; instead, *Bagley* assesses whether the exculpatory evidence could reasonably place the case in a different light by undermining confidence in the verdict;

(3) Once a *Bagley* violation is found, there is ***no need to inquire*** whether the error constitutes "harmless error;" by definition, it is not harmless error; and

(4) Undisclosed evidence should be ***viewed collectively with all undisclosed evidence known by the government*** because the prosecutor has a ***duty to learn*** of any favorable evidence known to other government agents and to gauge the cumulative effect of all exculpatory evidence before deciding whether to disclose, and this duty is absolute—not a good-faith effort test.

d. The *Strickler* Materiality Test

The Supreme Court subsequently summarized the materiality test as involving three components:

(i) The evidence at issue must be favorable to the accused because it is either exculpatory or impeaches a witness;

e.g. **Example:** The prosecution committed a *Brady* violation when it failed to disclose statements from the sole eyewitness linking the defendant with the killing of five people. The eyewitness's undisclosed statements directly contradicted his in-court testimony. Although evidence impeaching an eyewitness may not be material if the government's other evidence is strong enough to sustain confidence in the verdict, when the eyewitness's testimony is the only link to the defendant, the evidence is material. [**Smith v. Cain**, 565 U.S. 73 (2012)]

(ii) The evidence must have been suppressed by the prosecutor (either willfully or inadvertently); and

(iii) The defendant's case was prejudiced as a result.

[**Strickler v. Greene**, 527 U.S. 263 (1999)]

EXAM TIP

On an exam, if you see facts indicating that the prosecutor failed to disclose information to the defendant, remember: (i) a ***prosecutor's duty to disclose exculpatory information is automatic***; a defendant need not request the exculpatory evidence; and (ii) failure to disclose information that ***reasonably could have changed the result*** of the trial will result in a "Brady" violation and a reversal.

e. Duty Does Not Apply at Post-Conviction Proceedings

A prosecutor's obligation to disclose material, exculpatory evidence under ***Brady*** and its refinements does not apply at post-conviction proceedings. [**District Attorney's Office for the Third Judicial District v. Osborne**, 557 U.S. 52 (2009)—a convicted offender has no federal due process right to obtain post-conviction access to a state's evidence for DNA testing in the absence of any indication that available state post-conviction relief procedures are fundamentally unfair]

f. Witness Deals

Brady requires the disclosure of any deals made by the prosecution with a witness, because these are material to a witness's credibility. [**Giglio v. United States**, 405 U.S. 150 (1972)]

g. Exception—Confidential Reports

A defendant may obtain confidential reports only when they are favorable to the defendant and material to guilt or punishment. However, a trial judge is ***not*** required to perform an ***in camera*** review to decide which information is material to the defendant's case. [**Pennsylvania v. Ritchie**, 480 U.S. 39 (1987)]

e.g. **Example:** A defendant accused of molesting his daughter has no automatic right to obtain investigative reports made by the state's agency in charge of the welfare of children. [**Pennsylvania v. Ritchie**, *supra*]

h. Exception—Failure to Preserve Evidence

Unless a criminal defendant can show bad faith on the part of the police, failure to preserve potentially useful evidence does not constitute a violation of due process of law. [**Arizona v. Youngblood**, 488 U.S. 51 (1988)—failure to perform tests of semen taken from 10-year-old male victim of sexual assault and failure to refrigerate the boy's clothing to preserve the semen on it was negligent, but did not require reversal because no bad faith was shown]

3. Defense Obligation to Disclose Information

Some states provide that the prosecution may be entitled to receive information from the defense prior to trial.

a. Alibis

Some states require that a defendant give advance notice of alibi defenses (including the names of alibi witnesses) to the prosecution. Such requirements do not violate the Fifth Amendment privilege against self-incrimination. [**Williams v. Florida**, 399 U.S. 78 (1970)]

b. Reciprocal Discovery

If the state is entitled to discover information from the defense, the defense must be entitled to reciprocal discovery rights from the government or the Due Process Clause will be violated. [**Wardius v. Oregon**, 412 U.S. 470 (1973)]

(1) Federal Rules

Under the Federal Rules of Criminal Procedure, if the defendant requests that the prosecution produce documents and tangible evidence, reports of examinations and tests, or expert witness information, the defense must make a reciprocal disclosure. [Fed. R. Crim. P. 16(b)(1)(A)–(C)]

c. Witness Statements

In federal court, upon request of the opposing party, both sides must disclose prior written statements by a witness after the witness testifies on direct examination. [18 U.S.C. § 3500—Jencks Act]

4. Informants

Normally, the prosecution is under no obligation to reveal the identity of confidential informants. However, this rule is not absolute. If disclosure of the informant's identity is relevant and helpful to a defendant's case or essential to a fair determination of the case, a court may order disclosure of the informant's identity.

e.g. **Example:** Defendant was charged with transportation of narcotics. A government informant was the recipient of the narcotics and the only eyewitness to the transaction. Because the informant was the only witness who could contradict the testimony of the government witnesses, the Supreme Court held that it was harmful error to deny the defendant's request to disclose the informant's identity. [**Roviaro v. United States**, 353 U.S. 53 (1957)]

5. Notice of Evidence at Penalty Phase

The government is not required to give a defendant notice of what evidence will be used against the defendant in the penalty phase of a trial. [**Gray v. Netherland**, 518 U.S. 152 (1996)]

H. Competency to Stand Trial and at Time of Execution

1. Competency and Insanity Distinguished

Competency to stand trial must be distinguished from the insanity defense, although both rest on a defendant's mental health status.

Insanity is a defense to the criminal charge; a defendant acquitted by reason of insanity may not be retried and convicted, although she may be hospitalized under some circumstances. ***Incompetency*** to stand trial depends on a defendant's mental condition at the ***time of trial***, unlike insanity, which turns on a defendant's mental condition at the ***time of the crime***. Incompetency is not a defense, but a ***bar to trial*** during such time as a defendant remains incompetent. If a defendant who is incompetent to stand trial later regains her competency, she can then be tried and—unless she has a successful defense—convicted.

2. Basis of Claim

The incompetency claim is rooted in the Due Process Clause of the United States Constitution. A defendant may not be tried, convicted, or sentenced if, as a result of mental disease or defect, he is unable: (i) ***to understand the nature of the proceedings*** being brought against him; ***or***

(ii) ***to assist his lawyer in the preparation of his defense***. [**Dusky v. United States**, 362 U.S. 402 (1960)—Defendant is competent to stand trial if she can communicate with her attorney and has a rational and factual understanding of the proceedings] In determining competency, the court will consider factors such as the defendant's irrational behavior, the defendant's demeanor at trial, and medical opinions on the defendant's competency to stand trial. [**Drope v. Missouri**, 420 U.S. 162 (1975)]

a. Competency to Waive Counsel

The standard to measure competency to waive counsel is different. While the Supreme Court has not specified a precise standard (*see infra,* p. 157), it has noted that a defendant may simultaneously be competent to stand trial and incompetent to waive counsel. [**Indiana v. Edwards**, 554 U.S. 164 (2008)—in limited circumstances, a state may insist that a defendant proceed to trial with counsel, denying a right of self-representation, while also finding the defendant mentally competent to stand trial]

3. Determining Competency

The Due Process Clause prevents a defendant from being declared incompetent ***without notice and a hearing***. Many jurisdictions grant a right to a jury determination of competence. If evidence of a defendant's incompetency is before the trial judge, the judge has a constitutional obligation to conduct further inquiry and determine whether in fact the defendant is incompetent.

a. Assignment of the Burden of Proof

Requiring a criminal defendant to prove by a preponderance of the evidence that he is not competent to stand trial does not violate due process. [**Medina v. California**, 505 U.S. 437 (1992)] However, the state may not impose a burden on the defendant to prove incompetency by a standard higher than a preponderance of the evidence. [**Cooper v. Oklahoma**, 517 U.S. 348 (1996)—requiring defendant to prove incompetency to stand trial by clear and convincing evidence violates due process]

b. Raising the Issue

Failure to make a timely assertion of incompetence to stand trial does not prevent defense counsel from raising the issue later. Competency to stand trial may be raised at any time before or during trial. A competency hearing must be held whenever there is sufficient doubt as to the defendant's competency. [**Cooper v. Oklahoma**, *supra*; **Pate v. Robinson**, 383 U.S. 375 (1966)]

c. Court-Appointed Psychiatric Exam

Whenever (i) the defendant can make a colorable showing that he might benefit from the insanity defense, or (ii) the government is going to produce psychiatric evidence at sentencing to prove potential future dangerousness, an indigent criminal defendant is constitutionally entitled to a psychiatric evaluation at state expense. [**Ake v. Oklahoma**, 470 U.S. 68 (1985)]

4. Effect of Finding Incompetence

A finding of incompetence ***suspends the criminal proceedings*** and invariably results in ***commitment*** until such time as the defendant regains competence. But the defendant cannot be hospitalized indefinitely or for a long period of time simply because he is found incompetent. This can be done only if independent "civil commitment" proceedings are begun and result in commitment. [**Jackson v. Indiana**, 406 U.S. 715 (1972)] There is no comparable right to suspend a civil, habeas case when a state prisoner seeking federal habeas relief is incompetent to assist counsel. [**Ryan v. Gonzalez**, 568 U.S. 57 (2013)]

a. Forced "Cure"

Under the Due Process Clause, the government may administer antipsychotic drugs to an unwilling, mentally ill defendant facing serious criminal charges in order to make him competent to stand trial if: (i) the treatment is medically appropriate, (ii) the treatment is substantially unlikely to cause side effects that may undermine the fairness of the trial, and (iii) considering less-intrusive alternatives, the treatment is necessary to further important governmental trial-related interests. [**Sell v. United States**, 539 U.S. 166 (2003)]

5. Incompetency at Time of Execution

Just as a defendant cannot be tried if they are unable to understand the nature of the proceedings, a defendant may not be executed if they are incapable of understanding the nature and purpose of the punishment. [*See* **Ford v. Wainwright**, 477 U.S. 399 (1986); **Panetti v. Quarterman**, 551 U.S. 930 (2007)] Although modern statutes often specify that only the warden may raise the issue, some provide for a jury determination. A defendant may not be executed if he is incapable of understanding the nature of the proceedings, but there is no similar bar to execution when the defendant cannot remember the events from the offense. The Eighth Amendment may bar execution of a prisoner suffering from dementia or other mental disease, if he cannot comprehend his punishment. [**Madison v. Alabama**, 586 U.S. 265 (2019)]

6. *Miranda* Warnings

A defendant is entitled to *Miranda* warnings before being compelled to undergo a court-ordered psychiatric examination to determine competency to stand trial. The defendant may then refuse to submit to the evaluation or to answer certain questions. [**Estelle v. Smith**, 451 U.S. 454 (1981), *supra,* p. 103]

Chapter Five
The Trial

CONTENTS	PAGE

Key Exam Issues

A variety of constitutional issues involving the trial process may arise on your exam. Although you might see exam questions with issues concerning the fairness of a trial, joint trials, the right to a public trial, or the Confrontation Clause (and thus you should review those topics briefly), it is much more likely that your exam will cover the right to a jury trial, the right to counsel, the burden of proof, and affirmative defenses.

1. Right to Jury Trial

The constitutional bases for the right to a jury trial are found in the Due Process Clause and the Sixth Amendment. Recall that the defendant is entitled to a jury trial only in cases involving ***serious offenses*** (*e.g.,* where more than six months' imprisonment is authorized), and that unanimity is constitutionally required for decisions by juries. Remember too that the ultimate issue involving the jury is one of basic fairness. The jury venire or pool must represent a reasonable cross-section of society, the jury cannot be unduly prejudiced prior to hearing the evidence, and the jury must be reasonably instructed on the law by the judge.

2. Right to Counsel

The right to an attorney at trial is protected by the Sixth Amendment. The amendment has been interpreted to mean that defendants are entitled to the assistance of ***reasonably competent lawyers*** in cases where ***actual imprisonment is ultimately imposed***. This right applies at ***any "critical" stage*** of the proceedings (*e.g.,* preliminary hearing, lineups that occur after adversary judicial proceedings have begun, sentencing, and automatic appeals). But keep in mind that a lawyer is ***not*** required in connection with investigatory processes such as the grand jury. Also, remember that convictions are seldom set aside on the basis of ineffective assistance of counsel.

3. Burden of Proof

Our system is based on the notion that defendants are presumed innocent until proven guilty. Thus, beware of any statutory device or jury instruction that improperly ***shifts the burden*** onto the defendant to disprove ***elements*** of a crime. All elements of all crimes must be proved by the government ***beyond a reasonable doubt***.

4. Affirmative Defenses

True affirmative defenses do not simply challenge the proof of the government. Instead, they involve situations where the government has likely proved all of the elements beyond a reasonable doubt, but as a matter of policy, the defendant cannot be convicted. Two of the most important and complex defenses are the ***insanity defense*** and the ***entrapment defense***. Regarding these defenses, ask yourself the following questions.

a. Insanity Defense

(1) Does the jurisdiction recognize a defense of insanity?

(2) Is the defendant simply disproving the state of mind or ***raising a true defense*** involving insanity?

(3) Which of the four ***insanity tests*** is used in the jurisdiction?

(4) What ***burden of proof procedure*** is used? Does the burden shift to the prosecution?

b. Entrapment

(1) Two standards can be found in the United States: A subjective test—***predisposition of the defendant***—and an objective test—***conduct of the government***. The subjective test is the majority view.

(2) No matter what the standard, what was the ***nature of the government's involvement?***

(3) Under the majority standard, what were the defendant's ***earlier criminal activities*** and what was her ***state of mind*** prior to the government's conduct?

A. Fair and Impartial Trial

1. Constitutional Bases

The right to a fair and impartial trial is required by the concept of due process and the Sixth Amendment's guarantee of an impartial jury. The right operates to ensure that a defendant is tried only by an ***impartial judge or jury***.

2. The Judge

a. Right to Unbiased Judge

Due process is violated if the judge is significantly ***prejudiced*** against the defendant or has a ***financial interest*** in the trial resulting in a finding of guilt.

e.g. **Example—Personal Bias:** The Supreme Court has found personal bias where the judge who cited an attorney for contempt presided over the subsequent contempt proceeding. [**Taylor v. Hayes**, 418 U.S. 488 (1974)]

e.g. **Example—Personal Involvement:** "[U]nder the Due Process Clause there is an impermissible risk of actual bias when a judge earlier had significant, personal involvement as a prosecutor in a critical decision regarding the defendant's case." [**Williams v. Pennsylvania**, 579 U.S. 1 (2016)]

e.g. **Example—Personal Financial Interest:** A judge regularly took bribes from defendants in exchange for granting acquittals. To defray suspicion, the judge ruled very harshly in other criminal cases where he was not bribed. Under these circumstances, the judge's personal financial interest in defraying suspicion raised an inference that he had a pro-prosecution bias in cases where he was not bribed. [*See* **Bracy v. Gramley**, 520 U.S. 899 (1997)]

e.g. **Example—Other Financial Interest:** The Supreme Court has found bias where the judge who presided over trials for municipal fines was also mayor of the municipality, and half of the municipality's revenue came from fines imposed by the court. The system violates due process standards because the judge has too great a financial interest in the outcome. [**Ward v. Village of Monroeville**, 409 U.S. 57 (1972)]

cf. **Compare:** Defendant Jerome was tried by Judge Smith three months ago. At sentencing, the judge said to the defendant: "Jerome, I have been lenient this time, but if you come back here again, I promise you the maximum." Jerome has been arrested on a new charge and is to be tried by Judge Smith. Judge Smith is not prejudiced or biased in the sense used here, and she may preside at Jerome's new trial.

b. No Right to Have Judge Be a Lawyer

A defendant in a minor misdemeanor case has no right to a legally trained trial judge provided that, upon conviction, the defendant has a right to a trial de novo in a court with a judge who is legally trained as a lawyer. [**North v. Russell**, 427 U.S. 328 (1976)] However, in serious cases, it is likely that the judge must be legally trained.

c. Process for Removing Judge

In federal court cases and in most state cases, there are two ways in which a judge may be removed for financial or personal interest.

(1) Party's Motion

In the federal courts, a party alleging bias may exercise one peremptory challenge per case to the presiding judge. The judge must accept the disqualification if counsel presents an affidavit and a certification of good faith. [28 U.S.C. § 144; **Bracy v. Gramley**, *supra*, p. 137; **Berger v. United States**, 255 U.S. 22 (1921)] Many states have similar rules.

(2) Judge's Recusal

A judge may disqualify herself, with or without a motion for recusal by either party. [28 U.S.C. § 455]

3. The Jury

A defendant has a right to a jury or trier of fact free from unfair influences. Unfair influences can arise in several ways.

e.g. **Example:** A court bailiff's comments in the presence of jurors about the guilt of the defendant and the Supreme Court's ability to correct the jury should they find the defendant not guilty is unfairly prejudicial and violates the Sixth Amendment right to an impartial jury. [**Parker v. Gladden**, 385 U.S. 363 (1966)]

a. Trying Defendant in Prison Clothing

Trying the defendant while he is wearing prison clothing can result in unfair prejudice to the defendant. Thus, if a defendant makes a timely objection to standing trial in prison clothing, it is unconstitutional for the state to compel him to do so. [**Estelle v. Williams**, 425 U.S. 501 (1976)] Similarly, the Due Process Clause prohibits the use of visible shackles during the trial and penalty phase of a capital proceeding unless the court makes a specific finding that their use is justified by concerns about courtroom security or risk of escape. [**Deck v. Missouri**, 544 U.S. 622 (2005)] *Rationale*: Shackling was prohibited at common law and undermines the presumption of innocence, the defendant's ability to consult with counsel, and the dignity of the proceedings.

b. Jury Association with Prosecution Witnesses

Due process is violated if prosecution witnesses have constant and intimate association with jurors. For example, if two sheriffs are also prosecution witnesses, it violates due process if the sheriffs eat with the jurors or run errands for them. [**Turner v. Louisiana**, 379 U.S. 466 (1965)]

c. Trial Disruption

Due process is violated when a trial is conducted in a manner that interferes with the jury's ability to give the evidence reasonable consideration. For example, televising or

broadcasting parts of a trial may influence the jury by emphasizing the notoriety of the trial. [**Estes v. Texas**, 381 U.S. 532 (1965)] However, the state may constitutionally permit the televising of criminal proceedings over the defendant's objections ***as long as the televising does not prejudice the jury***. [**Chandler v. Florida**, 449 U.S. 560 (1981)] In any case, the trial judge has a duty to protect the defendant from inherently prejudicial publicity and to control disruptive influences in the courtroom. [**Sheppard v. Maxwell**, 384 U.S. 333 (1966)—"Given the pervasiveness of modern communications and the difficulty of effacing prejudicial publicity from the minds of the jurors, the trial courts must take strong measures to ensure that the balance is never weighed against the accused"]

d. Pretrial Publicity

Excessive pretrial publicity prejudicial to the defendant may require a change of venue or a retrial.

Example: Due process is violated if a trial is held before a jury that was familiar with the material facts in the case and that had formed an opinion as to the defendant's guilt before the trial. [**Irvin v. Dowd**, 366 U.S. 717 (1961)] However, due process is satisfied if the judge asks the venire persons whether they were exposed to pretrial publicity and if so, whether it would affect their impartiality and ability to hear the case with an open mind. The judge does not have to ask about the specific source or context of the pretrial information. [**Mu'Min v. Virginia**, 500 U.S. 415 (1991)]

Example: A new trial is required if the defendant is denied a change of venue and is then tried before a jury drawn from people who have seen an interview in which the defendant confessed. [**Rideau v. Louisiana**, 373 U.S. 723 (1963)]

Compare: No prejudice was found when: (i) a criminal trial was held in the large city in which the defendant allegedly committed a crime, (ii) news stories about the defendant contained no blatantly prejudicial information, (iii) media attention diminished in the four years between the alleged crime and the defendant's trial, and (iv) the jury that was chosen acquitted the defendant on a number of counts. [**Skilling v. United States**, 561 U.S. 358 (2010)]

(1) Misdemeanors

A state law that does not permit changes of venue for misdemeanor cases violates the right to trial by an impartial jury. Even persons charged with misdemeanors must be given the opportunity to show that a change of venue is necessary. [**Groppi v. Wisconsin**, 400 U.S. 505 (1971)]

e. Juror's Application for Job with Prosecutor

A juror's submission of a job application to the prosecutor's office during the defendant's trial does ***not*** alone show juror bias. To have the conviction reversed, the defendant must show at a post-trial hearing that the juror was ***actually biased***. [**Smith v. Phillips**, 455 U.S. 209 (1982)]

f. Biased Jurors

A defendant is entitled to a jury selected from a fair cross-section of the community. (*See infra,* pp. 147–149) Bias may be a legitimate basis on which to exclude a prospective juror, but bias is extremely tough to establish. [*See*, *e.g.*, **Love v. Texas**, 142 S.Ct. 1406 (2022) (denying *certiorari* in a death penalty habeas case in which defense counsel had moved unsuccessfully to exclude a prospective juror for cause who said during voir dire "that . . . non-whites commit more violent crimes than whites," "are statistically more violent than the white race," and "I believe in statistics."]

g. Venue

The Sixth Amendment guarantees "the right to a speedy and public trial, by an impartial jury of the State and district **wherein the crime shall have been committed**, which district shall have been previously ascertained by law . . . ." Thus, a criminal trial must be held where the crime was committed. The remedy for a conviction in the wrong venue is to vacate the conviction and retry the defendant in the proper venue and "not a judgment barring reprosecution." [**Smith v. United States**, 599 U.S. 236 (2023)]

B. Joint Trials

1. Joinder of Defendants

Generally, two or more defendants may be charged in the same indictment or information, and thus tried jointly, if they are alleged to have participated in the same act or transaction (or series of acts or transactions) constituting an offense or offenses. [Fed. R. Crim. P. 8(b)] Similarly, defendants charged under several indictments may be joined together if the offenses and defendants could have been joined in a single indictment. [Fed. R. Crim. P. 13] Improper joinder can be appealed, but is subject to a harmless error analysis. [**United States v. Lane**, 474 U.S. 438 (1986)]

2. Severance of Defendants

Even if joinder of the defendants is legally proper, if either is unfairly ***prejudiced*** by the joinder, the judge should grant a motion for separate trials—a ***severance***. The duty is a continuing one; *i.e.*, severance should be granted whenever prejudice appears—even during trial. [**United States v. Gooch**, 665 F.3d 1318 (D.C. Cir. 2012)] In federal court and in most state courts, severance may be made by the court sua sponte or on motion of the defendant or prosecution. [Fed. R. Civ. P. 14]

a. Preference for Joint Trials in Federal Court

Out of concern for efficiency in the judicial system, the Supreme Court has cited "a preference for joint trials of defendants who are indicted together." [**Zafiro v. United States**, 506 U.S. 534 (1993)] A federal district court should grant a severance only if "there is a ***serious risk that a joint trial would compromise a specific trial right*** of one of the defendants, or prevent the jury from making a reliable judgment about guilt or innocence." The rule is similar in most states as well.

b. Differences in Proof

Prejudice is often claimed where the proof against each defendant is significantly ***different***—*i.e.*, incriminating one defendant but not another. The test is whether the jury can keep the evidence relevant to each defendant ***compartmentalized*** so as to render a fair and impartial verdict as to each. [**United States v. Chan**, 981 F.3d 39 (1st Cir. 2020)] When the evidence cannot be compartmentalized appropriately, improper "spillover" is said to have occurred.

c. Confession by Co-Defendant

Prejudice may arise when the prosecution seeks to introduce an ***admission or confession*** made by one defendant that also ***implicates another defendant***. Such an admission or confession is admissible as evidence of guilt ***only*** against the defendant who made it. It is inadmissible hearsay as to any co-defendant. It is not covered under the hearsay exception to the rules of evidence for co-conspirator declarations, because it was not made during, or in furtherance of, the conspiracy. [*See* **Bruton v. United States**, *infra*]

(1) Traditional Approach

Until ***Bruton***, the traditional approach was to admit the admission or confession and instruct the jury to consider it only against the defendant who made it.

(2) General Rule—*Bruton*

In **Bruton v. United States**, 391 U.S. 123 (1968), the Supreme Court held that such an instruction to the jury would ***not*** afford the other defendants the protection to which they are entitled under the Confrontation Clause of the Sixth Amendment. Normally, there must be a ***severance*** of defendants or a ***deletion of references*** to the co-defendants.

e.g. **Example:** In a joint trial, Bruton and his co-defendant, Evans, were convicted of armed postal robbery. A postal inspector testified that Evans had confessed that both he and Bruton had committed the crime. Bruton's name was not redacted from the statement admitted at trial. Evans did not testify, and the judge instructed the jury that the testimony of the postal inspector was admissible only against Evans. The admission was found to violate Bruton's constitutional rights. [**Bruton v. United States**, *supra*]

(a) Exception—Unspecified References

Note that references to co-defendants that are not specific (*e.g.*, "we talked about killing our robbery victims," and references that do not indicate who "we" includes) need not be excluded. [**Richardson v. Marsh**, 481 U.S. 200 (1987); **Samia v. United States**, 599 U.S. 635 (2023) (in joint trial of three defendants, confession of non-testifying co-defendant was admitted after Samia's name was deleted and all references were to an "other person" (or other neutral pronoun), and trial court gave limiting instruction), but *see* **Gray v. Maryland**, 523 U.S. 185 (1998); *and see infra*, p. 165]

d. Exculpating Testimony of Co-Defendants

Where one co-defendant indicates a clear willingness to exculpate the other, a severance may be required to enable the latter to call the former as a witness or otherwise introduce the exculpatory statements to the jury.

e. Antagonistic Offenses

The mere fact that the co-defendants have conflicting defense positions does ***not necessarily*** mean that joinder is prejudicial, and that severance is automatically required. The question is whether the accounts of the defendants lead to "a danger that the jury will unjustifiably infer that this conflict alone demonstrates that both are guilty." [**United States v. Weckman**, 982 F.3d 1167 (8th Cir. 2020)] If so and if the conflict is prejudicial, there must be severance. [**People v. Flinner,** 476 P.3d 240 (Cal. 2020)]

3. Joinder of Offenses

Generally, two or more offenses may be charged as separate counts in the same indictment or information if the offenses—whether felonies, misdemeanors, or both—are of the same character, are based on the same act or transaction, or are parts of a common scheme or plan. [Fed. R. Crim. P. 8(a)]

4. Severance of Offenses

If the defendant is prejudiced by a joinder of offenses, the trial judge can grant a severance. As stated above, the decision is largely within the court's discretion and involves ***balancing the efficiency and economy*** of a joint trial ***against*** any ***prejudicial impact on*** the defendant. [**State v. Bluford**, 393 P.3d 1219 (Wash. 2017)]

a. Harmless Error Test Applies

Misjoinder is subject to a harmless error analysis and is not reversible error per se. For example, misjoinder of one count of mail fraud involving one defendant with other counts of mail fraud involving both defendants is harmless error. [**United States v. Lane**, 474 U.S. 438 (1986)]

EXAM TIP

On an exam question, if multiple defendants are accused of committing one or more crimes together, several issues may be involved. Probably the first to be addressed is whether the defendants ***may be tried together*** on one or more of the charges. Generally, in the interests of judicial efficiency, multiple defendants may be tried together on multiple charges, as long as the defendants and charges ***arose out of the same act, transaction, or series of acts and transactions***. Normally this occurs when the defendants are charged as co-conspirators. Do not assume that the defendants or charges have been misjoined, or that the joinder is prejudicial, unless there is a serious risk that the joinder will compromise a specific trial right of one of the parties. After trial, a conviction is rarely reversed for misjoinder, as the prosecution may show that the misjoinder was harmless. Another popular exam issue centers on the use, against a defendant, of a non-testifying codefendant's confession implicating the defendant. Be sure to analyze the "**Bruton**" issues to determine whether the confession, even when redacted, identifies the defendant. If so, the defendant's right to confront their accuser is violated, even if the trial judge gives a limiting instruction to the jury.

C. Right to a Jury Trial

1. Constitutional Bases

The right to trial by jury is guaranteed by Article II, Section 2 of the Constitution ("the trial of all crimes, except in cases of impeachment, shall be by jury"). The right is also guaranteed by the Sixth Amendment which states, "In all criminal prosecutions, the accused shall enjoy the right to . . . trial, by an impartial jury. . ."

a. Applies to States

The Sixth Amendment's right to a jury trial has been applied to the states via the Fourteenth Amendment. [**Duncan v. Louisiana**, *supra,* p. 2–3] In ***Duncan***, the Supreme Court held that the right to a jury trial is fundamental to the proper administration of justice. [*See also* **Ramos v. Louisiana**, 590 U.S. 83 (2020) (the Sixth Amendment right to a jury trial requires a unanimous verdict of guilt in all criminal trials)]

2. Purposes of Juries

Juries serve several purposes in our criminal justice system. Primarily, juries serve as a ***check against arbitrary or vindictive law enforcement***. The Supreme Court has recognized that juries also improve the ***fact-finding*** process. [**Duncan v. Louisiana**, 391 U.S. 145 (1968)] In addition, juries provide for ***public participation*** in the criminal justice system, which is essential in a democratic society.

3. When Right Attaches

The right to a trial by jury applies ***only to serious***, not petty, offenses. [**Baldwin v. New York**, 399 U.S. 66 (1970)]

a. Serious Offenses

(1) Imprisonment of More than Six Months Authorized

For purposes of the jury trial right, a serious offense is one for which ***more than six months' imprisonment*** is authorized. [**Baldwin v. New York**, *supra*]

(2) Other Serious Penalties

A prison term of six months or fewer, in combination with other penalties, is considered serious for the purpose of the right to jury trial only if the defendant can demonstrate that the combination of penalties is so severe that it ***clearly reflects a legislative determination*** that the offense in question is a ***"serious" one***. [**Blanton v. City of North Las Vegas**, 489 U.S. 538 (1989)—"driving while intoxicated" statute: (i) authorizing six months' prison term or 48 hours of community work while dressed in clothing indicating the person is a DWI offender; and (ii) requiring a 90-day suspension of license, \$200–\$1,000 fine, and attendance at an alcohol abuse course does ***not*** constitute serious offense; *and see* **United States v. Nachtigal**, 507 U.S. 1 (1993)—possibility of six months' imprisonment or \$5,000 fine and up to five years' probation is not sufficient to overcome the presumption that the crime is petty]

(3) Aggregation of Petty Offenses

The right to a jury trial does not arise when, in a single proceeding, sentences for multiple petty offenses result in an aggregate prison term of more than six months. [**Lewis v. United States**, 518 U.S. 322 (1996)]

(4) Distinguish—Right to Counsel

The standard for determining whether a defendant has a right to a jury trial differs from the standard for determining whether he has a right to counsel. There is a right to a jury trial only for serious cases, but there is a right to counsel ***whenever actual imprisonment is imposed*** (*see infra,* p. 153).

b. Contempt

Special considerations apply for imprisonment for contempt, depending on whether the contempt is civil or criminal.

(1) Civil Contempt

No right to jury trial attaches in cases of civil contempt. In such a case, the contemnor will be released from prison as soon as he complies with a court order. In this sense, the contemnor "carries the key to the jail in his pocket." Because there is no overtly punitive purpose to citation for civil contempt, no right to jury trial attaches. [**Maggio v. Zeitz**, 333 U.S. 56 (1948)]

(2) Criminal Contempt

In criminal contempt cases, there is rarely a statutorily authorized penalty. Instead, judges are given a great deal of discretion to impose whatever sentence is necessary for the proper administration of justice. When there is no statutorily authorized penalty, the duration of the ***actual sentence imposed*** after trial determines whether the defendant was entitled to a jury. [**Bloom v. Illinois**, 391 U.S. 194 (1968)]

(a) Multiple Contempt Situations

In ***post-verdict*** adjudications of contempt, if the sentences for multiple acts of contempt exceed six months, the contemnor is entitled to a jury trial—even though no sentence of more than six months is imposed for any one act of contempt. [**Codispoti v. Pennsylvania**, 418 U.S. 506 (1974)] However, if the judge summarily imposes punishment for contemptuous acts ***during trial,*** the penalties may aggregate to more than six months without a jury trial. [**Codispoti v. Pennsylvania**, *supra*]

(b) Appellate Modification

If an appellate court reduces a sentence imposed for contempt to six months or less, the contemnor cannot challenge the sentence as violative of his jury trial right. [**Taylor v. Hayes**, 418 U.S. 488 (1974)]

RIGHT TO JURY TRIAL IN CONTEMPT PROCEEDINGS IMPOSING IMPRISONMENT

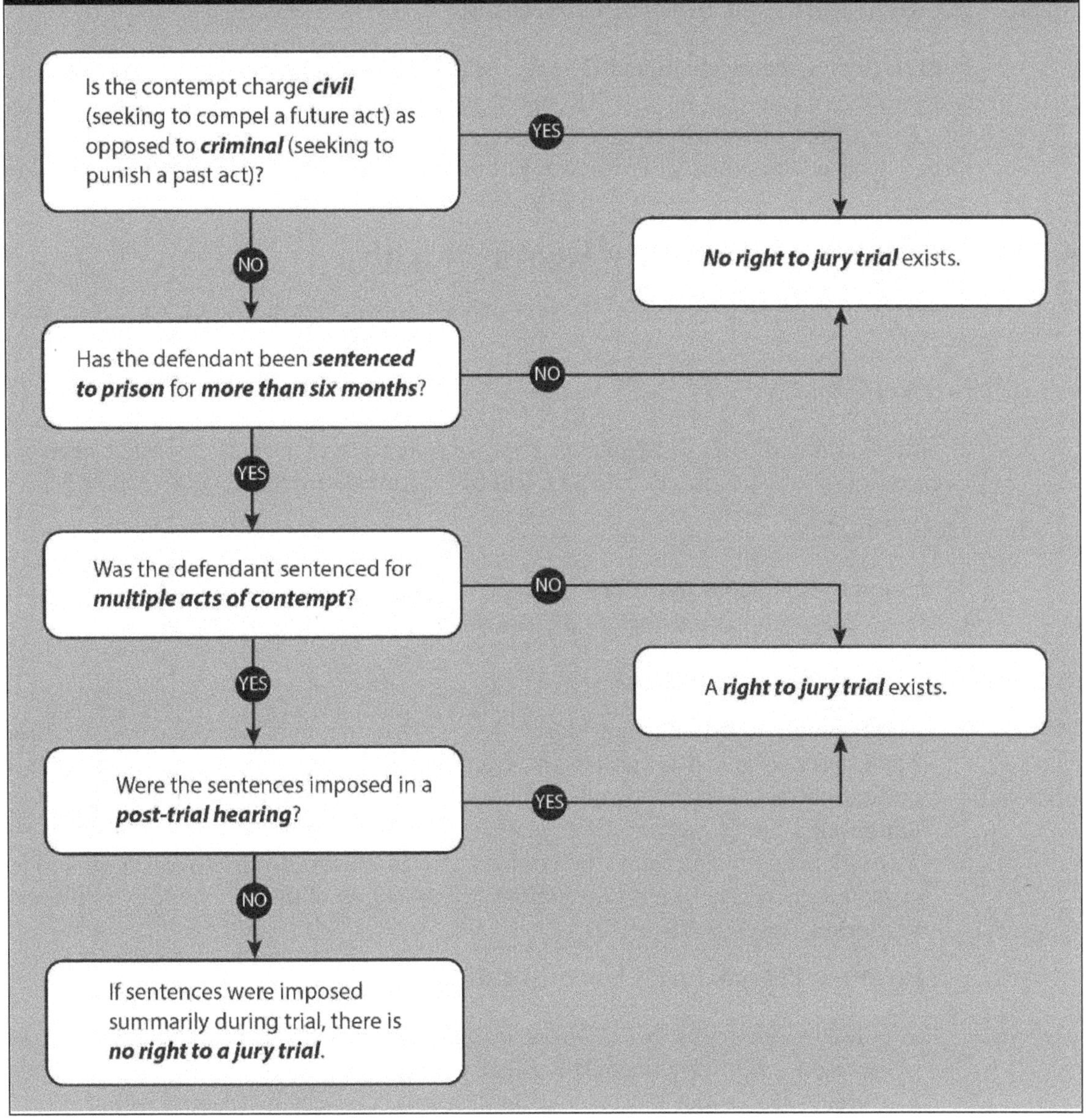

(c) Probation

A judge may place a contemnor on probation for a term of up to five years without affording him the right to a jury trial—so long as revocation of probation would not result in imprisonment for more than six months. [**Frank v. United States**, 395 U.S. 147 (1969)]

(d) Fines

Fines imposed for contempt can be civil or criminal, depending on the purpose of the fine. A fine primarily intended to coerce future conduct is civil, while a fine intended primarily to punish past conduct is criminal. If a criminal fine is serious, the right to a jury trial attaches. The Court has refused to set a bright-line test for determining what constitutes a serious fine, but has found a criminal contempt fine of $52 million to be sufficiently serious to give rise to the right to a jury trial. [**United Mine Workers of America v. Bagwell**, 512 U.S. 821 (1994)]

c. No Right to Jury in Juvenile Proceedings

In **McKeiver v. Pennsylvania**, 403 U.S. 528 (1971), the Supreme Court held that there is no right to a jury trial in juvenile delinquency proceedings. The Court reasoned that juries would materially disrupt both the nature and purpose of the state's separate juvenile justice system. Particularly, juries would undercut the confidentiality of the juvenile system.

4. Jury Size and Unanimity Requirements

The requirements regarding the size of the jury depend on whether the case is tried in federal or state court.

a. Federal Court

In federal criminal trials, a ***12-person*** jury is required, and the jury's verdict ***must be unanimous***. [Fed. R. Crim. P. 23(b)(3); **Ramos v. Louisiana**, 590 U.S. 83 (2020)]

b. State Court

Because the Supreme Court considers the 12-person jury a result of "a historical accident," the Court has ***declined to impose this requirement on the states***.

(1) Six-Person Minimum

The Supreme Court upheld a Florida jury system that permitted six-person juries. The Court reasoned that the size of the jury had little impact on its ability to act as a buffer between the accused and the state. The small size of the jury is not viewed as diminishing the community participation function of juries. The only limitation on jury size is that the jury must be large enough to ***ensure group deliberation*** and to ***provide a possibility of a representative cross-section*** of the community. [**Williams v. Florida**, 399 U.S. 78 (1970)]

(a) Five-Person Juries Unconstitutional

The minimum number of jurors is six. After *Williams,* the Court held that five-person juries were unconstitutional because they would not provide effective group discussion; they would diminish the chances of drawing a fair cross-section of the community; and they might impair the accuracy of fact-finding. [**Ballew v. Georgia**, 435 U.S. 223 (1978)]

(2) Unanimous Juries Are a Requirement of the 6th and 14th Amendments

In **Ramos v. Louisiana**, *supra*, the Court held that the Fourteenth Amendment incorporates the Sixth Amendment right to a jury trial against the states and requires a unanimous verdict of guilt in all criminal trials. Although 48 states and the federal court system already required a unanimous jury verdict of guilt, Louisiana and Oregon did not. *Ramos* makes clear that the practices in Oregon and Louisiana were unconstitutional.

EXAM TIP

Remember, a jury of 12 is ***not constitutionally required***; juries can be as small as six members. All jury verdicts ***must be unanimous***.

c. *Allen* Charge

If the jury foreperson reports to the trial judge that the jury is unable to reach a unanimous verdict, the judge might give an ***Allen*** charge. This instruction to the jury urges the jurors to examine the issues in the case and re-evaluate their opinions and the opinions of other jurors in an attempt to reach a verdict. [**Allen v. United States**, 164 U.S. 492 (1896)] Such an instruction is improper if it coerces jurors into reaching a verdict. [**Brewer v. Hetzel**, 913 F.3d 1042 (11th Cir. 2019)]

5. Fair Cross-Section Requirement

A defendant is entitled to have the jury selected from ***a fair cross-section of the community***. [**Carter v. Jury Commission of Greene County**, 396 U.S. 320 (1970)] A defendant may claim a violation of her rights if a certain group is excluded from serving on a jury. The defendant need ***not*** be a member of the group excluded to raise the claim. [**Campbell v. Louisiana**, 523 U.S. 392 (1998)—a white defendant has standing to raise an equal protection challenge of discrimination against Black persons in the selection of grand jurors; *and see* **Peters v. Kiff**, 407 U.S. 493 (1972)]

a. Basis of the Claim

To make out a prima facie case of unconstitutional jury discrimination, a defendant need only show ***the under-representation of a distinct and numerically significant community group*** and need not show an opportunity to discriminate in the jury selection process. Regardless of how exclusion occurred, any systematic exclusion of a significant and distinct community group from the venire (the large group from which juries are selected) states a cause of action under the present test. [**Taylor v. Louisiana**, 419 U.S. 522 (1975)]

b. No Right to a Particular Jury Composition

The defendant is entitled only to have the jury drawn from a ***venire representing a fair cross-section*** of the community. A defendant is not entitled to have all groups (*e.g.*, race or gender) in the community represented on the jury deciding her case.

c. Young Adults Need Not Be Represented

Young adults might not constitute a group entitled to be represented in the venire. Thus, a system that refills the jury list only every four years does not violate the fair cross-section requirement. [**Hamling v. United States**, 418 U.S. 87 (1974)] *But note*: *Hamling* predates ***Taylor*** (*supra*) and might come out differently if relitigated today.

d. Use of Peremptory Challenges for Racial or Gender-Based Exclusion

Under all jury selection systems, the parties may strike an unlimited number of potential jurors "for cause," if there is a basis to believe that they cannot properly perform their duties (*e.g.*, because of personal interest in the case or because of disclosed antipathy or affinity for a particular relevant group). The parties also have a limited number of peremptory strikes. In contrast to striking potential jurors for cause, a prosecutor or defense lawyer generally may exercise peremptory challenges for any rational ***or irrational*** reason. [**Thaler v. Haynes**, 559 U.S. 43 (2010) (demeanor-based peremptory strike is not by itself illegal)] However, the Equal Protection Clause forbids the use of peremptory challenges to exclude potential jurors solely based on their race or gender. [**Batson v. Kentucky**, 476 U.S. 79 (1989); **J.E.B. v. Alabama**, 511 U.S. 127 (1994); **Flowers v. Mississippi**, 588 U.S. 284 (2019)]

(1) Challenge Procedure

An equal protection-based attack on peremptory strikes involves three steps:

(i) The defendant must show ***facts or circumstances that raise an inference*** that the exclusion of potential jurors was based on race or gender.

(ii) If such a showing is made, the prosecutor must then provide a ***race-neutral explanation*** for the strike. The reason for the strike need not be reasonable, as long as it is race neutral. [**Purkett v. Elem**, 514 U.S. 765 (1995)—explanation that potential jurors were struck because of their long hair and beards was sufficient]

(iii) The judge then determines whether the prosecutor's explanation was the genuine reason for striking the juror, or merely a pretext for purposeful discrimination. [**Purkett v. Elem**, *supra*] The judge does not have to preside during voir dire and personally observe the juror's demeanor to allow the peremptory strike. [**Thaler v. Haynes**, *supra*, p. 147] *Note*: The defendant need not be a member of the group excluded to make a claim. [**Holland v. Illinois**, 493 U.S. 474 (1990); **Powers v. Ohio**, 499 U.S. 400 (1991)]

e.g. **Example:** That a stricken juror was young, had no ties to the community, and was disrespectful were sufficient grounds to support a peremptory strike. [**Rice v. Collins**, 546 U.S. 333 (2006)]

cf. **Compare:** During voir dire in a murder case, a Black college student voiced concern that the trial might interfere with his student teaching, which he needed to fulfill his graduate requirements. A court clerk called the student's dean and reported to the student that the dean would work with him on rescheduling. The prosecutor asked no further questions about the matter. Nevertheless, the prosecutor used a peremptory challenge to exclude the juror. Defense counsel challenged the peremptory strike, and the prosecutor explained that he was concerned that because of the student's pressing educational needs, he would find the defendant guilty of a lesser charge to avoid a lengthy capital sentencing hearing. As a result of peremptory challenges and challenges for cause, no Black jurors were included in the final jury. *Held:* Because white jurors who also stated that they had pressing needs were not struck, and because it is unlikely that one juror could shorten the trial (because of the necessity of convincing the other jurors to follow his lead), the prosecutor's rationale for the strike was a pretext, and the strike should not have been upheld. [**Snyder v. Louisiana**, 552 U.S. 472 (2008)]

(2) Defendants

It is unconstitutional for a criminal defendant or the defendant's attorney to use peremptory challenges in a racially discriminatory manner. [**Georgia v. McCollum**, 505 U.S. 42 (1992)]

(3) Court's Duty to Inquire

A court must inquire into a claim that the prosecution struck jurors on purely racial grounds. The court cannot claim that as long as the Sixth Amendment fair cross-section requirement is met, the jury selected is adequate. [**Alvarado v. United States**, 497 U.S. 543 (1990)]

e. Use of Peremptory Challenges to Strike Improper Jurors

A defendant's right to due process in exercising peremptory challenges is not violated when he is forced to use a peremptory challenge to remove a potential juror after the district court erroneously refused to dismiss the juror for cause. [**United States v. Martinez-Salazar**, 528 U.S. 304 (2000)—a prospective juror indicated that he would favor the prosecution, the district court declined to excuse him for cause, and the defendant exercised a peremptory challenge to remove the prospective juror] The Supreme Court reasoned that although peremptory challenges play an important role in reinforcing a defendant's constitutional right to trial by an impartial jury, these challenges are auxiliary and are not of federal constitutional dimension. The key here was that the ***juror was in fact removed*** and therefore the ***empaneled jury was not biased***.

f. No Automatic Exemption for Women

The Court has held that states are free to grant exemptions from jury service where special hardships would arise [*e.g.,* it would interfere with the person's occupation, which is critical to the community). [**Rawlins v. Georgia**, 201 U.S. 638 (1906)] However, the Court has rejected a law exempting all women from jury service, on request, under a special hardship category, holding that it is untenable that service would constitute a special hardship for every woman. [**Duren v. Missouri**, 439 U.S. 357 (1979)]

6. Right to an Impartial Jury

The Sixth Amendment guarantees defendants an impartial jury.

a. Objections to Capital Punishment

States may not exclude for cause potential jurors who express scruples against the death penalty. The resulting jury would be unable to speak for the community. [**Witherspoon v. Illinois**, 391 U.S. 510 (1968)] Similarly, states may not exclude potential jurors who are unwilling or unable to take an oath that a mandatory penalty of death or life imprisonment ***would not affect*** their deliberations. [**Adams v. Texas**, 448 U.S. 38 (1980)] In *Adams*, the Court indicated that a state may ensure that the jurors will consider and decide facts impartially and apply the law as charged by the court. But striking jurors who merely say that their deliberations will be "affected" by the mandatory penalty goes too far. The Court ruled that a juror "may not be challenged for cause based on his views about capital punishment unless those views would ***prevent or substantially impair*** the performance of his duties as a juror in accordance with his instructions and his oath."

(1) Distinguish—Refusal to Impose Capital Punishment

States ***may*** exclude potential jurors who indicate that they are morally opposed to capital punishment and would never return a verdict of death regardless of the evidence adduced at trial. *Rationale*: These individuals are indicating an unwillingness to follow a court's instructions. [**Witherspoon v. Illinois**, *supra*]

(2) Standard

The standard for determining when a prospective juror should be excluded for cause is whether the juror's views would ***prevent or substantially impair*** her duties in accordance with the judge's instructions and the juror's oath. [**Lockhart v. McCree**, 476 U.S. 162 (1986); *and see* **Wainwright v. Witt**, 469 U.S. 412 (1985)] If a juror is improperly excluded, a resulting death penalty must be reversed. [**Gray v. Mississippi**, 481 U.S. 648 (1987)] However, as indicated above, reversal is not required if a juror should have been excluded by the judge, was not, but was excluded by a peremptory challenge. [**Ross v. Oklahoma**, 487 U.S. 81 (1988)]

b. Favoring Capital Punishment

If a jury is to decide whether a defendant in a capital case is to be sentenced to death, the defendant must be allowed, upon request, to ask potential jurors during voir dire if they would automatically give the death penalty upon a guilty verdict. A juror who answers affirmatively should be excluded for cause, because such a juror has indicated the same type of inability to follow jury instructions (as to mitigating circumstances) as a juror who has indicated an inability to impose the death penalty under any circumstances. [**Morgan v. Illinois**, 504 U.S. 719 (1992)]

c. Failure to Exclude the Racially Prejudiced

Whenever racial matters are ***inextricably bound up in the controversy***, a defendant is entitled to questioning on voir dire specifically directed to ascertain whether racial prejudice exists among potential jurors. [**Ham v. South Carolina**, 409 U.S. 524 (1973)]

Example: Defendant was a well-known civil rights activist arrested for possession of marijuana. He claimed that he was being framed by the police. The Court held that questioning on racial bias should have been allowed because of the defendant's reputation as an activist, which he claimed was likely to intensify any prejudice that jurors might have against Black individuals. [**Ham v. South Carolina**, *supra*]

Example: Habeas petitioner produced sufficient evidence to proceed in forma pauperis and have his claim considered when he produced an affidavit from a trial juror who admitted saying during deliberations that "there are two types of black people: 1) Black folks and 2) N_ _ _ _ _ _," and that petitioner wasn't among the good Black folks and "should get the electric chair for what he did." [**Tharpe v. Sellers**, 583 U.S. 33 (2018)]

Compare: In noncapital cases, the mere fact that the defendant is Black and the victim is white is ***not*** enough to entitle the defendant to the special questioning of prospective jurors about racial prejudice. [**Ristaino v. Ross**, 424 U.S. 589 (1976)]

(1) Standard on Appeal

Failure to honor the defendant's request for questioning on racial bias is reversible error only if the circumstances indicate "a reasonable possibility that racial or ethnic prejudice might have influenced the jury." [**Rosales-Lopez v. United States**, 451 U.S. 182 (1981)]

(2) Capital Defendants

A capital defendant accused of an interracial crime is entitled to have prospective jurors informed of the victim's race and is entitled to voir dire questioning regarding the issue of racial prejudice without showing any other special circumstances. [**Turner v. Murray**, 476 U.S. 28 (1986)]

7. Chilling Assertion of the Right

The exercise of the right to jury trial may not be constitutionally chilled by statute. For example, a statute that provides for the death penalty only if recommended by the jury is unconstitutional as unnecessarily encouraging defendants to waive their right to a jury trial. [**United States v. Jackson**, 390 U.S. 570 (1968)]

8. Waiver of Jury Trial

A defendant may waive the right to jury trial as long as the waiver is ***expressly and intelligently made***. The government can require that the waiver be approved by the prosecution and the court. [**Singer v. United States**, 380 U.S. 24 (1965)]

a. Federal Court Rule

The Federal Rules of Criminal Procedure presume that the defendant will be tried by a jury "unless: (1) the defendant waives a jury trial in writing; (2) the government consents; and (3) the court approves." [Fed R. Crim. P. 23(a)]

9. Inconsistent Verdicts

An inconsistent jury verdict is normally not reviewable if the defendant was acquitted on one charge but convicted on a related charge. The reasoning behind this rule is that it is impossible to tell on which decision the jury erred; thus, any challenge of the verdict would be based on pure speculation. [**United States v. Powell**, 469 U.S. 57 (1984)] Remember in any event, an acquittal cannot be challenged as it is inviolate. [*See* **McElrath v. Georgia**, 601 U.S. 87 (2024)]

D. Right to a Public Trial

1. Constitutional Basis

The Sixth Amendment provides that "in all criminal prosecutions, the accused shall enjoy the right to a . . . public trial. . . ." The right to a public trial is rooted in the traditional Anglo-American distrust of secret trials, and its purposes are to protect the defendant's right to a fair trial, safeguard against any attempt to employ the courts as instruments of persecution, and inform the public of governmental actions against citizens. [**Press-Enterprise Co. v. Superior Court**, 478 U.S. 1 (1986)]

2. Closed Trial Proceedings

a. Excluding of Spectators from the Courtroom

In extremely ***limited*** situations, if the need arises, the judge has discretion to exclude members of the public from the trial. [**Globe Newspaper Co. v. Superior Court**, 457 U.S. 596 (1982)]

e.g. **Example:** A judge may properly exclude certain persons if it is shown that they are likely to intimidate a principal witness. [**United States v. Portillo**, 969 F.3d 144 (5th Cir. 2020)]

(1) Voir Dire of Prospective Jurors

The right to a public trial includes voir dire of prospective jurors. Trial courts must make every reasonable effort to accommodate public attendance. [**Presley v. Georgia**, 558 U.S. 209 (2010)—judge improperly excluded defendant's uncle from courtroom during voir dire, stating that prospective jurors could not mingle with the uncle and needed all of the rows of seats in the courtroom]

b. Exclusion of the Media

Even if the government, the defendant, and the judge all agree to closed proceedings, both Sixth and First Amendment concerns may be raised by members of the media.

(1) Trial

Members of the public (and the media representing them) have a First Amendment right to attend a criminal trial. [**Richmond Newspapers, Inc. v. Virginia**, 448 U.S. 555 (1980)] Therefore, a trial judge can order a trial closed only if specific findings are made that closure is necessary for a fair trial in the particular case. [**Globe Newspaper Co. v. Superior Court**, *supra*, p. 151] The extent of the closure must be "narrowly tailored" to remedy the specific problem behind the closure, and there must be a showing that closure is the least restrictive alternative available.

(2) Pretrial Hearings

(a) Preliminary Probable Cause Hearing

Preliminary hearings to determine whether there is probable cause on which to prosecute are presumptively open to the public and the press. [**Press-Enterprise Co. v. Superior Court**, *supra*, p. 151]

(b) Suppression Hearings

The Sixth Amendment right to a public trial extends to ***pretrial suppression hearings***. Such hearings may not be closed to the public unless:

(i) The party seeking closure shows an ***overriding interest likely to be prejudiced*** by a public hearing;

(ii) The closure is ***no broader than necessary*** to protect such an interest;

(iii) ***Reasonable alternatives to closure have been considered***; and

(iv) ***Adequate findings to support closure are entered by the trial court***.

[**Waller v. Georgia**, 467 U.S. 39 (1984)]

E. Right to Counsel

1. Constitutional Basis

The Sixth Amendment provides that "in all criminal prosecutions, the accused shall enjoy the right . . . to have the assistance of counsel for his defense." The Sixth Amendment is incorporated by way of the Due Process Clause of the Fourteenth Amendment to apply in state cases. [**Gideon v. Wainwright**, 372 U.S. 335 (1963)]

a. Generally There Is No Right to Counsel in Civil Proceedings

By its terms, the Sixth Amendment right to counsel does not apply to civil cases. In **Turner v. Rogers**, 564 U.S. 431 (2011), the Supreme Court acknowledged that indigent defendants facing incarceration in ***civil*** contempt proceedings lack a Sixth Amendment right to the appointment of counsel but stated that the ***Due Process Clause*** may sometimes require the appointment of counsel or alternative procedural safeguards when incarceration is threatened in such a proceeding.

e.g. **Example:** A state court ordered Defendant to pay child support. He failed to pay as ordered and was repeatedly held in civil contempt and jailed. At his last hearing to show cause why he should not be held in contempt, he appeared *pro se* and admitted that he had "done wrong," but the court made no finding that he was able to pay. The judge found Defendant in willful contempt and sentenced him to 12 months in a detention center. Defendant appealed, arguing that the Constitution entitled him to counsel at the "show cause" hearing. *Held:* There is no categorical right to counsel under the Due Process Clause, but Defendant's incarceration here violated due process because a "fundamentally fair" civil contempt proceeding is required. In deciding whether counsel is required, the Court applies a balancing test, evaluating fairness factors from **Mathews v. Eldridge**, 424 U.S. 319 (1976). Here, Defendant's incarceration violated due process because he did not receive counsel or alternative procedural safeguards such as (i) clear notice that his ability to pay was crucial in the contempt proceeding, or (ii) a finding that he was able to pay. [**Turner v. Rogers**, *supra*, p. 152]

2. Rights of Indigents to Appointment of Counsel

Defendants in many criminal trials are entitled to the appointment of a lawyer at trial regardless of their ability to pay. Few courts have set specific standards with respect to indigency. In most courts, it is not necessary to establish total destitution. In determining indigency, most courts will consider factors such as: (i) the defendant's income while in custody, (ii) the defendant's previous indebtedness, (iii) the defendant's assets, (iv) the defendant's dependents, (v) the nature of the charge against the defendant, and (vi) bond expenses.

a. Recoupment of Expenses

Some states have passed statutes that require, as a condition of probation, that the convicted defendant pay back to the state the fees of the appointed attorney. As long as the statutes provide exemptions for defendants who cannot afford repayment, these statutes are constitutional. [**Fuller v. Oregon**, 417 U.S. 40 (1974)] *Note*: A recoupment program requiring reimbursement only from defendants actually sentenced to prison violates equal protection. [**Rinaldi v. Yeager**, 384 U.S. 305 (1966)]

3. Cases in Which Right to Counsel Exists

a. Right to Counsel at Trial

The right to counsel at trial is violated in ***criminal prosecutions*** if an accused is not given the opportunity to have the assistance of counsel and any term of ***actual imprisonment*** or a ***suspended sentence with probation is imposed***. [**Argersinger v. Hamlin**, 407 U.S. 25 (1972); **Scott v. Illinois**, 440 U.S. 367 (1979); **Alabama v. Shelton**, 535 U.S. 654 (2002)]

(1) Actual Imprisonment

The right to counsel exists in situations in which imprisonment is ***imposed***—at any point—as a result of the conviction. Thus, if a crime is punishable by fine or imprisonment, the defendant's Sixth Amendment right is ***not violated*** if the defendant is denied counsel and ***only a fine*** is imposed.

(2) Suspended Sentence

A defendant is denied the assistance of counsel if counsel is not provided, and she receives a suspended sentence and probation. [**Alabama v. Shelton**, *supra*]

(a) Distinguish—Sentence Enhancement

A previous uncounseled misdemeanor conviction, valid because no imprisonment was imposed at the time, can be used to enhance a subsequent conviction in which imprisonment is ordered. [**Nichols v. United States**, 511 U.S. 738 (1994)]

(b) State Rules

Some states go further and grant indigent defendants the right to counsel regardless of whether actual imprisonment is imposed. [*See, e.g.,* Arizona, which provides an attorney if a conviction "may result in punishment involving a loss of liberty"—Ariz. R. Crim. P. 6.1; Oregon which requires an attorney if "the defendant is charged with a crime"—ORS 135.050]

(3) Assistance Other than Counsel

In federal court, by statute, the defendant may "obtain investigative, expert, or other services necessary for an adequate defense." [18 U.S.C. § 3006A(e)] More broadly, due process may require such services if necessary for a fair trial. [**Ake v. Oklahoma**, 470 U.S. 68 (1986)] Many states specifically give the judge discretion to provide assistance other than counsel, such as medical experts, investigators, etc. [N.C. Gen. Stat. §§ 7A–498 *et seq.*] Other states also have a procedure, similar to the federal rule, for appointed attorneys to secure, at public expense, "expert, investigative, or other services." [*See, e.g.,* Minn. Stat. § 611.21; Nevada Rev. Stat. § 7.135]

(4) Joint Representation

Defendants in a joint trial may have their own attorneys appointed, or in some cases, may share the services of one lawyer. If, however, the appointed attorney advises the trial court of a conflict of interest, the trial court ***must*** give separate counsel. [**Holloway v. Arkansas**, 435 U.S. 475 (1978)] For example, a conflict of interest would be present if defense counsel, representing two defendants, suspects that she can use testimony incriminating one of the defendants to exculpate the other.

(a) Defendant Must Object to Joint Representation

To establish a violation of the Sixth Amendment due to joint representation, the defendant ***must object at trial***. If no objection is made, on appeal it must be shown that an ***actual conflict*** of interest ***adversely affected the lawyer's performance***. [**Cuyler v. Sullivan**, 446 U.S. 335 (1980)]

(b) Court May Question Joint Representation

Many courts initiate inquiries as to the possible conflict of interest in multiple representation situations. While the Supreme Court has recommended this practice, it is not constitutionally required. [**Cuyler v. Sullivan**, *supra*]

(c) Joint Representation Is Not Necessarily Ineffective Assistance

Joint representation does not, on its own, constitute a violation of the constitutional guarantee of effective assistance of counsel. For joint representation to constitute ineffective assistance, a defendant must demonstrate that her counsel ***actively represented*** conflicting interests ***and*** that the conflict ***adversely affected*** the attorney's performance. [**Burger v. Kemp**, 483 U.S. 776 (1987)]

(d) Court May Refuse to Allow Joint Representation

The court may refuse to allow an attorney to represent a defendant when the attorney is representing two co-defendants and a serious potential for conflict is present. Even when all of the co-defendants waive their right to conflict-free representation, the court has discretion to refuse the joint representation.

[**Wheat v. United States**, 486 U.S. 153 (1988)—likely that defense would choose to call co-defendant represented by petitioner's counsel to testify for petitioner]

b. Right to Counsel in Nontrial Proceedings

The defendant is entitled to the assistance of counsel ***at any critical stage of the proceeding***, any time when the absence of counsel "might derogate from his right to a fair trial." [**Gilbert v. California**, 388 U.S. 263 (1967)]

(1) Pretrial Proceedings

The constitutional right to counsel arises upon the ***initiation of an adversary criminal prosecution***. [**Kirby v. Illinois**, 406 U.S. 682 (1972)] The defendant is thus entitled to counsel in the following situations:

(i) ***Post-adversary proceeding lineups*** [**Kirby v. Illinois**, *supra*];

(ii) ***Custodial interrogation*** [**Miranda v. Arizona**, 384 U.S. 436 (1966), *supra*, p. 97—*Note:* This right derives from the Fifth Amendment privilege against compelled self-incrimination rather than from the Sixth Amendment right to counsel];

(iii) ***Psychiatric examinations*** to determine the defendant's competency, amenability to rehabilitation, or future dangerousness [**Estelle v. Smith**, 451 U.S. 454 (1981), *supra*, p. 134; **Satterwhite v. Texas**, 486 U.S. 249 (1988)];

(iv) ***Pretrial arraignments*** [**Hamilton v. Alabama**, 368 U.S. 52 (1961)];

(v) ***Initial appearance to set bail*** [**Rothgery v. Gillespie County**, 554 U.S. 191 (2008), *supra*, p. 117]; and,

(vi) ***A preliminary hearing*** to determine the existence of probable cause against the accused [**Coleman v. Alabama**, 399 U.S. 1 (1970)]

The defendant is ***not*** entitled to counsel at ***grand jury proceedings***, which are deemed to be investigatory in nature. [**United States v. Mandujano**, 425 U.S. 564 (1976)] Neither is there a right to counsel at a pre-indictment lineup or a post-indictment, photo display. [**United States v. Ash**, 413 U.S. 300 (1973), *supra,* p. 114]

(2) Postconviction Proceedings

The defendant is constitutionally entitled to a lawyer at all ***sentencing*** hearings [**Mempa v. Rhay**, 389 U.S. 128 (1967)] and at the ***first***, automatic appeal [**Douglas v. California**, 372 U.S. 353 (1963)]. Under the Due Process and Equal Protection Clauses, a defendant, who is convicted based on a plea of guilty, is also entitled to appointment of counsel for a first-tier appeal. [**Halbert v. Michigan**, 545 U.S. 605 (2005)]

(a) Distinguish—Probation or Parole Revocation

The defendant is ***not*** entitled to counsel at ***probation or parole revocation*** proceedings where the trial has already been completed and sentence determined [**Gagnon v. Scarpelli**, 411 U.S. 778 (1973)], or at discretionary appeals (*i.e.*, where the courts may refuse to consider the appeal) [**Ross v. Moffitt**, 417 U.S. 600 (1974)]. In both situations it is discretionary whether to appoint counsel.

(b) State Postconviction Review

There is no constitutional right to counsel in state postconviction proceedings in either capital or noncapital cases. [**Murray v. Giarratano**, 492 U.S. 1 (1989)] However, some ***states*** do grant defendants access to counsel for postconviction review. Because this state-granted right to counsel is not constitutionally mandated, all of the procedural protections guaranteed to defendants at trial and on first appeal are not required. [**Pennsylvania v. Finley**, 481 U.S. 551 (1987)]

4. Impact of Violation of Right to Counsel

If the defendant was entitled to a lawyer at trial, the failure to provide counsel results in ***automatic reversal of the conviction*** even without any showing of specific unfairness in the proceedings. [**Gideon v. Wainwright**, *supra*, p. 152] Similarly, erroneous disqualification of privately retained counsel results in automatic reversal. [**United States v. Gonzalez-Lopez**, 548 U.S. 140 (2006)] *Rationale*: An element of the Sixth Amendment right to counsel is the right of a defendant to choose who will represent him. However, at ***nontrial proceedings*** (such as a post-charge lineup), the harmless error rule applies to deprivations of counsel. [**United States v. Wade**, 388 U.S. 218 (1967)]

EXAM TIP

When writing exam answers, you should keep in mind that while many deprivations of constitutional rights are judged under the ***harmless error standard*** (*i.e.,* the conviction need not be reversed if the prosecution can show that the error was harmless, because, for example, the great weight of the evidence indicates that the defendant would have been convicted even absent the unconstitutional conduct), this is not true for denial of the right to counsel at trial. If a defendant had a right to counsel ***at trial*** and counsel was denied, the conviction ***must be reversed***. Such errors are ***structural***, never harmless.

5. Waiver of Right to Counsel

The defendant may waive the right to counsel and represent herself at trial. This right of ***self-representation*** is not "inferior to the right of assistance of counsel." [**Faretta v. California**, 422 U.S. 806 (1975)] A defendant may also waive the right to counsel prior to trial. This often occurs after indictment, when a defendant may agree to respond to police questioning without the presence of an attorney. [**Patterson v. Illinois**, 487 U.S. 285 (1988); **Montejo v. Louisiana**, 556 U.S. 778 (2009)]

a. Requirements for Effective Waiver of Right to Counsel

To waive the right to counsel, the defendant must be advised of the right and be competent to ***intelligently and voluntarily*** abandon the right. The defendant must also be competent to proceed *pro se*. If these requirements are met, the court must allow the defendant to proceed without counsel. [**Johnson v. Zerbst**, 304 U.S. 458 (1938); **Indiana v. Edwards**, 554 U.S. 164 (2008)]

(1) *Miranda* Warnings Sufficient Notice

The *Miranda* warnings are sufficient to advise a defendant of the Sixth Amendment right to counsel, even though the warnings are based on Fifth Amendment protections. The *Miranda* warnings convey to a suspect the right to the assistance of counsel, thereby enabling the suspect to waive the right if he chooses. [**Patterson v. Illinois** and **Montejo v. Louisiana**, *supra*, p. 156]

(2) Waiver at Trial

At trial, it is not enough for a defendant to state in open court her desire to waive the right to counsel. The trial court must conduct a thorough inquiry to determine that the waiver is made knowingly, intelligently, and voluntarily and that the defendant is competent. [**Von Moltke v. Gillies**, 332 U.S. 708 (1948); **Indiana v. Edwards**, *supra*]

(3) Competency Standard

In determining whether a waiver of the right to counsel is knowing and intelligent, the court must scrutinize the waiver to ensure that the defendant has a rational and factual understanding of the proceeding against him. The Court has not established the standard for determining whether the defendant is mentally competent. However, the Court has noted that a defendant may be mentally competent to stand trial and yet incompetent to represent himself based on the trial judge's consideration of the defendant's emotional and psychological state. Still, competence in this setting does ***not*** mean that the defendant would be skilled at representing himself or would be wise to reject a lawyer. [**Indiana v. Edwards**, *supra*]

b. Assistance in Self-Representation

The defendant need not demonstrate legal expertise to be able to represent herself. However, to avoid difficulties with regard to trial complexities, some courts appoint lawyers to assist a defendant who has waived counsel. [**Silva v. State**, 190 So. 3d 151 (Fla. App. 2016)] Note that unsolicited participation by standby counsel does not violate a *pro se* defendant's Sixth Amendment right to present her own defense, as long as the defendant has actual control over the cases she chooses to present to the jury, and the jury has the perception that the defendant is representing herself. [**McKaskle v. Wiggins**, 465 U.S. 168 (1984)]

c. Cannot Generally Be Partial Self-Representation

All courts must allow the defendant to decide to represent himself or have a lawyer represent him at trial. Many courts do not allow the defendant to handle parts of the case while the lawyer handles other parts of it. [**People v. Silburn**, 98 N.E.3d 696 (N.Y. 2018)]

d. Appeal

There is no federal constitutional right to self-representation for oral argument before an appellate court. The Supreme Court held that states have discretion to conclude that the government's interest in ensuring integrity and efficiency of the appellate process outweighs the invasion of the defendant's interest in self-representation. [**Martinez v. Court of Appeal**, 528 U.S. 152 (2000)]

6. Ineffective Assistance of Counsel

The Sixth Amendment provides the right not merely to be represented by counsel, but also to be represented by effective counsel. If counsel's representation is ineffective, a resulting conviction may be overturned.

a. When Applicable

A claim of ineffective assistance of counsel often is based on an allegation that but for counsel's ineffective performance, ***defendant would not have been convicted***. A claim may also be made that counsel's ineffective assistance caused defendant to receive a sentence that was ***longer than it would have been*** with effective assistance. The claim can be based on any increase in jail time and on the basis that the death penalty would not have been imposed had counsel been effective. [*See* **Glover v. United States**, 531 U.S. 198 (2001)—increase in prison sentence from six months to 21 months is sufficient to constitute prejudice required for showing ineffective assistance of counsel; **Missouri v. Frye**, 566 U.S. 134 (2012)—counsel's failure to convey a prosecutor's plea offer to reduce a felony charge to a misdemeanor, which resulted in expiration of the offer, is covered by the Sixth Amendment's right to effective assistance of counsel; **Lafler v. Cooper**, 566 U.S. 156 (2012)—when counsel's ineffective advice leads the defendant to reject a favorable plea offer and subject himself to trial, resulting in conviction and a correspondingly longer sentence, the right to effective assistance applies; **Thornell v. Jones**, 602 U.S. 154 (2024)—rejecting claim that lawyer ineffectively presented mitigating circumstances to avoid sentence of death.] Ineffective assistance may also rest on counsel's failure to advise a criminal defendant of immigration consequences of his case. [*See* **Padilla v. Kentucky**, 559 U.S. 356 (2010)], and an ineffective assistance challenge can lie against retained, as well as appointed, counsel. An ineffective assistance claim cannot be raised with regard to a proceeding to which the right to counsel does not apply. [**Wainwright v. Torna**, 455 U.S. 586 (1982)—counsel's failure to apply for ***discretionary*** review did not deprive defendant of counsel; *but see* **Garza v. Idaho**, 586 U.S. 232 (2019), prejudice to the defendant is presumed, and counsel renders deficient performance when she fails to file a notice of appeal in response to the client's clear and repeated requests]

b. Standard of Reasonableness

Convictions are not often set aside on the ground of ineffective assistance of counsel. Failure to do what would appear to be good practice or even failure to know the law does ***not*** necessarily result in reversal of a conviction. The question is whether "counsel's representation fell below an objective standard of reasonableness." The Court has stated that "more specific guidelines are not appropriate. . . . Judicial scrutiny of counsel's performance must be highly deferential" [**Strickland v. Washington**, 466 U.S. 668 (1984); **Thornell v. Jones**, *supra* (an ineffective assistance of counsel claim requires a showing that counsel's performance was deficient **and** prejudice to the defendant, meaning a reasonable probability that absent counsel's errors, the outcome would have been different)]

c. Reasonableness and Deference

When, through a habeas petition, "a state prisoner asks a federal court to set aside a sentence due to ineffective assistance of counsel during plea bargaining . . . the [reviewing] federal court [must] use a 'double deferential' standard of review," giving both the state court and the lawyer "the benefit of the doubt." [**Burt v. Titlow**, 571 U.S. 12 (2013)]

(1) Application

A claim of ineffective assistance of counsel typically requires pointing out specific errors made by trial counsel. It cannot be based on an inference drawn from trial counsel's inexperience, lack of time to prepare, gravity of the charges, complexity of defenses, or accessibility of witnesses to counsel. [**United States v. Cronic**, 466 U.S. 648 (1984)] In fact, effective assistance of counsel ***is present unless*** the adversarial process is so undermined by counsel's conduct that the trial cannot be relied on to have produced a just result. An ineffective assistance claimant must show:

(i) ***Deficient performance*** by counsel; and

(ii) ***But for such deficiency***, there is a reasonable probability that the result of the proceeding would have been different.

[**Strickland v. Washington**; **Thornell v. Jones**, *supra*, p. 158]

(2) Instances in Which No Violation Was Found

Courts have held that the following did ***not*** necessarily constitute ineffective assistance of counsel:

(a) Failure to interview co-conspirators [**Dixon v. Warden**, 940 F. Supp. 2d 614 (S.D. Ohio 2013)];

(b) Trial counsel's failure to call witnesses. [**People v. Jurewicz**, 948 N.W.2d 448 (Mich. 2020)];

(c) An attorney's failure to raise a federal constitutional claim based on law at the time of the proceeding but that was later overruled [**Lockhart v. Fretwell**, 506 U.S. 364 (1993)];

(d) Appointed counsel's failure to meet with defendant until a few minutes before defendant's second trial, when appointed counsel was familiar with the first trial [**Chambers v. Maroney**, 399 U.S. 42 (1970)];

(e) The failure of an attorney to present mitigating evidence or make a closing argument at a capital sentencing proceeding where counsel asserted that the mitigating evidence had just been presented at trial, the defendant's mother and other character witnesses would not have been effective or might have revealed harmful information, and closing argument would have allowed rebuttal by a "very persuasive" lead prosecutor [**Bell v. Cone**, 535 U.S. 685 (2002)];

(f) In a capital murder trial, counsel's failure to obtain a client's affirmative consent to the strategy of going to trial and not challenging guilt (rather than pleading guilty) in hopes of having more credibility at sentencing [**Florida v. Nixon**, 543 U.S. 175 (2005)];

(g) In a capital murder sentencing hearing, counsel's failure to investigate further possible mitigating circumstances after his client refused to allow him to introduce any mitigating circumstances, even though such an investigation would have revealed, among other things, that the client's brain was injured [**Schriro v. Landrigan**, 550 U.S. 465 (2007)]; and

(h) In a capital case, counsel's failure to present evidence in mitigation regarding the defendant's family members and their criminal, mental, and substance abuse problems; the defendant's schooling; and the defendant's medical and mental health history including his epileptic disorder. [**Cullen v. Pinholster**, 563 U.S. 170 (2011)]

(3) Instances in Which a Sixth Amendment Violation Was Found

Courts have held that the following can constitute ineffective assistance of counsel:

(a) Failure of counsel to fully investigate viable defense. [**United States v. Glover**, 174 F. Supp. 3d 431 (D.D.C. 2016), *aff'd* 681 F.3d 411 (D.C. Cir. 2016)];

(b) Failure of counsel to file a statutory appeal [**State v. Uchima**, 464 P.3d 852 (Haw. 2020)];

(c) Failure of counsel to object to a prosecution when the charge was expressly barred [***In re* Williams**, 1 Cal. 3d 168 (1969)];

(d) Failure of counsel to file a timely motion to suppress [**Kimmelman v. Morrison**, 477 U.S. 365 (1986)];

(e) Failure of counsel to file a timely notice of appeal [**Evitts v. Lucey**, 469 U.S. 387 (1985)];

(f) In a death penalty case, failure of counsel to fully investigate the defendant's life history when counsel has reason to believe that the investigation could uncover mitigating facts [**Wiggins v. Smith**, 539 U.S. 510 (2003)]; and **Andrus v. Texas**, 590 U.S. 806 (2020) (per curiam) (finding defense counsel's failure to investigate unreasonable where it resulted from inattention, not strategy);

(g) In a capital prosecution, failure of counsel to look at the case file of defendant's prior crime that the prosecution had indicated would be central to proving aggravating circumstances justifying imposition of the death penalty, even when family members and the defendant himself have suggested that no mitigating evidence is available. [**Rompilla v. Beard**, 545 U.S. 374 (2005)—the file would have revealed leads that would have given counsel new mitigating information about the client, including that he suffered from mental illness, intellectual deficits, fetal alcohol syndrome, and had been seriously abused as a child];

(h) Counsel's strategic concession of defendant's guilt in attempt to save the defendant from the death penalty, over the defendant's adamant objection to such a concession, is ineffective assistance. [**McCoy v. Louisiana**, 584 U.S. 414 (2018)];

(i) Counsel was ineffective in a capital case when he failed to ask the judge for additional funding to hire an expert witness and failed to correct the judge's incorrect understanding that funding was capped by statute at an amount insufficient to hire a competent expert. Counsel was unaware of an amendment to the statutory fee limit and failed to adequately research the issue. [**Hinton v. Alabama**, 571 U.S. 263 (2014)—"An attorney's ignorance of a point of law that is fundamental to his case combined with his failure to perform basic research on that point is a 'quintessential' example" of unreasonable performance under **Strickland**]

d. No Right to Particular Lawyer

An indigent defendant is not entitled to the lawyer of his own choosing. The question is whether the lawyer assigned ***can render effective assistance*.** [**United States v. Mutuc**, 349 F.3d 930 (7th Cir. 2003)] Unless the relationship between the lawyer and the defendant is so strained that they cannot cooperate, the trial court is not required to appoint any particular attorney. [**State v. Jones**, 797 N.W.2d 378 (Wis. 2010)] Nor does the Sixth Amendment guarantee a "meaningful relationship" between counsel and defendant. There is no requirement that the defendant develop a certain "kind of rapport" with his attorney. [**Morris v. Slappy**, 461 U.S. 1 (1983)]

e. Right Only to Lawyer

The defendant is entitled only to have a lawyer represent him. Even in cases in which the defendant would prefer to have someone else handle the matter, only the presence of a lawyer is required. [**United States v. Noyes**, 2020 WL 5500433 (W.D. Pa. 2020)]

f. Trial Court May Not Interfere

The trial court may not unduly interfere with the lawyer's representation of the defendant. Lawyers must be given the opportunity to give a final summation of the evidence, even in nonjury cases. [**Herring v. New York**, 422 U.S. 853 (1975)] Furthermore, the trial court may not require counsel to have the defendant testify as the first defense witness. [**Brooks v. Tennessee**, 406 U.S. 605 (1972)]

g. Attorney-Client Interference

The presence of an undercover government witness at an attorney-defendant conference does not violate the Sixth Amendment if the witness does not disclose prejudicial information from that meeting to the prosecution. [**Weatherford v. Bursey**, 429 U.S. 545 (1977); **Hoffa v. United States**, 385 U.S. 293 (1966)]

h. Right Limited While Testifying

The Sixth Amendment right to counsel includes the right to consult with counsel during the trial; however, there is no right to consult with counsel while testifying. Whether a defendant has a right to consult with counsel during breaks in the client's testimony depends on the character of the break. Generally, the longer the break, the more likely the Court will find the right. [*Compare* **Geders v. United States**, 425 U.S. 80 (1976)—defendant must be allowed to talk with attorney during overnight break in defendant's testimony, because ordinary trial tactics can be, and usually are, discussed during such breaks—*with* **Perry v. Leeke**, 488 U.S. 272 (1989)—sequestration during 15-minute break between defendant's direct testimony and cross-examination permissible, because cross-examination of uncounseled witness more likely to lead to truth]

i. Appeal—*Anders* Rule

If appointed counsel on appeal genuinely believes that the case lacks merit, she may ***move to withdraw*** from representation if she ***prepares a brief*** "referring to anything in the record that might arguably support the appeal." [**Anders v. California**, 386 U.S. 738 (1967)] The court must then review the record to determine if any appeal would be wholly frivolous.

(1) Some States Prohibit *Anders* Withdrawals

To avoid the problems of appointed counsel seeking to withdraw even under ***Anders***, some state courts do ***not allow*** withdrawal on the basis that the appeal is frivolous or lacks merit. [*See* **State v. Wilson**, 83 N.E.3d 942 (Oh. 2017)]

(2) *Anders* Rule Applies Only to First Appeal of Right

The ***Anders*** rule applies only to the first appeal as of right. It is not constitutionally mandated in other postconviction situations where states have provided a right to counsel. [**Pennsylvania v. Finley**, 481 U.S. 551 (1987)]

(3) State Can Require Appointed Counsel to Discuss Why Potential Issues Lack Merit

The right to counsel is not violated by a state rule that requires appointed attorneys who are withdrawing to file a brief specifying why potential issues lack merit. [**McCoy v. Court of Appeals**, 486 U.S. 429 (1988)]

(4) Ethical Dilemma

Under ***Anders***, *supra*, p. 161, when confronted with a meritless appeal, defense counsel may be required either to file a no-merit brief against the client's interest or to present a potentially frivolous appeal before the court. As a consequence, the Supreme Court has adopted a flexible approach toward ***Anders***, allowing states to experiment with alternatives. [**Smith v. Robbins**, 528 U.S. 259 (2000)]

F. Right to Confront Witnesses; Compulsory Process

1. Confrontation

COMPONENTS OF CONFRONTATION RIGHT
A DEFENDANT HAS A RIGHT TO:
☑ Be ***present at trial*** unless waived (voluntarily or through disruptive conduct after warning).
☑ Be ***informed of the identity of prosecution witnesses*** unless anonymity is needed to protect witnesses from harassment, ridicule, etc.
☑ A ***face-to-face encounter with witnesses***, unless preventing such confrontation serves an important public purpose ***and*** the reliability of the witness's testimony is otherwise assured.
☑ ***Cross-examine witnesses*** and prevent admissions of co-defendants who are not subject to cross-examination.

a. Constitutional Basis

The Sixth Amendment provides: "in all criminal prosecutions, the accused shall enjoy the right . . . to be confronted with the witnesses against him."

(1) Purposes

The purposes of the confrontation requirement are threefold:

(i) ***To ensure reliability*** by means of the oath;

(ii) ***To expose the witness to the probative effects of cross-examination***; and

(iii) ***To permit the trier of fact*** (jury or judge) ***to weigh the demeanor of the witness*** in determining credibility.

[**California v. Green**, 399 U.S. 149 (1970)]

(2) Federal and State Prosecutions

Confrontation is deemed to be a ***fundamental right*** applicable to the states under the Due Process Clause of the Fourteenth Amendment. [**Pointer v. Texas**, 380 U.S. 400 (1965)]

(3) Limitation—Pretrial Proceedings

The right to confront witnesses is a ***trial-based right***. It does not necessarily apply in pretrial situations. For example, the Confrontation Clause is not violated by the defendant's exclusion from a pretrial hearing to determine the competency of two child witnesses, because such a hearing is not a critical proceeding dealing with the substantive issues of the trial. [**Kentucky v. Stincer**, 482 U.S. 730 (1987)] Nor does the Confrontation Clause give the defendant a right to obtain investigative reports made by a state agency investigating cases of sexual abuse. [**Pennsylvania v. Ritchie**, 480 U.S. 39 (1987), *supra*, p. 131]

b. Right of Accused to Be Physically Present

The right to confrontation means that the accused ***must have the right to be physically present*** in the courtroom during the trial. [**Snyder v. Massachusetts**, 291 U.S. 97 (1934)]

(1) Waiver

The right to be present may be waived by improper conduct of the accused.

(a) Deliberate Absence

If an accused is present at the start of trial but later voluntarily absents himself, most jurisdictions hold that the trial may continue in his absence—*i.e.,* that he has waived his right to be present. [**Taylor v. United States**, 414 U.S. 17 (1973)—the accused did not return to the court after the lunch recess, but claimed that his absence should not be viewed as a voluntary waiver; the Court disagreed]

(b) Disruptive Conduct in Courtroom

If the accused persists (after a warning) in disorderly or disrespectful conduct in the courtroom, he will be held to have waived his right to be present and may be excluded from his own trial. [**Illinois v. Allen**, 397 U.S. 337 (1970)—repeated instances of threatening remarks, talking out of turn, and "vile and abusive" language] However, the accused must be allowed to return to the courtroom, in accordance with his right to be present, if he later agrees to act appropriately.

1) Methods of Dealing with Disruptive Behavior

The Supreme Court in ***Allen*** approved the following methods for dealing with a disruptive defendant: (i) hold the defendant in ***contempt***; (ii) ***bind and gag the defendant*** in the courtroom; or (iii) ***remove*** the defendant altogether.

(2) Restrictions on the Right

The government may not place a burden on this right by requiring the defendant to appear in court in prison clothes or shackles without good cause shown. [**Estelle v. Williams**, *supra,* p. 138; **Deck v. Missouri**, *supra,* p. 138]

c. Right to Identity of Prosecution Witnesses

Witnesses who ***testify*** against the accused normally must reveal their true names and addresses (*i.e.,* they cannot take the stand as anonymous persons).

(1) Rationale

Such information may be crucial to the defense in investigating and cross-examining for possible impeachment. [**Smith v. Illinois**, 390 U.S. 129 (1968)]

(2) Exception

Pseudonyms (*e.g.,* John Doe) may be used to protect a person from harassment, injury, ridicule, or personal embarrassment. However, the surrounding circumstances requiring protection must be unusual or special. [**United States v. Guiterrez de Lopez**, 761 F.3d 1123 (10th Cir. 2014)]

d. Right to Face-to-Face Encounter with Witnesses

The Sixth Amendment generally includes a right to a face-to-face encounter between a defendant and the witnesses against him. [*See* **Crawford v. Washington**, 541 U.S. 36 (2004); **Smith v. Arizona**, 602 U.S. 779 (2014).] This rule often precludes the introduction of hearsay evidence, even when such evidence fits into an exception contained in the federal or state rules of evidence. When a witness is absent from trial, their testimony is inadmissible, unless the witness is unavailable (within the meaning of the evidentiary rules) and the accused has enjoyed a prior opportunity to cross examine the witness's testimony. In rare instances, the absence of a face-to-face confrontation does not violate the Sixth Amendment. Although this case predates ***Crawford***, face-to-face confrontation may be denied when: (i) Preventing such confrontation serves an important public purpose (such as lessening the serious emotional distress of young child witnesses). [**Maryland v. Craig**, 497 U.S. 836 (1990)]

e. Right to Cross-Examine Witnesses

An accused has the right to lead and impeach prosecution witnesses and defense witnesses who give damaging testimony on the witness stand. In this situation, traditional rules of evidence against impeaching "one's own" witness give way to the constitutional right of confrontation. [**Chambers v. Mississippi**, 410 U.S. 284 (1973)—when Defendant called witness who had previously confessed to the murder with which Defendant was charged, witness recanted confession; Defendant should be allowed to impeach by proving out-of-court confession]

(1) Scope of Cross-Examination

The scope of permissible cross-examination must be wide enough to be effective. Because the purpose of cross-examination is to inquire into the reliability of a witness's testimony, the accused must be allowed to show any matters that would reflect ***possible bias*** by the witness testifying against him. [**Davis v. Alaska**, 415 U.S. 308 (1974)—Defendant permitted to show that prosecution witness was on probation as a juvenile delinquent; any government interest in protecting anonymity of juvenile offenders must give way to right of confrontation]

f. Confessions of Co-Defendant

The admission of an out-of-court confession made by a co-defendant can present a right to confrontation problem because the nonconfessing defendant cannot compel the confessing co-defendant to take the stand for cross-examination.

(1) *Bruton* Rule

In **Bruton v. United States** (*supra*, p. 141), the Supreme Court decided that confessions of co-defendants cannot be used at joint trials when the confessions incriminate the defendant, and the confessor does not take the stand for cross examination. The Court held that juries cannot be expected to follow instructions that limit the use of the confessions to the confessing co-defendants.

(a) Note

In dissent, Justice White argued that the ***Bruton*** rule is too rigid and that a jury instruction to disregard the confession in relation to the non-confessing defendant is sufficient, but the Court has not retreated from its core holding.

(2) Limitations on Rule

The ***Bruton*** rule has had significant impact on the joint trials of defendants, but it is subject to numerous limitations.

(a) Harmless Error

The rule is subject to the harmless error principles; erroneous admission of the confession does not result in ***automatic*** reversal. [**Schneble v. Florida**, 405 U.S. 427 (1972)—admission of confession was harmless where there was other overwhelming evidence of defendant's guilt]

(b) Deletion of Reference

If references to the nonconfessing defendant are sufficiently deleted from the confession, no Confrontation Clause issue is raised, and the confession may be admitted. [**Richardson v. Marsh**, *supra,* p. 141]

1) Note

It is not sufficient merely to insert a blank or some other substitution for the name of the other defendant. The redaction should not indicate the defendant's involvement. [*Compare* **Richardson v. Marsh**, *supra*—after redaction, confession indicated that defendant and a third party (who was not a co-defendant) participated in the crime and contained no indication of co-defendant's involvement and **Samia v. United States**, 599 U.S. 635 (2023)—in which a DEA agent testified that one defendant confessed to "a time when the other person he was with pulled the trigger on that woman in a van" among other testimony that made reference to "the other person," *with* **Gray v. Maryland**, 523 U.S. 185 (1998)—redaction "me, deleted, deleted, and a few other guys [killed the victim]" which was found to clearly refer to the co-defendant]

(c) Defendant Testifies

The rule does not apply if the confessing defendant takes the witness stand at trial and testifies, because he is then subject to cross-examination and "confrontation." This is true even if the defendant denies ever having made the confession. [**Nelson v. O'Neil**, 402 U.S. 622 (1971)]

(d) Admitted for Limited Purpose

The rule does not apply if the confession is offered for a limited purpose, such as to rebut the defendant's claim that his confession was obtained by coercion. The jury must be instructed as to the purpose of the admission. [**Tennessee v. Street**, 471 U.S. 409 (1985)]

EXAM TIP

In an exam question, if one co-defendant has given a confession that implicates the other, remember that introduction of the confession will *violate the Sixth Amendment right of confrontation unless*: (i) all portions referring to the nonconfessing defendant can be eliminated; or (ii) the confessing defendant takes the stand and subjects himself to cross-examination; or (iii) the confessing defendant's confession is being used for a limited purpose, such as to rebut the other defendant's claim that his confession was obtained through coercion.

(3) Co-Conspirator Statements

In **Bourjaily v. United States**, 483 U.S. 171 (1986), the Court found that statements made "in the ***course of a conspiracy*** and in furtherance of it" fall within a firmly rooted hearsay exception, so that no independent indicia of reliability is necessary to establish their admissibility under confrontation analysis. Thus, in a conspiracy trial, a conspirator's statement can be used against a co-conspirator.

2. Compulsory Process for Obtaining Witnesses

a. Constitutional Bases

The Sixth Amendment expressly provides that the accused in any criminal prosecution shall have the right to compulsory process for obtaining witnesses in her favor. Taken with the Due Process Clause, this means that the ***defendant is given the same right as the prosecutor to present witnesses*** in state as well as federal criminal proceedings. [**Washington v. Texas**, 388 U.S. 14 (1967)]

b. Scope of Right

The right to obtain witnesses includes more than just the power to subpoena them. It encompasses the right to ***present a defense***, which includes the right of the accused to present her own witnesses and her own version of the facts. [**Washington v. Texas**, *supra*—"The right to offer the testimony of witnesses, and to compel their attendance, if necessary, is in plain terms the right to present a defense"]

(1) Intimidation by Judge

If the trial judge makes threatening remarks to the only defense witness, which effectively drives that witness off the stand, the accused is deprived of the right to present a defense. [**Webb v. Texas**, 409 U.S. 95 (1972)—trial judge singled out the lone defense witness and admonished him about the danger, likelihood, and repercussions of being convicted for perjury, specifically referring to the fact that this witness's present prison sentence would be significantly lengthened by such a conviction]

(2) Exclusion of Crucial Evidence

Exclusion by the trial judge of evidence crucial to the defense and bearing substantial assurances of trustworthiness impairs the right of the accused to present a defense—even if the evidence offered is technically ***inadmissible under appropriate local rules of evidence***. [**Chambers v. Mississippi**, 410 U.S. 284 (1973)]

e.g. **Example:** Defendant offered evidence of oral confessions by another witness. The trial court excluded the proffered evidence because this was inadmissible hearsay under local rules of evidence, but the Supreme Court reversed, holding that the evidence bore substantial assurances of trustworthiness, and that local rules could not be allowed to impair the accused's right to present a defense. [**Chambers v. Mississippi**, *supra*]

(a) Exception—Sanction for Violation of Discovery Rules

Exclusion of evidence can be proper as a ***sanction for the defendant's violation of discovery rules***. For example, a trial court can exclude the testimony of a witness who was known to defense counsel but not identified in counsel's response to pretrial discovery. While other sanctions are usually adequate, in some instances excluding testimony or other evidence is the only effective remedy for violation of the court's rules. [**Taylor v. Illinois**, 484 U.S. 400 (1988)]

(3) Exclusion of Accomplice Testimony

A statute providing that an accomplice cannot be used as a defense witness has been held to violate the accused's right to present a defense. The statute was based on the notion that "each [accused] would try to swear the other out of the charge," but even this legitimate concern could not be used to deprive the accused of relevant and material testimony. [**Washington v. Texas**, *supra*, p. 166]

(4) Deportation of Witnesses

A constitutional claim based on the government's deportation of a witness can be successful only if the defendant shows that the testimony of the deported witness would have been ***material and favorable*** to the accused's defense. [**United States v. Valenzuela-Bernal**, 458 U.S. 858 (1982)—defendant participated in criminal action with the deported accomplice, but defendant could not show how testimony of the deported accomplice would be favorable to his defense]

(5) Exclusion of Hypnotically Refreshed Testimony

A *per se* rule excluding all hypnotically refreshed testimony was invalidated by the Supreme Court because it impermissibly infringed on the defendant's right to testify in her own behalf. Although the Court acknowledged that hypnotically refreshed testimony may be unreliable in some cases, the majority concluded that a *per se* rule impermissibly excludes testimony that may contain sufficient indicia of reliability. [**Rock v. Arkansas**, 483 U.S. 44 (1987)] In ***Rock***, independent evidence corroborated the defendant's hypnotically refreshed testimony, and tape recordings of the hypnosis session existed so that the suggestiveness of the testimony could be shown on cross-examination.

(6) Claim That Third Party Committed Crime

A state cannot impose a rule prohibiting a defendant from suggesting that a third party committed the crime whenever there is strong forensic evidence of the defendant's guilt. [**Holmes v. South Carolina**, 547 U.S. 319 (2006)] Proffered evidence can be excluded if it is shown to be flawed, but not merely because of the perceived strength of the prosecutor's case.

G. Burden of Proof

1. General Standard

A basic part of the due process right to a fair trial is the requirement that the prosecution produce evidence of guilt and prove the defendant guilty of ***every element*** of the crime charged ***beyond a reasonable doubt***. [**Taylor v. Kentucky**, 436 U.S. 478 (1978)]

e.g. **Example:** When the government charges a defendant with unlawfully distributing heroin with death resulting, the government must prove beyond a reasonable doubt the causation element of the crime—that the heroin caused the victim's death. [**Burrage v. United States**, 571 U.S. 204 (2014)]

a. Presumption of Innocence

Under the Due Process Clause, the defendant is presumed innocent of all charges. The jury need not, however, be given one specific instruction that defendant is presumed innocent. Instead, the ***"totality of the circumstances"***—including all instructions to the jury, the arguments of counsel, the weight of the evidence—must be considered to determine whether such an instruction is necessary for a fair trial. [**Kentucky v. Whorton**, 441 U.S. 786 (1979)]

b. "Reasonable Doubt"

The Supreme Court has noted that the reasonable doubt standard "plays a vital role in the American scheme of criminal procedure" and "is a prime instrument for reducing the risk of convictions resting on factual error." [**Cage v. Louisiana**, 498 U.S. 39 (1990)] However, the Supreme Court and most other courts have been reluctant to adopt a definition. Mere probability of guilt clearly is not enough, but something less than absolute certainty is required.

e.g. **Example:** The Supreme Court struck down a conviction where the trial court's instructions on reasonable doubt equated it with "grave uncertainty" and "actual substantial doubt," because these require a higher standard of doubt than "reasonable doubt." [**Cage v. Louisiana**, *supra*]

c. Where "Reasonable Doubt" Is Inapplicable

It is only the ***defendant's guilt*** that must be established beyond a "reasonable doubt." Thus, in most courts, questions as to the admissibility of prosecution evidence—*e.g.*, whether it was obtained by "lawful" search or seizure, or whether defendant's confession was "voluntary"—need only be proved by a ***preponderance of the evidence***. [**Lego v. Twomey,** 404 U.S. 477 (1972)]

2. Presumptions

There are two kinds of presumptions. A ***permissive*** presumption ***allows*** the jury to infer an element of a crime from proof by the government of the basic fact, but the jury may ***elect to reject*** this inference. A ***mandatory*** presumption ***requires*** the jury to accept the element.

a. Permissive Presumptions Are Constitutional

To allow use of a permissive presumption, a ***rational connection*** must be established between the basic facts shown by the government and the ultimate fact to be presumed. The judge must also agree that the ultimate fact is likely to flow from the basic fact. [**Ulster County Court v. Allen**, 442 U.S. 140 (1979)] Of concern is the fact that presumptions cannot interfere with the fact-finder's duty to find the elements of the crime beyond a reasonable doubt. Permissive presumptions allow the factfinder to reject the presumption, protecting the reasonable doubt standard. It is also significant that the opposing party can challenge the validity of the presumption.

b. Mandatory Presumptions Are Unconstitutional

Mandatory presumptions may not be used by the prosecution, because they conflict with the requirement that the government prove each element of the offense beyond a reasonable doubt. [**Sandstrom v. Montana**, 442 U.S. 510 (1979)]

e.g. **Example:** The Court has held that an impermissible mandatory presumption was created by the following jury instructions in a "malice murder" trial: 1) "acts of a person of sound mind and discretion are presumed to be the product of a person's will, but the presumption may be rebutted"; and 2) a "person of sound mind and discretion is presumed to intend the natural and probable consequences of his acts, but the presumption may be rebutted." These instructions are unconstitutional because they would lead a reasonable juror to conclude that the state's burden of proof on intent to kill may be inferred from proof of the defendant's acts unless the defendant proves otherwise. [**Francis v. Franklin**, 471 U.S. 307 (1985); **Yates v. Aiken**, 484 U.S. 211 (1988)]

e.g. **Example:** A presumption is impermissible that an accused contemnor is able to comply with the court's order. Such a presumption places the burden of proof on the accused as to one of the key elements of a contempt charge, thus shifting the state's obligation to prove guilt beyond a reasonable doubt. [**Hicks v. Feiock**, 485 U.S. 624 (1988)]

e.g. **Example:** The Due Process Clause prohibits a statutory presumption that an individual has intended to commit theft when he fails to return leased personal property of another within 20 days after the owner makes a written demand for return of the property, because such a presumption establishes elements of the crime without the state fulfilling its burden of proving these elements beyond a reasonable doubt. [**Carella v. California**, 491 U.S. 263 (1989)]

3. Scientific Evidence in Federal Trials

Federal Rule of Evidence 702 provides the standard for admitting scientific evidence in a federal trial. Under Rule 702, scientific evidence offered by experts is admissible if it "will assist the trier of fact to understand the evidence or determine a fact in issue." There is no requirement that the scientific evidence has gained general acceptance in the scientific community, as is required in some state courts following the rule of **Frye v. United States**, 293 F. 1013 (D.C. Cir. 1923). [**Daubert v. Merrell Dow Pharmaceuticals, Inc.**, 509 U.S. 579 (1993)] Even if scientific evidence is admissible under Rule 702, it must also be admissible under the Sixth Amendment Confrontation Clause and **Crawford v. Washington**, *supra*, p. 164. *Note*: Several states have rules similar to the federal rule.

4. Review of the Sufficiency of the Evidence

When a jury has returned a finding of guilt, the court (whether at trial or on appeal) must decide that there was adequate evidence to justify the jury's finding of guilt beyond a reasonable doubt. [**Jackson v. Virginia**, 443 U.S. 307 (1979)] This is not the same as requiring the court to find that it believes that the evidence actually established guilt beyond a reasonable doubt. This standard of review is whether, "after viewing the evidence in the light most favorable to the prosecution, any rational trier of fact could have found the essential elements of the crime beyond a reasonable doubt."

5. Affirmative Defenses

Even if the government has proved all the elements of the crime, the defendant may still be acquitted if it is shown that the defendant had an ***excuse or justification*** for the commission of the crime (*e.g.,* self-defense, duress). This is referred to as an affirmative defense. The defendant may be required to ***prove*** the affirmative defense, including an insanity claim. [**Leland v. Oregon**, 343 U.S. 790 (1952)]

a. Caveat

In some cases what appears to be an affirmative defense is actually an element of the crime charged, so that the government must prove that fact beyond a reasonable doubt.

e.g. **Example:** It is unconstitutional to require the defendant to prove reasonable provocation that will reduce a killing from murder to manslaughter, as reasonable provocation is an element of the crime of manslaughter. [**Mullaney v. Wilbur**, 421 U.S. 684 (1975)]

cf. **Compare:** It is constitutional to require the defendant to prove "extreme emotional disturbance" where that is not an element of a lesser homicide crime. [**Patterson v. New York**, 432 U.S. 197 (1977)]

H. Insanity Defense

1. In General

Insanity ***excuses*** otherwise criminal acts of the defendant because of an abnormal mental condition at the time the act was committed. Insanity is a defense to all crimes, but not every state offers an insanity defense. In states that do not allow the defense, the accused is permitted to argue that the government is unable to prove beyond a reasonable doubt the required mens rea element of the crime(s).

2. Four Tests

Most jurisdictions use one of the following substantive tests of insanity. The majority of the states use either the ***M'Naghten*** or **irresistible impulse** test, or a combination of them. Only a few jurisdictions use the ***Durham*** test. A number of states use the **A.L.I.** test.

a. *M'Naghten* Rule

Under the ***M'Naghten*** rule, a defendant is insane if, at the time of the crime, he suffered from a disease of the mind that made him unable to ***know the wrongfulness of his actions*** or to ***understand the nature and quality of his acts***. [**M'Naghten's Case**, 8 Eng. Rep. 718 (1843)]

(1) **Federal Test**

The test for insanity in federal cases is whether, as a result of "severe mental disease or defect," the defendant was unable to appreciate the nature and quality or the wrongfulness of his acts.

b. **Irresistible Impulse Test**

A defendant is deemed insane under the irresistible impulse test if, because of mental illness at the time of the crime, the defendant ***lacked capacity for self-control*** or free choice. The inability need not be "impulsive" in the sense that it came upon the defendant suddenly. [**Parsons v. State**, 81 Ala. 577 (1887)]

c. ***Durham*** **(or Product) Test**

Under the ***Durham*** test, a defendant is deemed insane if the defendant's otherwise criminal action was the "***product*** of mental disease or defect"; *i.e.*, the crime would not have been committed ***but for*** some mental disease. [**United States v. Brawner**, 471 F.2d 969 (D.C. Cir. 1972)]

(1) **"Mental Disease or Defect" Defined**

"[A] mental disease or defect includes any abnormal condition of the mind which substantially affects mental or emotional processes and substantially impairs behavior controls." [**McDonald v. United States**, 312 F.2d 847 (D.C. Cir. 1962)]

d. **American Law Institute (A.L.I.) or Model Penal Code Test**

The American Law Institute approach combines the ***M'Naghten*** and **Irresistible Impulse** tests. Under this approach, a defendant should be acquitted if, as a result of suffering from a mental disease or defect, he lacked substantial capacity to either ***appreciate the wrongfulness*** of his conduct ***or*** to ***conform his conduct*** to the requirements of law.

Although most jurisdictions use one of these four tests as noted above, a few jurisdictions preclude the use of an insanity defense except where the accused's mental disease or defect prevents the accused from forming the mens rea for the crime charged. In ***Kahler v. Kansas***, 589 U.S. 271 (2020), the Court held that such a system is constitutional and that the Due Process Clause does not require that a defendant recognize the morally wrong nature of his acts.

SUMMARY OF INSANITY DEFENSES

TEST	DEFINITION
M'NAGHTEN	Because of mental impairment, defendant did not (i) ***know his acts were wrong*** or (ii) understand the ***nature and quality of his acts***
IRRESISTIBLE IMPULSE	Crime caused by insane ***impulse*** that ***overcame defendant's will***
DURHAM	Crime was a ***product of defendant's*** mental disease or defect
MODEL PENAL CODE	Because of mental impairment, defendant ***lacked substantial capacity*** to (i) ***appreciate criminality*** of conduct or (ii) ***conform it to the law***

3. Burden of Proof

a. Burden of Producing Evidence

A defendant is ***presumed sane*** until she comes forward with some evidence to show that she was insane at the time of the crime.

b. Burden of Persuasion

Once the accused raises an issue of insanity, in some states the ***prosecution*** must prove beyond a reasonable doubt that the defendant was sane. In other jurisdictions, the ***defendant*** must prove insanity by a preponderance of the evidence, and ***federal*** courts and some states require the defendant to prove insanity by "clear and convincing" evidence.

4. When the Defense May Be Raised

The insanity defense ***may*** be raised when the defendant pleads at the arraignment, but she is ***not required to raise it then***. A "not guilty" plea at the arraignment does not bar the defendant from raising the defense later. In some jurisdictions, if the defendant is going to raise the defense at trial, she must give the prosecution notice some number of days ***before trial*** to permit the state to counter the defense. Most courts do not allow a prosecutor or judge to assert the insanity defense when a competent and adequately represented defendant has chosen not to do so.

5. Psychiatric Examination

If an indigent defendant has made a preliminary showing that she is likely to be able to use the insanity defense, the state must provide a mental health expert for the preparation of the defense. A defendant is also entitled to expert examination and testimony in the sentencing proceeding if the state has presented evidence that the defendant is likely to be dangerous in the future. [**Ake v. Oklahoma**, *supra,* p. 154]

a. Use by Prosecution

Generally, the prosecution may not use evidence obtained during psychiatric examinations prepared to assist the defendant in his defense. However, when the defendant and the prosecution jointly request a psychiatric examination, the prosecution may use evidence from the examination solely to rebut the defendant's mental-status evidence. Such use does not violate the defendant's Fifth or Sixth Amendment rights. [**Buchanan v. Kentucky**, 483 U.S. 402 (1987)] The prosecution may also introduce evidence from a court-ordered mental examination to rebut the defendant's argument that she lacked the mental capacity to commit the charged offense. [**Kansas v. Cheever**, 571 U.S. 87 (2013)]

6. Post-Acquittal Commitment

If the defendant is acquitted by reason of insanity, she may be committed to a mental institution until she has recovered. In some jurisdictions, the commitment is automatic. In others, the defendant must be shown to be presently mentally ill or dangerous.

a. Commitment Standard

When a defendant acquitted by reason of insanity was required at trial to show insanity by only a "preponderance of the evidence," he cannot avoid commitment to a mental hospital even though the civil standard for commitment ("clear and convincing evidence") was not met. Because the jury found beyond a reasonable doubt that defendant committed a criminal act, indicating dangerousness, a preponderance of the evidence standard on the insanity issue is sufficient for commitment. [**Jones v. United States**, 463 U.S. 354 (1983)] Moreover, the defendant may be committed until she has recovered her sanity or is no longer dangerous—even though this may be for longer than she might have served in prison had she been convicted. [**Jones v. United States**, *supra*]

(1) Note

A defendant acquitted by reason of insanity who is determined to have recovered his sanity cannot be indefinitely committed in a mental facility merely because he is unable to prove himself not dangerous to others. Such a commitment violates due process. [**Foucha v. Louisiana**, 504 U.S. 71 (1992)]

7. Diminished Capacity

Many jurisdictions permit a defendant to offer evidence of mental illness short of insanity to show that the government has not proved the mental state for crimes requiring specific intent. This diminished capacity must be raised and proved by the defendant. The question is whether the defendant lacked the ability at the time of the offense to form the needed intent due to a mental disorder not amounting to insanity.

8. Bifurcated Trial

Some states determine sanity only after guilt has been proved. Insanity is addressed by the same or a new jury (depending on the judge's discretion) at a separate second stage of the proceeding.

I. Entrapment Defense

1. In General

Entrapment is an affirmative defense. It is ***not constitutionally based***. Rather, in the federal system, it is based on the Supreme Court's interpretation of congressional intent in enacting criminal statutes. The Court has held that it would be difficult to conclude that Congress intended to permit government officials to lure otherwise innocent persons into committing crimes so that the government could punish them. [**Sorrells v. United States**, 287 U.S. 435 (1932)—"the government cannot be permitted to contend that [the defendant] is guilty of a crime where the government officials are the instigators of his conduct"] Most states either follow such a view or rely on statutes establishing the defense.

2. Burden of Proof

In the federal system and in many states, if the defendant offers credible evidence of entrapment, the government must then disprove the defense beyond a reasonable doubt. In other states, the ***accused*** bears the burden of proving entrapment. In either case, it is well settled that the factual issue of whether the defendant was actually entrapped should normally be decided by the jury. [**Sherman v. United States**, 356 U.S. 369 (1958)] A defendant is entitled to a jury instruction on the issue of entrapment even when she denies one or more elements of the crime. [**Mathews v. United States**, 485 U.S. 58 (1988)]

3. Basic Test

a. Majority View

The majority view focuses on the ***predisposition of the defendant*** to commit the act alleged. According to this view, the entrapment defense applies only if the accused has ***no predisposition*** to commit the crime but committed it due to inducement of government agencies.

(1) Timing

The predisposition of the defendant must exist ***prior*** to the government's initial contact with the defendant. A mere "inclination" to engage in the illegal activity is not adequate proof of predisposition. [**Jacobson v. United States**, 503 U.S. 540 (1992)—defendant who ordered child pornography only after government solicited such a sale for *two* years was not predisposed]

b. Minority View

The minority view rejects the predisposition test and concentrates solely on an ***analysis of the conduct of the government agents***.

Example—Entrapment: Defendant and a government informant met at a narcotics clinic where both were undergoing treatment for addiction. Informant asked Defendant if he knew a supplier of drugs and then whether Defendant himself would provide the narcotics. After first attempting to avoid the issue, Defendant gave in under repeated requests, apparently based on informant's suffering and failure to respond to clinical treatment. Defendant thereafter supplied drugs to the informant at next to cost. The Court found entrapment as a matter of law. [**Sherman v. United States**, *supra*, p. 173]

Compare—No Entrapment: Defendant was supplied with heroin by a government informant. Defendant then sold the heroin to two government agents. The Court affirmed a jury finding of no entrapment because of Defendant's predisposition to commit the crime. [**Hampton v. United States**, 425 U.S. 484 (1976)]

Compare—No Entrapment: A government narcotics agent, posing as a narcotics manufacturer and distributor, offered to supply the defendants with one of the difficult-to-obtain ingredients for manufacture of the drug methamphetamine in return for half of the drug produced. The defendants accepted the offer. There was also evidence that the defendants had obtained the scarce ingredient from another source both before and after they obtained it from the narcotics agent. There was no entrapment. [**United States v. Russell**, 411 U.S. 423 (1972)]

4. Use of Defense

In line with other areas of criminal law, the Court has expanded the area of permissible activity for law enforcement officials. Thus, ***except in cases of unusual persuasion or inducement, the entrapment defense does not usually prevail***. [*See, e.g.,* **Jacobson v. United States**, *supra*—"where the defendant is simply provided with the opportunity to commit a crime, the entrapment defense is of little use because the ready commission of the criminal act amply demonstrates the defendant's predisposition"] However, if the government inducement is intense and especially lengthy, entrapment may be found, as in ***Jacobson***. In most places, the defendant's prior criminal record may be introduced into evidence, if she raises the defense of entrapment, for the purpose of demonstrating predisposition to commit the crime.

EXAM TIP

Most exam questions on entrapment are going to require you to consider the issue of the defendant's predisposition. Be sure to concentrate first on the *defendant's past conduct* and her *behavior in the transaction for which she was arrested.* Look for indications that she was predisposed to commit this type of crime. You may then want to examine the police activity involved for hints of a *lack* of predisposition, but don't lose sight of the fact that under this majority approach to entrapment, the focus is on the defendant's predisposition, not on the government's conduct.

Chapter Six
Punishment

CONTENTS	PAGE

Key Exam Issues

Criminal Procedure professors do not typically test heavily on punishment issues. However, there are a few topics in this chapter that may show up on your exam:

1. **Guilty Pleas**

   It is important for you to remember what the plea involves: The plea is an agreement by both sides, in which "consideration" is based on (i) the defendant giving up the right to go to trial, and (ii) the prosecution promising either to reduce charges or to recommend a lesser punishment. The defendant must be given ***all of the material facts*** in connection with this plea before the judge accepts the plea (the nature of the charge, the maximum penalty, knowledge of the relinquishment of the trial right, etc.) or the plea will not be upheld.

2. **Sentencing**

   At sentencing, the defendant has no right to confront witnesses against him (probation reports can be used by the judge), but he does have a right to have an attorney assist him. Note that much discretion is given to the sentencing judge, and essentially, if the sentence is within the statutory limits, appeals courts will normally ***not*** reverse.

3. **Death Penalty**

   The death penalty is a complex area with numerous considerations. You should be aware of three principal points:

   a. The Supreme Court has ruled that the death penalty is ***not*** inherently violative of the Eighth Amendment's prohibition against cruel and unusual punishment.

   b. The courts have given detailed directions to trial judges and juries with respect to the procedure for imposing the death penalty. Check that the sentencing body considers both ***aggravating and mitigating factors***, and that the statute provides for ***specific review procedures***.

   c. The death penalty cannot be mandatory punishment; yet, the sentencing body cannot be given too much discretion. There must be ***specific standards*** for the jury to follow.

A. Guilty Pleas

1. Alternative Pleas

Before trial, the defendant will be asked how she pleads. This hearing is called ***arraignment*** in many jurisdictions. At arraignment, the defendant can plead guilty, not guilty, and in some cases nolo contendere.

a. Guilty Pleas

Guilty pleas are waivers of the right to jury trial and all other rights that accompany a trial. The overwhelming majority of all cases resolve by guilty plea.

b. Nolo Contendere Pleas

A nolo contendere or no contest plea allows the accused, without admitting guilt, to forgo a trial and accept punishment as if he were guilty. Unlike a guilty plea, a nolo plea ***cannot be used against a defendant as an admission of guilt in a subsequent criminal or civil case***.

c. Failure to Plead

When a defendant fails to enter a plea or refuses to speak, the judge will enter a not guilty plea on the defendant's behalf.

2. Entering the Plea

a. Plea Must Be Voluntary and Intelligent

The judge must determine that the plea is voluntary and intelligent. The judge must address the defendant personally in open court on the record. [**McCarthy v. United States**, 394 U.S. 459 (1969)] Specifically, the judge must be sure that the defendant knows and understands:

(i) ***The nature of the charge*** to which the plea is offered [**Henderson v. Morgan**, 426 U.S. 637 (1976)—plea involuntary if defendant not informed that intent is element of crime of murder];

(ii) ***The maximum possible penalty*** for the offense and any ***mandatory*** minimum penalty;

(iii) ***The defendant has a right to plead not guilty*** or to persist in that plea if it has already been made; and

(iv) ***By pleading guilty, the defendant waives the right to a trial.***

[*See* Fed. R. Crim. P. 11(b)(1)]

(1) Attorney May Inform Defendant

The judge need not personally explain the elements of each charge to the defendant on the record. Rather, the constitutional prerequisites of a valid plea may be satisfied where the record accurately reflects that the nature of the charge and the elements of the crime were explained to the defendant by his own counsel. [**Bradshaw v. Stumpf**, 545 U.S. 175 (2005)]

(2) No Right to "Helpful" Information

Defendants are ***not*** entitled to be told of either impeachment evidence or evidence relevant to affirmative defenses prior to entering a plea agreement. Although failure to provide such evidence might be important in determining whether the defendant had a fair trial, it does not make a plea involuntary. A plea agreement can be voluntary even if it is based on incomplete information. [**United States v. Ruiz**, 536 U.S. 622 (2002)]

b. Competency Standard

The competency standard for pleading guilty is the same standard as for standing trial. The defendant must have sufficient present ability to rationally understand the proceedings, as well as the ability to consult with counsel. [**Godinez v. Moran**, 509 U.S. 389 (1993)]

c. Factual Basis

In all federal cases, before entering judgment, the court must determine that there is a factual basis for the plea. [Fed. R. Crim. R 11(b)(3)] This requirement is not constitutionally mandated in state cases, although some states by their own court rules require a showing of factual basis to support the plea.

(1) Admission of Guilt

An admission of guilt is ***not*** a constitutional prerequisite to imposition of a criminal penalty. [**North Carolina v. Alford**, 400 U.S. 25 (1970)] A defendant need not admit guilt in open court as long as the state has introduced strong evidence of the defendant's guilt, and the defendant's voluntary plea appears to be an intelligent choice from among his alternatives. The court may then accept the voluntary plea even though the defendant refuses to admit guilt.

EXAM TIP

Although it may seem odd, remember that an admission of guilt is *not a prerequisite to a guilty plea*. Thus, a defendant may proclaim innocence and still enter a guilty plea, provided it is voluntarily entered. However, in such a case the prosecution must have introduced strong evidence of the defendant's guilt to help assure that an innocent person is not being punished.

(2) Forfeitures

Even in federal cases, the rules do not require the court to establish a factual basis for a stipulation in a guilty plea that property is subject to forfeiture (because, *e.g.*, it was obtained with proceeds of drug sales). The rules require that a factual basis be established ***for a guilty plea***, and forfeiture is not part of a criminal offense to which a defendant pleads guilty; rather, forfeiture is an additional punishment for some offense to which the defendant has pleaded guilty. [**Libretti v. United States**, 516 U.S. 29 (1995)]

d. No Waiver of Subsequent Fifth Amendment Privilege

Neither a defendant's guilty plea nor her plea hearing functions as a waiver of the right to remain silent at sentencing. A waiver of a right to trial with its attendant privileges is not a waiver of the privileges that exist beyond the confines of the trial. [**Mitchell v. United States**, 526 U.S. 314 (1999)] A defendant may have a legitimate fear of adverse consequences from further testimony when the sentence has not yet been imposed.

3. Plea Bargaining

A high percentage of criminal cases are resolved through plea bargaining. Generally, plea bargains involve an agreement by the defendant to plead guilty to one offense in exchange for the prosecutor's agreement to dismiss other charges or to recommend a certain sentence. Because plea bargains avoid the delay and expense of trials, the Supreme Court and lower courts look favorably Upon them.

a. Disclosure to the Court

Federal Rule of Criminal Procedure 11(c)(2) requires disclosure of any plea agreement when the defendant pleads guilty. State courts have generally followed this procedure, requiring that counsel disclose any plea agreement and that the terms of the bargain become part of the record. A court might find the terms of a plea bargain unacceptable, in which case, the defendant must be informed and permitted to withdraw the plea.

b. Enforcing the Bargain

Once the court has accepted a guilty plea entered pursuant to a plea bargain, the defendant has a right to have the bargain enforced. If the ***prosecution*** does not keep the bargain, a court should decide whether the circumstances require ***specific performance*** of the plea agreement or whether the defendant should be granted an ***opportunity to withdraw the guilty plea.*** [**Santobello v. New York**, 404 U.S. 257 (1971)] If the ***defendant*** fails to keep her part of the bargain, the prosecution can have the plea vacated and can reinstate the original charges. [**Ricketts v. Adamson**, 483 U.S. 1 (1987)]

c. Withdrawing the Plea

A plea may be withdrawn after it is entered and before sentencing only if the court rejects the plea or for some other "fair and just reason" (*e.g.,* the plea was coerced, the defendant overlooked a defense that he would like to raise, etc.). [**United States v. Hyde**, 520 U.S. 670 (1997)]

d. Driving a Hard Bargain

A guilty plea is ***not*** involuntary even if it is entered in response to the prosecutor's threat to charge the defendant with a more serious crime if he does not plead guilty. [**Bordenkircher v. Hayes**, 434 U.S. 357 (1978)] Consistent with a contractual theory of plea negotiation, ***the state may drive as hard a bargain as the law allows***.

e.g. **Example:** To encourage a defendant to plead guilty, the prosecutor threatens to seek a recidivist indictment that could lead to a life sentence. As long as the threat fairly states the law, it does not render Defendant's guilty plea involuntary.

e. Admission of Statements Made in Connection with Plea Bargaining

Under the Federal Rules of Evidence and of Criminal Procedure, statements made by a defendant in the course of unsuccessful plea negotiations are inadmissible at trial. However, such statements can be admitted *if* the defendant has knowingly and voluntarily waived the Federal Rules' exclusionary provisions. [**United States v. Mezzanatto**, 513 U.S. 196 (1995)—statements used to impeach defendant's testimony at trial]

4. Collateral Attack on Guilty Pleas After Sentence

a. General Rule—No Collateral Attack

A defendant may not collaterally attack her guilty plea after sentence if it represents a "***voluntary and intelligent choice among known alternatives***." The Supreme Court has held that, after sentencing, defendants generally have ***no right to attack their pleas on the grounds of prior constitutional violations***. The Court has indicated that by pleading guilty, a defendant presumably has balanced the likelihood of success and the advantages of a guilty plea against the strength of the prosecution's case and the risks of going to trial. A guilty plea cannot be attacked simply because the defendant miscalculated her chances or the strength of the case against her. [**Brady v. United States**, 397 U.S. 742 (1970); **McMann v. Richardson**, 397 U.S. 759 (1970); **Tollett v. Henderson**, 411 U.S. 258 (1973)]

b. Exceptions

(1) State Rules

Some states have special provisions guaranteeing judicial review of certain constitutional claims even after a guilty plea. For example, in some states, the defendant may plead guilty and then appeal the denial of his motion to suppress evidence. [**Lefkowitz v. Newsome**, 420 U.S. 283 (1975)]

(2) Lack of Jurisdiction

A defendant can attack his guilty plea by showing that the court that took the plea lacked jurisdiction to do so. For example, if the court lacked jurisdiction over the defendant because of double jeopardy, the defendant can attack the guilty plea by petitioning, after sentence, for the writ of habeas corpus. [**Blackledge v. Perry**, 417 U.S. 21 (1974)]

(3) Ineffective Assistance of Counsel

A defendant may successfully attack a guilty plea on the ground that he received ineffective assistance of counsel if, but for counsel's errors, the defendant probably would not have pleaded guilty. [**Hill v. Lockhart**, 474 U.S. 52 (1985)] For example, if the defendant pleaded guilty when the only evidence against him was illegally obtained and his counsel failed to inform him of the possibility of excluding the evidence, the defendant can move to withdraw his plea as a product of ineffective assistance of counsel. A defendant may also attack a felony conviction for ineffective assistance when his lawyer fails to communicate a plea offer [**Missouri v. Frye**, 566 U.S. 134 (2012)] and when his lawyer provides ineffective advice leading the defendant to reject a favorable plea [**Lafler v. Cooper**, 566 U.S. 156 (2012)]. But counsel's performance will be viewed very deferentially. [**Burt v. Titlow**, 571 U.S. 12 (2013)]

(4) Failure to Keep Plea Bargain

Finally, failure of the prosecutor to abide by an agreed-upon plea bargain is a good basis for collateral attack.

e.g. **Example:** Defendant agrees to plead guilty in exchange for the prosecutor's promise to drop all but one charge and to make no sentence recommendation. All but one charge is dropped. Defendant pleads guilty. Then, the prosecutor recommends the maximum sentence. Defendant may withdraw his plea after sentence or collaterally attack the plea because the prosecutor failed to keep the bargain.

c. Collateral Effects of Guilty Pleas

The Supreme Court has held that a defendant is "convicted" within the provisions of the Federal Gun Control Act when the defendant pleads guilty to a state charge punishable by more than one year, even if no formal judgment is entered and the record is later expunged. [**Dickerson v. New Banner Institute**, 460 U.S. 103 (1983)] On the other hand, the Court has held that when a defendant pleads guilty to charges stemming from a police search, the guilty plea neither admits the legality of the search nor waives Fourth Amendment claims in a subsequent civil damages action challenging the constitutionality of the search. [**Haring v. Prosise**, 462 U.S. 306 (1983)]

B. Sentencing

1. Procedural Rights

a. Confrontation Clause

The defendant's rights under the Confrontation Clause of the Sixth Amendment are ***less strictly applied in the sentencing proceeding*** than in the trial itself.

(1) Only Limitation—Trustworthiness

The trial judge may consider out-of-court information regarding the circumstances of the crime and the defendant's personal life in determining a sentence. The only limitation is that the information be trustworthy. [**Williams v. Oklahoma**, 358 U.S. 576 (1959)]

(2) No Right to Confrontation or Cross-Examination

The defendant has no right to confront and cross-examine persons who have supplied adverse information to the court regarding sentencing. Even in a capital case, the sentencing procedure has a purpose different from the trial and confrontation rights are less weighty. [**Williams v. New York**, 337 U.S. 241 (1949)]

b. Due Process

In passing sentence, the judge may consider numerous factors ***beyond the record*** of the trial itself and may also consider the ***conduct of the defendant*** with regard to the trial.

e.g. **Example:** The trial judge may take into account her belief that the defendant committed perjury while testifying at trial. Such a factor would be important in determining whether the defendant was likely to be rehabilitated after trial. [**United States v. Grayson**, 438 U.S. 41 (1978)]

e.g. **Example:** The trial judge may also properly consider the defendant's refusal to assist officials in their investigation of a criminal conspiracy in which he was a confessed participant. [**Roberts v. United States**, 445 U.S. 552 (1980)]

(1) Erroneous Information

If the judge goes beyond the record, however, and ***uses erroneous information*** in passing sentence, due process rights have been violated. [**Townsend v. Burke**, 334 U.S. 736 (1948)—erroneous information regarding prior conviction voided the sentence]

(2) Defendant's Silence

A sentencing court cannot draw adverse inferences from a defendant's silence in determining facts relating to circumstances and details of the crime that bear upon the severity of the defendant's sentence. [**Mitchell v. United States**, *supra,* p. 180]

(3) Consideration of Alternatives

The judge is generally ***not*** required to state that she considered alternatives to incarceration. [**Black v. Romano**, 471 U.S. 606 (1985)]

c. Right to Counsel

Because the sentencing proceeding is deemed to be a critical stage of a criminal prosecution, a defendant is entitled to a lawyer, either retained or appointed, to render effective assistance at that hearing. [**Mempa v. Rhay**, 389 U.S. 128 (1967), *supra,* p. 155]

2. Sentence Imposed

The trial judge is ***given great discretion*** in many jurisdictions in determining the sentence, and when the sentence is within statutory limits, it is ***generally not reviewed or reversed*** on appeal unless the sentencing statute so provides. The discretion is not, however, completely unbridled. Some constitutional limitations are present. In some jurisdictions, trial judges are guided by suggested sentencing ranges. [*See infra,* p. 188]

a. Cruel and Unusual Punishment

The Eighth Amendment to the Constitution provides that "cruel and unusual punishments [shall not be] inflicted." Note that if the restriction or requirement imposed is not "punishment," it does not violate the Eighth Amendment, no matter how distasteful. Moreover, if the sentence is within the lengths authorized by statute, the courts are reluctant to apply the Eighth Amendment restriction—even in cases in which the sentence seems quite heavy for the nature of the offense. Nevertheless, in three situations, the Supreme Court has been willing to find sentences unconstitutional:

(1) Grossly Disproportionate Sentence

When the nature of the sentence was shocking, considering the minor nature of the offense, the sentence has been struck down. For example, a sentence of 12 years in irons at hard labor for falsifying public records, followed by constant surveillance by the authorities, was held unconstitutional. [**Weems v. United States**, 217 U.S. 349 (1910)]

(a) Length of Sentence

The length of a prison sentence cannot be grossly disproportionate to the severity of the crime. [**Solem v. Helm**, 463 U.S. 277 (1983)—life sentence without possibility of parole for seventh nonviolent felony is "grossly disproportionate"; *and see* **Graham v. Florida**, 560 U.S. 48 (2010)—juvenile offender may not be sentenced to life in prison without parole for a nonhomicide offense] But, substantial deference is given to sentencing decisions of legislatures and sentencing courts, and successful challenges based on the length of a sentence ***alone*** are rare. [**Rummel v. Estelle**, 445 U.S. 263 (1980)—upholding life sentence, ***with*** parole possibility, for multiple offense nonviolent offender]

e.g. **Example:** The Court held that a mandatory imposition of a life sentence for possession of a certain quantity of drugs is ***not*** cruel and unusual even though the statute allowed no consideration of mitigating factors. [**Harmelin v. Michigan**, 501 U.S. 957 (1991)]

e.g. **Example:** A California "three strikes" law requires imposition of an indeterminate life sentence after a person is found guilty of a felony if the person has previously been convicted of two or more serious or violent felonies. Ewing was convicted of stealing three golf clubs worth $399 each. Although the trial judge had discretion to treat the crime as either felony grand theft or a misdemeanor, she treated the theft as a felony and sentenced Ewing to 25 years to life because he had four previous serious felony convictions. *Held:* The sentence does ***not*** constitute cruel and unusual punishment. [**Ewing v. California**, 538 U.S. 11 (2003)]

(2) Death Penalty

"The Constitution allows capital punishment." [**Bucklew v. Precythe**, 587 U.S. 119 (2019)] Nevertheless, the imposition of the death penalty for a crime other than murder has been intensely scrutinized. For example, imposition of the death penalty for the crime of rape (even the rape of a child) is unconstitutional because—the

Supreme Court held—the penalty is disproportionate to the offense. [**Coker v. Georgia**, 433 U.S. 584 (1977); **Kennedy v. Louisiana**, 554 U.S. 407 (2008)]

(3) Status Crimes

The Eighth Amendment is violated by statutes that make it a crime to ***have a particular "status."*** The courts have been careful, however, to conclude that it is not a violation of the Eighth Amendment to make activities criminal merely because they are related to a certain status.

e.g. **Example:** It is unconstitutional to convict someone of the offense of being addicted to narcotics. [**Robinson v. California**, 370 U.S. 660 (1962)]

cf. **Compare:** It is constitutional to convict a chronic alcoholic of being drunk in public. [**Powell v. Texas**, 392 U.S. 514 (1968)]

b. Excessive Fines

The Eighth Amendment provides that excessive fines shall not be imposed. The Supreme Court has not decided whether this provision applies to the states through the Due Process Clause. It has held that this Excessive Fines Clause applies only to fines imposed as punishment, *i.e.,* penal fines. The Clause does not apply to civil fines. Thus, penal forfeitures are subject to the Clause, but civil forfeitures are not.

(1) Punitive Forfeitures

Generally, a forfeiture will be considered penal only if it is provided for in a criminal statute. In such cases, a forfeiture is excessive only if it is ***grossly disproportionate to the gravity of the offense***. [**United States v. Bajakajian**, 524 U.S. 321 (1998)]

e.g. **Example:** The Court held that forfeiture of $357,144 for the crime of merely failing to report that the sum was being transported out of the country was grossly disproportionate, because the crime caused little harm (it would have been legal to take the money out of the country; the only harm was that the government was deprived of a piece of information). [**United States v. Bajakajian**, *supra*]

(2) Nonpunitive Forfeiture

(a) Civil in Rem Forfeitures

Civil in rem forfeitures treat the property forfeited as a "wrongdoer" under a legal fiction. The action is against the property and not against an individual and, therefore, is ***not*** subject to the Excessive Fines Clause.

(b) Monetary Forfeitures

Monetary forfeitures (*e.g.,* forfeiture of twice the value of illegally imported goods) have been found to be remedial in nature where they are brought in civil actions. They are seen as a form of liquidated damages to reimburse the government for losses resulting from the offense. Therefore, they are not subject to the Eighth Amendment. [*See* **United States v. Bajakajian**, *supra*]

c. Restitution

Restitution to the victim of child pornography under the restitution statute (18 U.S.C. § 2559) is dependent on the amount of loss to the victim caused by the defendant's conduct. [**Paroline v. United States**, 572 U.S. 434 (2014)]

d. Equal Protection Clause

The Equal Protection Clause has been used to restrict the type of sentence that may be imposed. The claim is normally raised in connection with the sentence of imprisonment plus a fine, or a probation condition requiring the payment of money.

(1) Conversion of Fine to Imprisonment

It is a violation of the Equal Protection Clause of the Fourteenth Amendment to limit punishment to payment of a fine for those who are able to pay it, but to convert the fine to imprisonment for those who are unable to pay it. [**Tate v. Short**, 401 U.S. 395 (1971)] Likewise, a court may not revoke a defendant's probation and imprison him for the remainder of the probation term for failure to pay a fine and make restitution, unless there is a showing that the defendant was actually capable of making payment or that there were no alternative forms of punishment available to meet the state's interest in punishment and deterrence. [**Bearden v. Georgia**, 461 U.S. 660 (1983)]

(2) Additional Time for Nonpayment

An indigent defendant cannot receive additional time of imprisonment for failure to pay a fine or court costs so that the sentence exceeds the maximum period fixed by statute. [**Williams v. Illinois**, 399 U.S. 235 (1970)]

e. Right to Counsel

As a condition of probation, indigent defendants ***may*** be required to pay back to the state the ***costs of their appointed counsel***. Such a requirement is constitutional if exemptions are granted for those truly unable to pay back the costs. [**Fuller v. Oregon**, 417 U.S. 40 (1974)]

f. Due Process Clause

(1) Appealing Conviction

Under the Due Process Clause, a defendant may not be punished for appealing a conviction. Thus, if the defendant appealed, was retried, and again convicted, the resulting sentence may not be harsher than that originally imposed ***unless*** the harsher sentence was based on ***conduct*** of the defendant that ***occurred after the time of the original sentencing*** proceeding. [**North Carolina v. Pearce**, 395 U.S. 711 (1969)] Without the requirement of a showing of conduct justifying the harsher sentence, there would be a risk of judicial vindictiveness against a defendant who appealed.

(a) Subsequent Conviction

A harsher sentence is permissible if the judge relies on an additional criminal conviction that occurred ***after*** the initial sentencing hearing. [**Wasman v. United States**, 468 U.S. 559 (1984)]

(b) Exception—Jury Determination of Sentence

The requirement of new information applies only where the sentence is determined by the ***trial judge***. If the sentence is determined by a ***jury***, and the jury is not informed of the prior sentence, there can be no concern about "vindictiveness," and the jury on retrial can recommend or determine a harsher sentence with or without new information. [**Chaffin v. Stynchcombe**, 412 U.S. 17 (1973)]

(c) Exception—Retrial in Higher Court

A harsher sentence may also be imposed without new information in states that have a ***two-tier system*** (where, after a conviction or plea of guilty in an inferior court, the defendant has the right to a ***trial de novo*** in a higher court). In such cases, there is no risk of vindictiveness by the same court that imposed the sentence originally, and the due process considerations of **North Carolina v. Pearce** do not prevent imposition of a harsher sentence if the accused is found guilty after the second trial. [**Colten v. Kentucky**, 407 U.S. 104 (1972)]

1) Distinguish—More Serious Charge

The prosecutor ***cannot substitute a more serious charge*** in the trial de novo. Doing so would be precisely the kind of "vindictiveness" (here by the prosecutor) that could effectively deter the exercise of a defendant's right to appeal. [**Blackledge v. Perry**, *supra,* p. 182]

(2) Sentence Enhancement

A sentence may be increased beyond the statutory maximum for a crime, if additional facts (other than prior conviction) are proved. However, proof of such facts must be submitted to the jury and proved beyond reasonable doubt; the sentencing judge may not make the determination. [**Apprendi v. New Jersey**, 530 U.S. 466 (2000)—statute allowing defendant's sentence to be increased by 10 years if judge finds by preponderance of the evidence that the crime was motivated by hate is invalid under the Sixth and Fourteenth Amendments] The same is true if a fact (such as brandishing or discharging a firearm) will increase the statutory minimum sentence for a crime.

e.g. **Example:** A defendant was charged and convicted of robbery and using a firearm in relation to a crime of violence. The jury verdict form indicated that the defendant had used or carried a firearm but not that he had brandished the weapon. Based on a presentence report, the judge at sentencing made an independent finding that defendant had brandished the weapon. Using or carrying a firearm requires a 5-year mandatory minimum sentence. Brandishing requires a 7-year mandatory minimum sentence. Held, facts that increase a mandatory minimum sentence, like those that increase a statutory maximum, are "elements" that must be found by a jury. [**Alleyne v. United States**, 570 U.S. 99 (2003)]

e.g. **Example:** Defendant pleaded guilty to kidnapping. Based on the facts admitted, under state law, Defendant's maximum penalty was 53 months imprisonment. After the judge found that Defendant acted with deliberate cruelty—an additional factor that allowed adding time to the standard sentence range—the court imposed a 90-month sentence. Because the facts supporting Defendant's exceptional sentence were neither admitted by him nor found by a jury, his sentence violated the Sixth Amendment right to a trial by jury. [**Blakely v. Washington**, 542 U.S. 296 (2004)]

e.g. **Example:** A jury found defendant guilty of possession with intent to distribute 92.5 grams of crack cocaine, which by statute subjected the defendant to a minimum of 10 years in prison and, pursuant to guidelines, a sentence of between 210 and 262 months. The judge imposed a sentence above that range after finding at sentencing that defendant had possessed an additional 566 grams of crack and was also guilty of obstruction. The sentence violated the Sixth

Amendment because the judge imposed a sentence higher than the maximum authorized by the jury's verdict. [**United States v. Booker**, 543 U.S. 220 (2005)]

e.g. **Example:** After a defendant was convicted and served prison time, he was released on supervised release. The sentencing judge, sitting without a jury, found that he had violated the terms of supervision; therefore, the judge imposed additional prison time above and beyond the initial prison term imposed. A plurality in **United States v. Haymond**, 588 U.S. 634 (2019), held that the new sentence violated the Fifth and Sixth Amendments because the sentence was imposed in "the absence of a jury's finding beyond a reasonable doubt."

(a) Harmless Error Test Applies

In deciding whether to overturn a sentence for failure to submit a sentencing factor to the jury, the harmless error test applies. [**Washington v. Recuenco**, 548 U.S. 212 (2006)]

(b) Distinguish—Judge May Decide Whether Sentences Run Consecutively

The Supreme Court has refused to extend the *Apprendi/Blakely* doctrine to the decision of whether sentences for multiple crimes are to run consecutively or concurrently. A state legislature may give to its judges (rather than the jury) the power to make such a decision even though it is based on the facts of the case. *Rationale*: Historically, judges have been entrusted with such decisions. The framers of the Constitution probably did not intend the Sixth Amendment's right to a jury trial to supplant this practice. [**Oregon v. Ice**, 555 U.S. 160 (2009)]

g. Federal Sentencing Guidelines

In 1984, Congress adopted the Sentencing Reform Act, which delegated the power to establish sentencing guidelines to a sentencing commission. The Supreme Court has held that this delegation is constitutional. [**Mistretta v. United States**, 488 U.S. 361 (1989)] Many states have also adopted sentencing guidelines using a process similar to the federal process.

(1) Guidelines Advisory

The Supreme Court struck down provisions in the federal sentencing guidelines that had rendered the guidelines mandatory, leaving the guidelines advisory so that they did not violate a defendant's Sixth Amendment jury trial right. [**United States v. Booker**, *supra*] Thus, judges are no longer bound by ranges in the guidelines. Judges must take account of the proper range and consider Congress's sentencing goals, as enumerated in the Sentence Reform Act, but may choose a sentence outside the guidelines range. [**Cunningham v. California**, 549 U.S. 270 (2007)] When sentencing outside the Guideline range, the trial judge must make clear that she considered the § 3553(a) factors but does not have to write extensively with an explanation for the exact sentence. [**Chavez-Mez v. United States**, 585 U.S. 109 (2018). *See also* **Kimbrough v. United States**, 552 U.S. 85 (2007)—the sentencing judge maintains discretion to consider the disparity under the federal sentencing guidelines of the sentencing ranges between powder cocaine and crack cocaine when sentencing a defendant for an offense involving crack and to sentence below the recommended range for crack to account for the disparity]

(a) But Note—Federal Judge May Not Impose Longer Sentence for Rehabilitative Goal

The Sentencing Reform Act does not permit a sentencing judge to impose or lengthen a prison term in order to foster a defendant's rehabilitation. Therefore, where a district court judge imposed a longer incarceration period so that the defendant would qualify for the Bureau of Prison's drug treatment program, the Supreme Court held that the sentence was improper. [**Tapia v. United States**, 564 U.S. 319 (2011)]

(2) Prior Conduct

Under the United States Sentencing Commission Guidelines Manual, case precedent, and statute [18 U.S.C. § 3661], sentencing courts may consider prior conduct for which a defendant has been acquitted if the government establishes the conduct by a preponderance of the evidence. [**United States v. Watts**, 519 U.S. 148 (1997)]

(3) Review of Departures from Guidelines

Appellate courts should review sentencing court decisions that depart from the Sentencing Guidelines' sentencing range only for abuse of discretion and should not conduct de novo review. [**Koon v. United States**, 518 U.S. 81 (1996)] This abuse-of-discretion standard applies to all sentences, whether a sentence falls inside or outside a determinate sentencing guideline range. [**Gall v. United States**, 552 U.S. 38 (2007)] (If the trial judge selects a sentence within the guideline range, an appellate court may presume that the sentence is reasonable and that the sentencing judge did not abuse her discretion. [**Rita v. United States**, 551 U.S. 338 (2007)])

(a) Departure Below Minimum

A district court is justified in departing below the ***Sentencing Guidelines*** minimum sentence when a government motion attests to the defendant's assistance in a criminal investigation and requests the district court to depart below the minimum. However, the request does not permit the court to depart below the ***statutory minimum*** sentence for the offense without a government motion under 18 U.S.C. § 3553(e). [**Melendez v. United States**, 518 U.S. 120 (1996)]

(b) Departure Based on Policy Disagreement

After **United States v. Booker**, *supra*, which rendered the Federal Sentencing Guidelines advisory, sentencing courts are entitled to vary downward from the crack cocaine guidelines in a routine case to recognize an unwanted disparity between sentences for powder cocaine and crack cocaine. [**Spears v. United States,** 555 U.S. 261 (2009)]

(c) Departure Based on Defendant's Rehabilitation After Initial Sentencing

When a defendant's sentence is set aside on appeal, the judge may consider the defendant's post-sentencing rehabilitation efforts when resentencing and may impose a sentence significantly below the low end of the guidelines range. [**Pepper v. United States**, 562 U.S. 476 (2011)]

POSSIBLE LIMITATIONS ON SENTENCING	
THE FOLLOWING CONSTITUTIONAL PROVISIONS MAY LIMIT SENTENCING:	
EIGHTH AMENDMENT	• Prohibits ***cruel and unusual punishment***; has been used to strike sentences that: (i) are grossly disproportionate to the crime, (ii) make a particular status illegal, and (iii) impose death under a number of circumstances. • Prohibits ***excessive fines***; applicable only if fine is imposed as punishment; has been used where fine was grossly disproportionate to gravity of offense.
EQUAL PROTECTION CLAUSE	Prohibits imposing imprisonment merely ***because defendant is financially unable to pay*** a fine.
DUE PROCESS CLAUSE	Prohibits imposing harsher sentence on defendant ***entirely because he appeals*** his conviction.
SIXTH AMENDMENT	Prohibits a judge from imposing a sentence based on findings that lengthen a sentence beyond the level justified by facts reflected in the jury's verdict or admitted by the defendant.

C. The Death Penalty

1. As "Cruel and Unusual" Punishment

The death penalty is ***not*** cruel and unusual punishment under all circumstances. Capital punishment is permissible for adults under statutes meeting the following requirements:

(i) The sentencing body (judge or jury) is permitted to consider, and is given adequate guidance on both ***aggravating*** and ***mitigating*** factors (***about the crime*** and ***the background of the defendant***) relevant to sentencing; and

(ii) ***There is a review procedure*** to ensure against imposition of the death sentence for arbitrary or discriminatory reasons.

[**Gregg v. Georgia**, 428 U.S. 153 (1976); **Lockett v. Ohio**, 438 U.S. 586 (1978)] *Rationale*: "It is of vital importance to the defendant and to the community that any decision to impose the death sentence be, and appear to be, based on reason rather than caprice or emotion." [**Gardner v. Florida**, 430 U.S. 349 (1977)]

a. Method of Execution

A method of carrying out a death sentence is not cruel and unusual just because it might cause the condemned person some pain. A method of execution will be found to be cruel and unusual only if the condemned can prove that: (i) there is a substantial risk of inflicting ***severe pain***; or (ii) an ***alternative procedure*** is feasible, may be readily implemented, and in fact significantly reduces substantial risk of severe pain. [**Baze v. Rees**, 553 U.S. 35 (2008)]

e.g. **Example:** The mere possibility that the three-drug lethal injection protocol used by many states to carry out executions ***might*** be administered improperly and, thus, cause the condemned unnecessary pain does not make the procedure cruel and unusual punishment. [**Baze v. Rees**, *supra*]

e.g. **Example:** The fact that the state's execution protocol might cause the condemned substantial pain because of his existing medical conditions—an applied Eighth Amendment challenge—does not change the test. "To decide whether the state has cruelly "superadded" pain to the punishment of death isn't something that can be accomplished by examining the state's proposed method in a vacuum, but only by "compar[ing]" that method with a viable alternative." [**Bucklew v. Precythe**, 587 U.S. 119 (2019)]

b. Aggravating Factors

Aggravating factors include knowledge that the victim was a police officer, proof that the defendant committed the murder for financial reward, a showing that the defendant committed the crime while escaping from prison, proof that the defendant committed the murder during the course of a dangerous felony, and proof of a prior conviction for a crime involving force or violence. [**Jurek v. Texas**, 428 U.S. 262 (1976)] *Note*: If a death penalty is based on a prior conviction, the death sentence must be reversed if the prior conviction is reversed or vacated. [**Johnson v. Mississippi**, 486 U.S. 578 (1988)]

(1) Victim Impact Statement

Formerly, the Supreme Court banned consideration of a "victim impact statement" (*i.e.,* an assessment of how the crime affected the victim's family) during the sentencing phase of a capital case for fear that juries would impose the death penalty for improper reasons. [*See, e.g.,* **Booth v. Maryland**, 482 U.S. 496 (1987); **South Carolina v. Gathers**, 490 U.S. 805 (1989)] Now, however, the Court allows consideration of such statements. *Rationale*: The defendant has long been allowed to present mitigating factors, so the jury must be allowed to counterbalance by considering the impact on the victim's family in order to "assess meaningfully the defendant's moral culpability and blameworthiness." [**Payne v. Tennessee**, 501 U.S. 808 (1991)]. But, it violates the Eighth Amendment for the sentencing court to permit opinions from a victim or her family about the crime, the defendant, and the appropriate sentence. [**Bosse v. Oklahoma**, 580 U.S. 1 (2016)]

(2) Appellate Review

The application by a sentencing trial judge of an aggravating factor insufficiently supported by the facts is error unless an appellate court cured the error by reweighing the other aggravating and mitigating factors or by performing harmless error review. [**Sochor v. Florida**, 504 U.S. 527 (1992)] To cure the defect, it must appear that all aggravating and mitigating factors were considered. [**Richmond v. Lewis**, 506 U.S. 40 (1993)]. In **McKinney v. Arizona**, 589 U.S. 139 (2020), the Court held that once a sentencing error is identified during a habeas review of a death penalty case, at least when the error is one of a failure to appreciate a mitigating circumstance, the state appellate court may reweigh the mitigating and aggravating circumstances and sentence the defendant without additional input from a jury.

(3) Military Prosecutions

The Supreme Court has not resolved whether aggravating circumstances must be established to impose a death sentence on a defendant at a military court-martial proceeding. However, the Court has decided that assuming aggravating circumstances must be proved, the factors prescribed by executive order of the President, which are reflected in the Rules for Courts-Martial, are sufficient. [**Loving v. United States**, 517 U.S. 748 (1996)]

(4) Effect of Overturning Factor

The Supreme Court has held that a death sentence need not be overturned merely because one of several aggravating factors that were used to justify the death sentence were invalidated on appeal. The other aggravating factors may be relied upon if they were not tainted by the invalidated factor. However, where a defendant was sentenced to death based on two aggravating factors (high probability of future dangerousness and vileness of the murder), and the future dangerousness factor was invalidated because the defendant was indigent and not provided with a psychiatrist to aid him in rebutting this factor (as required by **Ake v. Oklahoma**, 470 U.S. 68 (1986), *supra,* p. 172), the jury might have been affected by this error. The "vileness" factor is not sufficiently independent and the sentence cannot stand on that ground alone. [**Tuggle v. Netherland**, 516 U.S. 10 (1995)]

c. Mitigating Factors

Mitigating factors include no significant prior record for the defendant, a showing of extreme mental or emotional disturbance, proof of minor participation in the criminal endeavor, and the youth of the defendant at the time of the crime. **Gregg v. Georgia**, *supra*, p. 190] *Note*: Most states list mitigating factors in their death penalty statutes. Nevertheless, the sentencing authority in a death penalty case must be able to consider ***any relevant mitigating*** evidence, regardless of whether it is listed in the state's death penalty statute. [**Hitchcock v. Dugger**, 481 U.S. 393 (1987)]

(1) Effect of Preventing Full Consideration

A death sentence must be reversed if the jury was precluded from considering any mitigating circumstance. Reversal also is required if the jury instructions might have caused the jurors to rest their decision on an impermissible view of how they were to proceed in assessing the presence of mitigating factors. [**Mills v. Maryland**, 486 U.S. 367 (1988)—jury instructions were unclear and jury might have thought that they needed unanimous agreement on the presence of the ***same*** mitigating factor to prevent imposition of the death penalty]

e.g. **Example:** The Eighth Amendment is violated when the jury at the sentencing phase of a capital case is not instructed about how evidence of the accused's intellectual disability and childhood abuse could be considered as possible mitigation of his offense. [**Penry v. Lynaugh**, 492 U.S. 302 (1989)]

cf. **Compare:** A statute that instructs jurors to impose the death penalty if they find it probable that the defendant would commit criminal acts in the future, considering all aggravating or mitigating evidence presented at trial, was upheld against an argument that the instruction foreclosed consideration of the defendant's youth. The court found that consideration of future dangerousness leaves open ample room for considering youth as a mitigating factor because "the signature qualities of youth are transient." [**Johnson v. Texas**, 509 U.S. 350 (1993)]

(2) Distinguish—Factors Not in Mitigation

Instructing a capital jury not to be swayed by "mere sentiment, conjecture, sympathy, passion, prejudice, public opinion, or public feeling" does not violate a capital defendant's right to have all mitigating evidence considered by the jury. [**California v. Brown**, 479 U.S. 538 (1987)]

2. Particular Statutory Schemes

a. Use of Presentence Investigation Report

The strict constitutional requirements are ***not*** satisfied when the trial judge imposes a death sentence on the basis of information in a presentence investigation report that is not disclosed to the defendant or counsel or made part of the record to be reviewed on appeal. [**Gardner v. Florida**, *supra*, p. 190]

b. Effect of Vague or Overbroad Statutes

Death penalties imposed pursuant to statutes that permit ***overbroad discretion***, and under which the penalty is ***selectively and capriciously applied***, violate the Eighth and Fourteenth Amendments. [**Furman v. Georgia**, 408 U.S. 238 (1972)]

Example: A state law that authorizes the death penalty for a killing that is "outrageously or wantonly vile, horrible, or inhuman in that it involved torture, depravity of mind, or an aggravated battery to the victim" is unconstitutionally vague—at least in the case in which there was no showing of torture, aggravated battery, or depravity. [**Godfrey v. Georgia**, 446 U.S. 420 (1980)] Similarly, a state statute that imposes the death penalty for murders that are "especially heinous, atrocious, or cruel" is unconstitutionally vague under the Eighth Amendment. [**Maynard v. Cartwright**, 486 U.S. 356 (1988)]

Compare: A statute that imposes the death penalty if the murderer displayed "utter disregard for human life" provides sufficiently clear and objective standards for imposition of the death penalty where the state supreme court had construed the statute to apply only where the killing was committed by a "cold-blooded, pitiless slayer." [**Arave v. Creech**, 507 U.S. 463 (1993)]

Compare: Statistical evidence that Black defendants who kill White victims are more likely to receive the death sentence does ***not*** establish that the death sentence is being imposed in an arbitrary, capricious, and discriminatory manner. Discretion is at the heart of the capital sentencing system and, absent exceptionally clear proof, an abuse of discretion will not be found. [**McCleskey v. Kemp**, 481 U.S. 279 (1987)]

(1) Advisory Juries

Allowing an advisory jury to consider recommending the death penalty based in part on an unconstitutionally vague, aggravating factor is constitutional error under the Eighth and Fourteenth Amendments. [**Espinosa v. Florida**, 505 U.S. 1079 (1992)]

c. Effect of Compulsory Capital Punishment

Where capital punishment is ***mandatory*** for a broad category of homicides (including killing a police officer), and there is no meaningful opportunity for considering mitigating factors, the death penalty is cruel and unusual. [**Woodson v. North Carolina**, 428 U.S. 280 (1976)] Similarly, a statute that mandates the death penalty for a particular category of defendants (prison inmates) is invalid. [**Summer v. Shuman**, 483 U.S. 66 (1987)]

(1) Distinguish—Judicial Override

Where a state's death penalty statute requires the jury to fix the punishment at death if a defendant is convicted of specific crimes with aggravation, but also requires the trial judge to hear evidence of aggravating and mitigating circumstances before sentencing the defendant, the statute ***is constitutional***. [**Baldwin v. Alabama**, 472 U.S. 372 (1985), *and see supra,* pp. 192–194]

d. Role of Jury

The jury must be given ***flexibility*** in reaching its verdict. The imposition of the death penalty is error if the jury is not allowed to reach a verdict on a lesser included offense. [**Beck v. Alabama**, 447 U.S. 625 (1980)]

(1) Judge Cannot Determine Aggravating Factors After Jury Adjudication of Guilt

Following a jury adjudication of a defendant's guilt of first degree murder, a trial judge is prohibited by the Sixth Amendment from determining whether aggravating factors justify imposition of the death penalty. The jury must make such a determination. [**Ring v. Arizona**, 536 U.S. 584 (2002)] *Rationale*: If a death sentence cannot be imposed unless an aggravating circumstance is found, in essence, the aggravating circumstance is one of the facts needed to prove the government's case for increased punishment, and under **Apprendi v. New Jersey**, *supra*, p. 187, if a sentence cannot be increased beyond the ***statutory maximum*** for a crime without proof of additional facts, the facts must be submitted to the jury.

(2) Ineligibility for Parole

If the only alternative to a death sentence is life imprisonment without a possibility of parole, due process requires that the jury be clearly informed of the defendant's parole ineligibility. An instruction that the jury's only choice is to sentence the defendant to death or life imprisonment does not clearly convey that the defendant will be ineligible for parole if he receives a life sentence. [**Kelly v. South Carolina**, 534 U.S. 246 (2002)]

(3) Jury Responsibility for Verdict

It is unconstitutional to diminish the jury's sense of responsibility of its role in determining a death sentence. Thus, comments from the prosecution that the jury's verdict is not the final decision, and that its verdict is reviewable by the court, are improper because they diminish the jury's "awesome responsibility" of imposing the death sentence. [**Caldwell v. Mississippi**, 472 U.S. 320 (1985)]

(a) Distinguish—Instruction Regarding Failure to Agree

On the other hand, even at the defendant's request, the court need not instruct the jury on the consequences of its failure to agree to a verdict. [**Jones v. United States**, 527 U.S. 373 (1999)—Eighth Amendment was not violated where court denied defendant's request that jury be instructed that judge would impose sentence if jury could not unanimously agree]

(4) Limitation on Death Sentence After Retrial

In a state in which the jury can impose the death penalty only if the government proves, beyond a reasonable doubt, that an aggravating circumstance exists, a decision by the first jury not to impose the death penalty precludes the imposition of the death penalty upon retrial. [**Bullington v. Missouri**, 451 U.S. 430 (1981)] *Rationale*: In effect, the first jury found that the prosecution did not prove an aggravating factor beyond reasonable doubt. Thus, it would constitute double jeopardy to retry the defendant on this issue. (*See infra,* pp. 238 *et seq.*)

3. Limitations on Death Penalty

a. Rape

It is unconstitutional to impose the death penalty for the crime of rape, because the Supreme Court has held that the penalty is disproportionate to the offense. [**Coker v. Georgia**, *supra*, p. 184—adult victim; **Kennedy v. Louisiana**, *supra,* p. 185—minor victim]

b. Minor Defendant

Execution of persons who were under 18 years of age at the time they committed their offense (including murder) violates the Eighth Amendment. [**Roper v. Simmons**, 543 U.S. 551 (2005); *see also* **Miller v. Alabama**, 567 U.S. 460 (2012)—automatically sentencing a juvenile offender to life in prison without the possibility of parole also violates the Eighth Amendment] However, it is constitutional for a trial judge to impose a life term in prison without parole for a minor, even if the sentencing judge does not make a specific finding that the defendant was "permanently incorrigible." [**Jones v. Mississippi**, 593 U.S. 98 (2021)]

c. Incompetency

The Eighth Amendment prohibits states from inflicting the death penalty on a prisoner who is insane (*i.e.,* one who was sane at the time the crime was committed and was properly sentenced to death, but is insane at the time of the scheduled execution). [**Ford v. Wainwright**, 477 U.S. 399 (1986)]. The death penalty may be imposed, however, on a condemned person who does not remember committing the crime because of a series of strokes or another medical condition occurring after the crime, provided he rationally understands the reasons for the death sentence. [**Madison v. Alabama**, 586 U.S. 265 (2019)]

d. Intellectual Disability

The Supreme Court has held that it is cruel and unusual punishment to impose the death penalty on a person who is intellectually disabled. [**Atkins v. Virginia**, 536 U.S. 304 (2002)] The Court in **Atkins** noted that what constitutes cruel and unusual punishment under the Eighth Amendment depends on contemporary values and found a trend against executing intellectually disabled persons because many states and the federal government had recently banned such executions. The Court left to the states the task of developing standards for determining who will be deemed intellectually disabled. States may not establish a rigid IQ cut off for determining intellectual disability. Such a rigid rule is unconstitutional because it "creates an unacceptable risk that persons with an intellectual disability will be executed." [**Hall v. Florida**, 572 U.S. 701 (2014)]

In assessing intellectual disability, courts must consider: (1) "deficits in intellectual functioning—primarily a test-related criterion"; (2) "adaptive deficits, assessed using both clinical evaluative and individualized . . . measures"; and (3) "the onset of these deficits while the defendant was still a minor[.]" [**Moore v. Texas**, 586 U.S. 133 (2019)]

e. Participation in Crime

Although the Supreme Court has overturned the capital sentence of a defendant who aided and abetted a robbery during which a person was murdered by a codefendant when the defendant did not himself kill, attempt to kill, or intend to kill, it is constitutional for the state to impose the death sentence on a defendant who neither killed nor intended to kill under limited circumstances. The defendant must have: (i) ***actively participated in a***

major way in a ***felony*** that resulted in murder ***and*** (ii) ***acted with reckless indifference to the value of human life***. [**Tison v. Arizona**, 481 U.S. 137 (1987)—death penalty is not disproportionate when imposed on brothers who brought weapons into a prison, supplied their father (a convicted murderer) and another convicted murderer with the weapons, helped their father and the other convict escape, and watched as their father and the other convict murdered a family whom they had abducted]

f. Note—Sentence Comparisons

The Eighth Amendment does not require a state appellate court, upon the request of a prisoner, to compare the death sentence in the case before it with the penalties imposed in similar cases. [**Pulley v. Harris**, 465 U.S. 37 (1984)]

Chapter Seven

Ex Post Facto Issues

CONTENTS	PAGE

Key Exam Issues

Traditionally, Criminal Procedure professors do not spend much time discussing ex post facto issues. Nevertheless, the Supreme Court has recently addressed a few such issues, making them slightly more likely to show up on a law school exam. The key point to remember is that if a law seeks to impose a more severe punishment than the punishment that was authorized when the criminal act was committed, the punishment likely violates the constitutional prohibition.

A. Constitutional Bases

1. Constitutional Provision

The Constitution includes two prohibitions against ex post facto laws: "No bill of attainder or ex post facto law shall be passed [by Congress]." [U.S. Const, art. I, § 9] "No state shall . . . pass any . . . ex post facto law. . . ." [U.S. Const, art. I, § 10]

B. Application

1. "Ex Post Facto" Defined

Central to the Ex Post Facto Clauses is a concern for the lack of fair notice. These provisions seek to restrain the government from increasing punishment beyond what was prescribed when an act was committed. For an act to violate the prohibitions of the Ex Post Facto Clauses, two critical elements must be present:

(i) The law must be ***retrospective*** (*i.e.,* apply to events that occurred ***prior to its enactment***); and

(ii) The law must ***disadvantage the offender*** affected by it.

[**Miller v. Florida**, 482 U.S. 423 (1987)] The Supreme Court has further refined this general definition and has held that a law violates the Ex Post Facto Clauses only if it:

(i) ***Punishes as a crime*** an act previously committed, which was innocent when committed;

(ii) ***Makes more burdensome*** the punishment for a crime after its commission; or

(iii) ***Deprives a defendant of a defense*** available under the law in effect when the act was committed.

[**Collins v. Youngblood**, 497 U.S. 37 (1990)]

a. Definition of "Punishment"

If a law's ***purpose*** is civil rather than punitive, it is not an ex post facto law unless its ***effect*** is so ***clearly*** punitive that it negates the legislature's intention.

e.g. **Example:** In 1994, Alaska adopted a statute—known as Megan's Law—requiring any sex offender within the state to register and give his name, address, place of employment, vehicle information, etc., to law enforcement authorities. The act provided that some of this information could be made public, and this provision was carried out through publication over the Internet. Failure to comply with the registration requirements could result in a criminal penalty. John Doe I and John Doe II pleaded *nolo contendere* to child abuse charges and were released from prison in 1990. They brought an action seeking to have Megan's Law declared void as to them under the Ex Post Facto Clause. Looking at the structure and text of the law, the Supreme Court found that the goal of the law is not to punish or stigmatize. Rather, the legislature had decided that sex offenders pose a high risk of reoffending and that the release of the information was intended to protect the public from sex offenders. That some of the law's provisions were found in the Code of Criminal Procedure was not dispositive in deciding whether the law was punitive because location and labels do not themselves transform a civil remedy into a criminal remedy. Moreover, the regulatory means were reasonable in light of the legislation's nonpunitive purpose. Any stigma resulted from dissemination of accurate information that was mostly public already. [**Smith v. Doe**, 538 U.S. 84 (2003); *and see* **Connecticut Department of Public Safety v. Doe**, 538 U.S. 1 (2003)—similar statute held not to violate the Due Process Clause; **United States v. Kebodeaux**, 570 U.S. 387 (2013) (applying Necessary and Proper Clause to uphold sex offender registration requirement that applied to persons convicted before the sex offender registration statute was enacted)]

2. Specific Cases

a. Sentence Guideline Revision

Florida has sentencing guidelines that restrict judicial discretion by creating a presumptive sentence for certain types of crimes. A judge may impose a sentence outside the presumptive sentence (either higher or lower), but she must explain her reasons. On the day Defendant committed sexual battery, the guidelines created a presumptive sentence of 3½–4½ years. Before Defendant was convicted, the guidelines were modified to provide a 5½–7-year presumptive sentence, and the longer presumptive sentence was imposed on Defendant. The Supreme Court held that imposition of the new guidelines violated the Ex Post Facto Clause because the guidelines imposed a higher presumptive sentence than had existed on the day the crime was committed. [**Miller v. Florida**, *supra,* p. 198; *see also* **Peugh v. United States**, 569 U.S. 530 (2013), finding Ex Post Facto Clause violated when defendant was sentenced under guidelines promulgated after defendant's crimes]

(1) Note

The ***Miller*** Court specifically rejected several arguments proposed by Florida, including: (i) a notice included in the old guidelines that they are subject to change provided adequate notice to satisfy Ex Post Facto Clause requirements; and (ii) the defendant did not prove that he actually would have received a lighter sentence under the old guidelines. The Court held that it was sufficient to show that he was substantially disadvantaged by the new guidelines.

b. Procedural Changes

There was no Ex Post Facto Clause violation under the following circumstances: Defendant was convicted of sexual assault. The statute provided that a prison term ***or*** a fine be imposed. Defendant was sentenced to a prison term ***and*** a fine, and the sentence was affirmed on direct appeal. Defendant then applied for a writ of habeas corpus, claiming that his sentence was unauthorized. The trial court recommended that the writ be granted. The appellate court, however, denied the writ and reformed Defendant's sentence to a prison term only, pursuant to a statute—adopted after Defendant's sentence was imposed—that allowed such reformation. Defendant appealed, claiming that the retroactive application of the statute allowing sentence reformation violated the Ex Post Facto Clause because it deprived him of a substantial procedural protection. The Supreme

Court held that there was no constitutional violation because the Ex Post Facto Clause is violated only by ***substantive*** changes in law, and not by procedural changes. [**Collins v. Youngblood**, *supra*, p. 198]

c. Cancellation of Prison Release Credits

After defendant was sentenced to 22 years' imprisonment, the state modified a statute awarding provisional early release credits to prisoners because of prison overcrowding. Defendant was released from prison after serving six years based, in part, on his provisional release credits. The state attorney general then interpreted a statute as having retroactively cancelled the provisional release credits which caused defendant to be rearrested and returned to custody. Defendant brought a habeas corpus petition for release. The Court found that despite the fact that the provisional release credits were an administrative remedy to relieve overcrowding and were not part of the sentencing scheme, retroactive cancellation of the credits effectively increased defendant's punishment and violated the Ex Post Facto Clause. Only the effect of the cancellation matters; the subjective purpose of the cancellation is irrelevant. [**Lynce v. Mathis**, 519 U.S. 433 (1997)]

d. Procedural Changes in Parole

No Ex Post Facto Clause violation was found when the Department of Corrections applied a new parole review procedure to petitioner after their conviction. Under the former procedure, the petitioner's eligibility for parole was reviewed every year. Under the new procedure, if parole was denied and the parole board decided petitioner was unlikely to be paroled within the next two years, a parole hearing could be, and in defendant's case was, postponed for three years. [**California Department of Corrections v. Morales**, 514 U.S. 499 (1995)] The Supreme Court reasoned that the petitioner's punishment was not increased; rather, there was merely a change in the procedure for determining eligibility for parole.

e. Civil Commitment

The Court held that no ex post facto concerns were raised by a "sexual predator statute" authorizing a sex offender to be committed to a mental institution upon being released from prison, whenever the state can prove that the offender is likely to engage in predatory acts of sexual violence. [**Kansas v. Hendricks**, 521 U.S. 346 (1997)] The Act does not criminalize conduct that was legal before its enactment or deprive a defendant of defenses that were available before the Act was adopted. The Act merely establishes procedures for ***civil commitment*** of persons with "mental abnormalities" who are likely to engage in predatory acts of sexual violence.

3. Indirect "Application" to Courts

By their terms, the Ex Post Facto Clauses prohibit only retroactive ***legislation***, but the Supreme Court has held that limited aspects of the clauses have been incorporated into the Due Process Clauses. This places some limitations on the power of courts to reinterpret law and to give the new interpretation retroactive effect. However, the due process limitation is much narrower than the ex post facto limitation. Specifically, due process prohibits courts from retroactively interpreting a criminal law in an unexpected and indefensible way. [**Rogers v. Tennessee**, 532 U.S. 451 (2001)]

e.g. **Example:** Defendant was convicted of murdering a victim who died while on life support systems 15 months after defendant stabbed the victim. Although the state murder statute did not mention the common law "year and a day" rule (under which a defendant could not be convicted of murder unless his victim died within a year and a day of defendant's criminal act), dicta in state judicial decisions presumed the rule applied. On appeal, the state supreme court upheld defendant's conviction and retroactively abolished the year and a day rule. The United States Supreme Court upheld the conviction, holding that abolition of the common law rule was not unexpected and indefensible because medical science has undermined its usefulness and it has already been abolished in most jurisdictions. [**Rogers v. Tennessee**, *supra*, p. 200]

EXAM TIP

If an exam question raises an ex post facto issue, remember the basics: The law is prohibited if it: (i) punishes as a crime an act that was ***legal when committed***; (ii) ***increases the punishment*** for a crime after its commission; or (iii) ***deprives a defendant of a defense*** that was available when the criminal act was committed. Note that the motivation for the change is irrelevant.

Chapter Eight

Post-Conviction Issues

CONTENTS	PAGE

Key Exam Issues

Only two legal issues tend to be examined in this area.

The first involves ***appeals***. While there is no explicit constitutional right to an appeal, all states have such procedures, providing for at least one "automatic" appeal. The key issue here is the ***rights of indigents***. An indigent's right to appeal cannot be limited due to his financial restrictions. Thus, to assure that equal protection is not violated, states must provide transcripts where necessary and a lawyer, at least for the first automatic appeal.

The second issue concerns ***habeas corpus***. The points you should remember about habeas corpus are:

1. Federal judges may grant the writ to ***both*** federal and state prisoners.
2. It is a ***civil action*** to challenge the legality of the defendant's detention and is a ***collateral attack*** by a defendant on her conviction, not a direct appeal of the criminal sentence.
3. To bring an action ***in federal court*** for habeas corpus:
   (i) The petitioner must demonstrate that ***federal rights*** have been violated.
   (ii) She must have ***exhausted all state remedies***.
   (iii) She must have complied with state procedural rules governing the manner for raising constitutional claims, unless she shows ***cause*** for the noncompliance ***and actual prejudice*** from the noncompliance or ***actual innocence***.

Note that Fourth Amendment issues cannot be relitigated.

A. Appeal

1. No Constitutional Right to Appeal

The Supreme Court has never held that there is a ***federal*** constitutional right to an appeal of a criminal conviction, and has cast doubt, in dicta, on any such right. [*See* **Ross v. Moffitt**, 417 U.S. 600 (1974)—"it is clear that the State need not provide any appeal at all"] However, state and federal ***statutes*** provide for appeals of criminal convictions.

2. Appellate Review

a. Preservation of Issue for Appeal

For appellate review, claims of error must be preserved at trial.

e.g. **Example:** At trial the judge ruled that if Defendant testified, the prosecution could impeach Defendant's testimony by use of Defendant's prior conviction. Defendant decided not to testify. The appellate court could not review the trial court's ruling regarding impeachment because unless Defendant testified, the claim of error was not preserved for appeal. [**Luce v. United States**, 469 U.S. 38 (1984)]

(1) Exception—Plain Error

There are exceptions to the requirement that objections be raised at trial. Specifically, when there is "plain error," an appellate court ***may*** reverse a conviction even though the error was not properly raised at trial. Whether there has been "plain error" depends on the facts of the case. [**United States v. Young**, 470 U.S. 1 (1985)]

An error is evaluated upon review by the appellate court and not when the error was made by the trial judge. [**Henderson v. United States**, 568 U.S. 266 (2013)]

e.g. **Example:** During closing arguments, defense counsel impugned the prosecutor's integrity and charged that the prosecutor did not believe his own case. During the prosecutor's closing argument, he stated that he believed Defendant was guilty (such statements of personal opinion are prohibited) and urged the jury to "do its job." Defense counsel did not object to the prosecutor's closing remarks. Therefore, to obtain appellate review, the prosecutor's remarks must be ***plain error***. *Held:* Although it was error to permit the prosecutor to give his personal opinion, taken in context, there was no plain error. Given defense counsel's repeated attacks on the prosecutor, the jury would have understood the opinions merely to be countering those personal attacks. Moreover, the evidence against the defendant was "overwhelming." [**United States v. Young**, *supra*]

b. Standard of Review—Harmless Error Doctrine

Not all errors made at trial result in reversal of a defendant's conviction. If the error was harmless beyond a reasonable doubt (*i.e.,* there is ***no reasonable possibility*** that the error contributed to the defendant's conviction) the conviction may stand. [**Chapman v. California**, 386 U.S. 18 (1967); **Brecht v. Abrahamson**, 507 U.S. 619 (1993)—"substantial and injurious effect" standard for habeas review]

(1) Issues That May Be Harmless Error

The issues listed below are assessed using the harmless error standard. Under the harmless error standard, the conviction will stand—even though the following rights have been violated—(if the error could ***not have contributed to the conviction***). The conviction will be reversed only if the error ***could have helped to convict the defendant.***

(a) Admission of ***evidence obtained through an illegal search and seizure*** [**Fahy v. Connecticut**, 375 U.S. 85 (1963)];

(b) Prosecutor's ***comment on defendant's failure to testify*** at trial (see *supra*, p. 87);

(c) The use of a ***coerced confession*** (see *supra*, p. 94–95);

(d) The denial of the ***right to counsel at non-trial stages***, such as during pretrial identification procedures (see *supra*, p. 115; *but see supra*, p. 156—automatic reversal for denial of counsel at trial);

(e) The ***improper joinder of defendants for trial*** [**United States v. Lane**, 474 U.S. 438 (1986)];

(f) A prosecutor's improper questions about a ***defendant's silence*** after receiving Miranda warnings [**Greer v. Miller**, 483 U.S. 756 (1987)] and other prosecutorial misconduct that does not rise to the level of fundamental unfairness;

(g) A jury instruction that ***omits an element of an offense*** [**Neder v. United States**, 527 U.S. 1 (1999)] or that fails to instruct the jury to find that the defendant had intent to commit or facilitate the crime [**California v. Roy**, 519 U.S. 2 (1996)];

(h) Admission of an improper aggravating circumstance in a death sentence hearing may be harmless if, absent the factor, the jury would have reached the same verdict or the result would have been the same had the invalid aggravating factor been precisely defined [**Jones v. United States**, 593 U.S. 98 (2021)];

(i) A magistrate judge's violation of Rule 11, Fed. R. Crim. P., which prohibits a judge from participating in plea discussions. [**United States v. Davila**, 569 U.S. 597 (2013)];

(j) Some ***Brady*** violations (*i.e.*, prosecutor's failure to disclose exculpatory evidence to the defense);

(k) Evidentiary errors including admission of evidence in violation of the Confrontation Clause, hearsay violations, improper admission of character evidence, and authentication errors; and

(*l*) Judicial misconduct that does not constitute structural error.

(2) Structural Errors Requiring Automatic Reversal

Structural errors require automatic reversal. [**United States v. Gonzalez-Lopez**, 548 U.S. 140 (2006)] The denial of the ***right to counsel at trial*** or denial of a paying defendant's choice of counsel is never harmless error and requires automatic reversal on appeal (*see supra,* p. 156). Similarly, a constitutionally deficient reasonable doubt jury instruction can never be harmless error. [**Sullivan v. Louisiana**, 508 U.S. 275 (1993)] Denial of the right to a public trial is not subject to the harmless error analysis. [**Waller v. Georgia**, 467 U.S. 39 (1984); **Presley v. Georgia**, 558 U.S. 209 (2010)] Neither is excluding from the grand jury a member of the defendant's race, [**Vasquez v. Hillery**, 474 U.S. 254 (1986)] nor allowing defense counsel in a death penalty case to concede the accused's guilt as a strategy to save the defendant's life over the defendant's strong objection. [**McCoy v. Louisiana**, 584 U.S. 414 (2018)].

3. Indigent's Right to Appeal

When a state grants the right to appeal (*i.e.*, the right to appeal is not automatic), it cannot do so in a way that discriminates against convicted individuals because of their poverty. ***Equal protection is violated*** if the state makes appellate review less accessible to the poor than to the rich. [**Griffin v. Illinois**, 351 U.S. 12 (1956)]

a. Procedural Requirements—Transcripts

If appellate review requires a transcript of the trial proceedings, such a transcript must be made available to a convicted indigent person free of charge. Thus, an Illinois rule that provided transcripts for indigent persons only in felony cases violated equal protection. Even in misdemeanor cases, an indigent defendant should be afforded as effective an appeal as a defendant who can pay. Where a complete transcript is needed, the state bears the burden of showing that something less will suffice. [**Mayer v. City of Chicago**, 404 U.S. 189 (1971)]

b. Right to Counsel—Automatic Appeals

When a state provides an appeal granted to all ***as a matter of right***, counsel must be appointed for indigent persons. [**Douglas v. California**, 372 U.S. 353 (1963)] In ***Douglas***, the Supreme Court struck down a California rule that allowed appellate courts to refuse to appoint counsel on appeals as of right when the court was of the opinion that counsel would be of no value. The Court held that equal protection principles were violated when "the rich man, who appeals as of right, enjoys the benefit of counsel's examination into the record, research of the law, and marshalling of arguments on his behalf, while the indigent [person], already burdened by a preliminary determination that his case is without merit, is forced to shift for himself."

(1) Effective Counsel

On a first appeal as of right, a defendant must be provided with ***effective counsel.*** [**Evitts v. Lucey**, 469 U.S. 387 (1985); *and see supra,* pp. 157–161] The attorney has no obligation to raise every nonfrivolous issue requested by the client. Strategic decisions rest within counsel's professional judgment and include the methods to use for a vigorous and effective advocacy. [**Jones v. Barnes**, 463 U.S. 745 (1983)] Nevertheless, a presumption of prejudice to the client applies when a lawyer fails to file an appeal as instructed by the client. The ultimate authority to decide whether to file an appeal rests with the client. [**Garza v. Idaho**, 586 U.S. 232 (2019)]

c. Right to Counsel—Discretionary Appeals

In most jurisdictions there is a two-tiered system of appellate review, with automatic review at the first tier and discretionary review at the second tier. Automatic appeals must be granted. By contrast, appellate courts may choose whether to grant discretionary appeals. The Supreme Court has held that the federal Constitution does ***not*** require the state to provide counsel for indigent persons for a discretionary appeal. The state also need not provide counsel for an indigent person on a petition for certiorari to the United States Supreme Court. [**Ross v. Moffitt**, *supra,* p. 204]

d. Recoupment Schemes

Many states require indigent persons to reimburse the state for the costs of their legal defense if they have been convicted and later become financially able to repay the state for supplied legal services. These recoupment schemes are valid as long as they do not arbitrarily discriminate against particular defendants or groups of defendants.

e.g. **Example:** A New Jersey statute that required only unsuccessful, incarcerated criminal appellants to reimburse the state for the costs of providing a trial transcript violates equal protection. Applying the statute only to incarcerated defendants, but not to those on probation or suspended sentence, constitutes invidious discrimination. [**Rinaldi v. Yeager**, 384 U.S. 305 (1966)]

e.g. **Example:** A state can require reimbursement of legal fees from indigent persons who are found guilty and later able to repay. The scheme does not violate equal protection, because the convicted indigent person is provided with all the exemptions and protections enjoyed by other judgment creditors and remission was allowed in the case of manifest hardship. In addition, the distinction between those found guilty and those acquitted is not irrational. By not requiring an acquitted indigent person to repay the costs of representation, the state is merely compensating them for the serious imposition of an unsuccessful prosecution. [**Fuller v. Oregon**, 417 U.S. 40 (1974)]

4. Retroactivity

Every rule announced by the United States Supreme Court on direct review (as opposed to collateral attacks, *infra*), even one that is a clear break with the past, applies retroactively to all other cases on direct review. *Rationale*: First, not to do so would put the Court in the position of acting like a legislature rather than a court. Second, failing to apply new rulings retroactively would unfairly allow the petitioner whose case was selected by the Court to benefit from the rule while others similarly situated might not, simply because their case was not chosen for review by the Court. [**Griffith v. Kentucky**, 479 U.S. 314 (1987)]

EXAM TIP

On your exam, if you are confronted with a defendant who is appealing a conviction, there are a few rules that you need to emphasize:

- Unless the error is plain and fundamental (*i.e.,* very obvious and basic), the appellate court will ***not reverse*** a conviction ***unless the defendant preserved*** the issue at trial, usually by raising an objection and stating the grounds for the objection.
- If an error is present, the conviction should ***not be overturned if the error was harmless*** (*i.e.,* there is no reasonable possibility that the error contributed to the defendant's conviction).
- Denial of the right to counsel ***at trial*** is ***never harmless***.
- If there is an ***automatic right to appeal***, such review must be accessible to the indigent defendant (*e.g.,* an attorney and required transcripts must be provided free-of-charge by the government).

B. Collateral Attack on Convictions—Habeas Corpus

1. Constitutional Basis

Article I, Section 9 of the Constitution provides that "the Writ of Habeas Corpus shall not be suspended, unless when in cases of rebellion or invasion the public safety may require it." The First Judiciary Act in 1789 empowered federal judges to grant the writ of habeas corpus to federal prisoners, and in 1867, federal judges were given authority to grant the writ to state prisoners as well.

2. Function of the Writ

The writ of habeas corpus is in the nature of a civil action. It requests the court to demand that a government agency confining an individual release her, because she is being held contrary to the Constitution or fundamental law. [**Preiser v. Rodriguez**, 411 U.S. 475 (1973)] A state criminal defendant can gain access to federal courts only when she alleges a ***violation of federal constitutional rights***. Access to federal courts can be achieved in one of two ways: (i) the defendant, after appealing through the state system, can petition the ***Supreme Court*** for direct review of the conviction; or (ii) the defendant can petition a ***federal district court*** to issue the writ of habeas corpus.

3. Historical Trend

Originally, the writ was used mainly to remedy cases in which the trial court was without jurisdiction to entertain the action. [**Rose v. Mitchell**, 443 U.S. 545 (1979)—*see* concurring opinion by Powell, J.]

a. Warren Court Expansion (1953–1969)

The scope of the writ expanded greatly with the federalization of criminal procedure during the Warren Court era. As the newly created federal constitutional rights of state defendants expanded, so did access of state prisoners to federal courts for vindication of those rights. The Warren Court was skeptical of relying solely on state courts for protection of these new federally protected rights. [*See* **Fay v. Noia**, 372 U.S. 391 (1963)]

b. Burger Court Restriction (1969–1986)

By contrast, the Burger Court's concern with federalism resulted in reduced availability of the writ. The Burger Court contracted the substantive constitutional rights of state criminal defendants and substantially limited their collateral access to federal courts for collateral attack on their state criminal convictions.

c. Rehnquist Court Restriction (1986–2005)

The Rehnquist Court further restricted availability of the writ by significantly narrowing the authority of the federal courts to announce "new" substantive constitutional rules in habeas cases, through a revision of the rules governing retroactivity [**Teague v. Lane**, 489 U.S. 288 (1989); *and see infra*, p. 211–212], and by limiting claims that may be brought in second or subsequent writ proceedings [*see* **McCleskey v. Zant**, 499 U.S. 467 (1991); *and see infra*, p. 216]

d. Roberts Court Maintaining Status Quo (2005–Today)

The Roberts Court has neither added nor restricted habeas review in significant ways. One study notes that habeas matters comprised between eight and 20 percent of the Court's certiorari docket each year with mixed results for petitioners. [*See* Aziz Z. Huq, *Habeas and the Roberts Court*, 81 U. Chi. L. Rev. 519 (2014)]

4. Procedural Issues

Because the habeas corpus proceeding is a ***collateral attack*** on a conviction [*See* **Wall v. Kholi**, 562 U.S. 545 (2011)], it is a separate ***civil*** proceeding in which the defendant challenges the lawfulness of her ***detention***. The person having custody of the defendant, often the prison warden, is named as respondent.

a. Burden of Proof

Generally, the petitioner bears the burden of proving by a ***preponderance of the evidence*** that her detention is unlawful. (This follows from habeas being a civil proceeding—not part of the criminal case to which it refers.) However, where the petitioner claims a constitutional error, the petitioner must be released if the error "had ***substantial and injurious effect or influence*** in determining the jury's verdict" considering the whole context of the case. [**Calderon v. Coleman**, 525 U.S. 141 (1993)] If the judge is in "grave doubt" as to the harm (*e.g.,* where the record is evenly balanced as to harmlessness), the petition must be granted. [**O'Neal v. McAninch**, 513 U.S. 432 (1995)]

EXAM TIP

If you have a question on habeas corpus on your exam, be sure that your answer mentions the fact that habeas corpus is a civil proceeding and so the ordinary criminal trial standard of proof (*i.e.,* beyond a reasonable doubt) does not apply. A petitioner may prove an unlawful detention by the lower *preponderance of the evidence* standard. However, the standard of proof is somewhat higher if the petitioner claims a *constitutional error*—in such a case, the petitioner generally must prove that the error had a *substantial and injurious effect or influence on the conviction.*

b. No Right to Counsel

An indigent person has no constitutional right to appointed counsel to help perfect a petition for a writ of habeas corpus, although a federal statute (18 U.S.C. § 3599) gives indigent defendants a right to counsel in capital cases, including habeas proceedings.

c. States May Appeal

Double jeopardy does not prohibit the state from appealing the grant of a writ, nor does double jeopardy bar retrial of the defendant for the same offense after a grant of the writ.

d. Timeliness

A petition for a writ of habeas corpus may be timely even if the statutory time for filing a direct appeal has expired, because the defendant is challenging the lawfulness of her detention. Moreover, no matter how late a first habeas petition is filed, its merits must be considered, even if this requires staying the petitioner's execution; delay in bringing the petition is not a ground for denying a stay. [**Lonchar v. Thomas**, 517 U.S. 314 (1996)] Nevertheless, in federal court the Antiterrorism and Effective Death Penalty Act ("AEDPA") [28 U.S.C. § 2244(d)(1)] imposes a one-year time limit for filing a habeas petition if the petitioner is "in custody pursuant to the judgment of a State court." The time during which a properly filed state habeas petition is pending does not count toward the one-year limit. And, the one-year statute of limitations on petitions for federal habeas relief by state prisoners is not jurisdictional and may be subject to equitable tolling in some cases. [**Holland v. Florida**, 560 U.S. 631 (2010); *see also* **McQuiggin v. Perkins**, 569 U.S. 383 (2013) (holding that AEDPA one-year statute of limitation can be excused with claim of actual innocence coupled with showing that trial counsel was ineffective)] A state post-conviction petition is not properly filed "if it was rejected by a state court as untimely." [**Allen v. Siebert**, 552 U.S. 3 (2007); **Christeson v. Roper**, 574 U.S. 373 (2015)—equitable tolling of statute of limitation is appropriate where defendant's attorney miscalculates the deadline and engages in ineffective assistance of counsel due to a conflict of interest]

e. Custody

Because habeas challenges the lawfulness of a detention, the defendant must be in custody. The term "custody" has usually been construed broadly, enabling individuals on ***probation*** or ***parole***, or ***out on bail***, to petition for the writ. Nevertheless, if a defendant attacks only the sentence in a federal habeas corpus proceeding, the challenge will become moot if the sentence has expired and there are no ***collateral consequences*** flowing from the sentence. [**Lane v. Williams**, 455 U.S. 624 (1982)] However, typically convictions have collateral consequences (*e.g.,* loss of voting rights, right to hold public office, etc.), so collateral consequences are presumed to arise from every conviction.

(1) Note

A petitioner is not in custody for habeas purposes if the sentence for the conviction she is attacking has fully expired—even if the conviction is being used to enhance a sentence she has yet to serve or is currently serving. [**Maleng v. Cook**, 490 U.S. 488 (1989)] A similar rule applies to parole revocations. [*See* **Spencer v. Kemna**, 523 U.S. 1 (1998)—habeas petition is moot if defendant is released on parole, parole is revoked, defendant files a habeas petition challenging the revocation, but is released before the petition is decided]

(2) But Note

A petitioner serving consecutive sentences ***is*** in custody for habeas purposes even though the sentence for the challenged conviction has expired. [**Garlotte v. Fordice**, 515 U.S. 39 (1995)]

EXAM TIP

Although it is said that habeas corpus is available only if a defendant is in custody, what constitutes "custody" for habeas purposes is far different from what constitutes custody for purposes of *Miranda.* If the petitioner is in prison, the custody requirement is, of course, met. But for purposes of habeas relief, a petitioner who is not incarcerated will be found to be in custody if there are any ***collateral consequences of conviction***, such as loss of the right to vote. Collateral consequences will usually be ***presumed*** to exist if the petitioner is challenging a ***conviction***, but not in other contexts (such as challenges to parole revocations).

f. Which Court May Grant the Writ

Federal prisoners can petition for the writ only in federal court. State prisoners may petition in state court or in federal court, subject to the requirements discussed below.

g. Retroactivity

As noted above (*supra,* p. 207), fairness demands that when the Supreme Court adopts a new rule (*i.e.,* one not dictated by precedent) on ***direct appeal***, the new rule should be applied retroactively to other pending cases. In contrast, the Court has sought to prevent such retroactive application in habeas corpus proceedings, holding that ***generally, new rules should not be announced or applied in habeas corpus proceedings***. Thus, habeas petitions seeking relief that was not supported by law in effect at the time the judgment was entered, probably should not be granted. [**Teague v. Lane**, *supra,* p. 15]

(1) Rationale

The Court has noted that the purpose of the writ of habeas corpus is not to substitute for direct appeals but to ensure that trial judges comply with the Constitution. This purpose is served by assessing ***whether the trial judge followed the law as it was at the time of the trial***. This purpose is not served by considering whether the law should have been different at that time. Moreover, considering and adopting or applying new rules in habeas corpus cases would undermine the concept of finality of judgment, which is essential in criminal law.

e.g. **Example:** At trial, Defendant admitted killing V, but presented evidence that he was guilty only of voluntary manslaughter. The jury received instructions modeled after state pattern jury instructions on murder and manslaughter and convicted Defendant of murder. After Defendant's conviction was final, he sought federal habeas relief, claiming that the pattern jury instructions violated his right to due process. While Defendant's petition was pending, the court of appeals found that the pattern jury instructions in question violated the Due Process Clause. Under these circumstances, Defendant cannot obtain habeas relief on this ground because it constitutes a new rule of criminal procedure. [**Gillmore v. Taylor**, 508 U.S. 333 (1993)]

cf. **Compare: *Teague*** does not bar a defendant's habeas petition claiming that his guilty plea was involuntary and unintelligent, because such a claim is not a "new" rule of criminal procedure. [**Bousley v. United States**, 523 U.S. 614 (1998)]

(2) Exceptions

A new rule can be adopted or applied in a habeas corpus proceeding only under limited circumstances. If the petition seeks application of a rule that falls within one of the following categories, the court may apply the new rule:

(i) ***It places primary, private individual conduct beyond the power of the criminal law-making authority to proscribe*** (*e.g.*, a rule prohibiting regulation of sexual relationships between adults married to each other) or changes the substantive definition of the crime; or

(ii) ***It is implicit in the concept of ordered liberty*** (which at least four members of the Court have defined as a rule closely associated with accurate fact finding).

[**Teague v. Lane**, *supra*]

EXAM TIP

Remember, in the interests of finality, a ***new rule of criminal procedure*** will ***not*** be announced or applied in a habeas corpus proceeding ***unless*** it:

- Places a proscription on individual conduct beyond the power of government (*e.g.*, a rule prohibiting regulation of sex between married people) or changes the substantive definition of the crime; or
- It is implicit in the concept of ordered liberty.

5. State Habeas Corpus for State Prisoners

State prisoners may collaterally attack their conviction or the lawfulness of their detention by petitioning the state courts for the state writ of habeas corpus. Usually, such petitions are filed in the court that entered the final judgment order of conviction. State habeas petitions challenge the lawfulness of any detention—pretrial, mental health, juvenile, or criminal sentence. Some states set time limits for filing habeas petitions in state court. [*See, e.g.*, 42 Pa. C.S. § 9545(b)—imposing one-year limit on state petitioners in Pennsylvania; *and see* Ala. R. Crim. P. 32.2—imposing one-year limit on state petitioners in Alabama]

6. Federal Habeas Corpus for State Prisoners

Concerns of federalism and comity have resulted in the development of specific rules that govern when federal courts may entertain petitions for the writ of habeas corpus filed by state prisoners.

a. Detention Must Violate Federal Rights

For a state prisoner to obtain a writ of habeas corpus, he must prove that he is being detained in violation of his ***federal*** rights. [**Wilson v. Corcoran**, 562 U.S. 1 (2010)] Mere error in the state prosecution does not entitle a state prisoner to federal habeas relief.

e.g. **Example:** A state prisoner who was sentenced to death and claims "actual innocence" based on newly discovered evidence cannot have his claim heard in a federal habeas corpus proceeding absent an accompanying claim that there was a violation of his federal constitutional rights. [**Herrera v. Collins**, 506 U.S. 390 (1993)]

(1) Statutory Limitation

The Antiterrorism and Effective Death Penalty Act (AEDPA) enacted in 1996 (*supra,* p. 210) permits federal habeas relief regarding a state court determination of law only if the determination is “contrary to, or involved unreasonable application of, clearly established federal law as determined by the Supreme Court. . . .” 1996 (*see* 28 U.S.C. § 2254(d)(1)), The AEDPA standard is a very high bar and intentionally difficult to meet.

(i) Law will be deemed to be “***clearly established***” by the Supreme Court only if it is a holding of the Court; law established by dicta is not clearly established.

(ii) A state court decision will be considered to be “***contrary to***” such precedent only if it: (1) arrives at a conclusion opposite of that reached by the Supreme Court on a question of law; or (2) decides a case differently from the Supreme Court on facts that are materially indistinguishable from the facts previously before the Supreme Court in the precedential case.

(iii) A state court decision will be deemed an ***unreasonable application of clearly established federal law*** only if the decision was “objectively unreasonable” (a term the Supreme Court has conceded is not capable of definition—making this a “you’ll know it when you see it” type standard).

[**Williams v. Taylor**, 529 U.S. 362 (2000); **Woods v. Donald**, 575 U.S. 312 (2015)]

e.g. **Example:** Defendant was charged and tried with others for felony murder and armed robbery. Defendant asserted that he was present at the scene of the killing but did not participate in the crime. While testimony was given tying three of Defendant’s co-defendants to phone calls on the day of the crime, Defendant’s lawyer was not in the courtroom, having said: “I don’t have a dog in this race.”

Held: No relief should have been granted by the habeas state appellate courts. The Supreme Court has never addressed whether the usual presumption—that an accused has suffered unconstitutional prejudice when he is denied counsel at a critical stage of trial—applies when an accused’s lawyer is absent from trial for about ten minutes while a witness testifies about a co-defendant. “Because none of our cases confront ‘the specific question presented by this case,’ the state court’s decision could not be ‘contrary to’ any holding from this Court.” [**Woods v. Donald**, *supra*]

e.g. **Example:** At his capital murder sentencing hearing, Landrigan’s attorney attempted to introduce some mitigating factors, but Landrigan refused to allow such evidence to be introduced and even encouraged the sentencing judge to impose the death penalty. After being sentenced to death, Landrigan brought a habeas corpus petition in federal district court alleging ineffective assistance of counsel for his attorney’s failure to investigate different mitigating factors. The district court refused to hold an evidentiary hearing on the ineffective assistance claim, finding that Landrigan could not make out even a colorable claim of ineffective assistance.

Held: To make out a claim for ineffective assistance of counsel, a claimant must establish prejudice (*i.e.*, but for counsel’s deficient performance, there is a reasonable probability that the result of the proceeding would have been different). [**Strickland v. Washington**, 466 U.S. 668 (1984), *supra,* p. 158] The Supreme Court has never addressed an ineffective assistance claim in which the claimant had himself interfered with counsel’s presentation of mitigating evidence. Therefore, it was not an unreasonable application of ***clearly established federal law*** for the district court to conclude that the petitioner here could not have established prejudice based on his counsel’s failure to investigate further possible mitigating evidence. [**Schriro v. Landrigan**, 550 U.S. 465 (2007), *supra,* p. 159]

e.g. **Example:** At trial, Defendant raised an affirmative defense of diminished capacity but was convicted. He later sought and obtained federal habeas relief and was retried. By Defendant's second trial, the state had abolished the defense of diminished capacity. Defendant sought habeas relief from the second conviction, arguing a violation of due process.

Held: Relief was denied. Defendant could not establish the "high standard" necessary to prevail (*i.e.*, that the state court's decision was contrary to or involved an unreasonable application of clearly established federal law). [**Metrish v. Lancaster**, 569 U.S. 351 (2013)]

b. Exhaustion of State Remedies

State prisoners must exhaust all available state court remedies. If a state prisoner files a petition that contains any claim for which state remedies have not been exhausted, the petition must be dismissed in its entirety, even if the exhaustion requirement has been met as to other claims in the petition. The petitioner may either strike the unexhausted claims and refile in federal court or return to state court to exhaust the state remedies. [**Rose v. Lundy**, 455 U.S. 509 (1982)]

(1) What Remedies Must Be Exhausted

In **Fay v. Noia**, *supra,* p. 208, the Supreme Court clarified that the exhaustion requirement is limited to petitioner's failure to exhaust state remedies still open at the time of filing. Thus, the Court allowed the petitioner's claim, even though he had not appealed his claim in state court, because the time for state court appeal had expired. However, the Court has retreated from this rule.

In **O'Sullivan v. Boerckel**, 526 U.S. 838 (1999), the Court held that a state prisoner must present his claims to a state supreme court in a petition for discretionary review if that review is part of the state's ordinary appellate review procedure. Moreover, failure to seek a discretionary review with the state's highest court violates the exhaustion principal, ***even if the time for the appeal has passed***, unless the petitioner can show cause for the failure and that the petitioner was actually prejudiced by it (*see* below).

c. Failure to Comply with State Procedural Rules

State prisoners will be denied federal habeas relief when they fail to comply with state procedural rules governing the manner in which federal constitutional claims must be raised. [**Wainwright v. Sykes**, 433 U.S. 72 (1977)] A state prisoner who does not comply with state procedural rules will get relief only if she can show: (i) ***cause for the noncompliance*** and ***actual prejudice*** [**Francis v. Henderson**, 425 U.S. 536 (1976)]; or (ii) ***actual innocence*** of the substantive offense. [*see* **Dretke v. Haley**, 541 U.S. 386 (2004); **House v. Bell**, 547 U.S. 518 (2006)] This rule applies to failures to take an appeal as well as other procedural defaults such as missing a state law time limit to file a state habeas claim. [**Coleman v. Thompson**, 501 U.S. 722 (1991); **Walker v. Martin**, 562 U.S. 307 (2011)] The cause and actual prejudice requirements apply even when the alleged constitutional error affected the truth finding function of the defendant's trial. [**Engle v. Isaac**, 456 U.S. 107 (1982)]

In more recent decisions designed to ensure that federal courts do not infringe on state sovereignty, the Supreme Court continues to restrict state prisoners' access to federal habeas. In **Shinn v. Martinez Ramirez**, 596 U.S. 366 (2022), the Court refused to excuse a prisoner's failure to develop the state habeas record, despite the fact that this failure was caused by postconviction counsel's negligence. Likewise, in **Shoop v. Twyford**, 596

U.S. 811 (2022), the Court held that the federal habeas court below had erred by granting the petitioner's request to travel to undergo neurological testing in hopes of establishing that he had suffered a brain injury as a teenager. The Supreme Court majority found the travel order erroneous because the death row inmate had not established that the results of such testing could be admissible in the habeas proceedings.

Nevertheless, "in exceptional cases where a state-court judgment rests on a novel and unforeseeable state-court procedural decision lacking fair or substantial support in prior state law, the decision is not adequate to preclude review of a federal question." [**Cruz v. Arizona**, 598 U.S. 17 (2023)]. In Cruz, the defendant was sentenced to death for murdering a police officer. During trial, he had contended that his due process rights were violated because he was precluded from telling the jury that a life sentence in Arizona made him ineligible for parole. After his death sentence was final, the U.S. Supreme Court, in an unrelated case, clarified that the Arizona law precluding arguments such as the defendant's was unconstitutional. *Held*: Defendant Cruz should have been able to pursue federal habeas relief notwithstanding the "adequate and independent state grounds doctrine."

(1) "Cause"

The cause requirements can be met by demonstrating that either the factual or the legal basis for a claim was not reasonably available to defense counsel when the claim should have been raised. [**Amadeo v. Zant**, 486 U.S. 214 (1988)]

e.g. **Example:** State has a rule that requires objections to be made at trial when allegedly inadmissible evidence is offered. If no timely objection is made, state procedure implies a waiver from Defendant's silence. Defendant fails to object to admission of an illegally obtained confession. After conviction, Defendant petitions in federal court for a writ of habeas corpus on the ground that her confession should have been excluded. The habeas petition will be denied because Defendant failed to comply with state procedural rules governing when objection must be made to exclude a confession.

e.g. **Example:** Defendant was brought for trial in his prison clothing. Neither he nor his attorney objected to the judge. Defendant was convicted and appealed within the state system on other grounds. His conviction was affirmed throughout the state courts. He then filed a petition for the writ of habeas corpus with the federal district court on the ground that trying him in his prison clothing was a denial of due process (a claim that he presented for the first time in federal court). His failure to raise the claim in the state courts was deemed a waiver that barred him from raising the claim for the first time in federal court on federal habeas. [**Estelle v. Williams**, 425 U.S. 501 (1976)]

e.g. **Example:** Tactical decisions of defense attorneys and inadvertent failure by competent counsel to raise a particular substantive claim do not meet the cause and prejudice standard. [**Smith v. Murray**, 477 U.S. 527 (1986); **Murray v. Carrier**, 477 U.S. 478 (1986)]

e.g. **Example:** Defendant was sentenced to death by a particular judge for his role in an execution-style murder. Subsequently, it was discovered that the judge who sentenced Defendant had close ties with organized crime, had often bribed judges when he was a defense attorney, and had solicited bribes while he was on the bench. Defendant alleged that his appointed trial attorney was a former partner of the judge, and that the lawyer had conspired to take Defendant's case to trial quickly in order to deflect suspicion that the judge was accepting bribes and fixing other ongoing cases. The good cause requirement was satisfied with such specific allegations because Defendant alleged that the judge was actually biased in Defendant's own case. [**Bracy v. Gramley**, 520 U.S. 899 (1997), *supra,* p. 137]

The cause requirement is also satisfied when an attorney abandons his petitioner-client without notice, causing the client to default on his habeas claim, [**Maples v. Thomas**, 565 U.S. 266 (2012)], and when the petitioner's attorney was ineffective at trial and during the first collateral proceeding designed to raise a claim of ineffective assistance of counsel. [**Martinez v. Ryan**, 566 U.S. 1 (2012)]

(2) Actual Prejudice

e.g. **Example:** Habeas petitioner produced a sworn affidavit from a white juror who helped convict petitioner, admitting that the juror believed that "there are two types of black people: 1. Black folks and 2. N______" and that petitioner "wasn't in the 'good' black folks category," among other related racially charged comments. The Court held that "jurists of reason could debate whether [petitioner] has shown by clear and convincing evidence that the state court's factual determination was wrong" and remanded for future consideration. [**Tharpe v. Sellers**, 583 U.S. 33 (2018)]

(3) Government Must Preserve Issue

Procedural default normally is a "defense" that the state must raise in response to the habeas corpus petition. If the state does not raise the issue, it may lose the right to assert the defense later. [**Gray v. Netherland**, 518 U.S. 152 (1996), *supra*, p. 132]

FEDERAL HABEAS CORPUS FOR STATE PRISONERS

THE FOLLOWING REQUIREMENTS MUST BE MET FOR FEDERAL COURTS TO GRANT HABEAS CORPUS PETITIONS FROM STATE PRISONERS:

- ☑ Detention must violate ***federal constitutional rights***.
- ☑ Petitioner must have ***exhausted all state remedies***.
- ☑ If petitioner failed to comply with a state procedural rule, petitioner must show ***actual innocence*** or a ***factual or legal cause*** for the failure and that the failure ***prejudiced*** petitioner's case.

d. Grounds Must Be Raised at First Opportunity

A state prisoner filing a petition for writ of habeas corpus must generally bring all claims for release in his first writ.

(1) Subsequent Petition on Same Grounds

The AEDPA (*supra,* p. 210) prohibits a habeas petitioner from filing successive habeas petitions based on claims that were presented in earlier petitions, and the Supreme Court has upheld the validity of the act. [*See* **Felker v. Turpin**, 518 U.S. 651 (1996)] However, not every subsequent petition raising the same claim as an earlier petition will be held to be "successive."

e.g. **Example:** The Court held that a petition was not successive when the first petition was dismissed on a technical ground (the first petition was premature). [**Stewart v. Martinez-Villareal**, 523 U.S. 637 (1998)]

Example: A Rule 59(e) motion, which gives the court a chance to correct mistakes before its judgment on a simple habeas application, is not a successive petition. [**Banister v. Davis**, 590 U.S. 504 (2020)]

Example: A petition that was refiled after the federal court recalled its mandate denying all habeas relief was not successive; the refiled petition was treated as a continuation of the first. [**Calderon v. Thompson**, 523 U.S. 538 (1998)]

Example: Defendant was sentenced to death for killing a sheriff. The state court denied both defendant's direct appeal and habeas petition. The federal district court conditionally granted the writ as to the defendant's sentence. The state trial court resentenced defendant again to death. Finding more constitutional defects, the federal district court again granted the writ as to defendant's sentence. The defendant's latest challenge to his sentence was not successive—even though it was his second federal petition to challenge a death sentence—because it challenged a new judgment for the first time. [**Magwood v. Patterson**, 561 U.S. 320 (2010)]

(2) Subsequent Petition on Different Ground

A line of cases had addressed the issue of whether a petitioner could file a second petition raising grounds for relief not raised in the first petition. [*See, e.g.,* **McCleskey v. Zant**, *supra,* p. 203; *and see* **Schlup v. Delo**, 513 U.S. 298 (1995)] The AEDPA seems to have replaced these cases, restricting successive petitions even further. Under the AEDPA, a second petition may be filed only in two very limited circumstances. It may raise a claim that relies on a ***new rule of constitutional law*** that the Supreme Court ***made retroactive*** to cases on collateral review (*see* **Banister v. Davis**, 590 U.S. 504 (2020) and the discussion of ***Teague****, supra,* pp. 211, 212). Alternatively, a petitioner may raise a new ground when new facts are discovered that clearly establish that a ***constitutional error led to the conviction of an innocent person***. [**Magwood v. Patterson**, *supra*]

(a) "Made Retroactive" Narrowly Construed

The Court has interpreted the phrase "made retroactive" very narrowly. It is equivalent to "expressly held" (*i.e.,* a case will be applied retroactively under this AEDPA provision only if the Supreme Court expressly holds that the case should be applied retroactively). *See* **Tyler v. Cain**, 533 U.S. 656 (2001)

e. State Court Findings of Fact Must Be Respected

Findings of fact by a state court are presumptively correct when reviewed in a federal habeas corpus proceeding. To challenge a state court finding of fact, the habeas petitioner must establish by convincing evidence that the determination by the state court was erroneous. [**Sumner v. Mata**, 449 U.S. 539 (1981); **Coleman v. Johnson**, 566 U.S. 650 (2012) (emphasizing the importance of paying due respect to the role of the jury and state courts)]; *see also* **Johnson v. Williams**, 568 U.S. 289 (2013) (holding that when state court rules against a prisoner in an opinion that rejects some claims but does not expressly address a federal claim, a federal court must presume, subject to rebuttal, that the federal claim was adjudicated on the merits]

Similarly, a federal court, in a habeas corpus review of a petitioner's state conviction, may not reassess the credibility of witnesses it has not viewed in order to reject the state court's factual conclusions as not "fairly supported by the record." [**Marshall v. Lonberger**, 459 U.S. 422 (1983)] And, in reviewing a petition for habeas corpus that has been adjudicated on the merits in state court, federal courts are restricted to reviewing the record that was before the state court that adjudicated the claim. [**Cullen v. Pinholster**, 563 U.S. 170 (2011), *supra,* p. 159]

(1) Allegations of *Miranda* Violations Reviewable

Although a federal court must respect state court findings of fact in a federal habeas proceeding by a state prisoner, whether a prisoner's rights under *Miranda* were violated is a mixed question of law and fact. The state court's findings regarding the circumstances surrounding an interrogation must be presumed correct, but the federal court can determine as a matter of law whether under those circumstances the prisoner was "in custody" during an interrogation. [**Thompson v. Keohane**, 516 U.S. 99 (1995)]

(2) Federal Fact-Finding

The Supreme Court has limited the habeas cases in which the federal courts may conduct their own fact-finding hearings. Federal courts may conduct fact-finding hearings in habeas petition cases from state courts only if: (i) the petitioner can show that she failed to raise the fact issue in state court because of ineffective assistance by counsel or because of the state's interference with the petitioner's ability to raise the claim, ***and*** (ii) the claim would have affected the outcome of the case (the so-called ***cause and prejudice rule***). [**Keeney v. Tamayo-Reyes**, 504 U.S. 1 (1992); **Shinn v. Ramirez**, 596 U.S. 366 (2022)—holding that federal courts cannot consider outside evidence in ineffective assistance of counsel claims] The AEDPA, as construed by the Supreme Court, by and large incorporates this holding.

(3) Constitutional Error Must Not Be Harmless

Even a constitutional error does not warrant habeas relief unless the government cannot show that the error was harmless. [*See* **Davis v. Ayala**, 576 U.S. 257 (2015) (assuming that petitioner's federal constitutional rights were violated when the prosecutor was permitted to explain his peremptory strikes of jurors of color with neither the accused nor the accused's lawyer present (ex parte), but finding the error harmless and rejecting petitioner's habeas petition)]

f. Fourth Amendment Claims Cannot Be Relitigated

The Supreme Court's most substantial limitation on federal habeas corpus relief arose in **Stone v. Powell**, 428 U.S. 465 (1976). In *Stone*, the Court held that a state prisoner in a federal habeas proceeding cannot relitigate a Fourth Amendment search and seizure claim when the state court has already provided an opportunity for full and fair litigation of the claim. According to the Court, the benefits of the exclusionary rule were outweighed by the costs of extending it to collateral review of Fourth Amendment claims.

(1) Distinguish—Sufficiency of Evidence Claims May Be Relitigated

After ***Stone***, *supra*, it was unclear what other claims might be subject to the bar against relitigation in federal habeas proceedings. In **Jackson v. Virginia**, 443 U.S. 307 (1979), the Court held that because proof beyond a reasonable doubt is an integral part of due process, habeas corpus **is** available for state defendants who raise claims regarding the sufficiency of the evidence used to convict them. The writ of habeas corpus should be granted if the court, after reviewing the evidence in the light most favorable to the prosecution, concludes that no rational trier of fact could have found the defendant guilty.

(2) Grand Jury Discrimination Claims May Be Relitigated

A claim of grand jury racial discrimination is cognizable in a federal habeas proceeding even when the state has provided a full and fair opportunity to litigate the claim. The Court distinguished grand jury selection claims from search and seizure claims. In search and seizure cases, the courts are supervising the conduct of the police, which state courts can do as well as federal courts, but with racial exclusion from the grand jury claims, state courts would be monitoring their own conduct without review, because the state courts regulate grand jury selection. [**Rose v. Mitchell**, 443 U.S. 545 (1979)]

(3) Sixth Amendment Claims May Be Relitigated

Unlike Fourth Amendment claims, Sixth Amendment ineffective assistance of counsel claims ***may*** be relitigated in a federal habeas corpus proceeding. Thus, a petitioner can relitigate a claim that his attorney was incompetent and ineffective. [**Kimmelman v. Morrison**, 477 U.S. 365 (1986)] But significant deference is given to both the state court's review of the ineffective claim and to counsel's conduct. [**Burt v. Titlow**, 571 U.S. 12 (2013); **Shinn v. Kayer**, 592 U.S. 111 (2020) (when ineffective assistance claim is presented in a federal habeas petition, a state prisoner "faces additional burdens," including establishing an unreasonable application of clearly established federal law and that counsel engaged in deficient performance that prejudiced the defense.)]

(4) *Miranda* Issues May Be Relitigated

The *Stone* restriction does not bar habeas corpus relief based on a claim that the prisoner's conviction rests on statements obtained in violation of ***Miranda***. [**Withrow v. Williams**, 507 U.S. 680 (1993)]

(5) Eighth Amendment Issues May Be Relitigated

Provided a criminal defendant makes an appropriate showing of evidence, he may seek relief from a sentence of death, arguing intellectual disability. [**Brumfield v. Cain**, 576 U.S. 305 (2015)]

(6) Note—*Stone v. Powell* Cannot Be Avoided by Use of Section 1983

A state prisoner who is barred from seeking a writ of habeas corpus to relitigate a Fourth Amendment claim is also barred from using a civil rights suit, under 42 U.S.C. § 1983, to relitigate the claim. [**Allen v. McCurry**, 449 U.S. 90 (1980)] Thus, when a state has provided a defendant with a full and fair opportunity to litigate a Fourth Amendment claim, the defendant's only federal remedy is direct appeal from the state court system to the U.S. Supreme Court. [*Compare* **Skinner v. Switzer**, 562 U.S. 521 (2011)—prisoner may pursue a post-conviction claim for DNA testing either though habeas petition or under a 42 U.S.C. § 1983 action]

EXAM TIP

Only ***Fourth Amendment search and seizure claims*** cannot be relitigated on habeas petitions. The courts may reconsider almost any other claim (*e.g.*, a claim that guilt was not proved beyond reasonable doubt, a claim that there was discrimination in selection of the grand jury, a claim of ineffective counsel, etc.).

7. Federal Habeas Corpus for Federal Prisoners

A federal prisoner seeking habeas corpus relief on the basis of errors at trial or grand jury racial discrimination must show both ***cause for failing to object*** contemporaneously to these errors and ***actual prejudice*** from the errors. [**United States v. Frady**, 456 U.S. 152 (1982); **Davis v. United States**, 411 U.S. 233 (1973)]

e.g. **Example:** Defendant is tried and convicted in federal court of first-degree murder. This conviction is upheld by the federal courts on appeal. Defendant later collaterally attacks the conviction in a federal habeas corpus proceeding, claiming for the first time that his jury was improperly instructed as to the meaning of malice. Defendant ***cannot*** obtain habeas relief merely by showing that the instruction on malice was ***plainly erroneous***. The "plain error" standard applies only to claims raised on direct appeal. In a habeas proceeding, Defendant must also show actual innocence or ***cause*** for his failure to raise the issue at trial ***and actual prejudice*** resulting from the erroneous instruction. [**United States v. Frady**, *supra*]

Federal habeas law creates separate procedures for state inmates seeking relief from state convictions and federal inmates seeking relief from federal convictions. Under 28 U.S.C. § 2255, federal inmates must meet certain preconditions to file a second or successive habeas petition. These requirements, which are set forth in § 2255(h), include certification by a panel of the appropriate court of appeal, as set forth in cross-referenced provision § 2244. The Court has held that the relevant provision, § 2244(b)(3)(E), applies ***only to state inmates and was not intended to strip the Supreme Court of jurisdiction***. Thus, ***federal inmates may seek Supreme Court review of a second or successive habeas petition*** even if the court of appeal's panel denied certification. [**Bowe v. United States**, 607 U.S. __ (2026), 2026 WL 70342]

8. Showing Innocence

When seeking habeas relief on grounds of innocence, the petitioner generally must show that it is ***more likely than not*** that, but for the constitutional error, no reasonable juror would have found the petitioner guilty beyond a reasonable doubt. [**Schlup v. Delo**, *supra,* p. 217] The same standard applies to challenges against a guilty plea. [**Bousley v. United States**, *supra,* p. 211]

e.g. **Example:** Defendant was charged with illegal "use" of a firearm. He pled guilty to the charges after being told by the judge and his attorney that the statute penalizing "use" of a firearm included mere possession of the firearm. Subsequently, the firearm statute was interpreted to not include mere possession. Defendant then filed for habeas relief, claiming that he merely possessed the firearm at the time of his offense. The Court held that he should prevail if he can show that he probably was not guilty of the using-a-firearm offense or guilty of any more serious offenses forgone by the prosecutor because of the guilty plea. [**Bousley v. United States**, *supra*]

In **Jones v. Hendrix**, 599 U.S. 465 (2023), the Supreme Court rejected Jones's habeas challenge to his conviction for unlawfully possessing a firearm as a felon. After Jones's federal conviction became final, the Court ruled in **Rehaif v. United States**, 588 U.S. 225 (2019), that "the Government must prove both that the defendant knew he possessed a firearm and that he knew he belonged to the relevant category of persons barred from possessing a firearm." Jones sought habeas relief, based on statutory innocence, relying on Rehaif, because he had admitted to his felon status, but believed that his record had been expunged. Despite the favorable Rehaif decision, the Court rejected Jones's petition reiterating that a federal prisoner may not "file a second or successive § 2255 motion based solely on a more favorable interpretation of statutory law adopted after his conviction became final and his initial § 2255 motion was resolved." The Court reasoned that the holding in Rahaif "satisfied neither of § 2255(h)'s gateway conditions for a second or successive § 2255 motion because the case was neither 'newly discovered evidence,' . . . nor 'a new rule of constitutional law[.]"

Chapter Nine

Juvenile Offenders

CONTENTS	PAGE

Key Exam Issues

The legal issues involved with juvenile proceedings are complex because the state does not proceed in an adversarial position against the child, but rather as ***parens patriae***. Because of this, the law sometimes treats juveniles differently from adults.

In this area you should note the procedural protections afforded juveniles under the Due Process Clause, but also understand the protections that are ***not*** available. Major constitutional rights are protected, such as the right to counsel and privilege against compelled self-incrimination, but in juvenile proceedings there is no right to a jury trial, and the judge may order the proceedings closed.

A. Introduction

1. State Acts as Parens Patriae

Traditionally, juvenile offenders have been handled quite differently from adult offenders. Based on the traditional belief that a child is better treated through rehabilitation than punishment, the state proceeds not as an adversary against the child, but as *parens patriae* (a substitute parent, literally "parent of the country" in Latin). [***In re*** **Gault**, 387 U.S. 1 (1967)]

2. Due Process Requirements

Despite the state's non-adversarial role, courts should scrutinize juvenile proceedings to ensure that due process requirements have been satisfied and unfairness to juveniles avoided. [***In re*** **Gault**, *supra*]

B. Procedural Protections

1. Juveniles Afforded Many Constitutional Rights

Many constitutional, procedural protections are now mandated in juvenile proceedings—whether in state or federal jurisdictions. [***In re*** **Gault**, *supra*; In re Winship, 397 U.S. 358 (1970)] The following rights have been recognized by the Supreme Court:

a. Right to written notice of charges;

b. Right to counsel;

c. Rights of confrontation and cross-examination;

d. Privilege against self-incrimination;

e. Right to proof beyond a reasonable doubt; and

f. Protection against double jeopardy.

2. Limitation—Certain Rights Inapplicable

Some rights that apply in adult criminal cases do ***not*** apply in juvenile matters, because the juvenile court traditionally contemplates concern and sympathy rather than punishment. This has created the assumption of a need for more ***flexibility*** for the government in dealing with youthful offenders. In turn, this creates a justification for denying the following constitutional rights in juvenile proceedings.

a. No Right to a Jury Trial

There is no right to a trial by jury in juvenile court. [**McKeiver v. Pennsylvania**, 403 U.S. 528 (1971)]

b. Double Jeopardy Limitation

There is no double jeopardy problem where a juvenile proceeding begins with a master's finding and finishes with a decision by a judge (jeopardy has not attached at the stage before the master). [**Swisher v. Brady**, 438 U.S. 204 (1978)]

c. Pretrial Detention

The Supreme Court has upheld a statute authorizing pretrial detention of an accused juvenile delinquent who has been found, after a hearing, to be a serious risk to society and likely to commit another crime before trial. [**Schall v. Martin**, 467 U.S. 253 (1984)] Under the facts of *Schall,* the detention was for a strictly limited time (no longer than necessary to obtain a formal trial). The statute also required the judge to state the reasons for the detention and the reasons had to be supported by the facts.

3. Limitation—Search and Seizure

Public school officials are, for the purpose of the Fourth Amendment, governmental officers. As state actors, the Fourth Amendment prohibition against unreasonable searches and seizures (*see supra*, p. 34) applies to their actions. However, unlike other governmental searches (which usually require a prior search warrant), routine searches by school officials are valid ***without a warrant if*** they are based on ***reasonable suspicion*** that a student violated the law or a school rule. [**New Jersey v. T.L.O.**, 469 U.S. 325 (1985), *supra,* p. 73]

a. Rationale

Public school officials stand *in loco parentis* ("in place of a parent"), so they may exercise such powers of control, restraint, and correction over students as is reasonably necessary to facilitate the educational functions of the school. [**Tinker v. Des Moines School District**, 393 U.S. 503 (1969)] Because the primary purpose of school searches is to protect the school environment by upholding school rules and local laws, the reasonableness standard applies to routine school searches. This lowers the level of suspicion required for a routine search from probable cause to ***reasonable suspicion***. [**New Jersey v. T.L.O.**, *supra*]

b. Unresolved Issue

After *T.L.O.*, the following issue remains unresolved:

Would the applicable standard be more stringent if the search were conducted in conjunction with or at the behest of ***law enforcement personnel***?

c. Strip Searches

Personal searches of students will be upheld only if they are not excessively intrusive in light of the age and sex of the student and the nature of the infraction. [**Safford Unified School District #1 v. Redding**, 557 U.S. 364 (2009), *supra*, p. 72—finding unreasonable a search in which a school nurse required a 13-year-old girl to pull her underwear away from her body to see whether the student was hiding over-the-counter pain medication based on a weak tip]

d. Drug Testing of Students

Recall that the Supreme Court has upheld a school district's drug testing of students who participate in extracurricular activities. (*See supra,* pp. 73.)

4. Closed Juvenile Proceedings

In many states, the appearances by a juvenile in court are in closed session and the reporting on the action is restricted.

a. Limitation

Note that statutes making it a ***crime*** to publish the lawfully obtained name of a youthful offender violate the First Amendment. *Rationale*: The state's interest in protecting the anonymity of the juvenile offender is outweighed by the public's right to be informed by the media. [**Smith v. Daily Mail Publishing Co.**, 443 U.S. 97 (1979)—newspaper published offender's name after hearing it on a police scanner radio despite state statute making it unlawful to do so]

C. Transfer to Adult Court

1. Transfer Hearing

Juveniles who allegedly have committed serious crimes can be tried as adults in adult criminal courts. Recently there has been increasing pressure to try many juveniles as adults. Because the decision to transfer a juvenile to criminal court affects their substantial rights, prior to such transfer, the juvenile is entitled to a hearing, an attorney to represent him, and a statement of reasons for the decision. [**Kent v. United States**, 383 U.S. 541 (1966)]

2. Limitations on Punishment

When a juvenile is tried and convicted in adult court, certain limitations are imposed on the punishment that the juvenile may receive. In nearly all jurisdictions, juveniles may not be incarcerated among adult prisoners and must be sentenced to separate facilities. Any defendant under the age of 18 when a murder occurred may not receive the death penalty [**Roper v. Simmons**, 543 U.S. 551 (2005), *supra,* p. 195] A sentence of life imprisonment without possibility of parole for a juvenile convicted of a non-homicide offense is unconstitutional [**Graham v. Florida**, 560 U.S. 48 (2010)]. In addition, mandatory life imprisonment without parole for those under the age of 18 at the time of their crimes violates the Eighth Amendment. [**Miller v. Alabama**, 567 U.S. 460 (2012)] However, a trial judge may impose a life term in prison without parole for a minor even if the sentencing judge failed to make a specific finding that the defendant was "permanently incorrigible." [**Jones v. Mississippi**, 593 U.S. 98 (2021)]

Chapter Ten

Prisoners' Rights

CONTENTS	PAGE

Key Exam Issues

There has been much litigation in recent years involving prisoners' rights. This topic is also increasingly nationally and internationally relevant and may be vital in practice. However, prisoners' rights will probably not be tested in your typical Criminal Procedure course. If your professor does test on prisoners' rights, questions will most likely focus on procedural rights in connection with ***parole and probation revocations*** (especially the requirement of a two-stage hearing), the ***notice and hearing requirements for disciplinary proceedings***, and various ***First Amendment considerations*** (*e.g.,* access to the press, censorship of mail, etc.).

A. Parole and Probation

1. Right to Parole or Commutation

Generally, prisoners have no right to be paroled or to have their sentence commuted. Even when a state commutes a large percentage of sentences, due process does not require a statement of reasons for denying commutation. This is because these decisions have little precedential weight (*i.e.*, decisions create no protected liberty interest). [**Connecticut Board of Pardons v. Dumschat**, 452 U.S. 458 (1981)]

However, if ***state law*** does provide a prisoner with a ***right to parole***, due process requires that the prisoner be given "fair procedures for its vindication." [**Swarthout v. Cooke**, 562 U.S. 216 (2011)] An opportunity to be heard and, if parole is denied, the right to a statement of reasons for such denial satisfies the requirement of a fair proceeding. [**Greenholtz v. Inmates of the Nebraska Penal & Correctional Complex**, 442 U.S. 1 (1979)]

a. When Parole Is a Right

State laws regarding parole provide prisoners with a right to parole when ***mandatory*** language (*e.g.,* prisoners "shall" be paroled when certain conditions are met) is used. [**Board of Pardons v. Allen**, 482 U.S. 369 (1987)]

b. Distinguish—Right to Good Time Credit

Good time credit is a reduction in a prisoner's period of incarceration awarded based on good behavior and compliance with institutional rules. A state cannot alter the formula for computing good time credit in such a way that reduces the "good" time gained. Enacting a formula that reduces credit and applying it to prisoners already serving their sentences would constitute an ex post facto law in violation of the Constitution. [**Weaver v. Graham**, 450 U.S. 24 (1981)—*and see supra,* pp. 198–200]

c. Distinguish—Revocation Hearing

Although mandatory parole implicates a due process liberty interest, the procedural safeguards required in a ***parole determination*** are not as stringent as those required in a ***parole revocation*** hearing (*see infra,* p. 229). [*See* **Greenholtz v. Inmates of the Nebraska Penal & Correctional Complex**, *supra.* Nebraska parole procedure, which affords an opportunity to be heard and informs the prisoner why parole was denied, satisfies due process requirements]

2. Parole and Probation Revocations

The Supreme Court has decided several cases regarding parole and probation revocations, focusing on the right to counsel and the right to notice and hearing.

a. Right to Counsel

In probation revocation cases, if the revocation also involves imposition of a new sentence, the defendant is entitled to counsel. [**Mempa v. Rhay**, 389 U.S. 128 (1967)] However, in all other probation and parole revocation cases, the right to counsel is not guaranteed and will be determined on a case-by-case basis. Counsel should be appointed whenever representation is necessary to ensure a fair hearing, as in cases where the defendant denies committing the alleged acts or asserts an argument that is "complex or otherwise difficult to develop or present." Defendants ***must be informed of their right to request counsel*** and, if the request is denied, the record must contain a statement succinctly explaining the denial. [**Gagnon v. Scarpelli**, 411 U.S. 778 (1973)]

EXAM TIP

Remember that in parole or probation revocation cases there is no set rule for when an attorney must be provided. The probationer/parolee must ***always*** be informed of the right to request counsel. However, counsel will be appointed only when representation is deemed ***necessary to ensure a fair hearing***.

b. Right to Notice and Hearing

A defendant threatened with parole or probation revocation generally is entitled to both:

(1) ***A preliminary hearing*** at which a hearing officer determines if there is probable cause to believe that the defendant violated parole; and

(2) ***A revocation hearing*** before a neutral and detached hearing body. Included within the right to this hearing is the right to written notice of the charges, the right to appear and present evidence, and a (limited) right to confront witnesses as long as such confrontation would not expose the witness to a risk of harm. [**Morrissey v. Brewer**, 408 U.S. 471 (1972); **Gagnon v. Scarpelli**, *supra*]

(a) *But note*: The fact finder at the revocation hearing is not required to consider alternatives to incarceration or to provide a written statement as to why no alternatives were considered or selected. [**Black v. Romano**, 471 U.S. 606 (1985), *supra,* p. 183]

(b) *Exception:* There is no right to a preliminary hearing for parole revocation when the reason for revoking parole is the parolee's commission of a crime while on parole for a different conviction. [**Moody v. Daggett**, 429 U.S. 78 (1976)]

B. Rights in Disciplinary Situations

1. Discipline Resulting in Solitary Confinement or Loss of Good Time Credit

The Supreme Court has indicated that a prisoner may be deprived of good time credit or placed in solitary confinement only if certain procedural requirements are met. [**Wolff v. McDonnell**, 418 U.S. 539 (1974)] The prisoner is specifically entitled to:

(i) ***Written notice of charges*** to enable preparation of a defense;

(ii) ***A hearing***;

(iii) The right to ***call witnesses and present evidence***, if prison safety is not endangered;

(iv) The right to ***a written statement of reasons*** for the disciplinary action;

(v) The right to ***seek assistance from prison staff or other inmates*** if the inmate is illiterate or the issues are complex, but a prisoner is ***not*** entitled to have either an appointed or retained lawyer participate on his behalf; and

(vi) ***A decision supported by "some evidence"*** [**Superintendent, Massachusetts Correctional Institute v. Hill**, 472 U.S. 445 (1985)]

a. Limitation on Protections

Not all disciplinary actions trigger due process protections. The protections of *Wolff* apply only to ***atypical, significant liberty restraints not within the expected range of confinement*** for the prisoner's sentence. [**Sandin v. Conner**, 515 U.S. 472 (1995)]

e.g. **Example:** Assignment for an indefinite period to a "supermax" prison (*i.e.,* a maximum security prison with highly restrictive conditions, designed to segregate the most dangerous prisoners from the general prison population), in which prisoners rarely have visitors, are deprived of almost any environmental or human contact, and from which there is no eligibility for parole, ***is*** "atypical and extreme hardship." Thus, due process protections must be given. [**Wilkinson v. Austin**, 545 U.S. 209 (2005)]

cf. **Compare:** Disciplinary segregation for 30 days does not implicate a liberty interest that triggers due process protections. [**Sandin v. Conner**, *supra*]

2. Discipline Resulting in Transfer

An inmate has no right to remain incarcerated in any specific institution. Thus, there are no procedural due process limitations on the transfer of an inmate, even when the transfer involves a substantial change in the conditions of confinement and is allegedly based on specific acts of misconduct by the inmate. [**Meachum v. Fano**, 427 U.S. 215 (1976); **Montayne v. Haymes**, 427 U.S. 236 (1976)] However, a prisoner may not be transferred to a ***mental hospital*** without the right to a hearing. [**Vitek v. Jones**, 445 U.S. 480 (1980)]

3. Request for Witnesses

When prison officials deny an inmate's request for witnesses for a disciplinary hearing, there is no constitutional requirement that officials provide reasons for such denial within the administrative record. However, the Constitution does require reasons to be stated at some point. If they are not stated at the time of the hearing, they may subsequently be stated in a judicial action. [**Ponte v. Real**, 471 U.S. 491 (1985)]

C. Other Rights of Prisoners

1. Access to Courts

Prisoners must have reasonable access to courts and to their lawyers. Inmates must also be allowed to consult with other inmates unless the prison provides a reasonable substitute, such as a law library. [**Bounds v. Smith**, 430 U.S. 817 (1977); **Johnson v. Avery**, 393 U.S. 483 (1969)] Subject to reasonable regulations, law students and other paraprofessionals must be permitted to interview inmates for lawyers. [**Procunier v. Martinez**, 416 U.S. 396 (1974)]

a. Proving Violation of Right to Access

The right of access recognized in *Bounds* does not create an absolute right to a prison library or legal assistance. Prisoners alleging a *Bounds* violation must identify how specific defects in the prison's access program prejudiced a particular legal claim. [**Lewis v. Casey**, 518 U.S. 343 (1996)]

e.g. **Example:** Even in cases involving complex legal issues and severe consequences, *Bounds* does not require the appointment of counsel to all death row inmates for preparing habeas petitions. [**Murray v. Giarratano**, 492 U.S. 1 (1989)]

(1) Note

Prisoners under investigation for a crime committed in prison have no right to counsel until after adversary judicial proceedings have been initiated. [**United States v. Gouveia**, 467 U.S. 180 (1984)]

(2) Access to DNA Testing

A prisoner also has no substantive due process right to potentially exculpatory evidence, including no access to DNA testing of evidence, following a conviction affirmed on direct appeal. Such denial also does not raise procedural due process concerns if the state provided an adequate procedural mechanism to challenge the conviction in a postconviction proceeding. [**District Attorney's Office v. Osborne**, 557 U.S. 52 (2009)]

e.g. **Example:** A defendant convicted of sexual assault in state court filed a civil rights suit years later. He claimed a due process right to access evidence from his criminal case to subject it to DNA testing at his own expense. The Supreme Court held that he had no constitutional right to post-conviction access to the state's evidence to conduct the DNA testing. [**District Attorney's Office v. Osborne**, *supra*]

2. First Amendment Rights

The Supreme Court has recognized that prison officials must have some discretion to impose rules on prisoners regulating their First Amendment activities to run a safe and secure prison. They generally may impose any restriction on any First Amendment activity that is ***reasonably related to legitimate penological interests***. [**Turner v. Safley**, 482 U.S. 78 (1987)]

a. Access to the Press

Prison officials can prohibit personal interviews by news reporters with specific inmates if other means of communication exist between the inmate and reporters. [**Pell v. Procunier**, 417 U.S. 817 (1974); **Saxbe v. Washington Post Co.**, 417 U.S. 843 (1974)]

b. Censorship of Mail

(1) Incoming Mail

Incoming mail to prisoners may be regulated as long as the regulation is ***reasonably related to legitimate penological concerns***, such as security of prisoners, good order and discipline of the institution, and preventing the facilitation of criminal activity. [**Thornburgh v. Abbott**, 490 U.S. 401 (1989)] Thus, prison officials can prohibit inmates from receiving specific types of materials (*e.g.*, sexually explicit magazines or those indicating homosexual orientation). Prison officials may even open letters from lawyers (to prevent outside persons from sending contraband under the guise of attorney mail), if this is done ***in the presence of the inmate and the lawyer's letters are not read***. [**Wolff v. McDonnell**, *supra,* p. 230]

e.g. **Example:** Pennsylvania housed its most dangerous inmates in a special unit in which inmates start at level 2 but can graduate to level 1 with good behavior. Level 2 prisoners are very restricted and are prohibited from receiving any newspapers, magazines, or photographs. A prisoner sued, claiming that these prohibitions deprived him of his First Amendment rights. The prison justified the ban as a tool to encourage better behavior and persuaded the Court that very few privileges could be eliminated, because these prisoners had very few privileges already and any additional restrictions served a legitimate penological interest. [**Beard v. Banks**, 548 U.S. 521 (2006)]

(2) Inmate-to-Inmate Correspondence

As long as the restrictions are reasonably related to legitimate penological interests, prison officials can limit inmate-to-inmate correspondence (*e.g.*, limiting correspondence among inmates to family members or to correspondence regarding legal matters). [**Turner v. Safley**, *supra*]

(3) Outgoing Mail

Prison officials have much more limited legitimate interest in outgoing mail because it usually has little or no effect on security of the prison. Therefore, prison officials have less discretion to regulate outgoing mail. Such regulation is unlawful censorship unless: (i) it furthers an ***important governmental interest*** unrelated to the suppression of expression; (ii) it is ***no more stringent than necessary*** to accomplish its objective; and (iii) prisoners have ***adequate opportunity to protest the censorship***. [**Procunier v. Martinez**, *supra*, p. 231]

c. No Right to Unionize

Prison officials can prohibit inmates from soliciting other inmates to join a prisoner's union and from holding union meetings. Officials may also refuse to allow bulk mailings about union activities to be delivered to prisoners. [**Jones v. North Carolina Prisoners' Labor Union, Inc.**, 433 U.S. 119 (1977)]

d. Marriage

A prison cannot require inmates to demonstrate compelling reasons before allowing them to marry. The Court held that although legitimate security concerns may justify restrictions on the inmate's right to marry, requiring the inmate to show compelling reasons is an exaggerated and unlawful response to those concerns. [**Turner v. Safley**, *supra*]

e. Religion

Prison administrators must attempt to accommodate the religious practices of inmates. However, ***under the Constitution*** prison regulations that allegedly infringe on these practices are valid if the regulations are ***reasonably related to legitimate penological interests***. [**O'Lone v. Estate of Shabazz**, 482 U.S. 342 (1987)—upholding regulation prohibiting prisoners from leaving their assigned work, despite the fact that the regulation prevented a prisoner from praying at certain times, as required by his religion]

(1) Special Statutory Standard

As a matter of federal ***statutory*** law (the Religious Land Use and Institutionalized Persons Act of 2000), the federal government and any state that accepts federal funding for its prisons (and all states do) may not place a burden on the ***religious exercise*** of prisoners unless the burden furthers a ***compelling government interest*** (*e.g.,* a restriction that is necessary to ensure safety or discipline) and does so by the least restrictive means. [**Cutter v. Wilkinson**, 544 U.S. 709 (2005); **Holt v. Hobbs**, 574 U.S. 352 (2015)—holding that the Arkansas Department of Correction infringed Muslim inmates' rights accorded by the Religious Land Use and Institutionalized Persons Act of 2000 by forbidding them from growing beards longer than ¼ of one inch] This standard is higher than the constitutional standard set in ***O'Lone***, *supra.*

3. Right to Adequate Medical Care

A state that deliberately refuses to tend to prisoners' medical needs engages in cruel and unusual punishment in violation of the Eighth Amendment. Simple negligence in providing medical care does not. [**Estelle v. Gamble**, 429 U.S. 97 (1976)] Deliberate indifference to a prisoner's medical needs means that a prison official "knows of and disregards an excessive risk to inmate health or safety." [**Farmer v. Brennan**, 511 U.S. 825 (1994)] Severe overcrowding within a prison that results in grossly inadequate medical and mental health care also violates the Eighth Amendment Cruel and Unusual Punishment Clause. [**Brown v. Plata**, 563 U.S. 493 (2011)]

4. Two Inmates Per Cell

The housing of two inmates in a single cell is ***not*** cruel and unusual punishment. [**Rhodes v. Chapman**, 452 U.S. 337 (1981)]

5. Visitation

The Due Process Clause does not directly guarantee an inmate's interest in unfettered visitation. However, prisoners have a liberty interest in governmental regulations or procedures that **explicitly contain mandatory language** creating such interests (*e.g.,* prisoners "shall be allowed visitors"). Thus, for example, where a regulation merely allowed visitation and promulgated a nonexhaustive list of visitors who could be excluded, this regulation failed to protect inmates' liberty interest in receiving visitors. [**Kentucky Department of Corrections v. Thompson**, 490 U.S. 454 (1989)]

a. Contact Visits

A county prison may prohibit all contact visits (*i.e.*, visits with no physical barrier between the prisoner and the visitor) with family and friends. [**Block v. Rutherford**, 468 U.S. 576 (1984)]

6. Place of Incarceration

The Due Process Clause does not protect a prisoner from being transferred against his wishes to a prison in another state [**Olim v. Wakinekona**, 461 U.S. 238 (1983)]. State prisoners have no liberty interest in their continued confinement in the general prison population rather than administrative segregation, unless a state statute creates such an interest. [**Hewitt v. Helms**, 459 U.S. 460 (1983)]

7. Fourth Amendment Rights

A prisoner has no reasonable expectation of privacy in his cell. Hence, he has no constitutional protection against unreasonable searches. [**Hudson v. Palmer**, 468 U.S. 517 (1984)] *Rationale*: Extending to prisoners a right of privacy would disserve legitimate penological interests.

a. Seizure and Destruction of a Prisoner's Property

The Due Process Clause is not violated by restricting remedies for the negligent or intentional seizure and destruction of a prisoner's property to state law tort actions. [**Hudson v. Palmer**, *supra*]

8. Social Security Benefits

A prisoner who is eligible for Social Security benefits is entitled to continue receiving those benefits even during imprisonment. Because federal law specifically exempts Social Security benefits from execution or attachment, the Supremacy Clause is violated by a state statute authorizing the state to seize a prisoner's benefits to pay for the cost of incarceration. [**Bennett v. Arkansas**, 485 U.S. 395 (1988)]

9. Involuntary Treatment with Antipsychotic Drugs

The treatment of a prisoner with antipsychotic drugs against his will does not violate substantive due process where the prisoner has been found dangerous to himself or others and where treatment is deemed by prison officials to be in the prisoner's best interest. [**Washington v. Harper**, 494 U.S. 210 (1990)]

EXAM TIP

Prisoner issues are unlikely to show up on your exam. If you keep these four governing principles in mind, you should be well-prepared to answer almost any question that arises:

- Prisoner disciplinary actions do not trigger due process protections unless they constitute ***atypical significant restraints on liberty*** beyond the expected range of confinement requirements.
- Prisoners have no substantive due process right to DNA testing of evidence if their conviction was affirmed on direct appeal.
- Prison officials may infringe on many First Amendment activities if the regulation is ***reasonably related to legitimate penological interests***.

- A prisoner has no reasonable expectation of privacy in his cell, thus prisoners have no Fourth Amendment protection against unreasonable searches and no remedy unless they can obtain civil damages.

Chapter Eleven

Double Jeopardy

CONTENTS	PAGE

Key Exam Issues

The Fifth Amendment right not to be "twice put in jeopardy" is a complex and difficult area, but one given relatively little treatment in most Criminal Procedure classes. There are four important points for you to review:

1. Jeopardy attaches (*i.e.*, the claim can be made) when the jury has been sworn in, or when the first witness in a nonjury trial is sworn.
2. The defendant usually waives double jeopardy claims when she moves for mistrial (unless goaded into the motion by the prosecution), or he successfully raises a substantive appeal.
3. The government cannot appeal acquittals. That surely is the clearest violation of the Double Jeopardy Clause. An acquittal is inviolate. But be careful with government appeals of other orders, such as a ruling by a judge setting aside a guilty verdict, or a request for a review of sentencing by the government, which may be appealed by the prosecution.
4. The Double Jeopardy Clause applies only if the defendant is tried twice for the same offense. There is no restriction on new trials for new offenses unless the new offense relies on proof of the same conduct proved in the old offense. Therefore, you must be careful in weighing the elements of the crimes involved in the two proceedings. Consider whether either offense requires proof of an additional fact, which the other one does not. If so, double jeopardy is not implicated. Also, it is not the same offense if the prosecution is initiated by a different sovereign. For example, a federal prosecution is different than a prosecution by a state or a Tribal Nation.

A. In General

1. Constitutional Bases

The Fifth Amendment to the Constitution provides that "no person shall be . . . subject, for the same offense, to be twice put in jeopardy." The Fifth Amendment is applicable only to federal prosecutions, but the double jeopardy prohibition is so fundamental to the constitutional heritage of the United States that it is incorporated into the Due Process Clause of the Fourteenth Amendment and is, therefore, binding on the states as well. [**Benton v. Maryland**, 395 U.S. 784 (1969)]

a. Basic Principle

A person who has committed a single criminal offense can be subjected to only one prosecution or punishment for that act. Accordingly, when a defendant has been prosecuted for a criminal offense and the prosecution has resulted in either a ***conviction*** or an ***acquittal***—or the proceeding has reached such a point that a dismissal is tantamount to a ***termination of the proceedings based on innocence of the accused***—any further prosecution or punishment for the same offense is barred unless the bar is removed or waived (*see infra*).

(1) Erroneous Acquittal

An acquittal operates as a bar to a subsequent prosecution ***even if the acquittal appears to be erroneous***. [**Green v. United States**, 355 U.S. 184 (1957)]

e.g. **Example:** Trial court directed a verdict for the defendant in a prosecution for arson, finding that the prosecution failed to prove that the burned building was not a dwelling house. The judge believed, erroneously, that this was an element of the charge subject to beyond-a-reasonable-doubt proof. Held: Double jeopardy barred retrial because judge held that prosecutor failed to prove a necessary element, even if, in fact, the element was not legally required. [**Evans v. Michigan**, 568 U.S. 313 (2013)]

(2) Dismissal May Act as an Acquittal

A midtrial ruling dismissing a particular charge on insufficiency of evidence grounds is also a judgment of acquittal for double jeopardy purposes, unless the judge reserves the right to reconsider the ruling or state law indicates that such judgments are not final until the end of trial. [**Smith v. Massachusetts**, 543 U.S. 462 (2005)]

(3) A Verdict of Acquittal Is Inviolate

Jury found the Defendant not guilty by reason of insanity on a charge of malice murder and guilty but mentally ill on two other counts, including felony murder. On Defendant's appeal, the Georgia Supreme Court nullified the verdicts as "repugnant" and remanded for a new trial. The U.S. Supreme Court found the malice murder charge barred by the Double Jeopardy Clause because once a jury issues a verdict of acquittal, it cannot be challenged. It is inviolate. [**McElrath v. Georgia**, 601 U.S. 87 (2024)]

(4) Declaration of a Mistrial Is Not an Acquittal

Typically, the Double Jeopardy Clause does not bar a second trial if the first trial ends in a mistrial. *See infra* pp. 241–242.

b. Purposes

The prohibition against double jeopardy is designed to ensure that the defendant will not be forced to live in a continuing state of anxiety and insecurity. The prohibition also avoids the possibility that by repeated prosecutions, an innocent person may be found guilty. The chances of a conviction at a second trial are greater than at the first, because the government will be able to learn the strengths of the defense case and the weakness of its own case, thereby allowing it to refine its case against the accused. [**Green v. United States**, *supra*, p. 238] Another goal of the Double Jeopardy Clause is to preserve the "finality of judgments." [**United States v. DiFrancesco**, 449 U.S. 117 (1980)]

c. Civil Actions

The Double Jeopardy Clause prohibits only repetitive ***criminal*** prosecutions. Thus, a state generally is free to bring a remedial civil action against a defendant, even if the defendant has already been criminally tried for the conduct out of which the civil action arises. Similarly, the government may bring a criminal action, even though the defendant has already faced a civil trial for the same conduct.

(1) Determining Whether an Action Is Civil or Criminal

The starting point for determining whether a statute is civil or criminal is the label provided by the legislature. Although the mere fact that an action is denominated "civil" does not necessarily make it so, the clearest proof is required to override legislative intent and conclude that an act labeled civil is punitive in purpose and effect. [**Kansas v. Hendricks**, 521 U.S. 346 (1997)] The Court has held that the determination should be made from the face of the statute, rather than merely the penalty imposed, and that in making the determination a court should consider whether the sanction: (i) involves an affirmative disability or restraint; (ii) historically has been regarded as punishment; (iii) comes into play only on a finding of scienter; (iv) promotes the traditional aims of punishment—retribution and deterrence; (v) applies to behavior that is already a crime; (vi) serves an alternative (*i.e.,* nonpunitive) purpose (*e.g.,* to reimburse the government for expenses caused by the fined person's conduct); and (vii) appears excessive to the alternative purpose. [**Hudson v. United States**, 522 U.S. 93 (1998)]

(a) Not an "as Applied" Standard

Once an act is determined to be civil, it will be treated by the courts as civil. A defendant will not be permitted to argue that a civil statute is criminal in nature as applied to him. [**Seling v. Young**, 531 U.S. 250 (2001)]

(2) Private Civil Actions

A private party (as opposed to the government) may seek punitive civil sanctions against a defendant, even if the defendant has already been tried on criminal charges arising from the same act.

EXAM TIP

A number of Supreme Court cases have focused on the double jeopardy effect of "civil" fines, and your professor might be inclined to test on it. Remember that a civil fine does not give rise to double jeopardy protections, *but be careful*. The label that the trial court assigns to a fine is not necessarily dispositive. Be sure to assess whether the fine was *really imposed as a criminal penalty*, considering factors such as whether the fine has historically been regarded as punishment, whether it was levied as a deterrent or for retribution, and whether it appears excessive to fill any nonpunitive needs.

2. When Jeopardy Attaches

Jeopardy attaches at the defendant's trial when the ***jury is empaneled and sworn in***, or, ***in a nonjury case, when the first witness is sworn***. The trial need go no further; a conviction or acquittal is not necessary. [*See* **Crist v. Bretz**, 437 U.S. 28 (1978)—invalidating state statute providing that jeopardy does not attach in jury trials until first witness is sworn; *see also* **Martinez v. Illinois**, 572 U.S. 833 (2014)—After the jury was sworn, jeopardy attached even though the defendant was never at risk of conviction because government's witnesses failed to appear at trial to testify despite being subpoenaed]

a. Distinguish

A judgment of dismissal granted ***before*** trial (before jeopardy has attached) is ***not*** a bar to a subsequent prosecution for the same offense.

3. Distinguish—Civil Doctrine of Res Judicata

The finality concern of the Double Jeopardy Clause is not the same as the finality concerns of res judicata, the civil equivalent of double jeopardy. Res judicata is intended to avoid the costs of redundant litigation and unburden crowded dockets. In contrast, double jeopardy is concerned solely with preventing oppression of the accused.

4. Juvenile Proceedings

Juvenile proceedings can constitute criminal proceedings for purposes of the Double Jeopardy Clause. Thus, the prosecution of a defendant as an adult, after an adjudicatory finding in juvenile court that he had violated the same criminal statute, is prohibited under the Double Jeopardy Clause. [**Breed v. Jones**, 421 U.S. 519 (1975)]

a. Limitation

It does not violate double jeopardy for the state to appeal, pursuant to state procedural rules, the proposed findings by a juvenile master that the juvenile is not guilty of the offense charged. [**Swisher v. Brady**, 438 U.S. 204 (1978), *supra,* p. 225]

B. Exceptions to Double Jeopardy Prohibition

1. When Jeopardy Not a Bar

Even though jeopardy attaches as indicated above, the prohibition of jeopardy may be removed or waived in the following cases.

a. Mistrials

(1) With Defendant's Consent

If a mistrial is ordered on the ***defendant's motion*** or with the defendant's consent, the jeopardy bar is generally ***waived***, and the defendant may be retried for the same offense. [**United States v. Dinitz**, 424 U.S. 600 (1976)] A defendant's motion for retrial is deemed to be a "deliberate election on his part to forgo his valued right to have his guilt or innocence determined before the first trier of fact." [**United States v. Scott**, 437 U.S. 82 (1978)]

(a) Limitation

Retrial is barred, however, if bad faith conduct by the judge or prosecutor was ***intended*** to goad the defendant into seeking a mistrial (thereby giving the prosecution a more favorable opportunity to convict). [**United States v. Dinitz**, *supra*; **Oregon v. Kennedy**, 456 U.S. 667 (1982)]

(2) Without Defendant's Consent

If the defendant objects to the mistrial, double jeopardy bars any retrial unless there was a "***manifest necessity***" for granting the mistrial, or it is otherwise dictated by the "ends of public justice." [**Illinois v. Somerville**, 410 U.S. 458 (1973)]

(a) "Manifest Necessity" Defined

"Manifest necessity" will be found where a scrupulous exercise of judicial discretion leads to the conclusion that the ends of public justice would ***not*** be served by a continuation of the trial. [**Illinois v. Somerville**, *supra*]

(b) Application

The most frequent cases of "manifest necessity" involve ***hung juries*** (unable to agree on a verdict) or mistrials granted because of ***death or illness*** of the judge, a juror, or the defendant. Other cases raise more difficult problems.

1) Defendant Caused Mistrial

If the defendant or her counsel has caused the mistrial (*e.g.,* by prejudicial conduct or remarks in front of the jury that lead the court to conclude that there can no longer be a fair trial), there is sufficient "necessity" and double jeopardy does ***not*** prevent the defendant's retrial. [**Arizona v. Washington**, 434 U.S. 497 (1978)]

2) No Acquittal After Jury's Oral Report of Probable Verdict on Some Counts and Deadlocked on Others

In **Blueford v. Arkansas**, 566 U.S. 599 (2012), the trial court declared a mistrial after the jury could not reach a final verdict. At the retrial, the defendant argued double jeopardy on the two murder charges. The Supreme Court held that the defendant could be retried for murder in addition to manslaughter and negligent homicide because the foreperson's oral announcement during deliberations that the jury was unanimously against the two murder charges "was not a final resolution of anything." The jury's deliberations had not yet concluded. "There were separate forms to convict on each of the possible offenses, but there was only one form to acquit, and it was to acquit on all of them."

3) Prosecutor's Drafting Error

If the first indictment was dismissed because of the prosecutor's error in drafting (and the error was jurisdictional, so that it could not be cured by amendment), a mistrial granted after the jury was sworn and over the objection of the accused ***does not bar retrial***. *Rationale*: "The ends of justice" would not be served by allowing the accused to escape trial simply because of an error in drafting. [**Illinois v. Somerville**, *supra*, p. 242]

4) Absence of Known Prosecution Witness

The absence of a prosecution witness when known is ***not*** a sufficient "necessity," and if the mistrial is granted solely on this ground, double jeopardy bars retrial of the accused. [**Downum v. United States**, 372 U.S. 734 (1963)]

5) Conflicting Roles

Manifest necessity exists to summon another jury after the trial judge discharges the original jury, over the defendant's objection, upon discovering that one of the trial jurors served on the indicting grand jury. [**Thompson v. United States**, 155 U.S. 271 (1894)]

b. Dismissals

(1) Before Trial

If the dismissal occurs before trial, the defendant can be reindicted or the prosecution can appeal.

(2) After Jeopardy Attaches but Before Conviction

A dismissal after jeopardy has attached but before a conviction does not preclude the prosecution from reindicting the defendant, if the dismissal is ***at the defendant's request and for reasons unrelated to guilt or innocence***. [**United States v. Scott**, *supra*, p. 241—dismissal due to judge's belief that pretrial delay violated due process]

(a) Distinguish—Dismissal Related to Innocence or Guilt

If the defendant has obtained termination of the trial on some basis ***related to guilt or innocence*** of the offense charged, retrial is ***barred*** by the Double Jeopardy Clause.

e.g. **Example:** If the judge orders dismissal because the government's case is insufficient to go to the jury, the defendant may not be charged—even if the judge's acquittal ruling was erroneous. [**Sanabria v. United States**, 437 U.S. 54 (1978); **Evans v. Michigan**, *supra*, p. 239] Similarly, a ***midtrial*** dismissal due to insufficient evidence may not be challenged. Dismissal constitutes an acquittal from guilt, and reversal would violate the Double Jeopardy Clause because continuing the trial would subject the defendant to further proceedings evaluating guilt or innocence. Thus, continuing jeopardy in this form is double jeopardy in substance. [**Smalis v. Pennsylvania**, 476 U.S. 140 (1986); *see also* **McElrath v. Georgia**, *supra*, p. 239]

(b) Comment

Given the purpose of double jeopardy protections (to prevent the government from subjecting a defendant to multiple trials), it makes little sense to differentiate between dismissals based on guilt or innocence and those based on other reasons. Indeed, in a dissent in *Scott,* Justice Brennan argued that all acquittals should bar retrials, because the underlying policy of the Double Jeopardy Clause is to prohibit the government from subjecting defendants to multiple trials, ***not*** that acquittals based on guilt or innocence are necessarily accurate and correct. But Justice Brennan's view has never swayed a majority of the Court.

(3) After Conviction

If the dismissal occurs after conviction, the prosecution ***can*** attempt to reinstate the conviction by appeal, because no further trial would be required. [**United States v. Wilson**, 420 U.S. 332 (1975)] Double jeopardy does not bar the reinstatement of a conviction because reinstatement does not implicate the primary policy concern of double jeopardy—multiple trials.

(a) Where Conviction Cannot Be Reinstated

If the conviction cannot be reinstated after a postconviction dismissal, a ***new trial is permitted*** if the postconviction dismissal is unrelated to guilt or innocence.

e.g. **Example:** Defendant is convicted of incest. The conviction is dismissed because, at the time of the assault, the victim (stepdaughter) was not yet covered by the incest statute. Because reversal was not related to guilt or innocence and because conviction cannot be reinstated, Defendant may be retried on the different charge of sexual assault. [**Montana v. Hall**, 481 U.S. 400 (1987)]

c. Appeals

(1) Appeal by Defendant

If the defendant appeals and is successful in overturning his conviction, retrial is permitted because by appealing, the defendant has implicitly waived the right to claim double jeopardy. Under an alternative rationale, the first jeopardy continues until the defendant is acquitted or his conviction made final. [**Green v. United States**, *supra,* p. 239]

(a) Reversal Because of Error at Trial

The general rule is that a defendant *can* be retried when the prior conviction is set aside on appeal because of errors committed during the trial. Here, there has not been "one fair opportunity" to litigate guilt or innocence, and the defendant has waived the double jeopardy claim by appealing. [**Burks v. United States**, 437 U.S. 1 (1978)]

1) Retrial Must Be for Same Offense

The defendant ***cannot*** be convicted of, or even charged with, a ***greater*** offense at the second trial, because of the bar of jeopardy. [**Price v. Georgia**, 398 U.S. 323 (1970)]

Example: Defendant, charged with murder, was convicted of manslaughter in the first trial; she appealed and won a new trial. She cannot be charged with murder in the second trial. *Rationale*: The finding of guilt on the lesser offense implies an acquittal finding on the greater offense.

2) Cannot Prosecute for Greater Degree of Same Offense

Prosecution for a greater ***degree*** of the same offense is also barred. Thus, *e.g.,* double jeopardy bars a later prosecution for murder in the first degree if the original conviction was only for murder in the second degree. [**Green v. United States**, *supra*]

(b) Reversal Because of Insufficient Evidence

A defendant cannot be retried when their conviction is reversed because the evidence is ***insufficient as a matter of law*** to sustain the conviction. [**Burks v. United States**, *supra*] *Rationale*: The prosecution should not have "another opportunity to supply evidence which it failed to muster in the first proceeding." [*Id.*]

1) Note

Burks applies even where the government has offered some evidence—as long as the judge determines that the evidence is legally insufficient. [**Hudson v. Louisiana**, 450 U.S. 40 (1981)] This is because the government has failed to prove its case as a matter of law, not because the judge acts as a "13th juror" evaluating the merits.

2) Distinguish—Reversal Based on Weight of Evidence

Burks does ***not*** apply if the reversal is based on the ***weight*** of the evidence, as where the appellate court disagrees with the jury's weighing of the evidence. [**Tibbs v. Florida**, 457 U.S. 31 (1982)] *Burks* also does not apply if the jury cannot agree as to the evidence. [**Richardson v. United States**, 468 U.S. 317 (1984)] This is because a reversal based on the ***weight*** of evidence is a "determination [by] the trier of fact that a greater amount of credible evidence supports one side of an issue or cause than the other." [**Tibbs v. Florida**, *supra*] However, a reversal based on the ***sufficiency*** of evidence is a determination that "no rational factfinder could have found the defendant guilty beyond a reasonable doubt." [*Id.*]

(c) Limitation on Sentencing After Retrial

If a defendant is convicted and sentenced, but appeals and obtains a new trial, and is then convicted a second time for the ***same*** offense, the Double Jeopardy Clause generally does not bar imposition of a more severe sentence on reconviction.

1) Special Rule for Death Penalty Cases

When there is a formalized, separate process for imposing the death penalty [*e.g.,* when guilt is first determined and then the jury is presented with evidence on whether to impose death), if at the first trial the jury finds that a death sentence is not appropriate, a death sentence cannot be imposed at the second trial. [**Bullington v. Missouri**, 451 U.S. 430 (1981), *supra,* p. 194] However, if the jury makes no such finding (*e.g.,* when a judge imposes a life sentence pursuant to a statute providing for such a sentence when the jury is deadlocked on sentencing), a death sentence can be imposed at a second trial. [**Sattazahn v. Pennsylvania**, 537 U.S. 101 (2003)—"the relevant inquiry . . . is not whether the defendant received a life sentence the first time around, but whether a first life sentence was an 'acquittal' based on findings sufficient to establish legal entitlement to the life sentence—*i.e.,* findings that the government failed to prove one or more aggravating circumstances beyond a reasonable doubt"] In any case, note that these special rules apply only to capital sentencing proceedings. [**Monge v. California**, 524 U.S. 721 (1998)]

2) Distinguish—Due Process Concerns

The Double Jeopardy Clause generally does not bar imposition of a harsher sentence on reconviction. However, the Due Process Clause prevents the ***trial judge*** from imposing a harsher sentence on reconviction absent a showing of identifiable facts occurring after imposition of the original sentence that constitute a basis for the increased sentence. Otherwise, there would be a risk of judicial vindictiveness, and a defendant might be afraid to appeal his original conviction because of the risk of receiving a harsher sentence on reconviction. [*See* **North Carolina v. Pearce**, 395 U.S. 711 (1969), *supra,* p. 186]

3) Exceptions

The rule in *Pearce, supra*, does not apply if the greater sentence follows a trial de novo after a trial in an inferior court [**Colten v. Kentucky**, 407

U.S. 104 (1972), *supra,* p. 187], or if the greater sentence is imposed by a jury rather than the trial judge [**Chaffin v. Stynchcombe**, 412 U.S. 17 (1973), *supra,* p. 186]

(d) Appeal After Guilty Plea

In general, a voluntary and intelligent guilty plea constitutes a waiver of defenses, even if there has been significant attorney or judicial error. [**Mabry v. Johnson**, 467 U.S. 504 (1984)] This includes defenses based on the Double Jeopardy Clause.

e.g. **Example:** On advice of his attorney, Defendant pled guilty to two charges of conspiracy for rigging bids on two separate highway projects. He wase sentenced on both counts. On double jeopardy grounds, Defendant appealed sentencing on the second count because although there were two acts, there was only one conspiracy. The Supreme Court held that Defendant's double jeopardy challenge was ***foreclosed*** by the guilty plea. [**United States v. Broce**, 488 U.S. 563 (1989)]

(2) Appeal by Prosecution

(a) Before Trial

The prosecution may appeal from orders issued by the trial court before trial commences (*i.e.,* before jeopardy has attached). [**Serfass v. United States**, 420 U.S. 377 (1975)—where judge ordered dismissal of the indictment at pretrial hearing and on appeal the order is reversed, Defendant may be required to stand trial]

(b) After Jeopardy Attached but Before Conviction

The prosecution may appeal rulings made after jeopardy has attached but before a conviction, if termination of the proceedings was ***not based on the innocence*** of the accused. [**United States v. Scott**, *supra*, p. 241—appeal of judge's order that pretrial delay violated due process]

(c) Appeal of Acquittal

The clearest case of double jeopardy occurs when a verdict of acquittal is appealed or sought to be set aside by the prosecution. The bar attaches whether the verdict of acquittal is rendered by the jury or the judge. [**United States v. Martin Linen Supply Co.**, 430 U.S. 564 (1977)—acquittal occurs "only upon a jury verdict of not guilty [or when] the ruling of the judge, whatever its label, actually represents a resolution [in the defendant's favor], correct or not, of some or all of the factual elements of the offense charged"; **McElrath v. Georgia**, *supra*, p. 243—a verdict of "not guilty by reason of insanity" for malice murder bars retrial on that charge, even if the jury renders an inconsistent verdict that also finds guilty but mentally ill on felony murder and aggravated assault.]

(d) Appeal Where Judge Sets Aside Guilty Verdict

Any ruling by the judge in the defendant's favor after a verdict of guilty can be appealed by the prosecution. The Double Jeopardy Clause applies only if the defendant may be subjected to a second ***trial*** for the same offense. It does not prohibit review of issues decided adversely to the prosecution that will not require a further trial. [**United States v. Wilson**, *supra*, p. 243—reversal of trial judge's dismissal of indictment after jury guilty verdict results in reinstatement of jury verdict, not new trial]

EXCEPTIONS TO DOUBLE JEOPARDY—A SUMMARY	
MISTRIAL	• If defendant ***consents*** to mistrial, retrial is generally permitted. • If defendant does not consent, retrial is permitted ***only*** if there was ***manifest necessity*** for granting the mistrial, such as a ***hung jury*** or ***death or illness*** of the judge, a juror, or the defendant.
DISMISSALS	• If dismissal occurs ***before trial***, defendant can be retried, as jeopardy has not yet attached. • If dismissal occurs ***after the jury is sworn*** (or in a nonjury trial, after the ***first witness is sworn***), retrial is permitted only if dismissal was at ***defendant's request*** and for reasons ***unrelated to guilt or innocence***, such as a dismissal based on running of the ***statute of limitations***.
APPEALS	• If ***defendant appeals*** a conviction and succeeds, retrial generally is permitted on the theory that the trial and appeal constitute ***continuing jeopardy*** for the same offense. However, defendant cannot be tried for a greater crime, or greater degree of crime, than that for which defendant was found guilty. Also, if the conviction is reversed for insufficient evidence, retrial is ***not*** permitted because the prosecution already had its chance. • If the ***prosecution*** appeals ***before conviction*** (*i.e.*, appeal of an interlocutory order), retrial is permitted unless the proceeding was terminated based on innocence. If defendant is convicted at trial, but the trial judge or appellate court overturns the conviction, ***double jeopardy generally does not bar a later reinstatement*** of the conviction, nor does the Double Jeopardy Clause prevent the prosecution from appealing to have a harsher sentence imposed.

(e) Appeal of Sentence

A government appeal of the sentence imposed after a guilty verdict (on the ground that the sentence is too lenient) does ***not*** violate double jeopardy policies against multiple prosecutions or multiple punishments for the same offense. [**United States v. DiFrancesco**, *supra,* p. 239]

d. Imposition of Additional Punishment

The Double Jeopardy Clause does not provide the defendant with a right to know exactly what the punishment will be. [**United States v. DiFrancesco**, *supra*]

e.g. **Example:** Defendant was convicted of an offense that authorized a mandatory fine and imprisonment. The trial court sentenced Defendant to imprisonment, but later on the sentencing day, the judge recalled Defendant to add a fine. The Supreme Court held that the fine did not violate double jeopardy because sentencing does not carry with it the same sense of "finality" as do verdicts. [**Bozza v. United States**, 330 U.S. 160 (1947)]

2. Jeopardy Is a Bar Only to Prosecution for "Same Offense"

Once jeopardy has attached, the defendant cannot normally be ***prosecuted for a second time*** for the same offense involved in the first trial, nor can she receive ***more than one punishment*** for the same offense.

a. Same Offense Defined

Two crimes are considered the same offense unless ***each crime requires proof of an additional element*** that the other crime does not require. [**Blockburger v. United States**, 284 U.S. 299 (1932)] The definition of "same offense" is important because if jeopardy attached on a certain charge and a double jeopardy exception is not applicable, reprosecution is barred not only on ***that*** specific charge, but also on any other charges which are considered the "same offense."

(1) Note

For a short time, the Supreme Court had two rules for determining whether two crimes constitute the same offense—differentiating between multiple punishments at a single trial and multiple trials. [*See* **Grady v. Corbin**, 495 U.S. 508 (1990)] However, ***Grady*** was soon overruled. [**United States v. Dixon**, 509 U.S. 688 (1993)] Now the definition is the same for both purposes.

(2) Application of *Blockburger* Test

(a) Crimes Related to Use of Automobile

A conviction of failure to reduce speed to avoid an accident does not necessarily prohibit the state from subsequently charging involuntary manslaughter. If manslaughter by automobile does not always entail proof of a failure to reduce speed, the two offenses are not the same for double jeopardy purposes. [**Illinois v. Vitale**, 447 U.S. 410 (1980)]

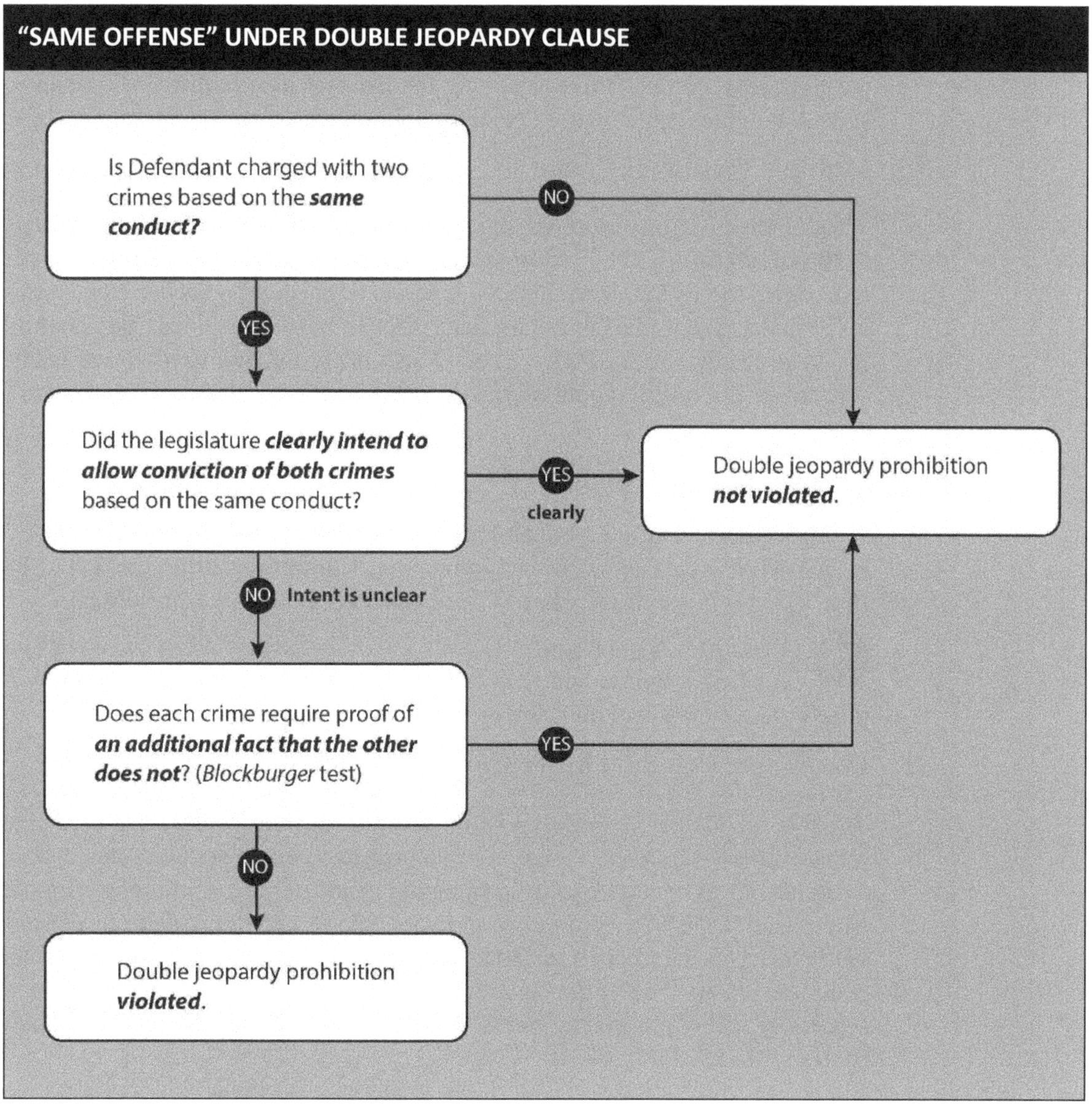

cf. **Compare:** After conviction for joyriding, the defendant could not be prosecuted for theft of a vehicle because no additional facts were needed for the second charge. [**Brown v. Ohio**, 432 U.S. 161 (1977)]

(b) Conspiracy and Substantive Offense

The commission of a substantive offense and a ***conspiracy*** to commit that offense are separate and distinct crimes. [**Iannelli v. United States**, 420 U.S. 770 (1975)] Conspiracy and the substantive offense are distinct for double jeopardy purposes because the "essence" of a conspiracy offense "is in the agreement or confederation to commit a crime." [**United States v. Bayer**, 331 U.S. 532 (1947)]

1) Note

An agreement that violates two separate and specific conspiracy statutes can be divided into separate offenses, if each conspiracy statute requires proof of different facts (*e.g.,* distribution and importation). [**Albernaz v. United States**, 450 U.S. 333 (1981)]

(c) Crimes with Different Elements

A single act might violate overlapping statutes that require different elements, such as burglary and larceny. This does not implicate double jeopardy.

(d) Multiple Victims of Crime

When there are two or more victims, there are two or more offenses. In **Ciucci v. Illinois**, 356 U.S. 571 (1958), the defendant was found guilty of the murder of his wife and two children in three separate trials, one for each victim. Juries at the first and second trials imposed imprisonment as punishment, but the third jury returned the death penalty. Even though the prosecutor tried the cases this way to have multiple opportunities to get a death penalty verdict, the third conviction was affirmed.

(e) Chronologically Discrete Acts

A single offense that may be separated into chronologically discrete acts may be considered separate offenses. [**Johnson v. Commonwealth**, 256 S.W. 388 (Ky. 1923)—75 hands of poker were considered to be separate offenses]

e.g. **Example:** A person who steals a gun, possesses it while breaking and entering a house, and then murders the occupant may be subjected to three separate trials and punishments.

(f) Continuing Criminal Enterprise

There is no double jeopardy violation when a separate ***substantive*** predicate crime is offered to prove violation of an organized crime statute. Thus, where a defendant was convicted of drug smuggling and later of a continuing criminal enterprise ("CCE"—a continuing series of felony violations done in concert with other persons), which included the prior conviction, which had not been completed at the time of the conviction, the two offenses could be prosecuted separately without violating the Double Jeopardy Clause. [**Garret v. United States**, 471 U.S. 773 (1985)]

(g) Lesser Included Offenses

If jeopardy has attached for the greater offense, a defendant may not be retried for any lesser included offense. [**Harris v. Oklahoma**, 433 U.S. 682 (1977)] Furthermore, being put in jeopardy for the lesser included offense bars retrial for the greater. [**Brown v. Ohio**, 432 U.S. 161 (1977)]

e.g. **Example:** Robbery has the lesser included offenses of larceny and assault. Being put in jeopardy for robbery bars retrial for either larceny or assault. Conversely, being put in jeopardy for larceny or assault would bar retrial for robbery.

1) Exception—New Evidence

If the defendant is tried for battery and later the victim dies, the defendant ***may*** be tried for murder. [**Diaz v. United States**, 223 U.S. 442 (1912)] The essential element for the greater offense did not develop until after prosecution of the lesser offense.

2) Multiple Punishments

If a person is convicted of two offenses, one of which is a lesser-included offense of the other, and receives separate punishment for each of the offenses, the multiple punishments generally will violate the Double Jeopardy Clause. The Clause is violated even if the sentences run concurrently. [**Rutledge v. United States**, 517 U.S. 292 (1996)] However, imposition of cumulative punishments for two or more statutorily defined offenses, ***specifically intended by the legislature to carry separate punishments***, even though constituting the "same" crime under ***Blockburger***, does ***not*** violate the Clause if the punishments are ***imposed at a single trial***. [**Missouri v. Hunter**, 459 U.S. 359 (1983)]

e.g. **Example:** Defendant robs a store at gunpoint. Defendant can be sentenced to cumulative punishments for both the robbery and under a "use a gun, go to jail" statute.

a) Presumption Against Multiple Punishments

Absent a clear intention by the legislature to the contrary, it will be presumed that multiple punishments are ***not*** intended for offenses constituting the same crime under ***Blockburger***. [**Rutledge v. United States**, *supra*—crime of conspiracy to distribute controlled substances is a lesser included offense of continuing criminal enterprise offense and multiple punishments are prohibited]

(h) When Defendant Requests Separate Trials

When the defendant opposes a consolidated trial of closely related criminal charges, the opposition may constitute a waiver of any double jeopardy claim as to multiple trials. [**Jeffers v. United States**, 432 U.S. 137 (1977)] The same is true when the defendant agrees to separate trials for different charges. [**Currier v. Virginia**, 585 U.S. 493 (2018)] In **Currier**, the defendant was indicted for burglary, grand larceny, and unlawful possession of a firearm by a convicted felon. He and the government agreed to sever the charges and try the substantive charges first. He was acquitted of burglary and larceny and sought to bar the unlawful possession charge. The Supreme Court rejected that double jeopardy argument, emphasizing that the defendant consented to multiple trials.

(i) Conspiracy and Substantive Offense

A prosecution for ***conspiracy*** is not barred merely because some of the alleged ***overt acts*** of that conspiracy have already been prosecuted. [**United States v. Felix**, 503 U.S. 378 (1992)]

(j) Prior Act Evidence

The introduction of evidence of a substantive offense as prior acts evidence is not equivalent to ***prosecution*** for that substantive offense, and therefore subsequent prosecution for that conduct is not barred. [**United States v. Felix**, *supra*]

b. Conduct Used as a Sentence Enhancer

The Double Jeopardy Clause is not violated when a person is indicted for a crime involving conduct already used to enhance the defendant's sentence for another crime.

[**Witte v. United States**, 515 U.S. 389 (1995)—defendant was indicted for conspiring to import cocaine after the conduct of the conspiracy was used to enhance his earlier sentence when he pleaded guilty to possession of marijuana]

c. Dual Sovereignties

The same act ***may*** be a crime under both federal and state law or under the laws of two different states. [**Heath v. Alabama**, 474 U.S. 82 (1985)] When this occurs, there are in effect ***two distinct crimes*** committed by the same act, so that the acquittal or conviction of the defendant in one jurisdiction does not bar prosecution in the other jurisdiction under double jeopardy provisions. [**Bartkus v. Illinois**, 359 U.S. 121 (1959); **Abbate v. United States**, 359 U.S. 187 (1959)] *Rationale*: An act denounced as a crime by both national and state sovereignties or by two states is an offense against the peace and dignity of both and may be punished by both. [**United States v. Lanza**, 260 U.S. 377 (1922)] Retrial by separate sovereigns is permitted regardless of whether a state proceeding precedes a federal action or the inverse.

(1) But Note—Municipalities Part of State

States and their municipal subdivisions are ***not*** separate sovereigns or jurisdictions for the purpose of the Double Jeopardy Clause. Municipalities are not considered sovereign entities because their power to adjudicate springs from the same law that created the state court. Thus, if a defendant has been convicted of violating the law by a ***municipality of the state,*** the ***state*** is barred from prosecuting acts constituting the "same offense." [**Waller v. Florida**, 397 U.S. 387 (1970)—D, convicted in municipal court, could not also be prosecuted in state court for the same crime based on the same acts]

(2) Tribal Courts

American Indian tribal nations are sovereign entities. Therefore a federal prosecution may follow a conviction in tribal court. [**United States v. Wheeler**, 435 U.S. 313 (1978); **United States v. Lara**, 541 U.S. 193 (2004)]

C. Collateral Estoppel

1. In General

Although neither a former conviction nor an acquittal necessarily bars a subsequent prosecution for a ***different*** offense arising out of the same criminal act (*see* above), the prosecution may still be estopped from relitigating issues of fact ***necessarily determined in the defendant's favor*** in the earlier trial. [**Ashe v. Swenson**, 397 U.S. 436 (1970); *and see* **United States v. Ford**, 371 F.3d 550 (9th Cir. 2003)]

e.g. **Example:** Six persons are robbed at the same time by the same criminal. Defendant is arrested and prosecuted for the robbery of one of the victims, but is acquitted. If the record ***establishes*** that the basis for Defendant's acquittal was the jury's finding that Defendant was ***not*** the robber, Defendant cannot later be prosecuted for robbery of any of the other victims. [**Ashe v. Swenson**, *supra*]

e.g. **Example:** Defendant was charged with, among other things, opening and maintaining a place of business for cocaine distribution. [21 U.S.C. § 841(a)(1)] He was acquitted on that charge. The court found that the government proved only one cocaine transaction, and one cocaine transaction does not establish distribution. Defendant was then charged with managing and controlling a place for the distribution of cocaine. [21 U.S.C. § 841(a)(2)] There is no double jeopardy violation here, because § 841(a)(1) and § 841(a)(2) each require different subjective intents: (a)(1) requires the owner to intend to distribute cocaine himself and (a)(2) requires the owner to intend to allow others to distribute cocaine. However, the government is collaterally estopped from prosecuting the second charge because each crime requires proof of the same objective element—distribution of cocaine—and that issue was already fully tried in the first case, and the trial court found that the prosecution failed to establish that element. [**United States v. Ford**, *supra*, p. 252]

a. Rationale

This is the doctrine of ***collateral estoppel***: Parties who have fully litigated an issue of fact in one proceeding are estopped from relitigating the ***same issue*** in any subsequent proceeding—even though it involves a ***different offense***. In the first example, above, the state litigated Defendant's identity as the robber in the first trial and lost. It cannot be permitted to harass Defendant by relitigating the issue in consecutive prosecutions—even though for a different offense (different victim of same robbery).

b. Inconsistent Verdicts

If the defendant has been charged with multiple counts and there is an inconsistency in the verdicts among the counts (*e.g.,* the jury acquitted the defendant on some and deadlocked on others), the focus should be on what was decided rather than on what was not decided. That is, the issues necessarily decided in the acquittal will have preclusive effect, even if the same issues were involved in the counts on which the jury deadlocked. [**Yeager v. United States**, 557 U.S. 110 (2009)]

e.g. **Example:** Yeager was charged with several counts of fraud and insider trading for his role in the collapse of a large, publicly held corporation—Enron. A necessary element in each count was that Yeager possessed material, nonpublic information and used it unlawfully. He was acquitted of fraud charges, but the jury failed to reach a verdict on insider trading charges. Retrial is barred on the insider trading counts under the issue preclusion component of the Double Jeopardy Clause. The jury's failure to decide the insider trading counts does not affect the preclusive force of the acquittals on the fraud counts, because both relied on the same factual element. [**Yeager v. United States**, *supra*]

2. Limitations

a. Issue Necessarily Determined

The collateral estoppel doctrine applies only if the issue of fact on which the present charge rests was **"*necessarily determined in defendant's favor*"** in an earlier trial.

(1) Note

It is often difficult to determine what the basis was for the defendant's acquittal in the earlier trial, because juries usually return only general verdicts ("guilty" or "not guilty"), without making any specific findings.

(2) Review by Court

It is up to the court in the later criminal proceeding to review the pleadings and evidence from the former trial to decide whether, as a practical matter, the jury verdict "necessarily determined" some crucial fact in the defendant's favor that is the ***foundation of the present criminal charge***. [**Ashe v. Swenson**, *supra*, p. 252—

Court found that the only conceivable basis for Defendant's acquittal was jury's conclusion that Defendant was not the robber]

e.g. **Example:** Two men entered W's home to rob her. Defendant was charged and at trial was acquitted. At Defendant's trial for an unrelated crime, W was permitted to testify that Defendant was one of the two men who had entered her home to rob her. The purpose of her testimony was to link Defendant to the other man who entered her home and was Defendant's suspected partner in the present case too. [**Dowling v. United States**, 493 U.S. 342 (1990)]

b. Issue Identical

The issue being estopped from relitigation must be identical to the issue in the first proceeding. [**United States v. Smith**, 470 F.2d 1299 (5th Cir. 1973)]

c. Issue an "Ultimate Issue"

Collateral estoppel applies only when the issue of fact determined was an "ultimate issue." The reviewing court must analyze the record of the original proceeding and conclude "whether a rational jury could have grounded its verdict upon an issue other than that which the defendant seeks to foreclose from consideration." If so, the finding is ***not*** "ultimate." [**Ashe v. Swenson**, *supra*, p. 252]

e.g. **Example:** A finding by the factfinder that the government's key witness was not credible does not refer to an "ultimate" issue. [**Schleiss v. State**, 239 N.W.2d 68 (Wis. 1976)] Conversely, a finding that the defendant was not the perpetrator in a multi-victim crime does involve an "ultimate" issue.

d. Same Sovereign

Collateral estoppel may be used only if the same sovereign is involved; it cannot be used in a proceeding brought by a different sovereign.

Review Questions and Answers

Review Questions

FILL IN ANSWER

CONSTITUTIONAL PRINCIPLES

1. Indicate whether the following statements are true or false: __________

   a. Because of its importance, the exclusionary rule applies at all stages of a criminal proceeding. __________

   b. To give effect to the exclusionary rule, the courts have applied it to evidence obtained directly or indirectly through the illegally obtained evidence. __________

   c. An accused can obtain an automatic reversal of conviction by showing that the trial court erroneously admitted evidence subject to the exclusionary rule. __________

   d. While not admissible to prove defendant's guilt, the exclusionary rule allows the government to use illegally obtained evidence to impeach the accused's trial testimony. __________

2. Defendant is arrested in his house by Officer Ogle without a warrant and taken into custody for embezzlement. Several hours later, at the station house, Defendant confesses to Ogle that he killed Victor two weeks previously. The arrest is later found to be unlawful. Is Defendant's statement admissible in proceedings against him for the murder of Victor? __________

3. Police officers, reasonably and in good faith, believing that their search warrant was valid, searched the home of Caitlyn and found narcotics. A later challenge to the warrant was successful, with the court finding that the magistrate had erred in finding probable cause. Because the evidence was found as the result of the unlawful warrant, it must be excluded at trial. True or false? __________

4. Police violate the Fourth Amendment when they execute a valid search warrant without knocking and announcing their presence before entering. As a result, the exclusionary rule will prohibit the introduction during the prosecutor's case-in-chief of any drugs or contraband found pursuant to the warrant after such an unlawful entry. True or false? __________

5. Police officers search a car based on an objectively reasonable good faith belief that their conduct is lawful. Soon thereafter, the law upon which the officers relied in conducting the search was changed, making such a search illegal. Should the evidence they found be suppressed under the exclusionary rule? __________

6. Supreme Court opinions are given full retroactive effect. True or false? ____________

FOURTH AMENDMENT

7. Police Officer chases a suspect and yells, "Stop immediately." The suspect continues to run until he is caught at a gas station. When was the defendant "seized" for Fourth Amendment purposes, at the time of the officer's command or at the gas station? ____________

8. Becca, a police officer, arrests Chandler in Chandler's home without a warrant, and subsequently conducts a search incident to the arrest. Although Becca had probable cause to make the arrest, there appears to be no reason why a warrant for the arrest could not have been obtained. Would the exclusionary rule apply? ____________

9. Warrantless entry to prevent the destruction of evidence is allowed where police do not create the exigency through an actual or threatened Fourth Amendment violation. True or false? ____________

10. Police stop a driver for a traffic violation and notice that the car is a rental and the driver is not listed on the rental agreement. Do police need consent, reasonable suspicion, or probable cause to search the car? ____________

11. The police enter Cleo's house pursuant to a valid arrest warrant to arrest Antony. Is this entry lawful? ____________

12. Police with an arrest warrant for Bob enter Bob's home and find Bob sitting in the front room on the couch. Police then conduct a cursory search of the entire home before removing Bob from the home. During the cursory search, police see a clear plastic bag of marijuana on a bedside table in the upstairs bedroom. Does the exclusionary rule bar admission of the marijuana? ____________

13. A police officer had probable cause to believe that a fleeing suspect had just committed a burglary. The officer aimed carefully at the suspect and shot and killed him as he was fleeing. Does the officer's conduct violate the Fourth Amendment? ____________

14. In determining reasonable suspicion, the fact of the suspect's flight from police officers by itself will satisfy the Fourth Amendment. True or false? ____________

15. Police officers received an anonymous tip that the defendant was on the corner of Fifth and Main selling drugs. Based solely on this tip, the officers went to the intersection, saw the defendant, frisked him, and found an illegal gun. Should the defendant's motion to suppress the gun be granted? ____________

16. Do routine sobriety checkpoints for drunk drivers violate the Fourth Amendment? ____________

17. Officer Olivia obtains a valid warrant to search Ashley's house for cocaine. While at Ashley's home and for the duration of the search, Olivia detains Ashley and her two friends.

    a. Is this detention permissible? ______________

    b. Is it permissible for Officer Olivia to search Ashley? ______________

18. Under the present law, the police may seize "mere evidence" if they have probable cause to believe it is related to criminal behavior. True or false? ______________

19. Logan, a private citizen, suspects Mason of stealing his tool chest. While Mason is away from his house, Logan breaks into Mason's locked garage and, while finding no tool chest, discovers a cache of drugs. Logan turns the drugs over to the police, who arrest Mason on a narcotics charge. Can Mason have the evidence (drugs) suppressed? ______________

20. Hotel owner is approached by police officers and directed to show her registry to the officers even though they do not have a warrant or a subpoena. Can the owner refuse to turn over the registry? ______________

21. A warrant is based on an affidavit that relies chiefly on the statements of an unidentified informer. The test for determining the validity of the affidavit, and thus the warrant, is whether under a totality of circumstances there is a fair probability that evidence will be found as indicated. True or false? ______________

22. As long as the judge or judicial officer issuing the search warrant has been duly appointed or elected, she is competent to act in the matter. True or false? ______________

23. The police apply for a warrant to search Amy's office. The court concludes that the facts presented in their affidavit constitute probable cause and issues the warrant. Subsequently, the affidavit is shown to contain errors and false statements. Will the warrant be deemed improperly issued? ______________

    a. Suppose the police affidavit is based on hearsay supplied by an informant. Although the statements are corroborated by the police, the informant is not identified. May the warrant nevertheless be issued? ______________

24. Officer Yolanda arrives at Zack's house to execute a search warrant. She does not knock or announce her presence and pushes open the front door. Is this lawful? ______________

25. The police generally may not, without a warrant, search digital information on a cell phone seized from an individual who has been lawfully arrested? True or false? ______________

26. Pursuant to the lawful custodial arrest of the occupant of a car, may the police search the passenger compartment of the car? __________

27. Police suspect defendant of drug distribution, so they ask his cell phone provider to give them historical cell phone data, showing his cell phone's location during various suspected drug sales. Because police obtain the information from a private company that gathers information relayed from Defendant's cell phone, defendant has no cognizable Fourth Amendment interest in the records. True or false? __________

28. The police lawfully stop Drake's car for speeding. They notice that Drake resembles the description of a certain murder suspect, and that he has a large amount of jewelry in his back seat. Jewelry was reported missing from the murder victim's home. Assuming that they have no warrant, may the police properly search the car? __________

29. To establish that a drug detection dog is reliable, the state need not, in every case, present an exhaustive set of records, including the dog's performance in the field. True or false? __________

30. The special automobile search rules do not apply to motor homes because individuals can actually reside in such vehicles. True or false? __________

31. After a 911 caller reported that a vehicle had run her off the road, a police officer located the vehicle identified during the call and executed a traffic stop. Does this satisfy the Fourth Amendment's reasonable suspicion requirement? __________

32. Officer Otto is sent late at night to investigate a reported robbery. Nearing the alleged scene of the crime, Otto spots Robert on the sidewalk. Robert fits the description of the robber. Otto stops Robert, frisks him, and feels what he believes to be a weapon, but instead is a clear humidor filled with marijuana in Robert's coat pocket. Otto thereupon arrests Robert on charges of possession. Was Otto's search permissible? __________

    a. Would the result change if the officer, in frisking Robert, felt what he believed to be a container of illegal drugs? __________

33. Officer Wilma stops Zach's car for speeding. May Wilma lawfully conduct a frisk of Zach's person to determine whether he is carrying a concealed weapon? __________

34. Alison admits Officer Bret into her apartment and consents to a search of the premises. Bret, who has no search warrant, discovers narcotics belonging to Alison's roommate, Caleb. Is the search proper? __________

    a. If Officer Bret later learns that Alison did not live in the apartment and did not have the authority to consent to a search of Caleb's apartment, is the search unlawful? __________

b. Officer Bret asks Alison for permission to enter and search her apartment. Caleb, a co-occupant of the apartment, is present too. While Alison tells Officer Bret that he is free to search, Caleb declares, "No way you are searching our home." If Officer Bret searches pursuant to Alison's consent, is any evidence found admissible? ______________

35. Police conduct a warrantless search of defendant's apartment following defendant's arrest and removal. The search is based on consent to the search by a person who also occupied the apartment. Does this violate the Fourth Amendment? ______________

36. Does the natural metabolization of alcohol in the bloodstream present a *per se* exigency that justifies an exception to the Fourth Amendment's search warrant requirement for nonconsensual blood testing in all drunk-driving cases? ______________

37. Does the Fourth Amendment allow police to conduct a warrantless breath test incident to a lawful arrest for suspected drunk driving? ______________

38. The police must obtain a warrant before using devices that record the numbers dialed from a particular telephone. True or false? ______________

39. Because the public welfare is involved, administrative searches are not subject to Fourth Amendment limitations. True or false? ______________

40. Public school officials reasonably believe that a student's locker has illegal drugs in it. Must the officials obtain a warrant before searching that student's locker? ______________

41. Because of the unique setting, searches of public school children conducted by school officials are not subject to Fourth Amendment limitations. True or false? ______________

42. A government employer wishes to conduct random drug tests on its employees. Does such testing violate the Constitution? ______________

43. A suspect has a bullet lodged in her arm, allegedly put there by a shopkeeper who shot at a robber. The prosecutor requests a court order, based on probable cause, directing that surgery take place to remove the bullet. The defendant claims that such an operation, over her objection, would violate her constitutional rights. Is the defendant correct? ______________

FIFTH AMENDMENT—SELF-INCRIMINATION

44. While the Fifth Amendment gives a criminal defendant the privilege of refusing to answer questions on the ground of compelled self-incrimination, it does not prevent the government from putting the defendant on the witness stand altogether. True or false? ______________

45. Beth claims that her Fifth Amendment rights were violated when the government offered into evidence her refusal to permit a blood test for intoxication at the time of the traffic violation. Is she correct? ____________

46. Abby and Brianna are on trial for armed robbery. During the trial, Abby does not take the stand, but Brianna appears as a witness on her own behalf.

    a. During her closing argument, the prosecutor notes several times that "Abby has offered you no explanation for her whereabouts at the time of the offense." Is this improper? ____________

    b. During the trial, Abby is requested to read a statement into a tape recorder as a voice sample for analysis by an expert witness. May Abby refuse to do so on the ground of self-incrimination? ____________

47. A defendant generally may invoke her Fifth Amendment privilege against compelled self-incrimination by remaining silent during police questioning. True or false? ____________

48. Witness Alexis is granted immunity from prosecution for her testimony in state proceedings. Can Alexis prevent her testimony from being used against her in a federal prosecution? ____________

49. Under present constitutional standards, the judge determines whether the confession of an accused was voluntary. True or false? ____________

50. Constitutional standards require that the voluntariness of a confession be established beyond a reasonable doubt. True or false? ____________

51. Allen is arrested for a crime. En route to the station house, the police tell Allen that he will not see his infant daughter until she is an adult unless he admits to the crime. Allen confesses. Is the confession admissible against Allen at trial? ____________

52. Involuntary confessions heard by the jury constitute automatic reversible error. True or false? ____________

53. Curt is suspected of murdering Victim. Curt is questioned at some length and gives an answer that both incriminates him and leads the police to find Victim's body. At no time was Curt given proper *Miranda* warnings.

    a. Is the statement admissible against Curt at trial? ____________

    b. Is the finding of the body, with incriminating evidence on it, admissible at trial? ____________

54. Defendant is arrested, told of her right to remain silent, and warned that she is entitled to counsel if and when she goes to court. Do these warnings violate the *Miranda* rule? ____________

55. Police officers cornered a suspect in a grocery store and asked him where the pistol was that he had used in connection with a robbery a few minutes earlier. He told them that the gun was under the produce bin, and the officers immediately went and found the gun. Would the defendant's statement and the gun be admissible in evidence at trial without any *Miranda* warnings having been given? ____________

56. Lori was arrested at her home and placed into custody. She then confessed to the crime in response to questioning by police officers. She did not receive *Miranda* warnings. The next day, after receiving *Miranda* warnings, she again confessed to the commission of the crime. The second confession may not be offered in evidence because it is the "fruit" of the first unlawful confession. True or false? ____________

57. Cathy is indicted on gun smuggling charges and released on bail after retaining counsel and receiving appropriate *Miranda* warnings, and without giving any statement. Two days later, an undercover agent posing as a gun buyer approaches Cathy and, in the course of discussing a possible purchase, obtains Cathy's statement that she engaged in a gun smuggling operation.

    a. Is this statement admissible at trial? ____________

    b. What if Cathy was initially charged with drug charges unrelated to gun smuggling? ____________

58. Does a suspect's age affect whether she is "in custody" for purposes of *Miranda*? ____________

59. A prisoner was escorted from his cell and interviewed in a conference room within the prison. He was offered food and water and the door was sometimes left open. He was told that he was free to leave and could go back to his cell whenever he wanted. Officers sometimes used harsh tones and language while questioning the prisoner for several hours, lasting past his normal bedtime. Was the prisoner in a custodial situation to which *Miranda* applies? ____________

60. After a defendant has asked for an attorney and questioning has ceased, the police may resume questioning without the attorney's presence if the *Miranda* rights are restated. True or false? ____________

61. If the defendant, in response to his *Miranda* warnings, says, "Maybe I should talk to a lawyer," must all questioning cease until counsel is provided? ____________

62. Andrea is arrested at her home, is immediately given a *Miranda* warning, and says that she understands her rights. Before leaving the premises, the police begin interrogating Andrea, who responds voluntarily. Has Andrea waived the right to remain silent? ____________

63. Adam is arrested and advised of his rights in compliance with *Miranda.* Then, Adam is questioned for three hours by officers. Does Adam invoke his right to remain silent if he sits without talking for almost the entire interrogation, answering "yes" only when asked whether he prayed for God to forgive him for his crime? ______________

64. Xander is arrested shortly after a burglary. The police do not give Xander *Miranda* warnings, but immediately question him about his involvement in the crime. Xander confesses that he committed the burglary. Can Xander's confession be used for purposes of impeaching his contrary testimony at trial? ______________

    a. Could Xander's confession be used to impeach the contrary testimony of a key witness if Xander does not testify at the trial? ______________

PRETRIAL PROCEEDINGS

65. Aaron is arrested for armed robbery. Prior to the filing of a formal charge, he is forced to appear in a police lineup where he is identified by Glenn, a witness to the robbery. Aaron is then charged with the crime and informed of his right to counsel. Does this procedure violate Aaron's rights? ______________

66. An accused is entitled to have counsel present at a post-arraignment identification from photographs. True or false? ______________

67. Demi is identified in a post-complaint lineup by Wilson. Assuming Demi was not apprised of her right to counsel, can she automatically exclude any identification testimony by Wilson at the trial? ______________

68. If Dotty is arrested and brought before a magistrate judge for an initial appearance but no prosecutor is present to represent the government's interests, is the proceeding an adversarial one in which Dotty is entitled to counsel? ______________

69. Xavier is arrested for accepting bribes as a public official. Will his right to a preliminary hearing depend on whether the arrest was made before or after a grand jury indictment? ______________

70. Because preventive detention focuses on the safety of the community rather than the likely appearance of the defendant in court, it violates the Constitution. True or false? ______________

71. Tyler is arrested on a charge of embezzlement. Is Tyler entitled to a grand jury hearing and indictment before prosecution begins? ______________

    a. Assume that a grand jury is called in Tyler's case. At the hearing, the prosecutor calls Witness Samantha, who purports to have overheard a conversation between Alex and Becky linking Tyler with the alleged crime. Can an indictment be handed down on the basis of Samantha's testimony? ______________

b. May Tyler refuse to answer questions before the grand jury on the ground of possible self-incrimination? __________

72. Dante is arrested for selling marijuana. At the preliminary hearing, the magistrate finds no probable cause. Is Dante acquitted of the charge? __________

73. Drew is indicted for criminal trespass. If Drew is not brought to trial on the charge for 18 months, has his constitutional right to a speedy trial been violated? __________

74. Donna is indicted for making illegal campaign contributions. While investigating the crime, the prosecutor interviews Carol, who asserts that she made the contribution in Donna's name "as a joke." Neither Donna nor her attorney knows about Carol or her comments. Must this evidence be disclosed to Donna? __________

75. Indicate whether the following statements are true or false:

    a. An accused has no constitutional right to discovery of the prosecution's case other than the right to exculpatory or mitigating evidence. __________

    b. Under present federal law, an accused is entitled to any physical evidence in the prosecutor's possession. __________

    c. The defendant in federal proceedings is never entitled to the pretrial statements of witnesses for the prosecution. __________

    d. An accused may be required to disclose the names and addresses of any alibi witnesses prior to trial if he intends to assert that defense. __________

76. A defendant is found guilty of murder based on one eyewitness's statements to police. The prosecutor finds police files in which the eyewitness made contradictory statements, which are favorable to the defendant, but the prosecutor does not disclose these statements to the defendant. Would this be a *Brady* violation? __________

77. If the government withholds evidence pre-trial that is favorable to the accused—either because it is exculpatory or impeaching—is a *Brady* violation automatic? __________

78. Defendant was required to prove that he was not competent to stand trial. Did this requirement violate the Constitution? __________

79. Henry is arrested and charged with various offenses. Psychiatric examinations indicate that Henry is mentally incompetent to stand trial. May Henry be committed by the court until he is competent for this purpose? __________

80. If Sally is found incompetent to exercise her right of self-representation during trial, it follows that she is incompetent to stand trial. True or false? __________

THE TRIAL

81. Media coverage of a criminal trial without the defendant's consent is an inherent denial of the defendant's due process right. True or false? __________

82. Wilton is charged with breaking and entering and with rape. Can those offenses be tried together in a joint trial against Wilton? __________

83. Indicate whether each of the following statements is true or false:

    a. A defendant tried before a nonattorney judge has been denied his right to a fair trial. __________

    b. In both state and federal courts, an accused is constitutionally entitled to a unanimous jury verdict. __________

    c. A defendant charged with an offense carrying a maximum penalty of $5,000 or five months in prison has no constitutional right to a trial by jury. __________

84. After being given immunity, Witness Wagner is ordered by the court to testify in a forgery trial. Wagner refuses, and the judge orders Wagner jailed until he agrees to testify or until the end of the trial. Does this deny Wagner's right to a jury trial? __________

85. A juror who opposes the death penalty might be excluded for cause in a capital case. True or false? __________

86. Evidence of racial bias during jury deliberations may be a sufficient basis to impeach a jury verdict of guilt when otherwise the rules of evidence prohibit such inquiry into the reasoning underlying the verdict. True or False? __________

87. Judge Jetson orders all members of the press barred from the courtroom during a particularly lurid segment of testimony in a murder trial. Can a news reporter, successfully challenge the order? __________

88. An accused has a constitutional right to counsel in any type of criminal prosecution. True or false? __________

89. An indigent defendant may obtain supplemental aid in preparing his defense. True or false? __________

90. Xavier and Yuri are tried for participating in an armed robbery. May attorney Zorba represent both defendants? __________

91. After an information is filed, Alicia is called into court for arraignment. Is Alicia entitled to counsel at the arraignment? __________

92. Is a defendant entitled to counsel at a preliminary hearing to determine probable cause? __________

93. Failure to provide counsel at any critical stage of a criminal proceeding results in an automatic reversal of conviction unless the defendant waives his right. True or false? ______________

94. At the time of arraignment, Dawn is informed by the court of her right to counsel. Dawn states that she does not want an attorney but wishes to represent herself. Is this an effective waiver of her right to a lawyer? ______________

95. Suppose that, during trial, the defense attorney enters no objections to the prosecutor's offers of evidence, even though much of it is blatant and prejudicial hearsay. Has the defendant necessarily been denied effective counsel? ______________

96. Defendant insisted on his innocence and objected to any admission of guilt by his attorney. But, reasonably believing that confessing guilt might help Defendant avoid the death penalty, during the guilt phase of the trial, counsel admitted to Defendant's guilt anyway.

    a. Ineffective assistance of counsel? ______________

    b. Violation of Defendant's Sixth Amendment rights? ______________

97. In a capital murder prosecution, defense counsel failed to request additional funds to replace a low cost expert because he mistakenly believed that available funding was capped at $1,000. The lawyer knew he needed more funding to make an effective rebuttal to the state's evidence, but he did not do any research on the relevant funding statute. Does this amount to ineffective assistance of counsel under the Sixth Amendment? ______________

98. Carl, a criminal attorney, is appointed to represent Tracy, an indigent defendant. Can Tracy successfully object to the appointment and request the appointment of Lawyer Linda? ______________

99. Face-to-face testimonial encounters at trial are always required for live witnesses under the Confrontation Clause. True or false? ______________

100. Sawyer and Viola are brought to trial for the murder of Trinity following a poker game.

    a. During the prosecutor's opening statement, Sawyer interrupts with vocal denials despite the court's warning to remain silent. May the judge order Sawyer excluded from the courtroom? ______________

    b. The prosecutor also seeks to introduce a prior confession by Viola that she "held Trinity while Sawyer worked her over." The court admits the confession, although Viola never takes the stand at trial. Does this constitute error? ______________

    c. Would the result be different if Viola took the stand and denied any involvement by herself or Sawyer with the crime? ______________

101. Drummond is charged with murder and pleads not guilty by reason of insanity. At the trial, Drummond's attorney introduces sufficient evidence to rebut the general presumption of sanity. Must the prosecution then prove Drummond's sanity beyond a reasonable doubt? ____________

102. Defendant was acquitted by reason of insanity, committed to a mental facility, and later determined to have recovered his sanity. Can the state continue to confine Defendant indefinitely if he is unable to prove himself not dangerous to others? ____________

103. Under the majority view, the question of police entrapment cannot be resolved by evidence of the defendant's predisposition to commit the crime in question. True or false? ____________

  a. Under the majority view, the predisposition of the defendant is determined prior to the government's initial contact with the defendant. True or false? ____________

PUNISHMENT

104. A plea of guilty or nolo contendere can be accepted if counsel for the accused assures the court that it is made voluntarily and with understanding of the charge and possible penalties. True or false? ____________

105. Dustin pleads guilty to a charge of manslaughter, but refuses to admit guilt. May the court accept Dustin's plea? ____________

106. Darla is arraigned for grand theft. Prior to the arraignment, the prosecutor tells Darla that if she insists upon a trial, former convictions will be introduced to increase the seriousness of the offense. Darla therefore pleads guilty at the arraignment. Does this violate due process? ____________

  a. Assume instead that Darla pleads guilty because she knows that the police have seized stolen goods that link her to the theft. Later, it turns out that the goods were taken in a clearly illegal search. Can Darla have the plea set aside? ____________

107. Nancy pleads guilty to an assault charge and is subsequently sentenced and imprisoned. Nancy later claims that she was pressured to make the plea. If she can show this, is she entitled to have the plea withdrawn? ____________

108. Tim is tried and convicted for possession of heroin. During the trial, substantial evidence is presented to show that Tim is an indigent addict. May the court properly sentence Tim to a prison term? ____________

  a. Suppose Tim appeals the conviction and obtains a new trial. If Tim is convicted again for the same offense, may the court impose a harsher sentence? ____________

  b. Can Tim properly be given a sentence of "$5,000 or five years in prison"? ____________

109. Maria is convicted of burglary. If Maria had appointed counsel, may the court condition her probation on repayment of costs of counsel? ______________

110. A state may properly permit the death penalty to be imposed at the discretion of the judge (or jury) without providing guidelines, as long as the offenses to which it applies are clearly specified. True or false? ______________

111. Does the Eighth Amendment allow a "victim impact statement" during the sentencing phase of a capital case that includes opinions from the victim's family member about Defendant's character and the appropriate sentence to be imposed? ______________

112. Does a statute imposing the death penalty satisfy constitutional requirements if it contains language indicating that the killer displayed "utter disregard for human life"? ______________

113. Can a defendant who was 16 years old at the time he committed a murder be sentenced to death? ______________

114. The state required, in capital cases, that defendants show an IQ test score of 70 or below before being permitted to submit additional intellectual disability evidence. Is this a constitutional standard? ______________

115. Does the Eighth Amendment prohibit execution of a defendant who, after suffering multiple strokes, cannot remember details of his death-penalty-eligible offense? ______________

EX POST FACTO CLAUSE

116. Defendant is about to be sentenced. May new sentencing guidelines (adopted after defendant committed her crime) be used to increase her penalty? ______________

POST-CONVICTION ISSUES

117. An erroneous reasonable doubt instruction is subject to the harmless error rule. True or false? ______________

118. Dan, an indigent defendant, is convicted of grand theft in state court proceedings and desires to appeal. Must Dan be furnished a copy of the reporter's transcript of trial? ______________

119. Suppose that Dan, an indigent person, wishes to challenge his conviction in a habeas corpus proceeding. Is he entitled to appointed counsel for this purpose? ______________

120. If a defendant pleads guilty based on his counsel's inaccurate assurances that he will not experience immigration deportation consequences, can the defendant effectively challenge his conviction based on ineffective assistance of counsel, even if the evidence against him was very strong? ______________

121. Indicate whether each of the following statements is true or false:

a. A state court has no power to issue writs of habeas corpus. ______________

b. If a state prisoner sentenced to death claims "actual innocence" based on newly discovered evidence, he will be able to have his claim heard in a federal habeas corpus proceeding. ______________

c. Federal habeas corpus is not available to a state prisoner unless the petitioner has complied with the state procedural rules. ______________

122. In a federal habeas corpus proceeding based on a violation of ***Miranda***, the trial judge may not consider the substantive Fifth Amendment claim, but may only look to whether the defendant was given a fair chance to raise the issue in state proceedings. True or false? ______________

123. True or False—Evidence of racial bias by a member of the petit jury that convicted defendant may be a sufficient basis to excuse defendant's procedural default sufficient to allow a federal habeas corpus proceeding. ______________

JUVENILE OFFENDERS

124. Deirdre, a 14-year-old girl, is arrested for shoplifting and turned over to youth authorities for juvenile court proceedings. Does Deirdre have the right to a jury trial on the charge? ______________

125. School officials are government agents and, therefore, may not search public school students without probable cause and a valid warrant. True or false? ______________

PRISONERS' RIGHTS

126. Does a defendant have a right to counsel in all cases of probation revocation? ______________

127. While incarcerated, Wilma is charged with misconduct in the prison and summoned before a prison disciplinary board for possible loss of "good time" credit. Is Wilma entitled to the assistance of counsel at this proceeding? ______________

128. Fanny, a convicted felon, is released from prison on parole. Shortly thereafter, Fanny is arrested and charged with violating the conditions of her parole. Fanny argues that she did not commit the alleged violations. May she be returned to prison without a hearing? ______________

129. May prisoners be treated against their will with antipsychotic drugs? ______________

DOUBLE JEOPARDY

130. A mistaken acquittal is an acquittal nonetheless, for double jeopardy purposes. True or false? ______________

131. Suppose Patience is brought to trial on a charge of possession of cocaine. Patience is convicted but has the verdict overturned on appeal. Can Patience be subjected to a second trial on the same offense? _______________

132. Jack is found guilty of murder and is sentenced to one year in prison. Does a successful government appeal of this sentence violate the Double Jeopardy Clause? _______________

133. The government can prosecute the defendant for conspiracy even though it earlier prosecuted her for crimes that are the alleged overt acts in connection with the conspiracy. True or false? _______________

134. Terri is tried in state court for counterfeiting and is acquitted. Will this bar Terri's subsequent prosecution for the same crime in federal court? _______________

Answers to Review Questions

1.	a.	**FALSE**	While the rule clearly applies at the ***trial*** stage, its deterrent purpose may be outweighed at other stages—such as grand jury proceedings—by the public policy favoring use of ***any*** relevant evidence. [**p. 6**]
	b.	**TRUE**	However, if there is a showing that the relationship between the "fruits" and the illegal search or seizure is so attenuated that the "taint" is dissipated (*e.g.,* that the evidence would have been obtained in any event), the evidence may be admissible. [**pp. 7–9**]
	c.	**FALSE**	Admission of such evidence is not always reversible error. But the prosecution has the burden of proving beyond a reasonable doubt that the error was harmless. [**pp. 14–15**]
	d.	**TRUE**	If the accused testifies, evidence that is otherwise inadmissible may be used to cast doubt on her credibility. Nevertheless, coerced statements may not be used, even for impeachment. [**pp. 10–10**]
2.		**DEPENDS**	If a defendant's confession is the "fruit" of his unlawful arrest, it is inadmissible. [**p. 8**]
3.		**FALSE**	If the police officers, in reasonable reliance and good faith, believed that the warrant was properly issued, the evidence may be admitted and used at trial, even if the warrant is itself invalid. [**pp. 11–13**]
4.		**FALSE**	Although the Constitution is violated by the unlawful entry, the exclusionary rule does not apply to exclude evidence from the subsequent search because a remedy of exclusion is said to be too attenuated from the purpose of the knock and announce rule, and the cost of excluding evidence is thought to be too great compared to the limited deterrent benefits. [**p. 13**]
5.		**NO**	Searches conducted in objectively reasonable reliance on then binding appellate precedent are not subject to the exclusionary rule. Suppression would do nothing to deter police misconduct in this circumstance, and it would come at a high cost to both the truth and the public safety. [**p. 11**]
6.		**FALSE**	Decisions apply retroactively generally only to cases that are not yet final or that are pending on appeal. [**p. 15**]
7.		**GAS STATION**	A seizure does not occur until a suspect is physically restrained or submits to an officer's show of authority. [**pp. 20–22**]
8.		**DEPENDS**	The exclusionary rule applies to evidence obtained from the house [**p. 23**], but not necessarily to confessions obtained later. [**pp. 8–9**]

9.	**TRUE**	Warrantless searches are allowed when the circumstances make it reasonable, within the meaning of the Fourth Amendment, to dispense with the warrant requirement. [**p. 24**]
10.	**PROBABLY YES**	Unlike a mere passenger in another's car, the driver of a rental car, even when not listed as an additional driver on the rental contract, has a reasonable expectation of privacy in the car. [**p. 6**]
11.	**NO**	Absent consent or exigent circumstances, a search warrant is required for the police officers to enter the home of a third party in order to arrest Antony, even though they have a valid arrest warrant. [**p. 25**]
12.	**DEPENDS**	Although police may search Bob and the area within his immediate reach to prevent him from concealing or destroying evidence or from obtaining a weapon to gain escape, police may perform a protective sweep of other areas in the home only if they have reasonable and articulable suspicion that accomplices may pose a threat to the police and may be present in the home. [**p. 49**]
13.	**YES**	The police may use deadly force to apprehend a suspect only when it is reasonable to do so. Here, there was no evidence that the fleeing suspect posed a threat to anyone. Under such circumstances, the Supreme Court has found the use of deadly force unreasonable. [**p. 25**]
14.	**FALSE**	Flight can be an important part of the individualized suspicion analysis, but other facts are needed to show reasonable suspicion. [**pp. 26, 28, 59**]
15.	**YES**	Generally an anonymous tip is, without more, insufficient to justify a stop and frisk. [**p. 28**]
16.	**NO**	The state's interest in preventing drunk driving outweighs the minimal privacy intrusion, but the roadblocks should be conducted pursuant to administrative polies and procedures to limit unfettered police discretion. [**p. 31**]
17.	a. **YES**	As long as the police have a valid warrant to search the premises for contraband, they may detain the occupants of the premises during the search. [**p. 32**]
	b. **NO**	Unless the police have or develop separate probable cause or reasonable suspicion to believe that Ashley is armed and dangerous, or they develop probable cause to arrest Ashley, they would need a search warrant to search Ashley. [**p. 32**]
18.	**TRUE**	Mere evidence—as well as contraband, fruits, or instrumentalities of crime—may be seized, but there is a probable cause requirement for seizure. [**p. 33**]

19.	**NO**	Evidence unlawfully obtained by private citizens is ***not*** subject to the Fourth Amendment, and hence will not be excluded unless the citizen is acting as a government agent. [**pp. 34–34**]
20.	**YES**	Even though the hotel industry is regulated, a more relaxed Fourth Amendment standard does not apply. [**p. 71**]
21.	**TRUE**	Although the court should consider the basis for the informer's reliability, ultimately the question involves a common sense totality of the circumstances approach viewing all the material facts. [**p. 42**]
22.	**FALSE**	The officer must also be ***neutral and detached*** from the case at hand. Thus, a magistrate who would also serve as investigator or prosecutor in the case could ***not*** validly issue a search warrant. [**p. 45**]
23.	**NOT NECESSARILY**	The affidavit need only be based on information that the police ***believe*** to be true—but if the defendant establishes deliberate or reckless use of false information, the warrant will be invalid if that information was necessary to establish probable cause. [**p. 43**]
a.	**YES**	Generally, the informant's identity does not have to be revealed. [**pp. 43–43**]
24.	**DEPENDS**	Yolanda's entrance is justified only if she reasonably believes, based on the facts specific to the entry, that proper announcement would be dangerous or futile or would inhibit the investigation. However, in either case, evidence obtained as a result of the entry will ***not*** be suppressed. [**p. 46**]
25.	**TRUE**	Without a search warrant, police officers may fully search a suspect, incident to that person's arrest, for personal items such as a wallet or a bag. Police may also seize a cell phone found on a suspect. However, with a phone, the invasion of privacy is much greater, so a search warrant is generally needed. [**p. 49**]
26.	**DEPENDS**	They may do so only if at the time of the search the arrestee is unsecured and officers reasonably believe the arrestee may access the passenger compartment to obtain immediate control of a weapon, or if officers reasonably believe that evidence of the offense of arrest may be found in the compartment. [**p. 51**]
27.	**FALSE**	The government conducts a "search" protected by the Fourth Amendment when it accesses historical cell phone records that provide a comprehensive picture of a cell phone user's past movements over time. Phones typically go everywhere their owners go, creating a novel challenge for privacy. The fact that the records are held by a third party does not remove the cell phone user's reasonable expectation of privacy in the records of his physical movements. [**p. 38**]

28. **YES** If stopping Drake's vehicle is lawful, things observed by the police during the stop can ripen into probable cause to believe that the car contains fruits and instrumentalities of crime, thus justifying a full warrantless search of the vehicle under the automobile exception to the warrant requirement. [**p. 53**]

29. **TRUE** That approach would be inconsistent with the flexible, common-sense standard of probable cause. It is sufficient if the state can show that the dog has passed a certification test for reliability or that the totality of the circumstances suggest reliability. [**p. 53**]

30. **FALSE** The automobile exception may apply to motor homes if they possess attributes of mobility similar to automobiles. [**p. 54**]

31. **YES** The police complied with the Fourth Amendment because, under the totality of the circumstances, the officer had a reasonable suspicion that the driver was intoxicated, and the officer could properly view a 911 caller as being reliable because she was communicating an eye witness account. [**p. 58**]

32. **PROBABLY** Assuming that Otto could reasonably conclude that Robert might be armed and dangerous (*e.g.*, near scene of reported robbery late at night), he is permitted to stop and frisk Robert for weapons without a warrant and without first arresting him. Police may seize anything reasonably believed to be a weapon and any item they have probable cause to believe is contraband based on its plain feel. [**pp. 58–61**]

a. **DEPENDS** The officer may seize any item that he reasonably believes is a weapon or has probable cause to believe—based on its plain feel—is contraband. It might be difficult to convince a judge that there was reason to believe a detainee had drugs merely because the officer felt an object like a humidor during a frisk. [**p. 61**]

33. **DEPENDS** A police officer who has lawfully stopped a vehicle for a traffic violation may order the driver to exit the vehicle without suspecting criminal activity. If the officer then reasonably believes that the driver may be armed and dangerous, the officer may conduct a frisk. Wilma would not be reasonable in believing that Zach was armed merely because he was speeding. [**p. 59**]

34. **DEPENDS** One of two persons who share an apartment can consent in the other's absence to a search of common areas, but not as to areas reserved to the other person. Thus, the lawfulness of this search depends on the location of the narcotics. [**pp. 62–63**]

a. **DEPENDS** As long as Officer Bret reasonably believed that Alison had a right to use and occupy the apartment, the search is reasonable and complies with the Fourth Amendment even though Alison lacked actual authority to consent. [**p. 63**]

b.	**DEPENDS**	The evidence should not be admissible against Caleb because police officers may not act based on the consent of a co-occupant if another co-occupant is present and objects. But the evidence is admissible against the consenting person. [**p. 63**]
35.	**NO**	The consent of one who possesses common authority over premises or effects is valid as against the absent, nonconsenting person with whom that authority is shared. While the police may not remove an occupant as a strategy to avoid the occupant's refusing consent, a lawful arrest is a legitimate reason to remove the occupant from the premises. [**p. 63**]
36.	**NO**	Exigency in this context must be determined case by case based on the totality of the circumstances. [**p. 65**] However, the exigent circumstances rule almost always allows police to obtain a blood test of an unconscious driver suspected of drunk driving.
37.	**YES**	If police have probable cause to suspect drunk driving, they may require a lawfully arrested suspect to take a breath test without first obtaining a warrant. Breath tests do not implicate significant privacy concerns. [**p. 65**]
38.	**FALSE**	Neither the Fourth Amendment, nor Title III, requires the police to seek judicial authorization before using pen registers. [**p. 68**]
39.	**FALSE**	Although warrant requirements are looser (and warrantless searches may be permitted in certain circumstances), the Fourth Amendment still applies in this area. [**p. 71**]
40.	**NO**	Neither a warrant nor probable cause is required for searches conducted by public school officials. Only reasonable grounds to believe that a student is violating a law or school rule are necessary. [**p. 72**]
41.	**FALSE**	While warrants are not needed and the individual suspicion standard has been reduced from probable cause to reasonable suspicion, the constitutional protection remains. [**p. 72**]
42.	**DEPENDS**	While drug testing by the government involves Fourth Amendment considerations, the Supreme Court has allowed it in certain limited situations. [**pp. 74–76**]
43.	**YES**	Normally the individual's interest in privacy outweighs the state's need for evidence in a case involving surgery for removal of evidence of a crime. [**p. 76**]
44.	**FALSE**	A criminal defendant has a right not to take the witness stand. [**p. 81**]
45.	**NO**	The Fifth Amendment does not prevent the government from offering into evidence a defendant's refusal to submit to a blood-alcohol test; only testimonial incrimination is covered. [**p. 82**]

46.	a.	**YES**	The prosecutor may not comment on the failure of a defendant to testify at trial. [**p. 87**] However, the prosecutor's comment will be permitted if it is a response to defense counsel's assertion that the defendant had no opportunity to tell her side of the story. [**p. 87**]
	b.	**NO**	The Fifth Amendment covers only ***testimonial*** compulsions; it does not encompass voice samples. [**p. 82**]
47.		**FALSE**	A defendant normally does not invoke the privilege against self-incrimination by remaining silent. A defendant who desires the protection of this privilege generally must speak and claim it unambiguously. [**p. 81**]
48.		**YES**	The same rule also applies to the use of federally "immunized" testimony in a state prosecution. [**p. 88**]
49.		**TRUE**	The jury cannot hear the evidence until a judge makes the appropriate finding. [**p. 91**]
50.		**FALSE**	The constitutional minimum is proof by a preponderance of the evidence. [**p. 91**]
51.		**NO**	Confessions must be ***voluntary*** to be admissible in evidence. If the police use severe threats or explicit promises to induce a confession, it is involuntary. [**pp. 89–94**]
52.		**FALSE**	Even involuntary confessions are subject to the harmless error rule. [**p. 94**]
53.	a.	**NO**	The statement is a direct result of unlawful questioning under *Miranda* and must be excluded. [**pp. 97, 98**] Nevertheless, the statement may be used to impeach Curt's contradictory testimony should he choose to testify. [**p. 108**]
	b.	**PROBABLY**	*Miranda* violations generally apply only to statements of the accused, not tangible evidence. The court would have to be convinced that the body was tainted evidence from the *Miranda* violation before exclusion would be possible. [**p. 109**]
54.		**PROBABLY**	While the precise wording in *Miranda* need not be followed, the question is whether the essence of *Miranda* has been communicated to the accused. When the right to counsel is tied to a future time, *Miranda* warnings have not "touched all of the bases" required. [**p. 98**]
55.		**YES**	When the purpose of the questioning was to determine the location of the gun for "public safety" purposes, *Miranda* does not apply and no warnings need be given. However, the lawful interrogation should be limited to questions necessary to secure the safety of the police and public. [**p. 99**]

56.		**FALSE**	The issue concerning the second confession is not whether it was the fruit of the first statement, but whether the second confession was obtained without coercion. [**pp. 89, 98**] The result should be different if the questioning in the home was part of an intentional scheme to circumvent the requirements of *Miranda.* [**p. 99**]
57.	a.	**NO**	Such "underhanded interrogations" violate Cathy's Sixth Amendment right to counsel, if she had previously been charged with the crime. This is true even if she has previously been given a *Miranda* warning. [**pp. 95, 99, 103**]
	b.		Because the indictment rests on a different crime than the one Cathy was later interrogated on, and confessed to, the police conduct does not violate the Sixth Amendment. The Sixth Amendment right to counsel is offense specific. [**p. 96**]
58.		**YES**	Although whether a suspect is deemed "in custody" is an "objective" inquiry, a person's age is one factor that may affect how a reasonable person perceives her freedom to leave and the coercive pressures of police questioning. [**p. 101**]
59.		**NO**	When an inmate is questioned, the determination of custody for the purpose of *Miranda* should focus on all of the features of the interrogation. These include the language used in summoning the prisoner to the interview and the manner in which the interrogation is conducted. The fact that the individual is incarcerated does not necessarily mean that he is in custody for *Miranda* purposes. [**pp. 101–103**]
60.		**FALSE**	Further interrogation without counsel can occur only if the defendant is provided with counsel, the defendant initiates the conversation, or there is more than a 14-day break between custodial interrogations. [**pp. 104–106**]
61.		**NO**	To trigger the constitutional requirement of counsel in this setting, the defendant must state unambiguously his desire to have an attorney present. Police have no duty to clarify a suspect's ambiguous comment about counsel. [**p. 105**]
62.		**PROBABLY**	An accused need not ***expressly*** waive her rights. Whether there was a waiver depends on the circumstances. However, the Supreme Court usually finds for the government when the validity of a waiver is in issue. This would be a waiver, provided Andrea's statement was not coerced. [**pp. 106–108**]
63.		**NO**	Remaining silent in the face of interrogation does not invoke the *Miranda* right to remain silent. Invocations must be unambiguous and sitting silently is ambiguous. [**p. 104**]

64.	**PROBABLY**	If Xander's statement was voluntary (*i.e.,* not coerced), it can be used to impeach Xander as a witness at trial—even though it is not directly admissible as evidence of his guilt in the prosecutor's case-in-chief. [**p. 108**]
a.	**NO**	The impeachment evidence can be used only against the defendant. [**p. 108**]
65.	**PROBABLY**	Aaron has no right to counsel at ***pre-complaint*** lineups. However, the circumstances of the identification (composition of lineup, etc.) might indicate a violation of Aaron's right to ***due process***. [**pp. 113, 115**]
66.	**FALSE**	Identification from "mug shots" is proper without counsel being present. Such an identification is not viewed as adversarial and is based on the assumption that it can be reconstructed at trial. [**p. 114**]
67.	**NO**	While failure to provide counsel precludes admissibility of evidence of the lineup itself, it does not automatically exclude the testimony of a witness who identified the accused at the lineup. The witness's in-court identification is valid if he can identify the accused at the trial, without having to rely on the lineup identification. [**p. 114**]
68.	**YES**	The initial appearance marks the start of adversarial judicial proceedings, and the right to counsel attaches. [**p. 117**]
69.	**YES**	In federal and most state courts, an arrest made ***after*** a grand jury indictment requires no preliminary examination (because the grand jury has already determined probable cause). If the arrest was ***before*** any indictment (or if it is a state where no grand jury is used), Xavier would be entitled to such an examination on the felony charge as long as no indictment is returned prior to the preliminary examination. [**pp. 117, 118**]
70.	**FALSE**	The Supreme Court has found that preventive detention does not violate the Due Process Clause or the Eighth Amendment. [**pp. 119–120**]
71.	**DEPENDS**	If a federal felony is involved, Tyler has a Fifth Amendment right to a grand jury indictment. There is no (federal) constitutional right to a grand jury indictment in state criminal prosecutions. [**p. 122**]
a.	**YES**	The testimony would be sufficient because, in most jurisdictions, the indictment can be based entirely on hearsay. [**p. 122**]
b.	**YES**	Unless Tyler has been granted immunity. [**pp. 80, 87**]
72.	**NO**	In most states, a finding of no probable cause by one magistrate does not preclude a prosecutor from presenting the case to another magistrate or to a grand jury. [**p. 125**]

73. **DEPENDS** Mere length of delay does not establish unreasonableness (and hence a violation of Drew's rights). The reasons for the delay, any assertion by Drew of his right to a speedy trial, and prejudice to Drew from the delay must also be considered. (Note that some statutes set forth specific time limits for the prosecution of criminal cases.) [**pp. 127–128**]

74. **YES** Such evidence is clearly favorable (exculpatory) to Donna, is material, and should be made available even without a specific request from the defense. [**p. 129**]

75. a. **TRUE** However, federal and state ***statutes*** or decisional law may grant a right to pretrial discovery by the defense. [**pp. 129–130**]

b. **FALSE** Although broad discovery is permitted under the federal rules, the defendant must show that such evidence is ***material to his defense***. [**pp. 129–130**]

c. **FALSE** The accused would be entitled to disclosure of any exculpatory evidence in such statements, even before trial. [**pp. 129–130**]

d. **TRUE** The Supreme Court has held that this requirement does not violate defendant's privilege against self-incrimination as long as the prosecution is ***also*** required to disclose any ***rebuttal witnesses*** it plans to call. [**p. 131**]

76. **YES** The eyewitness's statements were plainly material, and the State's failure to disclose those statements to the defense violates *Brady*. [**p. 129**]

77. **NO** To violate ***Brady***, the prosecutor must withhold evidence that is also "material," meaning that in the context of the entire record, there is a reasonable probability that the outcome of the proceeding would have been different. [**pp. 129–129**]

78. **DEPENDS** Requiring the defendant to prove incompetency by a preponderance of the evidence satisfies due process, but requiring a higher standard of proof is unconstitutional. [**p. 133**]

79. **NO** A defendant cannot be hospitalized indefinitely simply because he is found incompetent. Such a confinement can occur only following independent civil commitment proceedings. [**p. 133**]

80. **FALSE** A state may insist that Sally accept counsel to assist her at trial, denying her a right of self-representation, while also finding her competent to understand the nature of the proceedings and to assist her lawyer in her defense. Nevertheless, a finding of competency to stand trial coupled with a finding of incompetency to represent one's self would be unusual. [**p. 132**]

81.		**FALSE**	To establish a due process violation, the defendant must show that the media coverage (including television or radio) had a prejudicial effect on the trial participants or compromised the jury's ability to judge fairly. [**p. 138**]
82.		**DEPENDS**	Two or more offenses may be charged as separate counts in the same indictment or information if the offenses are of the same character, or are based on the same act or transaction, are parts of a common scheme or plan. Thus, if the two offenses were part of the same general conduct by Wilton (*i.e.,* forcing entry to the rape victim's residence), a joint trial would be appropriate. [**p. 141**]
83.	a.	**FALSE**	A trial before lay judges is permissible if the defendant has a right to a trial de novo in a court with a judge who is a lawyer. [**p. 138**]
	b.	**TRUE**	In 2020 the Court held that the Fourteenth Amendment incorporates the Sixth Amendment right to a jury trial against the states and requires a unanimous verdict of guilt in all criminal trials. [**p. 146**]
	c.	**TRUE**	Generally, the maximum potential sentence must be ***greater than six months' imprisonment*** before there is a constitutional right to trial by jury. [**p. 143**]
84.		**NO**	This is ***civil*** contempt (because Wagner can free himself by complying with the court order), and there is no right to a jury trial for civil contempt. [**p. 143**]
85.		**TRUE**	Cause would exist if the juror indicated that her attitude might prevent her from following a court's instructions. [**pp. 149–149**]
86.		**TRUE**	Normally a jury's verdict is given substantial protection from further inquiry into comments jurors made during deliberations, but the Court has made an exception for instances when a juror made clear statements indicating that racial animus was a motivating factor in his or her vote to convict. [**pp. 150, 216**]
87.		**YES**	The media (and the public) have a First Amendment right to attend a criminal trial. Thus, the trial judge can order the trial closed only if there are specific findings that closure is necessary for a fair trial in the particular case and there is no less restrictive alternative available. [**p. 152**]
88.		**FALSE**	The prosecution must be for an offense for which imprisonment is ultimately imposed. [**p. 153**]
89.		**TRUE**	Such aid may be required under the Constitution if necessary for the defense. In addition, many jurisdictions give the judge discretion to provide assistance other than counsel, such as medical experts, investigators, etc. [**p. 154**]

90.		**DEPENDS**	If there is any conflict of interest between Xavier and Yuri (*e.g.*, each blames the other, or an argument favorable to one may prejudice the other), Zorba's dual representation may be improper. [**p. 154**]
91.		**YES**	Adversarial judicial proceedings have begun, and this is a "critical stage" of the proceedings, because Alicia must plead to the offense. Thus, Alicia is entitled to be represented by counsel (appointed, if necessary). [**p. 155**]
92.		**YES**	This has been deemed a "critical stage" of the proceedings, giving rise to a constitutional right to counsel. [**p. 155**]
93.		**FALSE**	Failure to provide counsel at ***trial*** results in automatic reversal. Such failure is deemed a "structural error." A similar failure at other stages is judged by the "harmless error" standard. [**p. 156**]
94.		**NO**	In addition to Dawn's express waiver, the court must also determine that Dawn was ***competent*** to make the waiver—*i.e.,* it must make sure that Dawn understands the consequences and difficulties of self-representation and is emotionally and psychologically capable of self-representation. [**p. 156**]
95.		**PROBABLY NOT**	Failure to do what would appear to be good practice will not necessarily result in reversal of a conviction on the ground of ineffective assistance of counsel. If the attorney fails to object to leading questions or hearsay evidence, Sixth Amendment rights are ***not necessarily*** violated. A constitutional violation occurs only if the representation is sub-par and it affected the outcome of the trial. [**pp. 158–160**]
96.	a.	**NO**	The Court did not view the situation as one implicating counsel's competency but, rather, the client's autonomy. [**p. 160**]
	b.	**YES**	The defendant has a Sixth Amendment autonomy right to maintain her innocence at the guilt phase of a capital trial. Counsel may not waive that right over the accused's objection. [**p. 160**]
97.		**YES**	The attorney was ignorant of a point of law that was fundamental to the case, and he failed to perform basic research on that point. [**p. 160**]
98.		**NO**	While indigent defendants have the right to appointed counsel, they do not have the right to select a particular attorney. [**p. 160**]

99.		**FALSE**	Usually, face-to-face confrontation is required. But, the Supreme Court has held that the Confrontation Clause does not categorically require all witnesses to testify against the defendant in the defendant's physical presence. For example, the trial judge must balance the defendant's confrontation right against contrary policies in child sex abuse cases in which prosecutors seek to present child testimony via one-way closed circuit television. Notice, though, there has been a resurgence of confrontation rights cases over the past few decades that has solidified the defendant's confrontation rights. [**p. 164**]
100.	a.	**YES**	The court can order a defendant removed from court for disruptive conduct after making clear to the defendant that further disruption will not be tolerated. [**p. 163**]
	b.	**YES**	This is the clearest case of a denial of Sawyer's Sixth Amendment right of confrontation, and is not alleviated by a limiting instruction. [**p. 164**]
	c.	**YES**	Viola's testimony satisfies Sawyer's right of confrontation, so the prior confession can be used against both Viola and Sawyer, who may cross examine Viola. [**p. 165**]
101.		**SPLIT OF AUTHORITY**	Some jurisdictions impose this burden on the prosecution; others require the defendant to prove insanity by a preponderance of the evidence or even by clear and convincing evidence. [**p. 172**]
102.		**NO**	Such a commitment violates Defendant's constitutional rights if a showing is made that he has recovered his sanity. [**p. 173**]
103.		**FALSE**	The majority view ***does*** turn on predisposition, as well as the degree of inducement used by police. [**p. 174**]
	a.	**TRUE**	Even if disposition is formed prior to the crime, it must have been present prior to the government's first contact with the defendant. [**p. 174**]
104.		**FALSE**	Defendant must be ***personally*** addressed by the court, even though counsel is present. [**p. 179**]
105.		**YES**	Admission of guilt is not a constitutional prerequisite to imposition of a criminal penalty. If the prosecution introduces strong evidence of the defendant's guilt, and his voluntary plea appears to be an intelligent choice, the court may accept the plea even if the defendant refuses to admit guilt. [**p. 180**]
106.		**NO**	Because the prosecutor has discretion to plead such prior convictions, this would not be a threat rendering Darla's plea ***involuntary*** (hence it is not a violation of due process). [**p. 181**]

	a.	**DEPENDS**	If Darla was represented by counsel when the plea was entered, and her lawyer failed to inform her of the possibility that the goods could be excluded, Darla can move to withdraw her plea as a product of ineffective assistance of counsel. Nevertheless, the police's illegal actions are insufficient by themselves to invalidate the plea. [**p. 182**]
107.		**PROBABLY NOT**	Generally, a defendant may not collaterally attack her guilty plea after sentence if it represents a voluntary and intelligent choice among known alternatives. Here, if Nancy's plea was actually involuntarily coerced, she may be permitted to withdraw it. [**p. 182**]
108.		**YES**	While jailing a person merely for addiction may be "cruel and unusual punishment," prohibited under the Constitution, imprisonment of an addict for possession is not. [**pp. 184–185**]
	a.	**DEPENDS**	There must be a showing of "new data" to justify a more severe sentence, unless the sentence is determined by a jury, or the state has a two-tier trial system. [**pp. 186–187**]
	b.	**NO**	Authorizing imprisonment as an ***alternative*** to payment of a fine (or a fine as a means of reducing the term of a prison sentence) violates equal protection if the defendant is indigent. [**p. 186**]
109.		**YES**	Indigent defendants may be required to pay back to the state the costs of their appointed counsel as a condition of probation. However, exemptions must be granted for those truly unable to pay back the costs. [**p. 186**]
110.		**FALSE**	A discretionary death penalty without guidelines is unconstitutional. [**pp. 190–192**]
111.		**NO**	The Supreme Court allows victim impact statements that speak to the circumstances of the crime and the emotional impact of the crime on the victim's family, but such statements may not extend to opinions about the defendant or the appropriate sentence. [**p. 191]**
112.		**DEPENDS**	Such a statute may be sufficiently clear for a capital offense if the state courts have narrowed and clarified it (*e.g.*, stating that the statute will apply only when the killing was committed by a "cold-blooded, pitiless slayer"). [**pp. 193–194**]
113.		**NO**	The Eighth Amendment is violated by the imposition of the death penalty on minors under the age of 18. [**p. 195**]
114.		**NO**	It creates an unacceptable risk that persons with intellectual disabilities will be executed. Defendants must be able to present additional evidence of intellectual disability, including testimony regarding adaptive deficits. [**p. 195**]

115.		**NO**	As long as the defendant recognizes that he will be executed as punishment for his crime, he does not need to remember the details of committing it. [**p. 195**]
116.		**NO**	Retroactive application of such a change would have a disadvantageous impact on the defendant and would violate the Ex Post Facto Clause. [**pp. 198–199**]
117.		**FALSE**	Because a reasonable doubt instruction is central to the jury process, an error in the charge is always deemed to be prejudicial. [**p. 206**]
118.		**PROBABLY**	When a state grants the right to appeal, it cannot discriminate on the basis of poverty. If appellate review requires a transcript of the trial proceedings, such a transcript must be made available to convicted indigents free of charge. Thus, if this is an appeal as of right, and a transcript is required, Dan must be furnished a copy. [**p. 206**]
119.		**NO**	Because the criminal case has ended, an indigent person has no constitutional right to appointed counsel to help prepare a petition for a writ of habeas corpus. [**p. 210**]
120.		**YES**	Every ineffective assistance of counsel claim is difficult to prove. However, a defendant can establish that counsel's representation fell below an objective standard of reasonableness if he can show that counsel gave him incorrect information about deportation and establish a reasonable probability that, but for the erroneous legal advice, he would not have plead guilty. [**p. 158**]
121.	a.	**FALSE**	Both state and federal courts may issue the writ. [**p. 211**]
	b.	**DEPENDS**	The claim will be heard if it is accompanied by an assertion that the conviction is contrary to, or involved an unreasonable application of, clearly established federal law as determined by the Supreme Court. [**p. 212**]
	c.	**TRUE**	Absent a showing of cause and actual prejudice, petitioners must comply with state procedural rules governing the manner in which federal constitutional claims must be raised. [**p. 214**]
122.		**FALSE**	The restriction placed on federal judges in the Fourth Amendment area does not apply in the self-incrimination and *Miranda* context. [**p. 219**]
123.		**TRUE**	When the defendant produces an affidavit signed by the juror admitting to making blatantly racist comments about the defendant during deliberations, that may equate to clear and convincing evidence. [**p. 216**]
124.		**NO**	The right to jury trial is inapplicable in juvenile matters. [**p. 225**]

125.	**FALSE**	School officials may conduct some searches without a warrant, based on reasonable suspicion. [**p. 225**]
126.	**NO**	In a probation revocation case, the defendant is entitled to counsel when the revocation also involves imposition of a new sentence. In other probation revocation cases, the right to counsel is determined on a case-by-case basis. [**p. 229**]
127.	**NO**	While a prisoner in such proceedings has certain limited rights (*e.g.*, to call witnesses on her own behalf), she has no right to counsel. [**p. 230**]
128.	**NO**	Fanny is entitled to a ***two-stage*** hearing: A preliminary hearing on probable cause to detain her in custody while awaiting final disposition of the revocation, and a subsequent revocation hearing. [**p. 229**]
129.	**YES**	The Constitution is satisfied if the prisoner has been found to be dangerous and the treatment is in his best interests. [**p. 234**]
130.	**TRUE**	The Double Jeopardy Clause bars retrial following a court-decreed acquittal, even if the acquittal is "based upon an egregiously erroneous foundation." [**p. 238**]
131.	**DEPENDS**	A defendant can be retried when the prior conviction is set aside on appeal because of errors committed during the trial. However, a defendant whose conviction is reversed because the evidence is insufficient as a matter of law cannot be retried. [**pp. 244–244**]
132.	**NO**	Such an appeal by the government (on the ground that the sentence is too lenient) does not violate double jeopardy policies against multiple prosecutions or punishments for the same offense. [**p. 247**]
133.	**TRUE**	Because the agreement is central to the crime of conspiracy, the earlier prosecution for the crimes that are the overt acts do not serve to bar a later prosecution for conspiracy under the Double Jeopardy Clause. The agreement and the overt criminal acts are not the "same offense." [**p. 251**]
134.	**NO**	Two separate governmental systems (sovereigns) are involved, and acquittal (or conviction) on the state offense generally will not bar prosecution on the federal offense. [**p. 252**]

Exam Questions and Answers

Question I

Officer Felipe believed that Maria and Jasper were committing break-ins throughout the neighborhood. After receiving an anonymous tip consistent with this belief, Officer Felipe went to the restaurant where Jasper worked and asked the manager to bring Jasper to the employee lounge. The manager left and Felipe closed the door. He then said to Jasper, "We know it's you and Maria doing these break-ins." Jasper replied, "Well, who cares about these rich people anyway?"

Officer Felipe then told Jasper he was "under arrest," handcuffed him, and took him to the police station. After booking (*i.e.*, post-arrest processing), Felipe took Jasper into a separate interview room and said to him: "We know it's you and you already made that incriminating statement back at the restaurant. You should come clean now; it will go a lot easier for you if you do. Oh by the way, we've already arrested Maria. She confessed and said you were the brains of the group." Jasper responded, "I do not want to talk to you about this and yeah maybe I need to have a lawyer here." Felipe left while Jasper remained in the room by himself. Twenty minutes later, Felipe returned, warned Jasper of his *Miranda* rights, and asked Jasper if he wanted to confess. Jasper said, "OK you got me, but it was Maria who planned it. I was just there to help." Maria never was located by the police.

What problems, if any, will the prosecutor have using Felipe's two incriminating statements against him at trial to prove his guilt?

Question II

Victim is assaulted by two individuals. Several days later, at a police lineup, Victim identifies Michael and Stacy as her assailants. An indictment is issued charging both with the crime. The court appoints Dunn as counsel for the defendants. Although Stacy is broke, Michael has a $3,000 car. Before Dunn is appointed, at a meeting with the prosecuting attorney, the defendants tell the prosecution that they were at a football game at the time of the attack.

During defendants' sole pretrial meeting with Dunn, Stacy initially tells Dunn that it was all Michael's idea. Stacy also says that although she was present, she did not commit the attack and does not want to be found guilty for Michael's actions. Dunn tells Stacy not to worry because he will get them both acquitted. Afterwards, defendants tell Dunn that they were at a party with Stacy's family that evening and have witnesses to corroborate their story.

Just before the trial begins, Dunn asks the court for money to have an expert to: (1) construct a scale model of the vicinity and (2) testify that the defendants could not have reached the other side of town in time to assault Victim. The court denies Dunn's request.

At the joint trial, five witnesses testify that they saw the defendants running from the woods, at the time and place where the assault occurred. Near the end of the trial, after the prosecution's witnesses have been introduced and the defendants' testimony concerning their activities on the night in question have been impeached, Michael asks the court to dismiss Dunn from his case and to find him a new attorney. Michael claims that he has always hated attorneys and has no faith in Dunn. After the court refuses his request, Michael says that he would rather represent himself than have Dunn as counsel. The court makes no comment, and Dunn says nothing more. At the end of the trial, both defendants are found guilty.

On appeal, what issues may Michael and Stacy raise? Discuss.

Question III

Beth and Sam are involved in a conspiracy to kidnap the mayor of the town. Sam has been staying with Tim while in town and has permission from Tim to treat Tim's home like his own. One night, Sam calls Beth on Tim's home phone to discuss their plans. Suspicious that Tim is engaged in unrelated criminal activity, the police had previously attached a wiretap device to Tim's home phone. They did not obtain a warrant to do so. While listening to an incriminating conversation between Sam and Beth during the wiretap, the police learn that Beth will phone Sam on Sam's cell phone in three days with the kidnapping details. The police do not overhear that second conversation, and Beth disappears. They do, however, gather enough additional evidence to arrest Sam. When they arrest Sam, he has his cell phone. The officers take Sam into custody, seize the cell phone, and after searching the cell phone, locate several incriminating emails and text messages discussing the kidnapping plans.

What evidence gathered by the police will be admissible as evidence against Sam? Discuss.

Question IV

Officers Wright and Sane are approached in the street by Carlos. Carlos says that he has seen his next-door neighbor, Emily, sell cocaine from her house to high school students. Wright does not know Carlos, but Sane met him socially at a church gathering and knows he lives at 219 W. Fowler.

Later that day, Wright goes to the Fowler address and observes the only next-door house (221 W. Fowler) for an hour. During that hour, four questionable-looking characters enter and leave, but Wright sees no one young enough to be a high school student. The following day, the officers obtain a warrant from a local judge to "search Emily's house, 221 W. Fowler, for cocaine." The warrant is issued based on the sworn written affidavits of Wright and Sane, who attest to the above facts.

Upon arriving at Emily's house to execute the warrant, the police are greeted by her 21-year-old daughter. When they tell the daughter they have a search warrant, she tells them her mother is gone, but they can come inside and look around. Once inside, the police seize three pounds of cocaine lying on the kitchen counter, along with some illegal professional roulette wheels and craps tables set up in the basement. Emily is arrested and charged. The prosecution plans to introduce the cocaine and gambling paraphernalia at her trial.

Can Emily raise any persuasive arguments to exclude the evidence against her? Discuss.

Question V

The local police department wanted to reduce drunk driving. Pursuant to a specific, written regulation, the department created weekly nighttime roadblocks at various busy intersections and officers began stopping every car at the roadblocks to check for drunk drivers.

On Friday night at 10:05, James was stopped by Officer Ella and her partner, Officer Ken, at a roadblock. Ella believed that James was drunk because he smelled of alcohol, his speech was slurred, and he was speaking very loudly. When James failed the "walk the line" test, Ella arrested him for driving under the influence. Just before Ella and Ken transported James to the police station, James, who was not placed in handcuffs or otherwise restrained, was standing next to his car. Pursuant to standard department procedure, Ken seized James's car and searched its interior passenger compartment. Ken found an illegal gun under the front seat of the car. James was charged with driving under the influence and with possession of an illegal gun.

After his arrest, James was questioned at the police station by Ella and Ken without receiving ***Miranda*** warnings. James made an incriminating statement, indicating that he had been drinking heavily with friends just before the roadblock.

At trial, the government will seek to introduce evidence of Ella's observations of James and the illegal gun. James's lawyer has moved to suppress both items. As part of James's defense, his friend Wanda will testify that she and James had been together on that Friday night from 5 until 10 p.m. and that neither consumed any alcohol or drugs. The government has requested that it be permitted to impeach Wanda with James's incriminating statement.

How should the trial judge rule on these motions? Explain.

Question VI

Caine was charged in state court with the illegal sale of narcotics. His request for a jury trial was granted. During voir dire, the prosecution used all available peremptory challenges, with eight of the ten being used on prospective jurors under the age of 25. Caine's attorney, Brady, used only seven of her ten by the end of the jury selection.

During voir dire, Brady questioned a prospective juror about his knowledge of cocaine. The individual said he was unfamiliar with cocaine and that he has no real opinion on the use of illegal drugs. After the judge restricted Brady from asking any further questions concerning drugs, Brady dismissed the prospective juror using a peremptory challenge. Eventually, a panel of 10 was formed, comprised of seven men and three women. No juror was under the age of 25 (although one juror was 25) and three jurors were over 65.

At trial, Caine testified that he was holding the drugs for a friend, that he was not selling the drugs, and that he had merely been speaking generally about cocaine when he was arrested. At the close of trial, the judge instructed the jury as follows: "The burden of proof is on the government, but the key question for you will be whether the defendant raised a reasonable doubt as to his guilt."

After 10 hours of deliberation, the jurors returned and stated that they were deadlocked and almost evenly split. The judge instructed them on their duty to reach a decision and to avoid a hung jury. Thirty minutes later, they returned with a guilty verdict, nine votes to one, stating that a unanimous decision was impossible. Caine has filed a motion for a new trial.

On what ground(s) would Caine be entitled to a new trial? Discuss.

Answers to Question I

To determine whether Jasper's two statements ["rich people" and "you got me"] are admissible, you must examine: (1) whether the statements were voluntary; and (2) whether Jasper's Fifth Amendment rights under *Miranda* were violated.

Voluntariness: Confessions made by an accused are admissible at trial to prove guilt only if the prosecution can establish to the trial judge, by a preponderance of the evidence, that the statement was voluntary. A statement is voluntary if the speaker's will was not overborne by government pressure, threats, or promises. A voluntary statement must be the product of "an essentially clear and unconstrained choice by the maker."

Here, Jasper's first statement—made at the restaurant—appears to be voluntary. In determining whether a statement is voluntary, the court will look to factors such as police coercion and the defendant's age and intelligence, lack of food or sleep, etc. A confession will be deemed involuntary only under particularly egregious circumstances created by law enforcement, such as where there is physical brutality by the police, outrageous conditions of confinement, extremely protracted interrogations, unduly coercive threats, coercive promises, or trickery regarding the status of the defendant and her associates. False police statements alone rarely rise to the level of coercion required to show involuntariness. No egregious circumstances were present here.

Jasper's second statement—made at the police station—is a closer question. There was nothing especially outrageous about the questioning (*e.g.*, it was not extremely lengthy; Felipe made no physical threats). However, two voluntariness issues should be raised by counsel for Jasper. First, Officer Felipe lied to Jasper about Maria being arrested and implicating Jasper. This argument alone will probably be unpersuasive because the Supreme Court has consistently held that confessions are voluntary even if they were induced by police lies and deception regarding the evidence against the suspect. Second, Felipe suggested that if Jasper confessed, the confession would help him during the prosecution. This argument, even in combination with the first, will not likely prevail. This was not a firm promise. The judge should also weigh this suggestion against the defendant's earlier voluntary confession at the restaurant.

***Miranda*:** Even if Jasper's statement was voluntary, it will not be admissible if his Fifth Amendment rights as established in *Miranda v. Arizona* were violated. *Miranda* provides that a suspect in custody cannot be interrogated by the police until the suspect has been adequately warned of the right to remain silent, the right to an attorney, and the fact that any statement can be used against the suspect. If, after *Miranda* warnings, the suspect invokes the right to remain silent, the police must scrupulously honor that choice. This means that the police must refrain from questioning for a period of time, depending on the totality of the circumstances. Interrogation cannot be restarted unless the suspect has been warned again of his *Miranda* rights and has knowingly and voluntarily waived those rights. If, instead, the suspect invokes the right to counsel, all questioning must cease until the defendant has been provided with an attorney. A suspect's invocation of the right to counsel remains effective for at least 14 days. Both invocations of the right to remain silent and to an attorney must be explicit and unambiguous. Statements taken in violation of these rules will be excluded from the prosecutor's case-in-chief and cannot be used to establish guilt.

Here, whether Jasper's *Miranda* rights were violated is unclear. *Miranda* rights must only be given to a suspect who is both in custody and subjected to police interrogation. Jasper was likely not in custody at the restaurant. The test for custody is twofold: 1) whether a reasonable person would have felt she could end the interrogation and leave if she chose; and 2) whether the interrogation created the same coercive pressures as were present in the Miranda station-house interrogation. Here, the restaurant questioning seems less like the stationhouse, incommunicado interrogation in *Miranda* and more like the roadside questioning in Berkemer v. McCarty.

Furthermore, Jasper may not have been interrogated. While the facts say Officer Felipe told Jasper that there was evidence against him, it is not clear that this statement constituted interrogation. The test for interrogation is whether the officer knew, or reasonably should have known, that his statement would elicit an incriminating response. It is possible, but not certain, that a court would find that Officer Felipe knew, or should have known, that reminding Jasper of his incriminating statement at the restaurant, encouraging him to come clean now because it will be easier for him, and lying about Maria's confession, would elicit an incriminating response.

The other *Miranda* issue relates to continuing the interrogation at the police station after Jasper said he did not wish to talk and might want a lawyer. His request for silence ("I do not want to talk to you about this") was clear and unambiguous. Officer Felipe left, took a short break, and returned to ask questions. Here, the question is whether 20 minutes and renewed questioning by the same officer about the same crime would be a sufficient break in circumstances to "scrupulously honor" the invocation to allow additional questions once warnings are given and a waiver is obtained. The Supreme Court has not clearly addressed this point, although it has suggested that a break of two hours could be sufficient when a different officer questions the suspect about a different crime and in a different interview room. In any event, defense counsel will have a more difficult time showing that Jasper's reference to a lawyer ("yeah maybe I need to have a lawyer here") was an invocation of the right to counsel. Unfortunately for Jasper the request for counsel must be clear and unambiguous, and his remark is neither. If this was an invocation of Jasper's right to counsel, questioning could not be resumed, even after a break, unless the break was longer than 14 days.

Answers to Question II

Pretrial Right to Counsel: The first issue Michael and Stacy may raise is whether they were denied their right to counsel before trial. The right to counsel is guaranteed to Michael and Stacy by the Sixth and Fourteenth Amendments, regardless of their ability to pay. This constitutional right exists in criminal prosecutions where actual imprisonment is imposed. The constitutional right to counsel arises when there is an adversary criminal prosecution pending against the accused. At that point she is entitled to counsel at all critical stages of the proceeding. Critical stages are those stages of the proceeding at which substantial rights of the accused may be affected.

Michael and Stacy cannot claim the right to counsel at the lineup because they had not yet been indicted, and, thus, there was no criminal prosecution pending. They did have a right to counsel at the meeting with the prosecutor, because a post-indictment interrogation is a critical stage of a criminal proceeding. Nevertheless, the denial will not automatically result in a reversal. A pretrial denial of counsel is tested under the harmless error test. Here, the defendants will argue that, if they had been represented by counsel at the meeting, their alibi would not have been impeached at trial. However, because five witnesses testified (creating significant evidence) that they saw the defendants at the time and at the scene of the assault, the appellate court will likely find the error harmless beyond a reasonable doubt.

Joint Representation: Defendants may also claim a denial of the right to counsel based upon their joint representation. Joint representation is not *per se* a violation of the right to counsel. It is proper if the defendants have participated in the same act, but only if joint representation will not prejudice any party. To establish a violation of the Sixth Amendment from joint representation, the defendant must object at trial. If he does not object, on appeal it must be shown that an actual conflict of interest adversely affected the lawyer's performance. Here, Stacy told the attorney at the first meeting that it was all Michael's fault, but that claim was never repeated. Stacy never objected to joint representation during trial. Thus, the appellate court probably will not find an actual conflict that adversely affected her representation. An argument based on ineffective representation because of the dual representation will have a similar result (see below).

Right to Expert Assistance: Defendants might also argue that they were denied a right to assistance other than counsel, because their attorney was not given money to hire an expert to construct a model of the vicinity. The judge must provide indigent defendants with non-lawyer assistance when necessary for adequate representation. This argument will likely fail here. Today such an expert is generally unnecessary because the same point can be made with a local map or Internet site giving a geographic overview of the area. Thus, the model would not be deemed necessary for adequate representation.

Right to Self-Representation: Michael may also claim that he was improperly denied the right to self-representation. The right to represent oneself under the Sixth Amendment is as strong as the right to be represented by counsel. A defendant can have his conviction overturned if he is forced to accept representation when he is competent, and intelligently and voluntarily waives the right to counsel. However, there probably was no improper denial here. Michael did not choose to represent himself until near the end of trial, so an appellate court will likely find that he had waived his right to self-representation. Moreover, the facts do not clearly show that Michael wanted to represent himself because his statement was not made until after the court had denied his initial request for a new attorney.

Effective Representation: The right to counsel includes the right to effective representation. The standard is one of reasonableness. The defendant must show that counsel's performance fell below an objective standard of reasonableness and that, but for the deficiency, the result of the defendant's case probably would have been different. The defendants may raise several issues in this regard.

Defendants might claim that they were denied effective counsel because they met with counsel only once before trial. However, nothing in the facts indicates that this resulted in inadequate representation, so this argument will likely fail.

Similarly, Michael's complaint regarding his hatred of lawyers will likely not prevail. An indigent defendant is not entitled to a lawyer of his own choosing. A judge may appoint a new lawyer if irreconcilable differences arise between appointed counsel and the client. However, Michael has not identified any basis for his claim or any deficiency in Dunn's representation that would justify a finding of ineffective assistance. Thus, his claim will fail.

Finally, Stacy may raise a concern about her joint representation with Michael. As stated above, joint representation is improper if it prejudices one of the parties. Arguably Dunn should have investigated Stacy's initial claim of a lesser role in the crime, and his failure to do so and to recommend separate representation constitutes inadequate representation. However, Stacy never raised this claim in court. Moreover, given the evidence presented at trial, the appellate court would likely find that any alleged error was harmless.

Answers to Question III

The wiretapped home phone conversation between Sam and Beth is not admissible against Sam.

Wiretapping of Tim's Home Phone: The wiretapping of Tim's phone was an unreasonable search under the Fourth Amendment. It is a *per se* violation of the Fourth Amendment to wiretap without a judicial authorization unless one party to the conversation has consented. There is no evidence of consent here. The requirements for a valid judicial authorization to wiretap are akin to those for a search warrant. For the wiretap of Tim's home phone to be reasonable, the police would have needed to provide an authorizing court with a summary of the evidence supporting probable cause to believe that Tim was using the phone in violation of the law and a specific time period for surveillance. This was not done.

Sam's Standing to Object to the Unlawful Wiretap: Under the Fourth Amendment, Sam likely has standing to object to the unlawful wiretap of Tim's home. As an overnight guest in Tim's home, Sam has a right to privacy in the home that is protected against unreasonable intrusion (search and seizure) by the government. Here, Sam had a reasonable expectation of privacy when using Tim's home and Tim's home phone. Sam was temporarily living in Tim's home as Tim's overnight guest, and Tim had given Sam permission, to "treat Tim's home like his own." Thus, any evidence obtained through the wiretap should be inadmissible against Sam in a federal or state proceeding.

Evidence from Sam's Cell Phone: The emails and texts taken from Sam's cell phone would not be admissible against him. The Supreme Court in Riley v. California held that cell phones taken incident to a valid arrest may be properly *seized* without a warrant and physically examined. However, unlike other forms of personal property, officers must get a search warrant to examine the contents of cell phones (even incident to a lawful arrest), unless there is an exigent circumstance justifying that action. Because there was no emergency here, the officers should have obtained a search warrant before searching the emails and texts on Sam's cell phone.

Answers to Question IV

Because Emily was the owner of the home that was searched, she has a sufficient privacy interest (*i.e.*, standing) to raise search and seizure concerns pursuant to the Fourth Amendment.

The Search Warrant—Probable Cause: Emily can claim that the search warrant was improperly issued, making the search unreasonable. A valid search warrant must be: (1) issued by a magistrate or judge; (2) based upon sworn testimony or affirmation establishing probable cause; and (3) must describe with particularity the place to be searched and the items to be seized.

Here, Emily could argue that the warrant was not based on probable cause. A warrant lacks probable cause if the affidavit lacks sufficient evidence or if it contains false statements knowingly or recklessly made by the police, which when removed leaves the affidavit lacking in probable cause to believe that a crime is being committed or that evidence will be found. Because Officer Wright made no false statements about what he saw at Emily's house, her only substantial challenge is the lack of evidence supporting probable cause. Officer Sane knew Carlos (the informant) from church, but whether he knew him well enough to have an opinion as to Carlos's trustworthiness is unclear. Because Wright could not be sure that Carlos was reliable, he attempted to corroborate Carlos's statement by watching Emily's house. However, Carlos had told the officers that his neighbor was selling cocaine to "high school students." Wright did not observe any high school students at the house. Instead, he only saw four "questionable-looking characters," not young enough to be in high school. The mismatch between Carlos's information and Wright's observations makes this incomplete or even inadequate corroboration.

The Search Warrant—Particularity: A search warrant must also identify the items that are the object of the search with particularity. If Emily's argues that the warrant lacked the necessary specificity, her argument should fail. It is sufficient for the warrant to identify "cocaine." Although the warrant did not say where in the house the police could search, this information was impossible to provide and unnecessary because cocaine could have been anywhere within the house.

The Plain View Doctrine: Emily could challenge the admissibility of the gambling paraphernalia because this evidence was not mentioned in the warrant. However, the gambling paraphernalia is admissible under the plain view rule. Under this rule, because the police officers were lawfully entitled to enter or search the house, they may seize evidence they observe, if the nature of the evidence, as contraband, fruits, or instrumentalities of a crime, is readily apparent. The gambling paraphernalia is obviously contraband, and it was found while the police lawfully searched for the cocaine. The fact that some cocaine was found in the kitchen does not mean that the police had to stop searching the rest of the house, because they had no idea how much cocaine might be present. Assuming the search warrant is valid, both the cocaine and the gambling evidence should be admissible against Emily.

Consent to Search: If the search warrant is found to be invalid for lack of probable cause, the state may argue that the evidence should still be admitted because Emily's daughter consented to the search. Warrantless searches are valid if they are conducted pursuant to voluntary consent given by a person with an apparent right to use the premises searched.

Here, this prosecution argument should fail. It was reasonable for the officers to assume that Emily's daughter had a right to use the premises, because she was 21 (*i.e.*, not a child), answered the door, and appeared to be living on the premises. The problem is that, if the police announce that they have a warrant, any consent given to the police to search pursuant to the warrant will be considered involuntary if the police did not actually have a valid warrant.

The *Leon* Good Faith Exception: Finally, even if the warrant was invalid and there was no consent, the evidence may still be admissible at trial. The Supreme Court has held that evidence can be admitted if it was obtained by a police officer acting in objectively reasonable good faith reliance on a facially valid search warrant, even if a court later finds the warrant lacked probable cause. The "good faith exception" is a major limitation on the exclusionary rule.

Answers to Question V

Three separate issues must be resolved by the trial judge in the case against James.

The Roadblock: James will argue that his Fourth Amendment rights were violated because there was no individualized suspicion justifying the officer's stop of his car. This argument will fail if the roadblock was designed to serve purposes closely tied to a particular problem related to automobile safety (*e.g.*, drunk driving), and cars are stopped using some neutral, articulable standard (*e.g.*, every car, every third car, etc.). The Supreme Court has held that no individualized suspicion is required in such situations, balancing the relatively limited intrusion on the individual's privacy against the great public need to stop drunk driving. Here, the roadblock appears to have been lawful. Because the stop was lawful and Officer Ella's observations of James (*i.e.*, that he smelled of alcohol, his speech was slurred, and he was speaking very loudly), which provided the probable cause for his arrest, were pursuant to that stop, her testimony will be allowed at trial.

Seizure of the Gun: James will again argue that the police acted without individualized suspicion. That is, he will contend that the police searched his car without any reason to believe they would find evidence of a crime within the car. Here, too, the defense argument will fail. The Supreme Court has held that after a person in a car is arrested, the police may conduct a warrantless search of the passenger compartment of the car incident to arrest without individualized suspicion under two circumstances—either of which might apply here. First, police may search if the arrestee is unsecured and might be able to reach inside the car at the time of the search. Here, James was standing next to his car without handcuffs immediately following his lawful arrest. Second, police may search if it is reasonable to believe that evidence of the crime of arrest could be found in the car. Here, James was arrested because Ella had probable cause to believe he was drunk, so alcohol could have been found inside the car. Because the gun was found in the interior of the car pursuant to a lawful search incident to James's arrest, it can be admitted into evidence.

James's Statement: The statement cannot be used as evidence against James in the government's case in chief, as it violates Miranda v. Arizona. Because the emergency exception to *Miranda* does not apply here, the police must inform a suspect of their right to remain silent, their right to an attorney and the risk that any statement may be used against them as evidence before any custodial interrogation. Statements taken in violation of *Miranda* generally are inadmissible at trial to prove guilt, under the exclusionary rule, although statements obtained in violation of *Miranda* may be used for impeachment purposes. Thus, if James were to testify in a manner inconsistent with his earlier unwarned statement, the confession could be used to impeach his credibility. The Supreme Court has held that such impeachment is permitted only if the defendant himself testifies at trial. James's unwarned statement may not be used to impeach a witness testifying on his behalf. So, the government cannot use the statement to impeach Wanda.

Answers to Question VI

Caine can raise three issues in his motion for a new trial: the method of jury selection, the validity of the judge's jury instruction, and the sufficiency of the verdict.

Jury Selection: The Sixth Amendment guarantees a defendant an impartial jury. Although this requires a jury *selected from* a representative cross-section of the community, the selected jury members need not be proportionately representative of the community. Here, a reversal would be required only if Caine could show that the prosecution used its peremptory challenges to exclude a segment of the community that would have normally been represented. Caine can argue that excluding people under the age of 25 excludes a segment of society, but this is probably not a valid complaint. The segments of society protected against exclusion from juries, thus far, have been those the Supreme Court treats as suspect or quasi-suspect class members (*i.e.*, race, gender, or ethnic background). Age is not a suspect classification. Moreover, the jury in Caine's case included at least one juror 25 years old; thus, it was somewhat representative of the younger members of the community.

In addition, it is unclear whether the defendant must exercise all of his peremptory challenges to object to the impartiality of the jury. While courts are split on this issue, the actions of the prosecution may suggest that Caine should have the right to move for a new trial without having exhausted his challenges. The prosecution was attempting systematically to exclude a certain group of people, and Caine's peremptory challenges could not prevent these actions. Caine may also argue that it was error for the judge to restrict counsel's questioning of the prospective juror. Such restrictions, however, are reversible error only when they relate to challenges for cause, and this challenge was peremptory. Not only did Brady fail to attempt a challenge for cause, but she also already knew that the prospective juror had said he was neutral and could not have been excused for cause.

Jury Instruction: Caine will argue that the judge incorrectly instructed the jury concerning the burden of proof he must bear on his defense. The prosecution has the burden of proving that the defendant is guilty beyond a reasonable doubt of each element of the crime. Here, the actual selling of drugs is an essential element of the crime charged. The burden of proving the sale remains on the prosecution—not the defendant.

Because the defendant is presumed innocent, the judge's comment could be seen as error by suggesting that the defendant bears the burden (because it is the "key question") of establishing reasonable doubt. Improper conduct, such as prejudicial comments by the judge, constitutes ground for a mistrial. Although this was only one remark, stated just once, it could have prejudiced the jury, especially since it was part of the jury instructions. The jury naturally puts great weight on a judge's statements, particularly when the judge is instructing the jurors on the law and their duties.

Guilty Verdict: Caine will obtain a new trial based on the facts surrounding the verdict in his case. There is no constitutional requirement that the number of jurors be 12. Although this minimum is mandated in federal court by statute, state rules permitting a lesser number are valid. If Caine's state had such a rule, the use of 10 jurors would be permitted. However, there is a constitutional right to a unanimous verdict. Here, even though Caine's verdict was based on a substantial majority of the jury, the result was not unanimous and, therefore, must be overturned. Caine may, nevertheless, be retried.

Caine's final argument would be that the judge's second instruction to the jury, concerning the duty to reach a decision, is unlawful. Such an instruction is unlawful only if it is shown to be coercive, but the judge here made no threats or intimidating statements to the jury. The fact that the judge did not mention each juror's individual right to vote according to his or her conscience may be inappropriate, but it does not constitute coercion. The jury's speed in reaching a verdict suggests that some of the jurors may have been intimidated by the judge's statement. However, the fact that one juror refused to vote "guilty" shows that they probably understood they were still free to vote according to their consciences.

Table of Cases

Index